Deference and Defiance in Monterrey

The first comprehensive history of labor relations and the working class in twentieth-century Monterrey, *Deference and Defiance in Monterrey* explores how both workers and industrialists perceived, responded to, and helped shape the outcome of Mexico's revolution. Snodgrass's narrative covers a sixty-year period that begins with Monterrey's emergence as one of Latin America's preeminent industrial cities and home to Mexico's most powerful business group. He then explores the roots of two distinct and enduring systems of industrial relations that were both historical outcomes of the revolution: company paternalism and militant unionism. By comparing four local industries – steel, beer, glass, and smelting – Snodgrass demonstrates how workers and managers collaborated in the development of paternalistic labor regimes that built upon working-class traditions of mutual aid as well as elite resistance to state labor policies. *Deference and Defiance in Monterrey* thus offers an urban and industrial perspective to a history of revolutionary Mexico that remains overshadowed by studies of the countryside.

Michael Snodgrass is Assistant Professor of Latin American History at Indiana University–Purdue University Indianapolis. His essays have appeared in anthologies on Latin American labor history, the Mexican Revolution, international media studies, and in such journals as *International Labor and Working-Class History* and *Latin American Research Review.*

88
Deference and Defiance in Monterrey
Workers, Paternalism, and Revolution in Mexico, 1890–1950

Deference and Defiance in Monterrey

Workers, Paternalism, and Revolution in Mexico, 1890–1950

MICHAEL SNODGRASS

Indiana University–Purdue University Indianapolis

DAMAGED

CAMBRIDGE
UNIVERSITY PRESS

PUBLISHED BY THE PRESS SYNDICATE OF THE UNIVERSITY OF CAMBRIDGE
The Pitt Building, Trumpington Street, Cambridge, United Kingdom

CAMBRIDGE UNIVERSITY PRESS
The Edinburgh Building, Cambridge CB2 2RU, UK
40 West 20th Street, New York, NY 10011-4211, USA
477 Williamstown Road, Port Melbourne, VIC 3207, Australia
Ruiz de Alarcón 13, 28014 Madrid, Spain
Dock House, The Waterfront, Cape Town 8001, South Africa

http://www.cambridge.org

First published 2003

Printed in the United States of America

Typeface Garamond 3 11/12 pt.   *System* LaTeX 2$_\varepsilon$ [TB]

A catalog record for this book is available from the British Library.

Library of Congress Cataloging in Publication Data
Snodgrass, Michael.
Deference and defiance in Monterrey : workers, paternalism, and revolution in Mexico,
1890–1950 / Michael Snodgrass.
p.   cm. – (Cambridge Latin American studies ; 88)
Includes bibliographical references and index.
ISBN 0-521-81189-9
1. Labor relations – Mexico – Monterrey – History.   2. Working class – Mexico – Monterrey –
History.   I. Title.   II. Series.
HD8120.M66 s658   2003
331'.0972'13–dc21   2002034953

ISBN 0 521 81189 9 hardback

To my mother, Carol Anne Snodgrass,
and to Richard Pryce Snodgrass and Reed Capen Foster,
two friends who worked hard and left their marks on our world

Contents

Acknowledgments

Researching and writing this book were as much personal endeavors as collaborative efforts that benefited from the guidance and inspiration of countless friends and scholars. My interests in Latin American and labor history were first cultivated in the classrooms of two professors who later became colleagues at the University of Iowa, Charles Hale and Shelton Stromquist. As a graduate student at The University of Texas, my skills as a historian were honed in the seminars of professors Susan Deans-Smith, Richard Graham, Michael Hanchard, Aline Helg, Alan Knight, Standish Meacham, and David Montejano. I am particularly grateful to Jonathan Brown for not only guiding me to the study of Mexican history, but for his inspiring comments and masterful editing of the dissertation upon which this book is based. Kevin Kenny and David Montgomery both offered critical advice on an early version of this study. I am also indebted to Chris Boyer, Greg Crider, John French, Mark Healy, John Lear, Steve Lewis, Myrna Santiago, Mary Kay Vaughan, and Barbara Weinstein for the insights and critiques they offered over the years that this work was in progress. I thank Barry Carr and an anonymous reader for Cambridge University Press for their expert commentary and suggested revisions on the initial manuscript. And I owe Scott Seregny my heartfelt thanks for reading and commenting upon a final draft of the book.

A number of individuals and institutions helped make this investigation possible. Historians all owe great professional debts to the generations of archivists who have preserved our primary sources and guide us to them. That caveat holds especially true for Mexico, where such public servants support their families as well as our scholarly endeavors on rather meager salaries. I thus extend my gratitude to the staffs of the Archivo General de la Nación and the Hemeroteca Nacional in Mexico City. I am equally appreciative of the dedicated archivists at the Archivo General del Estado de Nuevo León and the Archivo Histórico Fundidora Monterrey. While conducting research, I enjoyed collegial guidance and valuable institutional support from Mario Camarena Ocampo at the Instituto Nacional de Antropología e Historia and Mario Cerutti at the Universidad Autónoma de Nuevo León.

Finally, I hope that this book does credit to the lives and stories of the retired workers I interviewed in Monterrey. Those interviews resulted not only in priceless source material but in enduring friendships as well. Fellowships from the Fulbright-García Robles Commission and the Institute of Latin American Studies at The University of Texas helped fund initial research in Mexico. Follow-up research in Monterrey and Washington, D.C., was financed by grants from the School of Liberal Arts and the Office for Professional Development at Indiana University–Purdue University Indianapolis.

Researching this study was more rewarding for the time spent outside the archives among the friends whom I discovered in Mexico. I owe a special thanks to Elisa Servín and to the family of Quinta Roberts and the late Manuel Cuevas for the home and hospitality they provided during my stays in Mexico City. Life in Monterrey is always a memorable experience for the time I enjoy in the company and homes of Jesús Avila, Raúl Rubio, and Lila Espinosa and Mark Miller. *Gracias a todos*. Finally, I wish to thank my family, friends, and colleagues in the United States for their inspiration during the course of this project. This book is dedicated to my mother, Carol, and to two friends who passed away before its completion: my father, Richard, and my friend, Reed Foster. *Que descansen en paz*.

Introduction

Only a decade after the onset of Mexico's 1910 revolution, the people of Monterrey, Nuevo León could celebrate the class harmony that reigned in their preeminently industrial city. The *regiomontanos* attributed this aura of industrial peace to the unique character of their city's workers and the inherent benevolence of their employers. They took special pride in both. Monterrey's workers carried a reputation for their hard work, industriousness, and staunch independence. They manifested the latter through their renowned autonomy from the national unions organized in the revolution's wake. The industrialists earned local acclaim for having built their companies with Mexican capital. Moreover, such pillars of local industry as the Cuauhtémoc Brewery and the Fundidora steel mill provided their employees with welfare benefits unique by Mexican standards. Since the early 1920s, civic boosters insisted, company paternalism had established the cornerstone of labor peace and economic prosperity. Then, just as General Lázaro Cárdenas assumed the presidency in 1935, class struggle seemingly engulfed their hometown. In a startling development, the steel workers broke from the Independent Unions of Nuevo León and affiliated with the national Miner-Metalworkers Union. Ten days later, workers at the brewery's subsidiary glass plant, Vidriera Monterrey, struck in support of militant unionism.

The industrialists blamed this outbreak of militance on the Cárdenas government's intrusive labor policies. Indignant at this perceived threat to their social hegemony, the industrialists orchestrated a mass antigovernment rally. They punctuated their resistance with a two-day lockout, shutting down their factories in a display of economic might.[1] Falling as it did on Mexico's Constitution Day, the march's organizers portrayed the event as a patriotic response to the "highly dangerous intrusion of communist agitators." That the agitators had arrived from Mexico City only sharpened local indignation. On the days preceding the protest, radio broadcasts and

---

[1] The following paragraph is based upon *El Porvenir*, Monterrey, January 10–February 7, 1932; *Excélsior*, Mexico City, February 2–6, 1936.

flyers posted about town reminded the *regiomontanos* that the "Communist Government of Mexico" threatened their jobs and their families' well-being. The message resonated powerfully. On the morning of February 5, 1936, approximately 50,000 protestors marched in the largest antigovernment demonstration to that point in Mexico's history. With thousands of loyal workers at their side, the city's captains of industry led a cross-class, multigenerational procession that caught the nation's attention. The movement proved a stunning success for Mexico's most powerful group of industrialists, a vivid display of their workers' inherent loyalty toward their employers.

Two days later, President Cárdenas arrived in Monterrey. Over the course of the following week, he met with local businesspeople and rival union leaders, listening attentively to their respective positions. Then, on February 11, he addressed thousands of supporters from the balcony of Nuevo León's Palacio del Gobierno. Outlining his government's labor policy, Cárdenas reiterated his promise to unify all Mexican workers into a national labor federation. Monterrey's company-controlled unions – the so-called independents – impeded that unity. He blamed the labor unrest upon the industrialists and their refusal to recognize the workers' right to elect their union leaders. Then, as if to confirm the *regiomontanos'* fears of communism, the president resolved that employers who resisted unionization "hand their industries over to their workers or the government." "That would be patriotic," he concluded, "the industrial lockout is not."[2] Cárdenas's veiled expropriation threat never materialized. But his government's labor policies tested the limits of Monterrey's unique system of industrial paternalism, offering workers two clear alternatives: "stay on the company's side" or "go with the reds," as locals referred to militant unions. Some workers forsook unionism for the security of paternalism; others embraced it for its promises of industrial democracy. The outcome separated the *regiomontano* workers and their families into two opposed camps, a division that endured for decades to come. This is the story of those workers and their experience of paternalism and revolution.

Deference and Defiance examines how the workers and industrialists of Monterrey perceived, responded to, and helped shape the course of Mexico's revolution. It builds upon and complements the "postrevisionist" scholarship on the period. Whereas an earlier generation of historians downplayed the grassroots nature of the revolution by positing the state as the era's dominant protagonist, scholars have since revised our understanding of the revolutionary process. By examining the revolution from a peripheral and largely rural perspective, the postrevisionists show that policy making and implementation entailed a "negotiation of rule" among state agents, local elites, and popular classes. The revolutionary government's economic, social, and

---

2 Jose P. Saldaña, *Crónicas históricas* (Monterrey, 1982), 250.

cultural projects encountered resistance at the local level. Regional developments in turn forced the ruling party to revise its policies of state formation to forge the most durable political consensus in twentieth-century Latin America.[3] This study examines that process from an urban and industrial perspective. Mexico remained a predominantly agrarian society into the 1940s. Yet within a single generation, rapid industrialization shifted the nation's demographic profile and economic base. Subsequent generations of workers and employers inherited the legal institutions, corporate policies, and union practices bequeathed by the labor struggles of the era.

Deference and Defiance sheds new light on Mexican working-class and labor history. For decades, the literature remained overshadowed by political narratives that highlighted organized labor's integration into Mexico's ruling party.[4] Meanwhile, social histories of working-class Mexicans focus on the prerevolutionary era and/or the foreign-owned export enclaves.[5] This study of urban workers provides a regional perspective to organized labor, its leaders, and its relation to the state. It revises our conception of those institutions and activists by assessing the interrelated struggles surrounding local politics and Mexican labor law, a crucial yet understudied outcome of the revolution. It enlivens the history of labor by exploring the culture of the local union hall and the workers who inhabited it. We also travel from the political arenas and union assemblies to the worlds of work and leisure, exploring the camaraderie and antagonisms that developed on the factory floors and in the blue-collar neighborhoods of Monterrey.

From there, *Deference and Defiance* departs from traditional studies of Mexican labor and the revolution by highlighting new issues and extending our coverage beyond the Cárdenas presidency and through that key transitional decade of the 1940s. We explore the experiences and perspectives of Monterrey's nonunion workers, the men and women who never struck nor attended a union assembly. These were laborers for whom consensual

3 See Gilbert M. Joseph and Daniel Nugent, eds., *Everyday Forms of State Formation: Revolution and the Negotiation of Rule in Modern Mexico* (Durham, 1994); Alan Knight, "Cardenismo: Juggernaut or Jalopy?" *Journal of Latin American Studies* 26:1 (February 1994), 73–107.

4 A cross-generational survey would include Rosendo Salazar, *Las pugnas de la gleba, 1907–1922* (Mexico City, 1923); Marjorie Ruth Clark, *Organized Labor in Mexico* (Chapel Hill, 1934); Joe Ashby, *Organized Labor and the Mexican Revolution under Lázaro Cárdenas* (Chapel Hill, 1967); Arturo Anguiano, *El estado y la política obrera del cardenismo* (Mexico City, 1975); Kevin Middlebrook, *The Paradox of Revolution: Labor, the State, and Authoritarianism in Mexico* (Baltimore, 1995).

5 Examples include Rodney Anderson, *Outcasts in Their Own Land: Mexican Industrial Workers, 1906–1911* (Dekalb, 1976); Jonathan Brown, "Foreign and Native-Born Workers in Porfirian Mexico," *American Historical Review* 98 (1993), 787–818; William E. French, *A Peaceful and Working People: Manners, Morals, and Class Formation in Northern Mexico* (Albuquerque, 1996); Juan Luis Sariego, *Enclaves y minerales en el norte de México: Historia social de los mineros de Cananea y Nueva Rosita, 1900–1970* (Mexico City, 1988). A recent exception is John Lear, *Workers, Neighbors, and Citizens: The Revolution in Mexico City* (Lincoln, 2001).

industrial relations remained the predominant feature of their working lives. As contemporary *regiomontanos* proudly proclaimed, labor relations in Monterrey were harmonious relative to other regions of Mexico. Those contemporaries rightly acknowledged that "class harmony" was the product of company paternalism. We examine paternalism as an institutionalized system of industrial relations that "intended to extend non-wage benefits . . . and create an identifiable corporate culture" among factory operatives.[6] Monterrey's industrialists offered their employees a range of welfare benefits like company housing, schools, and leisure activities. They did so in order to check labor unrest, instill work discipline, and foster company loyalty. We examine how paternalism assumed different forms at the companies under study and ask why workers responded in divergent ways to their employers' benevolent pretensions.

A comparative study of shop-floor relations illuminates the limits to paternalism. It explains why some working people opted to support militant unions and untangles a seeming paradox: why a city with a conservative reputation became a stronghold of communist labor activism in the 1930s and 1940s. The issue of unionism also sheds light on the contrasting ways in which Monterrey's employers acquiesced to or resisted the state's shifting labor policies. Due to their adversarial relation to the central government, the captains of industry appear prominently in the literature on revolutionary Mexico. But as the author of a seminal study of the industrialists notes, historians have limited their treatment of Monterrey to the elite's critical interventions in national politics.[7] We explore their antagonisms with the state as well as their everyday interactions with popular classes. In particular, we examine how both state labor policy and working-class pressures forced the industrialists to repeatedly revise their managerial strategies. In the process, the Monterrey elite themselves developed a class consciousness and created new and enduring forms of corporate solidarity. Meanwhile, they

---

6 Paternalism was a pervasive factor in the lives of Mexico's popular classes. It infused social relations in the countryside and remained embedded in the political culture of Porfirian and postrevolutionary Mexico. As employed in this study, the terms *company paternalism*, *industrial paternalism*, and *welfare capitalism* refer synonymously and specifically to managerial practices. Manifestations of patriarchy, benevolence, and personalism characterized the paternalistic practices of Monterrey's employers, just as they did the life of the hacienda and relations between the Mexican state and popular classes. But these characteristics, as Flamming notes, "were not so much the essence of paternalism as they were patterns of behavior that operated within and further complicated the system." Douglas Flamming, *Creating the Modern South: Millhands and Managers in Dalton, Georgia, 1884–1984* (Chapel Hill, 1992), 360–61.

7 Alex Saragoza, *The Monterrey Elite and the Mexican State, 1880–1940* (Austin, 1988). Regional histories sympathetic toward, if not commissioned by, the industrialists dominate the field. The classic is José P. Saldaña, *Apuntes históricos sobre la industrialización de Monterrey* (Monterrey, 1965). Two critical interpretations are Máximo de León Garza, *Monterrey: Un vistazo a sus entrañas* (Monterrey, 1968) and Abraham Nuncio, *El Grupo Monterrey* (Mexico City, 1982).

attempted to mobilize their employees' opposition to unions by fashioning working-class identities in tune with their own political outlooks.

Our study of working-class identity formation defers to Emilia Viotti da Costa's call to analyze not only the construction of multiple, overlapping, and competing identities but also how and why "one comes to prevail over the others."[8] Monterrey's workers perceived their world through a multiplicity of lenses. *Deference and Defiance* explores how material life and discourses of power and resistance shaped and reflected distinct political identities – be they regional, occupational, gendered, or class. Theoretically indebted to the writings of Antonio Gramsci, scholars like Stuart Hall recognize identity as "a matter of 'becoming' as well as 'being.'"[9] Identities are products of history and, as such, undergo constant transformation. Gramsci's own writings challenged the Marxist orthodoxy of his day: that class identities retain a level of uniform, objective purity. His own experiences during the rise of fascism in 1920s Italy informed Gramsci's understanding that working-class political identities may be divided, intersected, and subdued by a host of extraeconomic discourses. He thus invoked the notion of "contradictory consciousness" in recognition of the ambivalent and intertwined character of working-class identities. Gramsci perceived that such identities resulted from structural, ideological, and historical forces. Perhaps most importantly, he recognized that identity formation was a product of human agency and interventions.[10]

We analyze the mutual construction of subjective identities at and away from the workplace to explain workers' divergent perceptions of their employers, unions, and the state. For example, the practices of company paternalism both constructed and reinforced regional identities as part of an explicit managerial effort to undermine feelings of class or allegiances to organized labor. Meanwhile, a radical labor culture beyond the paternalistic grasp of the industrialists contested the workers' loyalty by drawing upon languages of class and revolution. Indeed, throughout this period of study both militant and more conservative worker-activists attempted to

---

8 Emilia Viotti da Costa, "Experience versus Structures: New Tendencies in the History of Labor and the Working Class in Latin America – What Do We Gain? What Do We Lose?" *International Labor and Working-Class History* 36 (1989), 4–24.

9 Stuart Hall, "Cultural Identity and Diaspora," in Jonathan Rutherford, ed., *Identity: Community, Culture, Difference* (London, 1990), 222–37.

10 Antonio Gramsci, *Selections from the Prison Notebooks*, edited by Quinton Hoare and Geoffrey Nowell Smith (New York, 1971). Among other studies that informed my analysis of identity formation are Leonard Berlanstein, ed., *Rethinking Labor History: Essays on Discourse and Class Analysis* (Urbana, 1993); Leela Fernandes, *Producing Workers: The Politics of Gender, Class, and Community in the Calcutta Jute Mills* (Philadelphia, 1997); and Lewis H. Siegelbaum and Ronald Grigor Suny, eds., *Making Workers Soviet: Power, Class, and Identity* (Ithaca, 1994). For a comparative case see Christopher Boyer, "The Threads of Class at La Virgen: Misrepresentation and Identity at a Mexican Textile Mill, 1918–1935," *American Historical Review* 105 (2000), 1576–98.

mobilize rank-and-file laborers through discursive appeals to their regional, patriotic, and gendered identities. The activists' capacity to transmit their political ideas and cultural values to fellow workers depended on their ability to earn the rank and file's trust and respect. We therefore invest considerable attention in the patterns of sociability and human relationships forged between rank-and-file workers and labor activists on and away from the factory floor. *Deference and Defiance* thus helps conceptualize the role these intermediaries performed in the (re)ordering of the political and cultural universes of the Mexican working class.

These issues are examined through a comparative study of four companies. Aside from the railway yards, Monterrey's first large-scale employer was the American Smelting and Refining Company (ASARCO). The smelter's foreign ownership made it unique because in contrast to national trends, Mexicans largely financed the city's industrialization. That distinction lent those industrialists a unique place in local society and national politics. In the 1890s, Monterrey's Garza Sada family launched their industrial empire with the Cuauhtémoc Brewery. A decade later, they opened the first of many subsidiary companies, Vidriera Monterrey. The glass company first manufactured bottles for the brewery. By the 1920s, the firm's workers were also producing crystal ware and plate glass for an expanding domestic market. Today those beer and glass companies anchor two of Latin America's largest multinational conglomerates, FEMSA and Vitro. But the company for which Monterrey first earned national renown was the Fundidora Iron and Steel Works, the first and only integrated mill in Latin America until the 1940s. Founded in 1900 by a consortium of local and national industrialists, the Fundidora would establish its headquarters in Mexico City to be near its principal client, the federal government. These four companies shared common traits, notably their scale of operations and their paternalistic labor regimes. But key distinctions in their ownership and managerial styles, their work regimes, and their peculiar relations to the state make them outstanding cases for comparative analysis.

Like many histories of urban labor in Latin America, the focus here is upon factory and (occasionally) railway workers. It regrettably but necessarily ignores the domestics, retail clerks, building tradesmen, and workshop hands whose voices remain muted in the archives that made this study possible. Several of those collections will prove invaluable to future historians. Given their concerns in Mexico, the United States consular staff left a repository of reports on local economies, politics, and labor disputes. State Department officials also enjoyed privileged access to the thoughts and organizational activities of the local elites whose company they often kept. In Mexico City, a visit to the National Archives should begin with its Labor Department holdings. Established early in the revolution, the agency gathered records on industrial accidents, costs of living, and labor market conditions. Its federal labor inspectors also traveled to the provinces to mediate disputes. Their reports offer keen insights into state labor policy and the bureaucrats charged with implementing it. The voices of managers, workers, and local government officials are logged in the extensive case files produced by Nuevo León's labor arbitration boards. Housed in the state archive, these well-catalogued labor court records emphasize the causes and outcome of workplace conflicts from 1923 onward. But they also illuminate the working lives of the claimants and their shop-floor interactions with managers and fellow workers.

This researcher also discovered a wealth of insights from the retired workers who opened their hearts and homes to an inquisitive gringo. Their stories, personalities, and voices bring the human experience to life in the pages that follow. Conducted upon completion of archival research, their interview narrowed gaps in the empirical record by untangling the bewildering events and intriguing characters from Mexico's ever-changing past. Their oral histories also illuminate the experiences, values, and traditions that fashioned individual consciousness and collective identities.[11] Despite their subjective and fragmentary character, memories do persist, often with remarkable (if selective) clarity. Moreover, unlike traditional sources, informants punctuate their oral testimonies with emphatic gestures, sighs of remorse, and tones of nostalgia. Tenses shift as speakers build their narratives and recollect the past with an eye to the present. Readers should therefore be aware that, when the interviews were recorded, organized labor had evolved into a corrupt appendage of the Mexican state. That widespread sentiment certainly informed retired workers' views of unionism and union leaders of the past. Furthermore, Mexicans were struggling through a deep economic depression. Such circumstances reinforced the sense of nostalgia with which any retiree reminisces about his or her past. Thus did one informant recall of his working days: "Times were rough, but I'll always remember the good."[12]

---

11 Among the methodologies and case studies that informed my use of oral history are Alessandro Portelli, *The Death of Luigi Trastulli and Other Stories: Form and Meaning in Oral History* (Albany, 1991); David Thelan, "Memory and American History," *Journal of American History* 75 (1989), 1117–29; Daniel James, *Doña María's Story: Life History, Memory, and Political Identity* (Durham, 2000).

12 Interview with Salvador Castañeda Medina, July 13, 2001.

I

Porfirian Progress in "Mexico's Chicago"

When General Porfirio Díaz became president in 1876, Monterrey was a city of merchant houses and workshops servicing northeastern Mexico's mining and agricultural economy. By 1910, when revolution forced the elderly dictator into exile, Monterrey had emerged as the nation's preeminent industrial center, "Mexico's Chicago." Monterrey symbolized and exemplified the Porfirian dream of industrial modernity. The Mexican people had accepted Don Porfirio's dictatorship as the price for peace. Union and Progress became the hallmark slogans of a regime that parlayed political stability and social order into economic development. Courted by the state, foreign investors financed railroads, factories, a mining revival, and oil exploration. The railroads spurred commercial agriculture, and a land grab ensued. Displaced peasants became rural laborers or rode the rails to find work in fast-growing industrial cities like Monterrey. By 1910, the capital of Nuevo León was the transportation hub of northern Mexico, the region that benefitted most from economic modernization. The railroads helped transform the frontier trading post into a modern city of banks, commerce, and industry. But Porfirian Progress carried a heavy and unacceptable price for the people of Mexico. As Don Porifirio grew old and his regime more repressive, a younger generation clamored for honest elections, workers agitated for industrial democracy, and peasants struggled for the restitution of lands. The wedding of those diverse grievances and social actors prompted the 1910 revolution that drew the old regime to a close.

Regiomontanos and the Regionalist Narrative

As the twentieth century dawned, the people of Monterrey – the *regiomontanos* – had developed a unique sense of themselves and their place in Mexican society. This regionalism reflected and fostered a proud, self-conscious identification with the city. It manifested itself in cultural, sentimental, and discursive fashions, percolating through regional lore, poetry, folk ballads, and political manifestoes. Regional identity built upon the presumably unique qualities shared by the locals, cultural values that were said to transcend

8

class boundaries and differentiate the *regiomontanos* from other Mexicans. For generations, Monterrey's civic boosters, captains of industry, public intellectuals, and working-class activists would all promote a regionalist discourse that is a key to understanding the city's history. Regionalism's capacity to resonate with effect owed to the specific moments, social settings, and political arenas in which it operated. To be sure, regionalism's promotion was very often an elite project used to mobilize locals in defense of their own economic interests. But its capacity to cultivate deference among workers or defiance among locals owed to its generalized embracement by all *regiomontanos*. Monterrey was not alone as a prosperous Latin American city where a sense of regional chauvinism would be built upon claims to greater modernity and industrial progress. What made it unique was that this regionalist discourse became meaningful not only for its elite and middle-class proponents – as in São Paulo – but for working-class people as well.[1] Be they workers or businessmen, men or women, old or young, the *regiomontanos* all came to share a regional identity founded on their northern Mexican heritage and a patriotic commitment to industrial progress.

As *norteños*, they shared common values and a distinct way of life that distinguished inhabitants of the northern states from other Mexicans. The northerners take a boastful pride in being independent, hardworking, self-sufficient, and rebellious. Having lived at the margins of central government authority since colonial times, they came to cherish their autonomy and to resent bureaucratic meddling from Mexico City. Theirs became a society "of the self-made man where, compared with central Mexico, achievement counted for more than ascription, where the rich (both Mexican and foreign) could expect bonanzas, and where even the poor enjoyed some mobility and opportunity."[2] While rarely articulated in an explicit fashion, the *norteños'* vision of themselves built upon their critical views of central and southern Mexico: lethargic, submissive, economically backward societies weighed down by an oppressive colonial heritage. Scholars generally attribute these northern "peculiarities" – in varying and often conflicting degrees – to the region's natural environment, its frontier past, or its proximity to the United States.[3] All of these factors played roles in the region's distinct

---

1 See Barbara Weinstein, *For Social Peace in Brazil: Industrialists and the Remaking of the Working Class in São Paulo, 1920–1964* (Chapel Hill, 1996).

2 Alan Knight, *The Mexican Revolution*, (2 vols., Cambridge, 1986), I, 10–11. A veteran *New York Times* reporter later characterized the *norteños* as "more daring and efficient, more outspoken and informal, even taller and whiter than most Mexicans . . . [They are] no less proud of their achievements than they are jealous of their independence." Alan Riding, *Distant Neighbors: A Portrait of the Mexicans* (New York, 1984), 283.

3 Given the vastness of a region stretching from Tijuana to Tampico, the degree to which ethnicity, the environment, and North American influences weighed on regional identity formation owes as much to scholarly interpretations as to local historical variants. See Anna María Alonso, *Thread of*

pattern of economic development and the relative prosperity of the North. Monterrey's own chroniclers have fashioned a local version of the *norteño* narrative that bridges centuries of frontier struggle to a twentieth-century story of industrial modernity.

Regional folklore holds that the Spanish colonists who founded Monterrey in 1596 came in search of silver and discovered instead a barren, arid land devoid of natural resources. The colonial outpost languished for generations as an isolated presidio, a fortified trading post that supplied mining towns of the interior with merchandise and contraband from the Gulf Coast. The inhabitants suffered political neglect from Mexico City, weathered a harsh climate, and struggled against hostile, seminomadic Indians. These *indios bárbaros*, it is said, "gave [the settlers] not a moment of rest," causing "the stagnation of progress."[4] By the mid-nineteenth century, the region's original inhabitants had succumbed to conquest and assimilation. Indeed, come the twentieth century, census takers would count the smallest indigenous population of any state in Mexico, prompting Governor Porfirio González to boast that, "There are no Indians in Nuevo León!" Despite the governor's remark, ethnic "whiteness" played no well-articulated role in regional identity formation in late-nineteenth and twentieth-century Monterrey, as it did in the northern states of Sonora or Chihuahua, and certainly had among Monterrey's Spanish-American colonists in the colonial period.[5]

Meanwhile, the locals' heroic resistance during the American occupation (1846–47) and their struggles during the French intervention (1860s) secured their patriotic credentials as Mexican liberals. By then, other chroniclers emphasize, "Nature's hostility forged a spirit of industry," and tempered an "enterprising, dynamic, vigorous, [and] sober" character among the *regiomontanos*. Faced with poor soil and a scarcity of minerals, "the makers

---

Blood: Colonialism, Revolution, and Gender on Mexico's Northern Frontier (Tucson, 1995), 15–16; Miguel Tinker Salas, *In the Shadow of the Eagles: Sonora and the Transformation of the Border during the Porfiriato* (Berkeley, 1997); Barry Carr, "Las peculiaridades del norte mexicano," *Historia Mexicana* 22 (1973), 320–46.

4 José P. Saldaña, *Apuntes históricos*, 2–3.

5 Rather, despite the relatively large "white" population recorded by census takers – 20 percent – the *regiomontanos* seemed to have shared a common sense of *mestizaje*, the European-Indian roots that most Mexicans claim. Thus did one *regiomontano* proclaim to his American wife upon witnessing a procession of "Indians" in a local parade: "But this is odd. . . . Because we have no Indians like this here in the North. Our people are all mestizo, and mostly they are factory workers or ranch hands, and they dress in blue jeans and wear shoes." The region's history of indigenous–settler relations is told by Abraham Nuncio, *Visión de Monterrey* (Mexico, 1997), 19–59, and Juan Mora-Torres, *The Making of the Mexican Border: The State, Capitalism, and Society in Nuevo León, 1848–1910* (Austin, 2001), 14–20; census figures from Departamento de Estadística Nacional, *IV Censo de la Poblacion*, Vol. 5 (Mexico City, 1927), 17; Governor Porfirio González quoted in *El Porvenir*, June 17, 1926; Elizabeth Borton de Treviño, *My Heart Lies South* (New York, 1953), 186–87 (quoted above).

of modern Monterrey" discovered commerce and then industry as the only viable roads to progress.[6] By the 1880s, the city had become a commercial boomtown and the emergent railroad hub of the North. Monterrey thus attracted migrants – from neighboring states and foreign lands – who complemented the *regiomontanos'* repute for being "risk takers . . . hard workers . . . industrious and ambitious."[7] Through hard work, thrift, and perseverance, the city's merchant clans overcame the region's lack of natural resources to make the desert bloom into the prosperous city that became the "Sultan of the North."

The preindustrial frontier experience thus produced the "values oriented toward modernity . . . that have made the city of Monterrey different from the rest of the nation."[8] Like other regionalist narratives, Monterrey's local variant rests on a foundation of factual inaccuracies, exaggerated claims, folklore, and myth. Moreover, it is very much a story less of the city's working class than its captains of industry. In contrast to the city's well-known local chroniclers, academic scholars now attribute Monterrey's unique development less to the cultural values of its makers and more to its proximity to and borrowing from North American markets, capital, technologies, and business cultures.[9] Indeed, their central Mexican rivals often translate the locals' renown for hard work and thriftiness into the commonplace stereotype of the penny-pinching, workaholic, "Americanized" *regiomontano*.[10] The locals dismiss these charges as a jealous response to their hard-earned prosperity and take patriotic pride in their hometown's status as Mexico's industrial capital. In their eyes, the enterprising spirit of the city's businessmen made Monterrey the vanguard of a new Mexico, the standard of industrial modernity to which the rest of Mexico aspired. The workers, for their part, took pride in manufacturing the products that would liberate Mexico from economic dependency on foreign imports. They, too, would be celebrated by civic boosters and outside observers as a breed apart from workers elsewhere in Mexico. More important, Monterrey's dominant narrative provides a historical seed whence sprout the cultural values shared by workers and employers

6 Salvador Novo, *Crónica regiomontana: Breve historia de un gran esfuerzo* (Monterrey, 1965), 5; Saldaña, *Apuntes históricos*, 13–14, 30–31.

7 Isidro Vizcaya Canales, *Los orígenes de la industrialización de Monterrey, 1876–1910* (Monterrey, 1969), 72–73.

8 Juan Zapata Novoa, *Tercos y triunfadores de Monterrey* (Monterrey, 1993), xiv.

9 Mario Cerutti, *Burguesía, capitales, e industria en el norte de Mexico: Monterrey y su ámbito regional* (Monterrey, 1992); Nuncio, *El Grupo Monterrey*, 41–53; Menno Vellinga, *Industrialización, burguesía, y clase obrera en México: El caso de Monterrey* (Mexico City, 1979).

10 Some also refer to Monterrey's business elite as the "Jews of Mexico," a generally mean-spirited, anti-Semitic reference to the allegedly Sephardic roots of the original settlers. See Riding, *Distant Neighbors*, 285.

alike. It thus bolsters a sense of regional identity that would ameliorate the antagonisms of class and unite the *regiomontanos* in the collaborative project called industrial progress. By the 1930s, the regionalist narrative linked a frontier past to an urban present where industrial pioneers and their blue-collar allies overcame the challenges posed by the modern equivalent of the *indios bárbaros*: revolution, economic crises, communists, and a meddlesome federal government.

Early in the twentieth century, Porfirian Mexico beckoned travelers as never before. In Monterrey, they discovered indisputable evidence of the peace and progress that Don Porfirio had promised. Having witnessed Mexico's impoverished countryside, they universally acknowledged Monterrey's prosperity. They attributed that well-being to its industrial base. "This," one visitor wrote, "is the manufacturing center of the Republic, progressive and modernized." "This city," another remarked, "is an example of a prosperous and growing Mexican community, largely supplying its own wants in raw materials and manufactured articles."[11] Unfamiliar perhaps with local lore, they often attributed Monterrey's relative affluence less to the character of its people than to those factors that made Mexico's economy grow during the Porfiriato: the railroad boom and foreign capital. Both abounded in a city served by four major railway lines and inhabited by several thousand foreign immigrants. Echoing the *regiomontanos'* own optimism, Mrs. Alec Tweedie observed that "Monterrey promises hereafter to become the great business centre of Mexico, and judging from the number of Americans, English and Germans already settled in the place . . . it is almost as cosmopolitan as Chicago, to which prosperous town Mexicans ambitiously liken it." Indeed, in a refrain that became commonplace in coming decades, travelers frequently suggested that "Monterrey has become more Americanized . . . than any other Mexican town." Certainly for that reason did another visitor conclude that, "It is not so interesting for the tourist looking for the real Mexican atmosphere."[12]

These travelers unknowingly disputed local myths of an arid, hardscrabble landscape. Indeed their accounts acknowledged the bountiful supplies of minerals, timber, and water that helped attract industry to Monterrey. Industrial growth and urban sprawl had only begun to consume the "productive valleys, copious streams, and picturesque scenery" that one traveler contrasted to "the appalling deserts" to the west. Nestled along the banks of the Santa Catarina river, Monterrey sat at the geographic intersection of

11 C. Reginald Enock, *Mexico, Its Ancient and Modern Civilizations* (London, 1909), 311–12; Percey F. Martin, *Mexico of the 20ᵗʰ Century* (New York, 1907), 311.

12 Mrs. Alec Tweedie, *Mexico As I Saw It* (New York, 1910), 62; Alfred Conkling, *Appletons' Guide to Mexico* (New York, 1886); Martin, *Mexico of the 20ᵗʰ Century*, 311.

the coastal plains and the Sierra Madre mountains. "These mountains," one visitor beheld, "surround a lovely valley, watered by clear running streams and carpeted by the green of fertile fields."[13] Typically arriving from Texas, travelers saw rolling farmland give way to urban-industrial flatlands backed by jagged mountain peaks. Rising in a semicircle to the south and west of the city, the pine-forested mountains ascended nearly 4,000 feet in a few miles, offering a refreshing escape from the hustle and summertime heat of the city below. The mountains became the natural symbol of Monterrey. Thus did the inhabitants of this *región montañosa* earn the name *regiomontanos*. Yet it was a man-made landscape of smokestack industry and bustling commerce that came to define the locals' way of life. Indeed industry became so much a part of Monterrey's identity that visits to the foundries, the glass factory, and the brewery became mandatory stops on any tourist's itinerary.[14]

Industrialization

A North American visiting in the late 1800s beheld Monterrey's railroad yards, its smokestacks, and its bustling workers and labeled the city "Mexico's Chicago." Others would stamp Nuevo León's capital with distinct foreign referents; but Pittsburgh and Birmingham never stuck. Monterrey's boosters embraced the namesake and did so with pride, for other upstart northern cities like Torreón had earlier claimed the mantle for themselves.[15] The correlation makes sense when reduced to scale. Like Chicago, the railways helped transform Monterrey from a regional commercial hub to a city of industrial barons and blue-collar workers. At mid-nineteenth century, the city's merchant houses were supplying the region's farm towns and mining camps with products from home and abroad. By 1883, Monterrey's 1,300 workers and artisans labored in three textile mills, dozens of metal-working and carpentry shops, and a number of small factories and mills producing food, liquor, tobacco, and leather goods. Government economic planners then set out to lure heavy industry. During his twenty years in office, Governor Bernardo Reyes built on federal policy and boosted the city's economy with protective tariffs and tax exemptions for enterprising industrialists. But it was the arrival of the railroads that sealed Monterrey's destiny as "Mexico's Chicago." By 1890, four major lines and dozens of feeders tied Monterrey to rich coal and iron fields, provincial capitals, the United States, and the Gulf Coast port of

13 Enock, *Mexico*, 311; Reau Cambell, *Complete Guide and Descriptive Book of Mexico* (Chicago, 1907), 211–12.
14 Martin, *Mexico of the 20th Century*, 87; *La Voz de Nuevo León*, Monterrey, Feb. 7, 1903.
15 *El Economista Mexicano*, Mexico City, June 9, 1903; *El Porvenir*, Monterrey, January 20, 1920.

Tampico. The capital of Nuevo León became the transportation hub of the North.[16]

As Stephen Haber notes, the years 1890–1910 marked the nation's first stage of industrialization, "the epoch when manufacturing became big business . . . [and] the basic structures of modern Mexican industry were established."[17] During that period the companies that became the industrial pillars of Monterrey would open to great local and national fanfare. Flush with capital and lured by incentives, local merchant–financiers and foreign investors launched an array of industries. Some were typical to Latin America's early stage of industrialization. A growing population of workers and middle-class consumers became the principal market for such nondurable goods as pasta, beer, cigarettes, furniture, and work apparel. Yet in contrast to São Paulo, Buenos Aires, or Medellín, Monterrey became a center of heavy industry as well. Its smelters answered the world's growing demand for industrial metals, while its steel mill, brick factories, glassworks, and cement plant supplied building materials to a modernizing Mexico. It was this concentration of both manufacturing and heavy industry that made Monterrey unique by Latin American standards.

The city first earned renown for its smelters. By the late-nineteenth century the railway hub hosted the regional offices of several dozen mining companies. From Monterrey they coordinated mineral exports to American smelters. In 1890, the McKinley Tariff Act imposed protectionist duties on Mexican ore imports to the United States. What began as a setback to the nation's principal export industry prompted a scramble to build smelters on Mexican soil. Within weeks of the act's passage, Meyer Guggenheim had dispatched his sons to Mexico. They first scouted the nearby city of Saltillo because rivals were already constructing a smelter in Monterrey. But Coahuila's governor vetoed their project, fearful of the environmental damage that such an industry would incur on his pristine capital. Motivated by a twenty-year tax exemption from the state of Nuevo León, the American metal barons therefore chose Monterrey as the site of their first Mexican plant. It became the largest of three local smelters. The plants transformed Monterrey into the smelting capital of the Americas and the most polluted city in Mexico. For the next twenty years, the American Smelting and Refining Company's 1,200 workers toiled around the clock and the Guggenheim family reaped profits unprecedented in Porfirian

16 For Monterrey's industrialization, see Vizcaya Canales, *Los orígines de la industrialización*; Cerutti, *Burgesía, capitales e industria*; Saldaña, *Apuntes históricos*; Saragoza, *The Monterrey Elite and the Mexican State*, 30–71; and Vellinga, *Industrialización, burguesía, y clase obrera*.
17 Stephen Haber, *Industry and Underdevelopment: The Industrialization of Mexico, 1890–1940* (Stanford, 1989), 3–4.

Monterrey.[18] Meanwhile, ASARCO began buying Mexican mines, added four more smelters, and became Mexico's largest private employer by the 1920s.

ASARCO's foreign ownership proved exceptional to the city's pattern of industrial development. Unlike Mexico's other centers of industry, where French, Spanish, and American interests dominated, Monterrey's industrialization depended chiefly on the homegrown capital of local merchant–financiers. By the early 1900s, Mexicans accounted for 80 percent of local industrial investments.[19] Their capacity to finance industry was owed to a forty-year period of capital formation that began with the end of the Mexican American War. Mexico's new northern border elevated Monterrey's role as the commercial hub of northeastern Mexico. The city's merchants reaped a bonanza during the American Civil War, when Monterrey's products became the primary exchange for smuggled Confederate cotton and rebel provisions. Intimately linked through business and intermarriage, the city's merchant clans divested their wealth into banking, landholding, and mining.[20] When the railroads arrived in the 1880s, the merchants' extensive knowledge of regional markets and their access to capital and credit poised these traders to become producers. At the vanguard of the local elite marched the Garza Sada family. Their two bedrock companies, the Cuauhtémoc Brewery and Monterrey Glassworks, became the pillars of an industrial dynasty in the making.

The brewery launched operations in 1890. The firm began as a joint venture between the *regiomontano* merchants and Robert Schnaider, the son of a Saint Louis brewer whose products the locals had distributed. The American supervised operations until 1895, when his Mexican partners purchased Schnaider's interest in the firm. Like all successful brewers, the Garza Sadas mastered the art of public relations, thereafter promoting Cuauhtémoc as a national enterprise founded by Mexican capital.[21] While the brewery's history belies the claim, few ever questioned the patriotic

---

18 While Nuevo León's mines produced but 2 percent of Mexican ore in the late 1890s, Monterrey's smelters refined 23 percent of the nation's output, more than double the capacity of any other state. Harvey O'Connor, *The Guggenheims: The Making of an American Dynasty* (New York, 1937), 88–99; *La Voz de Nuevo León*, Mar. 7, May 30, June 30, 1891; *El Economista Mexicano*, Nov. 23, 1901, Nov. 15, 1902; Cerutti, *Burguesía*, 178.

19 Viscaya Canales, *Los orígenes de la industrialización*, 78.

20 Saragoza, *The Monterrey Elite*, 16–30; Mario Cerutti, "Monterrey and Its Ambito Regional, 1850–1910: Historical Context and Methodological Recommendations," in Eric Van Young, ed., *Mexico's Regions: Comparative History and Development* (San Diego, 1992), 145–65.

21 Barbara Hibino, "Cervecería Cuauhtémoc: A Case Study of Technology and Industrial Development in Mexico," *Mexican Studies* (Winter 1992) 2–35; Gerónimo Dávilos, et al. *Cuarenta años son un buen tiempo* (Monterrey, 1930); on foreign capital's role in Cuauhtémoc's development see Raúl Rubio Cano, "Ideas Centenarias, Realidades Históricas," *El Financiero* (Monterrey edition), Nov. 7, 1990.

credentials of a company named for an Aztec emperor. Cuauhtémoc grew into Mexico's largest brewery by the turn of the century. The quality of its product earned it national esteem and the first of many blue ribbons at the Chicago World's Fair. Spurred on by keen marketing, a vast distribution network, and the high cost of imports, annual beer production soared from a modest half million to more than thirteen million liters in 1910.[22] As the brewing business boomed, the Garza Sadas diversified their holdings by producing for themselves such foreign imports as malt, packaging, and bottle tops. Opening in the 1920s, those subsidiaries – Malta, Titán, and Famosa – became Mexico's largest suppliers of their respective products.

The Monterrey brewery gained its greatest competitive edge when the Garza Sada family ventured into glass production. An initial foray into bottle making collapsed in 1903 after a contract dispute with the firm's German glass blowers. The owners then supplanted craftsmen with technology. In 1909, they purchased the exclusive Mexican rights to the Owens automated bottle-making process. The reconstituted plant soon produced 40,000 bottles per day and Vidriera Monterrey parlayed its ownership of the patent into a national monopoly. The Garza Sadas' ownership of Mexico's sole automated bottle plant played a major factor in Cuauhtémoc's drive to capture a dominant position in the Mexican brewing industry.[23] Moreover, the family-owned firm continued acquiring new technologies in the United States and Europe, expanding their lines into crystalware and plate glass in the 1920s. Like the brewery, the glassworks evolved into a major holding company in its own right. Its subsidiaries produced chinaware and ceramics (Troqueles y Esmaltes), and even bottle-making machinery designed and patented by company engineers (FAMA). The Vidriera became one of Mexico's first and largest multinational companies, with markets throughout the republic and into Central and South America.[24]

A handful of *regiomontano* families with names now synonymous with Mexican wealth – Garza, Sada, Mugüerza, Zambrano, Salinas, and Rocha – emerged as the industrial magnates of the North, the Monterrey Group. Following the Garza Sadas' lead, these enterprising merchants and landowners invested their capital in cement, cigarette, furniture, apparel, textile, and food-processing factories. They insured their firms' future by sending their sons to study business and engineering in the United States. They forged ties of blood and business with regional elites from nearby cities like Saltillo and Torreón. And they earned local acclaim for pioneering the industries that made Monterrey prosper. Their businesses thrived as Mexican

22 Saragoza, *The Monterrey Elite*, 62–68.
23 Roberto G. Sada, *Ensayos sobre la historia de una industria* (Monterrey, 1988), 60–63; Haber, *Industry and Underdevelopment*, 89–91; Hibino, "Cervecería Cuauhtémoc," 33–35.
24 The corporation today known as Vitro is among the world's largest glass producers.

markets grew, consumers adopted new tastes, and the state provided a cushion against foreign competition. Indeed, their business success owed as much to their capacity to lobby as to their enterprising spirit. Like all industry in Porfirian Mexico, that of Monterrey enjoyed government patronage, notably that extended by Nuevo León's preeminent industrial booster, Governor Bernardo Reyes. Reyes encouraged federal authorities to impose the high tariffs that priced imported beer and bottles out of the domestic market. He also exempted Cuauhtémoc from taxes even as the brewery's profits soared. As an otherwise sympathetic biographer notes, "a higher tax could have been placed on the lucrative brewing business, but Reyes was too interested in keeping established companies content and attracting new industries to Monterrey."[25] Determined to promote and protect their interests, Monterrey's businessmen would play leading roles in the national employers' associations formed in coming years.[26] But not until the 1940s would the *regiomontano* industrialists again reap the benefits of a government so in tune with their interests.

No local industry would depend more on state patronage than the Fundidora Iron and Steel Works. With the rolling of its first steel rails in 1901, the Fundidora launched operations as Latin America's first integrated mill, a distinction it retained for the next four decades. Its emergence therefore marked the crowning moment of Porfirian industrialization, symbolizing Mexico's intent to produce for itself that most basic product of modernization, steel. The Fundidora's own development would parallel that of Mexico's economy. Following a period of steady growth that lasted until 1911, steel production became as erratic as national demand. Indeed, the mill did not turn a profit until the mid-1930s, after which time the mill and its workers enjoyed four decades of expansion and prosperity. Those who witnessed its inauguration marveled at the plant's installations and the immense workshops, "housing the grandest, most modern, and most powerful machinery ever seen in Mexico."[27]

Capitalized by a consortium of *regiomontano* and Mexico City–based financiers, the Fundidora proved unique from its inception. Its principal

---

25 E.V. Niemeyer Jr., *El General Bernardo Reyes* (Monterrey, 1966), 133.

26 Directors of Monterrey industry presided over the first boards of the National Federation of Chambers of Commerce (Conacaco, Enrique Sada Müegerza, 1917) and the National Federation of Chambers of Industry (Concanin, Adolfo Prieto, 1918). Roderic Camp, *Entrepreneurs and Politics in Twentieth Century Mexico* (New York, 1989).

27 On the founding of the Fundidora, see Manuel González Caballero, *La Fundidora en su tiempo* (Monterrey, 1989), 11–51; Haber, *Industry and Underdevelopment*, 45–46, 62–67, 71–82; *El Economista Mexicano*, Oct. 25, 1902 (quoted); company histories include Victor Cavazos Pérez, Rosana Covarrubias Mijares, et. al., *Tierra, fuego, aire, agua . . . Un estudio sobre el devenir urbanístico y arquitectónico de la Fundidora de Monterrey* (Monterrey, 2000); Marcela Guerra and Alma G. Trejo, *Crisol del temple: Fundidora de fierro y acero de Monterrey* (Monterrey, 2000).

client became and remained the federal government. Unlike the local, family-owned brewing and glass industries, the Fundidora established its corporate headquarters in Mexico City. Moreover, among the steel company's administrators were many European-born managers and engineers, and very few sons of Monterrey. While the *regiomontano* elite shared a begrudging *norteño* contempt for Mexico City, the steel mill's direct dependence on the state underpinned its directors' cooperative relationship with central government authority. In the meantime, Monterrey became as synonymous with steel as it was famous for beer. Set before the dramatic backdrop of Monterrey's Saddle Mountain, the Fundidora's towering blast furnace, sprawling workshops, and belching smokestacks became the visual symbols of "Mexico's Chicago."

Monterrey thus emerged during the Porfiriato as the preeminent industrial center of a predominantly agrarian country. With but 80,000 inhabitants, the city remained small, but its potential huge. It counted less than one-fifth the population of Mexico City. But Monterrey surpassed the capital's industrial capacity and produced nearly 14 percent of the nation's output.[28] A generation born in the 1880s saw their hometown transformed from one of merchants and artisans to a blue-collar city of factory workers and their families. Much like the industrial towns of Torreón and Orizaba, Monterrey exemplified the modern Mexico that Porfirian policymakers had set out to fashion. Foreign observers shared their optimism. Reporting from Monterrey, the United States consul noted, "Railroads are being built in every part of the Republic, [as are] steel plants, smelters, and factories of every kind, affording increased wages to the laboring men; giving them better homes, better food, better clothing, education for their children, [and] delivering them forever from the spirit of discontent." He thus foresaw on the horizon a self-sufficient nation that would export its manufactured wares to Latin America and the Caribbean. More importantly, the diplomat echoed what became a common refrain among Monterrey's industrialists: Industry offered jobs to Mexico's downtrodden people, reforming them into citizens "who can be counted upon as loyal and upright."[29] Indeed, what civic boosters described as "this singular vision" of the city – "one of chimneys, immense chimneys, and smoke, columns of smoke" – attracted migrant workers by the thousands.[30]

---

28 Cerutti, *Burguesía*, 178; John Lear, *Workers, Neighbors, and Citizens: The Revolution in Mexico City* (Lincoln, 2001), 55.

29 Hanna, Consul General, Monterrey, to United States State Department, May 26, 1904, National Archives Washington, Record Group 59: Consular Despatches, 1849–1906 (hereafter SD/RG 59). (Subsequent references to State Department records will cite only name of official and date of despatch. All reports are from Monterrey Consulate, unless indicated otherwise.)

30 *El Porvenir*, Mar. 18, 1926.

The Workers

In many regards, the men and women who became Monterrey's first-generation working class were as diverse in background as the industries that employed them. Some came from the city, others from nearby farms. The locals worked alongside migrants from neighboring states and a few immigrants from afar. But compared to other industrial cities of the Western Hemisphere, they were much alike in that nearly all Monterrey's workers came from within one-half day's train ride from the city. Aside from these largely *norteño* origins, Monterrey's proletariat shared traits with workers in other industrializing regions of Mexico.[31] Common laborers often came from the rural hinterlands. These so-called *peones* challenged employers with their propensity to quit. Some returned home for the harvest. Others continued on to Texas. Indeed Monterrey became a labor clearinghouse that attracted migrants as well as labor contractors for the railroads, northern Mexican mines, and North American employers. But high and steady wages, the chance to learn a trade, and the promise of social mobility all helped resolve an early shortage of hands. Consistent with findings elsewhere, many of Monterrey's workers came from nonagrarian backgrounds and brought skills and experience with them to the job. But the city's smelting, steel, and glass industries demanded specialized tradesmen unavailable in Mexico. Monterrey's industrialists therefore tapped into foreign labor markets to recruit the skilled workmen who transmitted their knowledge of the industrial arts to native-born workers. By 1910, they had largely accomplished that task.

The railroads that brought industry to Monterrey transported migrants as well. By the turn of the century, the local press reported the frequent arrival of trains "coming loaded with families emigrating to Monterrey." These "poor working people" had arrived to a city "that currently offers vast employment opportunities to laboring men." A notable quantity of these "operatives" came from nearby San Luis Potosí, where hard times in the mines produced "a people destined to toil in this city's foundries."[32] Generations of *potosinos* found their destiny in Monterrey. Local chronicles

---

31 For working-class formation in the textile, mining, railway, and oil industries of both central and northern Mexico see Bernardo García Díaz, *Un pueblo del porfiriato: Santa Rosa, Veracruz* (Mexico, 1981); Lief Adleson and Mario Camarena Ocampo, eds., *Comunidad, cultura y vida social: Ensayos sobre la formación de la clase obrera* (Mexico City, 1991); Lear, *Workers, Neighbors, and Citizens*, 51–54; William French, *A Peaceful and Working People: Manners, Morals, and Class Formation in Northern Mexico* (Albuquerque, 1996), 34–51; Jonathan Brown, "Foreign and Native-Born Workers in Porfirian Mexico," *American Historical Review* 98 (1993), 787–818; Brown, *Oil and Revolution in Mexico* (Berkeley, 1993), chs. 1 and 5; and Mryna Santiago, "Huasteca Crude: Indians, Ecology, and Labor in the Mexican Oil Industry, Northern Veracruz, 1900–1938," (Ph.D. diss., University of California-Berkeley, 1997), ch. 5.

32 *La Voz de Nuevo León*, Monterrey, Apr. 27, 1901, Dec. 17, 1903.

date their large-scale migration to at least 1895, when Nuevo León's government contracted dozens of masons from that state's red granite quarries to build its majestic Palacio del Gobierno. Coming to stay, they arrived with family and belongings and settled into the riverside barrio that became known as Little San Luis.[33] Many a *regiomontano* family would trace its roots to the state. Some came via recruitment. Born in the high sierra town of Real de Catorce, the father of Gabriel Cárdenas began working in the mines at the age of eleven. In 1906, the eighteen-year-old miner embraced a recruiter's offer and joined the first generation of Mexican steel workers at the Monterrey mill. Likewise, María de Jesús Oviedo's father brought her family to Monterrey after the brewery recruited them from a small ranch near Matehuala. "That is why we came," she later recalled, "because they summoned us. . . . [T]hey used to go to the villages to bring people [to Monterrey]." The prospect of steady and relatively high-paying factory jobs beckoned migrants from a state of poor soils and boom-and-bust mine towns.[34]

"Mining was Matehuala's life," Manual Carranza recalled of his hometown. Speaking of his fellow *potosino* migrants, he observed that "they came to Monterrey because here is where one saw the greatest activity, the most jobs, more than any place else. Yes indeed, there was more than enough work here, and a great demand for hands." Carranza followed a typical route to the factories. His working life began early. Leaving school at the age of nine, he helped sustain his widowed mother by shining shoes, washing cars, and hauling produce in Matehuala's market. By his thirteenth birthday, they had migrated to Monterrey and moved in with Carranza's brothers. After stints in construction ("like everyone") and an apprenticeship as a welder, Carranza would find full-time work with a maintenance crew at the brewery. Family ties brought Salvador Casteñeda to Monterrey as well. Forsaking a mining job in Aguascalientes for fear of his health, the admittedly "restless" young man returned to his city of birth. In certainly typical fashion, Castañeda then labored on highway construction crews, worked the cotton harvest in South Texas, and then learned metal-working skills in the local railroad shops. After a six-month stint at ASARCO's smelter, he embarked on a forty-year career as an iron worker at the steel mill.[35]

The migrants who stayed on helped double Monterrey's population to 80,000 inhabitants between 1890 and 1910. By then, one in three residents

33 Francisco Javier González Medellín and Lilia Maldonado Leal, *San Luisito: Recuerdos de mi barrio* (Monterrey, 1996), 10–17.
34 Interviews with Gabriel Cárdenas Coronado, June 18, 2001, and María de Jesus Oviedo, May 23, 1996.
35 Interviews with Manual Carranza, Jan. 4, 1996 and Salvador Castañeda Medina, Mar. 13, 1996, both of whom migrated to Monterrey in the 1930s.

was born out of state, a figure that remained consistent for decades. If the origins of the steel workers are indicative of city-wide trends then such migrants figured even greater among the working class.[36] By 1926, 60 percent hailed in equal numbers from Monterrey or the farm towns of Nuevo León. Out-of-state migrants made up the remaining 40 percent of the Fundidora's workforce. Of the migrants, more than 60 percent hailed from San Luis. The others came mainly from nearby Coahuila and Zacatecas. The majority of the migrants were of nonagrarian backgrounds. Indeed, 70 percent came from those state's principal cities or from districts with established mining traditions. That so many workers hailed from nonrural backgrounds may reflect the nature of steel, an industry where some 60 percent of the workers were typically skilled or semiskilled operatives in the early 1900s.[37] Thus we shall later see that the Cuauhtémoc Brewery's limited demand for skilled operatives permitted it to recruit more rural migrants. That so many workers came from urbanized origins is consistent with John Lear's findings for Mexico City. What distinguished Monterrey from other Mexican cities was the high level of wage earners who found employment in manufacturing, transport, and construction rather than service industries, commerce, or small workshops.[38]

No other northern city attracted more migrants than Monterrey. One nonetheless finds persistent claims of labor shortages throughout the Porfirian era. One observant traveler found "the condition of labor [to be] extremely unsatisfactory . . . the demand for able-bodied workmen being far in excess of the supply." The dilemma, one paper claimed, "has forced each and every industry in this city to resort to foreigners."[39] Both the degree and causes of the shortages remain unclear. High turnover and employer competition certainly played a role. Labor contractors arrived to Monterrey from as far as Texas and Sonora. Moreover, summertime public works projects could occasion "immense legions of workers" to abandon the factories to toil in the fresh air.[40] Thus did the business press report as late as 1906 that "despite the more than acceptable wages paid [in Monterrey], the scarcity of labor continues and the various businesses have suffered greatly." Faced

36 Juan Mora-Torres, *The Making of the Mexican Border*, 126–36; profile of 400 steel workers based on figures in Archivo General de la Nación (AGN), Mexico City, Departamento del Trabajo: Accidentes, 1925–1926.

37 David Montgomery, *The Fall of the House of Labor: The Workplace, the State, and American Labor Activism* (Cambridge, 1987), 64.

38 Lear, *Workers, Neighbors, and Citizens*, 53. The percentage of local workers employed in the three industrial sectors rose from 57 to 70 percent between 1921 and 1930. Secretaría de la Economía Nacional, *Quinto censo de la población* (Mexico, 1934).

39 Martin, *Mexico of the 20th Century*, 86; *La Unión*, Monterrey, May 17, 1899.

40 Archivo General del Estado de Nuevo León (AGENL): Trabajo – Associaciones y Sindicatos, 1908–1912, box 2; *Monterrey News*, July 12, 1907.

with competition from the city's higher-paying employers, many a smaller factory and workshop certainly found it difficult to retain employees. Yet as more astute observers noted Monterrey's employers faced a very specific labor scarcity, that of skilled tradesmen versed in the arts of modern manufacturing.[41] By the early 1900s companies like ASARCO had resolved high labor turnover by hiring workers with families, by instituting attendance bonuses, and by raising basic wage rates. Indeed, over the course of twenty years, Monterrey evolved from among the lowest-paying to one of the highest-paying urban labor markets in Mexico.[42]

By 1910, the city's largest industries had begun supplementing those salaries to retain their most highly skilled operatives. However, contrary to earlier histories of Monterrey, the systems of industrial paternalism for which Monterrey earned renown developed only an embryonic form during the Porfiriato. In fact the city's major industries offered such nonwage incentives as company housing to very few workers. Unlike Mexico's isolated mining camps and oil fields, which had to recruit workers from afar, turn-of-the-century Monterrey housed an impressive quantity of skilled labor. The city's 1900 industrial census counted 650 native-born mechanics, blacksmiths, electricians, and sheet metal workers and more than 1,700 carpenters and bricklayers. The constant influx of mine workers and village artisans supplemented the local supply. The mid-1900s also saw the Mexican National Railways transfer its northern shops from the Texas border to Monterrey. With the shops came hundreds of Mexican mechanics, boilermen, machinists, and metal workers, a good many of whom belonged to Mexico's first generation of union activists. We will see that the native-born railroaders often found their career opportunities limited by immigrant American workers. Many in northeastern Mexico therefore packed their union cards into their bags of skills and traveled to other industries. Around Tampico they found jobs in the refineries and oil fields. In Monterrey higher wages and greater occupational mobility led many to careers at the steel mill and smelters.[43]

But few workers trained in the specialized arts of smelting, steel making, or glass production existed within Mexico's native-born proletariat. Local industrialists therefore turned to the United States and Europe to meet this demand. In addition to competitive wage rates, they offered an array of nonwage benefits to retain their prized recruits. ASARCO established

---

41 *El País*, Mexico City, Nov. 9, 1906 cited in Saragoza, *The Monterrey Elite*, 90.

42 The ASARCO smelter raised base wages for common laborers from $0.25 pesos (1892) and $1.00 (1894) to $1.60 (1903), and offered a $0.50 daily bonus to workers able to toil twenty-five consecutive days. O'Connor, *The Guggenheims*, 97–98; *La Voz de Nuevo León*, Sept. 15, 1907; Mora-Torres, *The Making of the Mexican Border*, 136–46.

43 *Censo de la municipalidad de Monterrey*, Oct. 28, 1900 (Monterrey, 1902), 7; *Monterrey News*, May 6, 1903; Santiago, "Huasteca Crude," ch. 6.

the early precedent. The American managers and foremen who arrived to Monterrey from the company's Colorado smelter would reside with their families in the "Colonia Americana," a settlement of spacious homes with well-groomed lawns, tennis courts, and a bowling alley. ASARCO also built several blocks of two-story brick apartment blocks for its skilled American and Mexican smeltermen, waiving rents for those who maintained steady attendance at work.[44] A half mile to the west stood Monterrey's "German Quarter," a block of tidy homes constructed by the glassworks for their craftsmen from Hamburg. No local industry depended more on imported labor than steel. The Fundidora turned to Europe to recruit "experts in their fields to take charge of production and serve as teachers to the workers of [Mexico]."[45] During its first decade, a Frenchman supervised the blast furnace crews. A Czech oversaw the rolling mill and a crew of Hungarian rollers. An Italian directed the plant's bricklayers. And American, Irish, English, Belgian, and German recruits rounded out the most ethnically diverse labor force of its day in Mexico. They were joined from the start by Mexican mechanics, carpenters, and machinists. To accommodate its prized recruits, who worked a mile east of the city center, the Fundidora constructed its Colonia Acero. Steel Town became a self-sufficient neighborhood of cottages, company stores, and a fifty-five-room hotel to house single workers.[46] The foreign recruits performed an indispensable role in Monterrey's early industrialization. But their employers saw them as a short-term solution to a scarcity of skilled labor.

From the outset Monterrey's industrialists committed themselves to the thorough Mexicanization of their work forces. They publicly portrayed their endeavor as a patriotic and benevolent mission to morally uplift the Mexican masses. But a cost-conscious, managerial pragmatism further motivated a policy shared by *regiomontano* and foreign capitalists alike. Not only did the foreign workers command high wages, they were troublesome as well.[47] For example, the Garza Sadas' first endeavor in bottle manufacturing concluded when a contract dispute with their imported glass blowers led to a strike. In an early display of its managerial style, the company ejected the workers from their "German Quarters," filed a $15,000 suit for "damages," and rescinded its obligation to cover their transport to Hamburg. The Germans returned home after six unhappy months in Monterrey. Upon arrival, they

44 O'Connor, *The Guggenheims*, 96–99; *Monterrey News*, Oct. 11, 1898.

45 *La Voz de Nuevo León*, May 16, 1903.

46 Manuel González Caballero, *La Maestranza de ayer, la Fundidora de hoy* (Monterrey, 1979), 17–19.

47 ASARCO paid its skilled American workers daily salaries up to $8.00–$10.00 ($4.00–$5.00 in U.S. currency) at a time when average factory laborers earned $1.00 in Monterrey. Generally, American workers commanded wages 25–30 percent higher than their home market offered. Luis Cortez and Alfredo de León to Governor Zambrano, May 22, 1918, in AGENL: Trabajo – Conciliación y Arbitraje, 1/6; Brown, "Foreign and Native-Born Workers," 797.

launched a negative publicity campaign in the French and German press that allegedly stymied the *regiomontanos'* efforts to recruit replacement workers.[48] North American recruits proved as unruly in Monterrey as in other parts of Mexico. Some of those employed by the local railways and smelters organized ethnically exclusive unions and doggedly protected their monopoly on high-paying jobs. In 1898, American railroad shop workers struck to protest the promotion of a Mexican. Governor Reyes threatened the foreigners with arrest under the state's antiunion vagrancy law and ordered troops to quell the railwaymen's protests. The issues of unfair promotions and unequal wages would soon prompt the Mexican railroad employees to organize and strike as well. At ASARCO, manager James Feeney complained that his attempts to promote native-born workers met resistance from a "well-organized union" of "resentful" Americans, who taunted Feeney as a "Mexican lover." Feeney nonetheless promised Governor Reyes that ASARCO would provide Mexican workers the same "salary, rights, and guarantees" as foreigners. By 1904, he declared "with great satisfaction that this goal has been accomplished."[49] The native-born workers would soon dispute these claims.

The gradual replacement of immigrant with native-born employees occurred despite the foreigners' resistance and because Mexican workers shared their employers' goal. Persistent conflicts in the railroad yards and the Americans' propensity toward unionism heightened the sensitivities of local employers and Mexican authorities alike.[50] Perhaps for that reason, the steel mill recruited Europeans to "serve as teachers to the workers of this country." Their contractual obligations were likely similar to those of the glass blowers. The Germans' three-year contracts stipulated that a failure to instruct their Mexican apprentices "with good will and decent treatment" would be grounds for dismissal.[51] The vocational training of Mexican steel workers transpired rapidly and smoothly at the Fundidora. In contrast to the railroad shops, the mill's European craftsmen mainly occupied supervisory rather than production jobs. Even the most hard-learned skills, like those of the rollers, were passed down in six months and then practiced to perfection. Through improvisation and the aid of interpreters, the foreigners transmitted their valuable skills to Mexican workers like Flavio Galindo. Galindo began as an apprentice in the blast furnace in 1901. Six years later,

48 AGENL: Correspondencia con el Ministerio de Relaciones Exteriores, 1903–1904, 58.
49 *La Voz de Nuevo León*, Mar. 23 and Apr. 2, 1898; James Feeney to Bernardo Reyes, February 29, 1904, in AGENL: Correspondencia Local del Gobernador, 1903–1904, 77.
50 Lorena M. Parlee, "The Impact of United States Railroad Unions on Organized Labor and Government Policy in Mexico (1880–1910)," *Hispanic American Historical Review* 64 (1984), 443–75.
51 Contracts in AGENL: Correspondencia con el Ministerio de Relaciones Exteriores, 1903–1904, 58; Brown, "Foreign and Native-Born Workers," details the conflictive ethnic relations in the railroad and mining industries

the company promoted him to foreman and, in 1911, named him supervisor of the mill's foundry. Veteran steel workers later lauded Galindo as an early "exponent of what the 'bronze race' can achieve when given the opportunity to develop its skills."[52]

In less than a decade, the foreign workers completed the task for which they were brought to Monterrey: imparting their knowledge and skills to Mexican apprentices. Some would stay on. They learned Spanish, married Mexican women, and even became naturalized citizens. By the 1930s, a handful still supervised Mexican workers in local plants, residing in the same neighborhoods and socializing with *la raza* after work.[53] But the majority departed during the 1910s, when political upheaval paralyzed the local economy. By the close of that decade a total of only fifteen foreign production workers were employed by ASARCO, the steel mill, and the brewery.[54] In the meantime, local employers had launched educational endeavors meant to supply *regiomontano* workers with the skills to survive in the modern industrial world.

Working-Class Culture and Politics in Porfirian Monterrey

Since the late 1890s, the local press had voiced concern that Monterrey industry was in an "embryonic state" due its workers' lack of skills. "Is it not a shame to see our brothers born into the most crass ignorance," editors asked, "because they have no source from which to drink knowledge?" They promoted vocational schools as the answer to industry's dilemma. A national business journal echoed their views. "Disciplined" laborers would never emerge from the nation's "disorganized, anarchic, and primitive workshops, [because] the master tradesmen are . . . as indolent and vice ridden as their operatives." From the businessman's point of view, the shortage of "educated, sober, and able-bodied" workers caused low productivity. Therefore, it was concluded, a shorter working day was not then feasible. Nuevo León's reform-minded Governor Reyes responded to these calls. In 1903 his government allocated funds for Monterrey's first vocational night school.[55] Shortly thereafter, the brewery opened its own Cuauhtémoc Polytechnic School to instruct the operatives and their children in "the culture and skills

52　González Caballero, *La Maestranza de ayer*, 17–20; *Colectividad*, Monterrey, July 1926 (quoted).

53　Linda Rodriguez, a glass worker who had lived north of the border, thus recalls of ethnic relations, "It wasn't like in the United States, where they had [segregated] colonias americanas and colonias mexicanas. . . . [Here] the foreigners got along well with *la raza*." Interview with Linda Alba de Rodrigúez, Apr. 25, 1996.

54　AGN: Departamento del Trabajo (DT), Labor Inspectors' Reports, 166/2 (1919), 436/3 (1922), and 625/6 (1923).

55　*La Unión*, Monterrey, July 1, 1899; *El Economista Mexicana*, Sep. 13, 1902; Niemeyer, *El General Bernardo Reyes*, 138.

required at work." In 1911 the Fundidora started its Escuela Acero (Steel School) to train "Mexican personnel." Both companies also developed scholarship programs that sent promising sons of their workers to study in Mexico City and abroad.[56] Nuevo León's government would continually expand its educational response to the "urgent need to make expert workers for this eminently industrial city." By the 1920s, some 2,000 working men and women were attending evening classes in the industrial arts.[57] We will later see that these initiatives demonstrated a common private/public sector interest in structuring a labor market favorable to Monterrey's industrial demands. But educational reform was not merely a top-down initiative.

The popular appeal of vocational training revealed the workers' own desire to assert their respectability and enhance their career opportunities. Notably, Governor Reyes patronized the city's first night school at the behest of local workers. Moreover, it was housed in the Mexican Mechanics Union hall and mainly benefited the well-organized railwaymen. Thus by the mid-1910s other workers began pressuring the city council to open more night schools "so that we may acquire the knowledge necessary to make ourselves useful to society." With their children's future in mind, they proposed vocational training programs for the city's public schools as well.[58] By the close of the Porfiriato, such workers had accepted the permanency of industrial capitalism. Younger members of this first-generation proletariat sought to emulate those like Flavio Galindo who earned the community's respect as the first Mexican workers to master specialized trades. Like Galindo they aspired to learn a vocation and achieve occupational mobility. Workers thereby pressured the state to make that opportunity possible. Soon they would begin organizing to demand the same "salary, rights, and guarantees" enjoyed by their foreign workmates.

It was during this period of working-class formation that Monterrey's more skilled workers developed their own working-class variant of a regional identity. It built on a blue-collar foundation of craft dignity and social respectability. The *regiomontano* workers derived a patriotic pride from their employment in nationally renowned industries that fostered Mexico's economic independence. They came to enjoy a *norteño* repute for hard work and industriousness. Thus did a veteran Fundidora manager – who entered the mill in 1920 – note the locals' reputation as "hard workers and quick learners." Such qualities, he suggests, facilitated the mill's efforts to

56 Saragoza, *The Monterrey Elite*, 90–91; González Caballero, *La Maestranza de ayer*, 69–72; AGN: Trabajo, Labor Inspector's Report, 444/10 (1922).

57 *El Porvenir*, Oct. 24, 1923 AGENL: *Informe del Gobernador Juan M. García*, 1920–1921, 18, and *Informe del Gobernador Jerónimo Siller*, 1926–1927, 16–17.

58 Niemeyer, *El General Bernardo Reyes*, 138; ASARCO workers to city council in Archivo Municipal de Monterrey (hereafter AMM), Acta no. 43, Sep. 10, 1917.

"Mexicanize" its work force. Referring to their levels of skill, literacy, and political awareness, other retired workers distinguished the *regiomontano* proletariat for being "more cultured" than other Mexicans of their class.[59] By the mid-1910s, the local press had launched its tradition of celebrating these unique qualities. "The Monterrey worker," one writer boasted, "has earned a place far superior to that of workers elsewhere in the Republic, who still find themselves in a very backward condition." Visitors to the city discerned the distinction as well. One thus observed of Monterrey that "here one does not encounter that unwashed, ill-clad mob which, unfortunately, one observes in some parts of the Republic . . . in general, everyone has a decent appearance: the worker and the artisan display well-being and an appearance of dignity and personal decorum."[60] So did this Mexican traveler distinguish the locals from their central Mexican brethren, far fewer of whom enjoyed the kinds of economic opportunity offered in Mexico's Chicago. The more skilled and affluent workers like those of the railroad shops or metal foundries flaunted their status with their fine attire and rubbed elbows with the merchants who belonged to the same Masonic lodges. Judging by these portrayals, Monterrey's skilled industrial workers shared a culture in common with many northern Mexican miners. Both groups of workers would assert their respectability through patterns of dress, self-improvement, hard work, and sobriety. By doing so, William French concludes, they demanded "to be accepted as equal members of [middle-class] society."[61]

Like other Mexican workers, those of Monterrey sought to improve their social and economic standing by forging networks of solidarity. Consistent with national trends, they organized working-class associations that largely deferred to acceptable standards and rarely defied government authority. As would be expected of a newly industrialized society, labor activity was rare in Porfirian Monterrey. Indeed, when compared to the central Mexican textile belt, levels of unionization remained low outside the city's one union stronghold, the Mexican National Railways shops. But mutual-aid societies proliferated. Artisans, industrial workers, and the city's immigrant communities established some two dozen by the early 1900s. Evidence on these *mutualistas* offers no indication of whether they offered typical benefits like accident and burial insurance. But the archival record does tell a story of "honorable" workers and their "respectable" societies.[62] That is because these self-help organizations enjoyed the patronage of Governor Reyes. For

59 Interview with Manual González Caballero, July 5, 1995 and Castañeda.
60 *El Liberal*, Monterrey, Sep. 4, 1917, cited in Zapata Novoa, *Tercos y triunfadores*, 6; Alfonso Dollero, *México al día* (1911) cited in Knight, *The Mexican Revolution*, I, 42.
61 French, *A Peaceful and Working People*, 134.
62 AGENL: Trabajo – Asociaciones y Sindicatos, 1901, 1906–1912.

example, the Sociedad Mutualista Benito Juárez received books for their library, a bust of President Juárez, and funds to construct a meeting hall. The workers in turn adorned their hall with Reyes's portrait "to show our appreciation for the help and protection you offer the working class." Some of their *mutualisas* also doubled as political clubs, mobilizing the members in public support of Reyes.[63] As a result of such activity, Monterrey workers earned their local repute as peaceful, orderly, and "dignified citizens." Thus did the a local paper praise these advocates of temperance and education as "vice-free men . . . [who] work for the future of their families and the fatherland's greatness." Such organizations, the government-owned press suggested, would counter attempts by radicals to "deviate honorable workers [by] exciting their spirits with ideas of anarchy."[64]

Unions of ostensibly anarchist inspiration were indeed active in Monterrey.[65] The government's own preoccupations suggest as much. During his tenure, Governor Reyes became particularly concerned with the infiltration of radical ideas among Monterrey's one group of well-organized workers, the railwaymen. Monterrey hosted the nation's largest locals of both the Unión de Mecánicos Mexicanos and the Great League of Mexican Railroad Employees (Gran Liga), a federation of craft unions. By the early 1900s, these unions counted smelter and steel workers among their members as well. The Gran Liga remained under the watchful eye of Governor Reyes. Government agents infiltrated the union and attempted to channel its activism away from "anarchist and socialist tendencies" and toward moral and educational reform. Reyes himself claimed to have revised the union's statutes. But government intervention failed to quell the causes of worker discontent. During 1906–07, falling real wages, the hiring of nonunion workers, the issue of unequal pay, and the promotion of American workers with less seniority than Mexicans all prompted walkouts in Monterrey's railroad shops and smelters. While Reyes patronized the railway workers' unions, his government also answered their protests by sending troops into the workshops and ordering the dismissal of militants.[66] Nonetheless, by

63 Sociedad Mutualista Benito Juárez to Governor Reyes, July 22, 1907, AGENL: Trabajo – Asociaciones y Sindicatos, 1906–1912, 2/8; Sociedad Mutualista Cuauhtémoc to Reyes, Oct. 20, 1907, AGENL: Trabajo – Associaciones y Sindicatos, 2/76; see Lear's insightful analysis of working-class *mutualismo* in *Workers, Neighbors, and Citizens*, 106–23.

64 *The Monterrey News*, July 13, 1907; *La Voz de Nuevo León*, Mar. 26, 1903.

65 Anarchist labor activists organized among the printers, bakers, tramway drivers, smeltermen, and construction workers. They all declared their affiliation with the Mexico City–based House of the World Worker (Case del Obrero Mundial) in the early 1910s, by which time Monterrey became the COM's most active provincial chapter. John M. Hart, *Anarchism and the Mexican Working Class* (Austin, 1987), 84, 115, 127.

66 Niemeyer, *El General Bernardo Reyes*, 136–38; Javier Rojas Sandoval, *Antecedentes históricos del movimiento oberero en Monterrey* (Monterrey, 1987), 22–24.

1910 a tendency toward unionization had clearly emerged in Monterrey's factories and railyards.

The same grievances that provoked worker protest elsewhere in Mexico provided the cause. Mario Cerutti's pioneering study demonstrates that the wages earned by a typical industrial worker in 1902 provided for a subsistence lifestyle at best. Workers depended upon family labor as a means of survival due to Monterrey's high cost of living. Moreover the travelers who marveled at Monterrey's modern industry and "handsome mansions" found that workers in the rapidly growing city lived in "the most terrible native huts." One Englishwomen recounted that, "the men working in some of the large factories live in hovels built of bamboo reeds, which are often so small and low that a man cannot stand upright in his own home.... If a man possesses a pig, he is considered wealthy, and that pig shares his home.... If he has a bed he is much to be envied."[67] Workers who thus struggled economically also encountered arbitrary authority in the workplace. Managers levied fines for tardiness or faulty workmanship. Foremen bribed workers who sought promotions. The twelve-hour day, seven-day week, and unchecked occupational hazards were commonplace as well.[68] The mutual-aid societies did work in defense of working-class interests, helping procure work for the unemployed and lobbying government authorities to enforce compliance with the accident law on their members' behalf. Otherwise workers like the fired German glass blowers relied on more short-term forms of solidarity to survive hard times. Their return voyage to Hamburg had been funded with donations from local steel workers, Monterrey's German colony, and Governor Reyes himself.[69]

Rodney Anderson's conclusions regarding labor's plight in Porfirian Mexico hold true for Monterrey. For a time, workers placed faith in a government that some came to perceive as benevolent and protective. But the state lacked the "desire, understanding, or instruments" to resolve labor conflicts because authorities refused to confront the men "who formed the financial backbone of the economy." Governor Reyes exemplified the trend. He earned working-class sympathies for his patronage of labor and his promotion of industry and education. He furthered his progressive credentials by enacting one of Mexico's first worker compensation laws. Such efforts earned a governor with aspirations to the vice presidency some blue-collar support.[70] Yet those sympathies proved stronger in distant Mexico City

---

67 Mario Cerutti, "Industrialización y salarios obreros en Monterrey (1890–1910)," *Humanitas* 21 (1980), 443–74; Martin, *Mexico of the 20th Century*, 87; Tweedie, *Mexico As I Saw It*, 62–63.
68 Mora-Torres, *The Making of the Mexican Border*, 213–28.
69 AGENL: Correspondencia con el Ministerio de Relaciones Exteriores, 1903–1904, 58.
70 Rodney Anderson, *Outcasts in Their Own Land: Mexican Industrial Workers, 1906–1911* (Dekalb, 1976), 211, 279; Niemeyer, *El General Bernardo Reyes*, 138–39.

than in Reyes's own backyard, where the Accident Law went unenforced and Reyes maintained labor peace through antiunion laws that criminalized collective action.[71] Indeed Reyes's alleged neglect of Monterrey's workers became a major point of contention for the opposition that emerged to his 1903 reelection. The student-led opposition hardened when the repression of a political rally left eight protestors dead. That incident would convince Francisco Madero – a young *norteño* whose family owned a home and businesses in Monterrey – to embark on a political career that soon led him to the presidency.[72] In the meantime, Monterrey's workers continued appealing to the state to seek recourse for their grievances. In 1908 local mechanics called on Governor Reyes to organize a government board to arbitrate workplace disputes in consultation with union delegates. The governor rejected their proposal.[73] Ten years later a government more attuned to working-class demands would initiate the reforms advocated by the mechanics.

Meanwhile, as the 1910 national elections approached, Reyes disappeared from the political scene and Monterrey emerged as a stronghold of Maderista opposition to the Díaz government. Madero's campaign promised to support unionization, expand vocational education, and institute a constitutional democracy, elevating his appeal among working-class Mexicans. In 1910, as Madero's campaign swung through central Mexico and back into the North, his local working- and middle-class support swelled to levels that led to the anticipated crackdown by the Díaz government. Thousands of Maderista activists were imprisoned on the eve of national elections. Madero himself was arrested in Monterrey. Shipped off to San Luis and forbidden to leave that city, Madero saw his quixotic drive to defeat the Díaz regime peacefully conclude with fraudulent elections. Three months later, Madero disguised himself as a worker, skipped bail, and rode the rails back through Monterrey and into political exile in Texas. From there he issued the call to arms that would prompt the downfall of Porifirio Díaz. The Mexican Revolution had begun.[74]

---

71 Nuevo León's vagrancy law permitted authorities to arrest striking workers and sentence them to jail, fines, or forced labor. Another code forbade the use of "moral or physical force" to demand higher wages, to win shorter hours, or "impede the individual's right to work." Javier Rojas Sandoval, "Conflictos obreros y legislación obrera en Nuevo León (1885–1918)," *Siglo XIX* 3:6 (1988), 190–91.

72 Saragoza, *The Monterrey Elite*, 87; Hanna, Monterrey, SD/RG 59, Apr. 29, 1903; Knight, *The Mexican Revolution*, I, 56.

73 Unión de Mecánicos Mexicanos to Governor Reyes, Oct. 17, 1908, in AGENL: Trabajo – Asociaciones y Sindicatos, 1906–1912, 5/12; Niemeyer, *El General Bernardo Reyes*, 137–38.

74 Hanna, Feb. 11, 1911, SD 812.00 NL/858 (National Archives Washington, Record Group 84, United States State Department Records Relating to the Internal Affairs of Mexico, 1910–1929, 1930–1939, hereafter SD); Knight, *The Mexican Revolution*, I, 56–64, 74–77, 137–39.

2

Revolution Comes to Monterrey

The Mexican Revolution began as an armed rebellion meant to overthrow the dictatorship of Porfirio Díaz. The Díaz government fell quickly and, in 1911, Francisco Madero became Mexico's first freely elected president in generations. But his 1913 assassination by counterrevolutionary forces unleashed a civil war that would ultimately cost an estimated one million lives. The revolutionary insurgency concluded four years later with the emergence of what promised to be a new political order. The 1917 Constitution became a blueprint for the revolutionary government's designs to forge a new Mexico though social, economic, and cultural reforms that both built upon and diverged radically from Porfirian precedents. The revolutionary government faced an immediate quandary. Years of political upheaval had recast popular consciousness and galvanized demands for far-reaching reforms in the countryside and cities of Mexico. But the civil war also devastated the economy. The federal government therefore instituted policies of national reconstruction while also addressing the basic social issues that led so many peasants, workers, and middle-class Mexicans to support the revolutionary movement. Labor became a key issue on its agenda. Indeed the emergence of an organized labor movement became one of the earliest and most consequential outcomes of the revolution. The years that followed saw the government court working-class support while attempting to rein in the sort of militancy that might damage Mexico's unstable economy. By the time that political stability was tenuously reestablished, in 1917, Monterrey's workers had seized upon the realignment of government authority to protest long-held grievances and launch their own struggle to draw the Porfirian order to a close.

The Revolutionary Insurgency

Monterrey's workers experienced the armed stage of the revolution much like urban proletarians elsewhere in the republic: as bystanders rather than protagonists.[1] A few local workers left the city to fight with rebel forces. Others certainly joined the rebels on the two occasions they occupied Monterrey. But we know neither how many fought nor why they did so. With the exception of the Red Battalions organized by Mexico City unionists, Mexican workers who became rebels did so as individuals rather than an armed and organized working class. Given the strategic nature of their industry, only the railroad workers played a collective role in the revolution's outcome. Most working people simply struggled to survive the tribulations of war. As refugees from the countryside sought sanctuary in Monterrey, other working-class families headed to the United States in search of peace and work.[2] But the majority stayed home and ultimately experienced the revolution as victims of unemployment, food shortages, and epidemic disease. A revolution that first elicited jubilation and great expectations thus begot hardship and uncertainty as civil war interrupted the security and prosperity of Porfirian times. The experience seemed even harder after the hopes that accompanied President Madero's brief term in office.

The fall of Díaz portended good times ahead because it coincided with a buoyant economy and ushered in the promise of democracy. The years 1910–12 witnessed a continuity of the industrial boom registered during the final years of the Díaz regime. Monterrey's steel mill and brewery produced record levels of output under the Madero government. ASARCO's Mexican operations likewise recorded unprecedented profits.[3] Despite the strong economy, the local industrialists were apprehensive about the unraveling of the Porfirian order. Only weeks before his fall, with much of the North under rebel control, they had telegraphed their "unconditional support" to the faltering dictator. However, it was soon clear to the United States Consul that "the anti-government majority in the locality is very large." "As a rule they are conservative," he observed, "[but] a very large majority ... sympathize with the revolutionary cause." Like other urban *norteños* they supported Madero's promise to restore constitutional order and "effective suffrage." Thus could Monterrey be "accused of being the headquarters of the revolutionary element ... [but remain] the most peaceable, conservative, and well-governed city in northern Mexico." So it became for a time after Madero's election. The first free elections in memory generated

1 Alan Knight, "The Working Class and the Mexican Revolution, c. 1900–1920," *Journal of Latin American Studies*, 16:1 (1984), 51–79. General overviews of the period 1910–20 in Monterrey are offered by Oscar Flores Torres, *Burguesía, militares y movimiento obrero, 1909–1923* (Monterrey, 1991), 37–160; Saragoza, *The Monterrey Elite*, 96–110; Rodrigo Mendirichaga, *Los 4 tiempos de un pueblo: Nuevo León en la historia* (Monterrey, 1985), 321–26.
2 AGN: Trabajo, 1914, 91/21.
3 Hanna, Apr. 12, 1911, SD 812.00 NL/1367, Dec. 28, 1912, 812.5045/44; Haber, *Industry and Underdevelopment*, 126; French, *A Peaceful and Working People*, 153.

keen competition and elicited unprecedented turnouts in Monterrey. Several old-guard politicos returned to congress and the state house under a new "Maderista label."[4] But in a sign of times to come, citizens also elected a steel worker and a railroad union leader to Monterrey's city council. Moreover, labor activism now flourished in this climate of political openness and economic prosperity. By the summer of 1911 local railroaders, smeltermen, and textile workers were unionizing and testing the new political waters by striking for higher wages and shorter hours. The transition from dictatorship to democracy seemed secure.

In October 1911 President Madero returned to the city where he had been imprisoned only fifteen months before. Sensing the shifting political winds, the local elite celebrated his visit with a lavish reception, "their earlier support for Díaz apparently forgotten, if not forgiven."[5] Madero's entourage soon moved from the banquet hall to city streets, where thousands of workers turned out to honor their new president with a *fiesta popular.* During a rally before the Government Palace a steel worker recited a poem penned for the occasion, assuring the "Apostle of Democracy" that "you are the people's hope." His former rebel allies soon thought otherwise. Interpreting a slow pace of reform as political betrayal, they revolted against Maderismo. Regional rebellion now threatened the economic boom. The *regiomontanos* rallied behind the president. Marching under banners calling for "peace, prosperity, and patriotism," business and working people joined in a "patriotic demonstration . . . for the upholding of the constituted government."[6] But one year later, in 1913, federal generals sought to impose political stability on Mexico by arresting and then assassinating President Madero. General Victoriano Huerta declared himself president. The military's attempt to restore the Porfirian order set off a civil war that engulfed Mexico in revolutionary violence until 1917. For most *regiomontanos* the jubilation caused by Madero's triumph gave way to a deep uncertainty about the future.

A four-year period of collective hardship settled upon the city. Within months of Madero's assassination, Constitutionalist forces loyal to Venustiano Carranza began engaging government troops in northeastern Mexico. Federal forces remained entrenched in urban centers as rebels opened fronts across the countryside, sacked rural towns, and beat at the doors of the North's major cities. As it drew near, the war disrupted railroad transport and sporadically deprived Monterrey of food, fuel, and industrial raw materials. The fighting also isolated Monterrey from its principal

---

4 Saragoza, *The Monterrey Elite*, 97; Hanna, Mar. 20, Aug. 11, 1911, SD 812.00 NL/111, 2256; Knight, *The Mexican Revolution*, I, 401, 424.
5 Saragoza, *The Monterrey Elite*, 97.
6 Poem in Mendirichaga, *Los 4 tiempos*, 321–22; Hanna, Mar. 22, 1912, SD 812.00 NL/3364.

consumer markets. Factory production declined accordingly. The Fundidora
closed its blast furnace for three years and produced minimal quantities of
fabricated steel. ASARCO ceased its Mexican mining and smelting operations for two full years. Cuauhtémoc saw its annual beer sales fall from
more than sixteen million liters to less than three million. Managers thereby
cut the brewery's workforce from 1,500 employees to less than 300. Those
fortunate enough to keep their jobs labored no more than three days weekly.[7]
In April 1913, it was reported that "thousands of men have been turned
out of employment and many of them have been leaving for the United
States." To compound these hardships, rural fighting, a regional drought,
and a flood of refugees from the countryside soon threatened Monterrey
with famine. Meanwhile, "wild rumors" circulated that "desperate bands
claiming to be followers of Carranza were intending to sack the city."[8]

   Monterrey did not pass unnoticed by rebel armies fighting to overthrow
the Huerta regime. In late 1913 they first reached the city's outskirts.
Locals watched from below as they drove federal forces from Topo Chico
Hill. They then ran for cover as artillery shells pounded the city. Over the
next three days, rebels engaged federal troops through Monterrey's deserted
streets. They set fire to homes and businesses "of those who the *Carrancistas*
considered enemies of the revolutionary cause." Forced to retreat, the rebels
vandalized the strategic railroad yards, putting the torch to sixteen locomo-
tives and hundreds of railcars. As federal troops departed the city in pursuit,
they followed the rebel lead, burning and looting homes of suspected rebel
sympathizers. A British journalist recalled the aftermath: "High in the sky
I saw vultures flying, drawn by dead horses and men who laid ghastly and
rigid in the dusty streets. [Rebel] bodies hung from many telegraph posts
as a hard warning to dissidents. . . . The dead lay scattered all about and
nearly every home [in the northern working-class neighborhoods] showed
signs of the armed struggle."[9] The rebels finally took the city in May
1914, their forces augmented over six days of fighting by local volunteers
from the working-class barrio of San Luisito. Huerta resigned shortly thereafter. By the end of the year Constitutionalist rule brought "good order" to
Monterrey, "where the people generally are hopeful and expect permanent
peace."[10]

7 Archivo Histórico de la Fundidora Monterrey (AHFM): Compañía Fundidora de Fierro y Acero de
   Monterrey, 1950 *Informe*, Mar. 10, 1951, 2–29 (hereafter AHFM: Informe); French, *A Peaceful and
   Working People*, 153–59; Haber, *Industry and Underdevelopment*, 126; Pablo Salas to Governor Raúl
   Madero, Mar. 17, 1915 in AGENL: Industria y Comercio, 1900–1921, 2/4.
8 Hanna, Apr. 10, 1913, SD 812.00 NL/7159.
9 Hamilton Fyfe, *The Real Mexico* (London, 1914) cited in Mendirichaga, *Los 4 tiempos*, 322 (translated
   from Spanish); Isidro Vizcaya Canales, *Monterrey bajo sitio: Octubre 23 y 24 de 1913* (Monterrey, 1988),
   45–51.
10 Viscaya Canales, *Monterrey bajo sitio*, 63; Hanna, Nov. 27, 1914, SD 812.5045/79.

The arrival of constitutionalist authority brought relief to a city experiencing the gravest economic consequences of the revolutionary insurgency. It also brought retribution from military leaders in need of provisions, arms, and pay for their troops. Hefty "fines" thus fell on Monterrey's leading businesspeople, many of whom found themselves briefly imprisoned in the "aristocrats' hotel," as the local penitentiary became known. The Garza Sadas, in particular, would come to share "an enduring, deep-seated resentment of the Constitutionalist cause."[11] Their Cuauhtémoc Brewery became an early and logical target of occupying forces. The Constitutionalists despised its owners because their family had openly supported the counterrevolutionary Huerta regime. Moreover its beer was in high demand by the troops. One revolutionary veteran recalled that when they seized the brewery, "it seemed as if we had crossed a sandy desert and arrived suddenly to a cool refreshing oasis . . . [of] ice-cold, freshly-brewed, glistening beer." While their employees mounted a courageous but short-lived attempt to defend the workplace, the brewery's owners had wisely joined their exiled family in Texas. Constitutionalist authorities therefore ordered the resumption of brewing operations to collect unpaid fines from the Garza Sadas. They would be punished, according to General Pablo González, for their "very active participation in efforts detrimental to the constitutionalist cause and in favor of the usurpers of the people's power." Unlike other local businesses, the brewery remained under a government intervener. Meanwhile, Saragoza notes Monterrey's most prominent captains of industry spent two embittered years in exile, "each day a reminder of dispossession, each day a reason to idealize the past."[12] They would return to a city where working people who shared their longings for economic recovery would nonetheless resist any return to a neo-Porfirian past.

Anecdotal evidence suggests that Monterrey's working class eagerly supported the coming of constitutionalist rule. One veteran remembered arriving at the brewery in 1914 and finding that "the company's workers seemed to sympathize with the Revolution, or perhaps they felt obligated to do so." Another recalled less ambiguously that "the brewery's people were splendid, giving us whatever they had, from a pleasant smile to their beer and cigarettes."[13] Like Monterrey's businesspeople, working people embraced the semblance of order and security that authorities established in the city. But under the surface of common aspirations swirled mounting labor grievances. As elsewhere in the republic, workers did not hesitate to

---

11 Saragoza, *The Monterrey Elite*, 107.

12 Francisco Urquizo, *Memorias de campaña* (Mexico, 1985); Saragoza, *The Monterrey Elite*, 107–09.

13 Francisco Vela González, *Diario de la revolución* (Mexico, 1971); Urquizo, *Memorias de campaña*, 45; Union Fraternal de Obreros of La Fama to Departamento del Trabajo, Aug. 2, 1914, AGN: Trabajo, 75/37.

capitalize on promises of real labor reform.[14] For help they turned to the new Labor Department that President Madero had established. In particular, they appealed to a small force of federal labor inspectors, men whose influential roles in Mexican labor history is belied by the little we know about them. They arrived to Monterrey entrusted with several tasks: collecting data, counseling workers, and mediating their disputes. The end of Porfirian rule had brought forth a number of strikes. Most were defensive responses to layoffs and inflation. But workers also challenged customary labor practices with demands for the eight-hour day, union recognition, improved workplace safety, and their supervisors' dismissals.[15]

At best the strikers achieved short-lived economic gains. But they also created enduring networks of solidarity. The railroaders stayed at the vanguard in local organizing. Their unions also represented workers at Monterrey's steel mill and smelters. Bakers, streetcar drivers, printers, textile operatives, and building tradesmen also unionized. By the mid-1910s, Monterrey was said to have the largest regional branch of the Casa del Obrero Mundial (House of the World Worker), the nominally anarchist labor central that had sent its Mexico City organizers out to the provinces early in the decade.[16] Despite the organizational gains workers often saw their aspirations dashed by constitutional authorities who perceived labor unrest as a challenge to their own sense of order. Interim Governor Antonio Villarreal thus informed streetcar workers striking for higher wages and union recognition that "now is not the opportune moment for strikes" and that what Monterrey needed was more industry and jobs. They swiftly challenged what they perceived as a throwback to the old order: "It is certain, Mr. Governor, that the more industry the country has, the more jobs there will be . . . but what good are a lot of factories if the wages they pay do not meet the proletariat's needs. No, Mr. Governor, we are not going back to Porfirian times, dazzling the entire world with material progress while the people remain in ignorance and poverty."[17]

Meanwhile, in mid-1914, working-class hopes for a "permanent peace" were interrupted again when a split in the revolutionary leadership plunged Mexico into another civil war. A relative and enduring peace proved elusive until 1916, when Pancho Villa's defeat on the northern battlefields sent him off the revolutionary stage and his nemesis, Venustiano Carranza,

---

14 Knight, *The Mexican Revolution*, I, 433–36; French, *A Peaceful and Working People*, 141–72; Lear, *Workers, Neighbors, and Citizens*, 143–241; Santiago, "Huasteca Crude," ch. 6.

15 AGN: Trabajo, Labor Inspector's Report, 34/9–11, 37/15; Flores Torres, *Burguesía, militares y movimiento obrero*, 116–18.

16 Hart, *Anarchism*, 84, 115, 127.

17 Quoted in Javier Rojas, *Movimiento obrero y partidos políticos en Nuevo León, 1910–1920* (Monterrey, 1982), 10–13.

assumed the presidency. The interim had seen Monterrey occupied by Villa's forces, convulsed by food riots, and so threatened by fears of looting that merchants had closed and barred their shops.[18] By late 1916, as delegates drafted Mexico's new constitution in Querétaro, urban working people were suffering the gravest consequences of the war. For most *regiomontano* workers the economic crisis spawned by fighting in the North brought their first experience of sustained unemployment. The fortunate few who had stayed on the job saw steeply rising prices and a devalued currency render their wages useless. Hunger became severe as fighting depopulated Nuevo León's countryside and drought ruined crops for three consecutive years. Efforts by local companies and the city to procure shipments of food met resistance by military authorities in other states. Death, privation, and malnutrition so weakened the war-weary population that epidemic disease swept through the city. By 1918 outbreaks of smallpox and Spanish influenza had killed several thousand *regiomontanos*.[19]

Destitution yielded slowly to economic revival. Weak domestic markets, a volatile global economy, and political instability made for an erratic recovery. Ironically, it was another war – that in Europe – that sparked the first rebound. Workers eager to get back to the factories would return with a newfound militancy. The seedlings of unionization planted during the late Porfiriato had extended their organizational roots during the armed revolution. Labor would test the political waters stirred by revolution to express a host of long-held grievances as well as the more immediate demands for higher wages and job security fostered during the hard times of 1913–16. Local labor militancy paralleled the unrivaled degree of industrial unrest that swept through Latin America in the late 1910s. But in Monterrey worker protest developed within the unique context of the Mexican Revolution. The old regime had fallen and the upstart revolutionaries who sought to fashion a new order "favored the workers' interests to an unprecedented extent."[20] The troops would still heed the call to maintain order and production. But repression became the response of last resort, as civilians and generals alike found mediation and legislation to be the politically correct means of handling labor disputes. Times were changing – and workers understood this. Their defiant attitude gained newfound legitimacy with the passage of the 1917

---

18 Hanna, May 24, 1915, SD 812.00 NL/15078; Knight, *The Mexican Revolution*, II, 288, 416; Gilberto Alvárez Salinas, *Pancho Villa en Monterrey* (Monterrey, 1969).

19 Knight, *The Mexican Revolution*, II, 406–23; Mendirichaga, *Los 4 tiempos*, 324–26; AGENL: *Memoria del Gobernador Nicéforo Zambrano, 1917–1919* (Monterrey, 1921); for efforts to procure food, fuel, and raw materials during the war see AGENL; Industria y Comercio, 1900–1921, box 2. Estimated deaths due to epidemic disease range from 1,500 (Mendirichaga) to 5,600 (Zambrano).

20 Knight, *The Mexican Revolution*, II, 430.

Constitution, an event that signaled the arrival of a new era of labor relations in Mexico. Indeed, over the next two decades Mexican workers struggled to fashion this blueprint for reform into effective workplace and government policy.

"The Rights the Revolution Bequeathed to Us"

Constitutional Article 123 provided mobilized workers the legal muscle to press their grievances and express their aspirations. The labor code promised radical change. The right to strike and the right to union representation now became law. So did the eight-hour day, seven-hour night shift, and six-day work week. Overtime pay would be mandatory on the "seventh day of the week," which for workers meant Sunday. Employers did retain strict workplace authority and the power to discharge workers for such insubordinate acts as fighting, drunkenness, and distributing "propaganda" on the job. But the labor code's authors sought to foster occupational security and limit arbitrary dismissals. Workers subjected to unjust firings earned the right to select reinstatement or a severance package equal to three months wages. Dozens of other clauses addressed the issues of child labor, workplace health and safety, seniority rights, profit sharing, and minimum-wage standards. Large employers were assigned the responsibility to provide housing, schools, scholarships, and "cultural and sport activities" for workers and their families. Finally, Article 123 mandated the establishment of labor arbitration boards to mediate industrial disputes in accordance with the law. Representatives elected by labor and employer associations served on these tripartite bodies presided over by a government appointee. The law, according to one legal scholar, "recognize[d] the theory of class struggle."[21] Starting from that theoretical assumption, it assigned to the state the corporatist role of establishing social equilibrium between "labor" and "capital." The state came to be the final arbiter of industrial relations and Mexico's became one of the most advanced labor codes in its time. Monterrey's leading daily noted shortly thereafter that, "the entire working class agrees firmly with these fixed regulations, which are sure to produce genuine industrial conflicts."[22] But the industrialists would gain a measure of relief from what for a time proved to be the law's most consequential stipulation. Article 123's opening clause assigned each state the duty to legislate their own labor codes in "accordance with local conditions." Consistent with Latin American constitutional tradition, the 1917 Constitution essentially set forth a blueprint of ideals toward which the government should strive rather than iron-clad guarantees that

21 Nestor del Buen L., *Derecho del trabajo* (Vol. I, Mexico, 1974), 343.
22 *El Porvenir*, Mar. 19, 1918.

it would be obligated to enforce. The labor law became effective to the extent that working-class mobilizations pressured the government to make it so.

Regiomontano labor activists quickly developed an intimate familiarity with specific clauses and the broader implications of Article 123. This emergent "legal consciousness" provided the ideological foundation upon which their struggles to achieve justice at the workplace would build.[23] Erstwhile unionists had long harbored their own understanding of Mexico's 1857 Constitution, fashioning its ambiguous guarantees of individual rights into a defense of collective interests. During the early stage of the armed revolution, striking workers readily enveloped their appeals in the patriotic discourse of constitutional liberalism. Thus did strike leaders at the La Fama textile mill protest to the new government that "our boss hates us . . . [because] seeing how all the Republic's workers are organizing, we who love our fatherland followed their example and believe ourselves protected by our magna carta that grants just guarantees to all citizens." They signed off their 1913 appeal with the deferential flourish common to an era when workers requested the state's "benevolence" as "your most humble servants." But their recourse to a language of the past masked their firm understanding of the rights established by the revolution's first national labor agreement: one that established in 1912 to regulate and standardize labor relations in the textile industry.[24]

By mid-decade, Monterrey's workers would perceive themselves as "fellow citizens" and increasingly dress their appeals in the language of class. The textile unionists, for example, decried nonunion workers as "tools of the bourgeoisie" and put forth demands for a closed shop. Sent to Monterrey to mediate a rash of industrial disputes, a federal labor inspector contemplated the union demand to dismiss workers who resisted unionization. "In the present circumstances," he replied, "I do not think it appropriate to impose such strong measures against said workers, and will instead advise you to adopt more persuasive means of convincing your workmates . . . to join your union." He went on that, "we must not forget that one of the ideals of the revolution is respect for freedom in all its various forms, and [that] the freedom of association is never a man's obligation, but his right." Workers

---

23 For a comparative perspective from which I borrow the concept of legal consciousness, see John D. French, "Drowning in Laws But Starving (For Justice?): Brazilian Labor Law and the Workers' Quest to Realize the Imaginary," *Political Power and Social Theory*, 12 (1998), 181–218.

24 Union Fraternal de Obreros de La Fama to Labor Department, Jul. 9, 1913, AGN: Trabajo 37/13; Ramón Eduardo Ruiz, *Labor and the Ambivalent Revolutionaries: Mexico, 1911–1923* (Baltimore, 1976), 35–36. The La Fama workers protested their employers' noncompliance with key clauses of the labor accord, including the establishment of minimum wage and overtime rates and bans on both child labor and company stores.

were therefore counseled to "illustrate the benefits of social solidarity to the comrades by means of a newspaper or the soap box (*la tribuna*)."[25] Mexico's labor inspectors – who often evinced a genuine sympathy for working-class interests – would have to balance their understanding of revolutionary "ideals" with workers' embracement of their newfound constitutional rights. For a new generation of local union activists the labor code came to be seen as the workers' revolutionary inheritance. From their perspective, the fact that their new labor rights were enshrined in the constitution lent a moral foundation to their struggles.

The constitution's passage coincided with a renewed outbreak of industrial conflict in Monterrey's metallurgical industries, which experienced three protracted strikes over the next six years. During that time, workers, managers, and the state struggled incessantly over the labor code's applicability given "local conditions" in Monterrey. A boom-and-bust economy served as the structural backdrop to the labor struggles. By January 1917, when Article 123 became law, the steel mill and silver-lead smelters lit their furnaces to meet the wartime demands for industrial metals. Both industries boomed. During the period 1916–20, global lead prices quintupled while annual sales of finished steel jumped from roughly 1.6 million to 8.1 million pesos. Then, the postwar recession caused sharp contractions in prices and demand, an economic downturn accompanied by hyperinflation. Production remained erratic until 1924, as railroad strikes, mining conflicts, and political rebellion threatened the metal plants' access to raw materials.[26] During this period managers continually sought to readjust their workforces in rhythm with fluctuating markets. Occupational instability emerged as a particular concern to the smelter and steel workers employed in the furnaces and foundries. Upholding customary practice, supervisors in these so-called continuous production departments asserted the need either to maintain round-the-clock schedules or to extinguish the furnaces (and lay off workers) to avoid damaging the kettles. The conflicts that ensued illuminated how the nature of metallurgy shaped the workers' lives.

Months after the constitution's passage, supervisors of the city's smelters and steel mill wrote to the governor and elicited their collective distress with the new constitutional order. Since the government had yet to formalize a state labor code, they sought an "exact interpretation" of new labor laws that stipulated the payment of overtime and severance compensation for dismissed workers. Would the laws be applied rigidly to

25 Sindicato de Obreros y Obreras Libres de La Industrial to Labor Department, AGN: Trabajo 130/36; Union Fraternal de Obreros de La Fama to Labor Department, and the inspector's response of Dec. 21, 1915, AGN: Trabajo 105/11.
26 AHFM: *Informe*; Knight, *The Mexican Revolution*, II, 429.

their industries? And if so, were they applicable to all workers? They subtly demanded exemptions and based their claims on the peculiarities of metallurgy. The nature of their industries demanded the employment of "variable quantities of labor" in conformity with fluctuating mineral supplies and market demand. By "obligating the employment of a fixed numbers of workers," the new law would compel them to retain and pay idled labor. On this point the governor agreed. He found it "natural and undeniable [that] any employer should have the right to deny employment to a worker for whom no position exists." He concluded that "this would be the most justified of causes [to dismiss workers without severance pay]." The employers also resisted the payment of overtime wages, which the workers "mistakenly interpret as meaning double pay on Sundays." The industrialists noted that "our foundries must operate on Sundays" and stated erroneously that workers who labor on that day "always receive a day off during the week." Thus did the industrialists draw forth conditions specific to their industry to win exemptions from the labor law. The governor declined to address the overtime issue, suggesting that the industrialists consult "the legislators who wrote the law."[27] The metal workers promptly forced the government to decide, as they found nothing ambiguous about Article 123.

Labor conflicts erupted shortly after the constitution's passage. By early 1917, skilled workers at the steel mill and smelters had unionized and began pressuring local authorities to enforce their new labor rights. In March the government successfully pressured the steel mill to shorten the workday from twelve to eight hours. Three months later, the ASARCO smelter workers struck for three weeks before management yielded to a petition that also stipulated an eight-hour day. ASARCO also conceded 10 percent wage hikes and agreed to a union demand to provide workers with basic foodstuffs at below-market cost. But management refused to concede overtime pay. Moreover, two strike leaders later protested that ASARCO punitively dismissed "nearly the entire executive board of our union, throwing workers into the street with a stroke of the pen."[28] Meanwhile, one year after the constitution's passage, Governor Nicéforo Zambrano convened Nuevo León's first labor arbitration court. He authorized Monterrey's largest employers and a federation of twenty-nine local unions to appoint respective delegates to the board. The industrialists accepted the idea with reluctance

---

27 C.L. Baker (ASARCO), Jesús Ferrara (Smelter #2), and León Schwitzer (Fundidora) to Interim Governor Alfredo Ricaut, July 5 and 7, 1917, and the governor's response of July 13, 1917 in AGENL: Trabajo – Conciliación y Arbitraje, 1/546–547.

28 Javier Rojas Sandoval, "Poder político, cerveza y legislación laboral en Monterrey (1917–1922)," in Mario Cerutti, ed., *México en los 1920s* (Monterrey, 1993), 108; AGENL: Trabajo – Conciliación y Arbitraje, 1/17; Luis Cortez and Alredo de León to Governor Zambrano, May 22, 1918, in AGENL: Trabajo – Conciliación y Arbirtraje, 1/6.

until Zambrano apparently convinced them that a mediating agent with a "'fair' image . . . would undermine the appeal of radical labor elements."[29] After more than two months of deliberations, the employers elected their delegates. One of them was the Cuauhtémoc Brewery's Luis G. Sada, an emerging ideologue of the *regiomontano* elite who became a pioneer of corporate resistance to federal labor policies. In contrast to the hesitant employers, organized labor embraced the court's creation. They promptly elected as their delegates two union militants fired months earlier by ASARCO.

The board's labor delegates utilized their official posts to call the governor's attention to frequent violations of the labor code at Monterrey's steel mill and smelters.[30] Evoking specific clauses of Article 123, they protested the refusal to pay overtime, pressed for the provisioning of doctors and clinics within the workplace, and demanded the industrialists' compliance with Nuevo León's Accident Law, a Porfirian reform that remained unenforced twelve years after its passage. The former smelter workers also parlayed ASARCO's foreign ownership into a means of courting the governor's patriotic favor. They decried that while "this powerful company exploits the nation's men and natural resources, [ASARCO] tramples all over our brand new Constitution." The smelter's personnel director, John Geaham, earned special attention as a "pernicious foreigner and extortionist of the worker." The unionists charged that ASARCO paid Geaham a cut of the savings that he had earned for the company by driving down wages. Their allegations suggest a significant reduction in labor costs as ASARCO nationalized its work force, paying skilled Mexican workers 25 to 50 percent less than Americans had earned.[31] They added that the North American firm once recognized "the foreigners' union, but the Mexicans do not have that right either." They concluded their letter with a prophetic warning: "Conflicts between workers and bosses here [in Monterrey] will not be resolved by any labor arbitration board, [because the industrialists] consider themselves our Masters . . . and will refuse to recognize any intermediaries on our behalf." Weeks later, the labor tribunal faced its first significant test.

On the very day the labor delegates had communicated their protest to the governor, the headlines of a leading Mexico City daily announced the coming of record production levels at the nation's only steel mill. Wartime demand promised to rescue the Fundidora from seven years of limited

29 AGENL: *Memoria del Gobernador Nicéforo Zambrano, 1917–1919*, x–xviii; Saragoza, *The Monterrey Elite*, 111–112 (quoted).
30 Luis Cortez and Alredo de León to Governor Zambrano, May 22, 1918 in AGENL: Trabajo – Conciliación y Arbirtraje, 1/6.
31 When queried by the governor, the plant manager confirmed the charges. He then added that "what the Mexicans earn is just retribution . . . [and] if they believe they will find better opportunities elsewhere then they are free to go do so." L.B. Harrison to Secretario General del Gobierno, June 6, 1918 in AGENL: Trabajo – Conciliación y Arbirtraje, 1/8.

output and record losses. By May 1918 the company had signed lucrative contracts with a stabilized Mexican government and purchasers from Cuba and the United States. Management scheduled six months of uninterrupted production and started hiring 800 new workers. The mill's union activists soon learned of an unprecedented disclaimer signed by the new hires. The waivers stipulated that, "In accordance with accepted rules for all cases of continuous production, those who want to work in the furnaces and rolling mill should agree to labor the entire [seven-day] week, without exception, for regular pay."[32] Union officials protested to the labor board. They acknowledged their eagerness to resume steady work. But the waiver forced the steel workers to "abdicate their constitutional rights as a term of employment." They also reminded the authorities that workers at the state-owned National Railway shops received double pay for overtime. "If the government complies with the Labor Law," they asked, "then why should the same not be demanded of private companies?" The mill's supervisor countered that it had not "deprive[d] them of any right," because the seven-day week "has always been the established custom [at the mill]." Efforts by government officials to establish an accord reached an impasse when rank-and-file steel workers voted down a company offer to pay time and a half on Sundays. Several days later a federal labor inspector arrived from Mexico City and met with union leaders. According to his report, he "made the workers see that it was impossible to demand exact compliance with [the law] given the country's present [economic] state." He added that, "Article 123 is not yet even formalized (*reglamentado*), and that for the sake of patriotism, they should let some of their pretensions go."

The Fundidora's supervisor expressed no apparent concern when union leaders declared their intent to strike the mill. He perceived the resistance as the "work of a minority of radicals" who did not represent the steel workers' "genuine interests." Government officials did worry, however, when union broadsides appeared on city walls. Flyers posted about town announced the strike, outlined its causes, and demanded the "moral solidarity of the Monterrey working class." "We hope," it went on, "that all Workers and the People in general take these developments into consideration and help rescue the rights that the Revolution bequeathed to us at the cost of so much blood." The government's final attempt to mediate the dispute elicited no response from the company. Labor authorities convened with union leaders and expressed their "hope that, while the walkout transpires, [the unionists] act to maintain order and public tranquility, as befits the workers of Nuevo León." On July 5, 1918, all but 300 of the steel mill's 1,200 workers walked out. As the labor inspector later concluded, the steel workers were "jealous of

---

32 Unless indicated otherwise, the following account comes from AGN: Trabajo, 125/34; AGENL: Trabajo – Conciliación y Arbitraje, 1/3; Flores, *Burguesía, militares y movimiento obrero*, 170–80.

the rights and prerogatives granted them by our constitution, and watchful less the industrialists trample on those precepts." Therefore, "seeing [the waiver] as a violation of their rights, [and] feeling their dignity undermined, they launched a strike that was as thoughtless as it was violent."

Upon exiting the mill, strike leaders marched directly to the city's two smelters and convinced those workers to adhere to a previous solidarity accord. Within days the Fundidora conflict had evolved into "a menacing sympathy strike of about twelve thousand laborers" from local factories and the railway shops.[33] The metal workers now added union recognition to their list of demands. By mid-July, mass demonstrations in downtown Monterrey grew unruly. The ASARCO workers commandeered trains to stop lead shipments from the smelter. Steel workers used iron bars to prevent strike-breakers and office workers from entering the Fundidora. Confounded by the causes of these developments, the press circulated rumors that "German agents" had provoked the strike to prevent wartime steel shipments to the United States.[34] The government proved to be far more concerned with the potential influence of anarchist labor activists. The Carranza regime perceived their espousal of general strikes as a threat to government authority and its policies of economic reconstruction. While the revolutionary government pledged to support union rights – and began to patronize more moderate labor leaders – radical union organizers suffered considerable repression during these years of intense labor activity in Mexican industrial centers. Several days after a strike rally at Monterrey's Juarez Theater, federal police arrested two such "agitators" from Tampico at a downtown hotel. Having trailed them to Nuevo León, the government charged them with "inciting the workers to violence" and expelled them from the state. By this time the type of anarchist labor movement that thrived in Tampico had apparently sunk roots in Monterrey. Among the anarchists resident in "Mexico's Chicago" were Bartolomeo Sacco and Nicola Vanzetti. They and sixty fellow Italian anarchists had arrived via the eastern United States and worked in the factories, bakeries, and mines around Monterrey. Like most immigrant workers, Sacco and Vanzetti found steady employment elusive and they left Mexico in 1917.[35] Ten years later, some of the striking metal workers would be back in the streets demanding the acquittal of the two Italian workers who became martyrs of the international left.

Meanwhile, after three weeks of daily but failed negotiations, the labor board's president declared the strikes illegal and ordered the strikers back to their jobs. In his correspondence to the union leaders, he scolded the workers for "assuming truly hostile and violent attitudes" and reprimanded

33 Dickensen, July 8, 11, 1918, SD 812.504/160, 161.
34 *Nuevo País*, Mexico City, July 6, 1918, in AGN: Trabajo, 125/34.
35 Paul Avrich, *Sacco and Vanzetti: The Anarchist Background* (Princeton, 1991), 36–39.

them for "failing to understand your duties and rights." He then concluded that "by alarming the public, annoying the authorities, and causing great damage to the companies . . . you have violated the very labor law invoked on your behalf." Strike leaders ended their movement when company officials agreed to negotiate a settlement, a process that would be mediated directly by the government rather than the tripartite labor court. The industrialists' eventual willingness to bargain collectively with the unionists in itself marked a radical break from prerevolutionary practices. It reflected the workers' unique level of bargaining power as economic conditions pressured the companies to settle or see their wartime profits lost. The employers not only agreed to pay overtime "in accordance with the labor law," but to reinstate union workers fired before the strike. They also acquiesced to the workers' long-standing demand and agreed to comply with the state's Accident Law. Finally, in an unprecedented concession, the industrialists pledged "to recognize representatives of unions formed or to be organized among the workers." Nuevo León's governor later lamented the use of "executive power" rather than the labor board to settle the strike. "Realizing the rhetoric of agitation could influence the spirit of the labor delegates," he explained, the government had "conciliated the interests of workers and employers without the treacherous influence of agitators setting a cancerous precedent for the future."[36]

"A Principle of Solidarity"

The 1918 steel workers' strike – and the sympathy walkouts in response – illuminated a growing culture of solidarity among Monterrey's workers. The metal workers' cohesion was born of their common commitment to make their new labor rights effective. Their unity stemmed from their membership in the craft unions that were first organized in the city's railroad shops. Yet as company officials certainly recognized, the near totality of the walkouts demonstrated the unionists' capacity to mobilize unorganized laborers. We shall later discuss how the trust that younger and less-experienced workers developed for Monterrey's proud, dignified, and politically active tradesmen made such mobilizations possible. The latter now extended their labor activism beyond the workplace. In the strike's aftermath, fourteen local trade unions unified as the Federation of Railroad Brotherhoods, a name reflective of the vanguard role played by the railway workers in local labor activity. Months later 120 railroad and metal workers founded the Worker Socialist Party of Nuevo León, a vehicle that several workers soon drove into local political office. The party's statutes established the legislation of state labor laws and unionization of all workers as

36 Governor Zambrano cited in Saragoza, *The Monterrey Elite*, 112.

its top priorities. Sixteen Monterrey unionists also traveled to the nearby city of Saltillo for the founding convention of a new national labor association, the Regional Confederation of Mexican Workers (CROM). In 1919, the CROM's political wing signed an electoral pact with General Alvaro Obregón, the presidential candidate who pledged to recognize the federation as labor's sole representative. Most historians agree that Obregon's election helped deliver the young Mexican labor movement "into the trammels of the revolutionary state."[37] But not in Monterrey – not just yet. As a swift economic downturn settled across northern Mexico, Monterrey's workers mobilized once again to secure their jobs and defend the conquests won during the 1918 strike. Ensuing strikes at the steel mill, smelter, and railway shops would severely strain the *regiomontano* workers' tenuous alliance with the federal government and its newfound ally, the CROM.

It is hardly surprising that job security became a paramount concern for an entire generation of northern Mexican workers. The civil war first introduced them to the hardships of unemployment. Regional rebellions (1920, 1923) could swiftly resurrect the specter of joblessness. But over the long run, it was the region's reliance on fickle export markets that made economic stability as elusive for *regiomontanos* as it was for northeastern mine and oil workers. For the migrants who arrived before the revolution, learned a trade, and stayed on in Monterrey, the issue of steady employment was of paramount importance. If ASARCO's 1,200 workers are reflective of citywide trends, then 90 percent of *regiomontano* workers lived with family.[38] Their shared aspiration for occupational stability is manifested in the words and actions of Monterrey's skilled metal workers. When the smelter dismissed Tomás Lozano during a 1919 production slowdown, the company sent him away with a letter of good service. His manager found this "more satisfactory" than dividing a limited workload among all such machinists. After all, the National Railway shops hired Lozano the very next day. Lozano's union disagreed. His dismissal violated a strike settlement made with local industrialists earlier that year. The agreement stipulated that all machinists accept shorter hours rather than see a fellow unionist dismissed. Lozano went before the labor board to win his reinstatement. In one of the first successful claims filed by an individual worker, he argued that, "As workers, we live by our labor and as a Principle of Solidarity we arranged that all [machinists] receive equal though less work so that we all have equal [wages] upon which to subsist."[39] Skilled workers like Lozano

37 Bowman, July 30, 1920, SD 812.504/225; Rojas, "Movimiento obrero," 23–28; Knight, *The Mexican Revolution*, II, 488 (cited).
38 AGN: Trabajo, Labor Inspector's Report, 1919, 166/2.
39 L.B. Harrison to Secretario del Gobierno, Dec. 3, 1919; Unión de Forjadores y Ayudantes Mexicanos to Governor González, Nov. 25, 1919, AGENL: Trabajo – Conciliación y Arbitraje,

could and did switch employers with relative ease. But it was in their interest to accumulate seniority because occupational mobility conferred higher wages and more prestigious jobs. After the revolution, they looked to their unions to protect their job security.

In mid-1920, falling metal prices, the threat of layoffs, and rampant inflation renewed labor activity throughout northern Mexico. *Regiomontano* metal workers joined the protests. Union leaders representing steel and smelter workers demanded 100 percent wage hikes, expanded medical care, and a closed shop to protect union jobs. They also insisted that management respond to falling demand by reducing hours "but without dismissing workers." The companies rejected the petition. They also refused to negotiate with union representatives who were not "their own workers," an indirect reference to the railway workers who led the unions. "We are ready for anything," the steel mill's director threatened, "including the indefinite closure of the Monterrey plant. We will only negotiate with our own workers and never, for any reason, with people we do not know but act as if they are the apostles of our operatives."[40] For the second time in two years, Monterrey's metal workers struck the steel mill and smelters. Threats by the railroaders to second the walkout prompted swift intervention by federal authorities. They convinced the metal workers to reduce their wage demands and permit nonunion laborers to enter the plants. But operations slowed to a standstill because the industrialists refused to negotiate until the union workers returned.

Despite a dearth of union funds, the strikers held out for four weeks.[41] Efforts by a federal labor inspector to mediate the dispute proved futile because the companies resisted state intervention. Union officials accused the steel mill's Mexico City directors with leading the resistance. As they wrote to the governor, "the Fundidora is the most obstinate [of the companies] and the one that has schemed hardest to undermine not only ourselves but a government that is now focused on national Reconstruction." The federal labor inspector agreed. His daily reports adopted a notable tone of concern when a North American labor contractor arrived to Monterrey. Indeed, one week into the strike, one dozen of the steel mill's skilled Mexican rollers emigrated to Michigan. "This class of artisans is in short supply and indispensable to the region's industry," he advised the Labor Department. Rumors that upward of 500 local metal workers had prepared to migrate led

1/4. ASARCO's first-, second-, and third-grade machinists earned daily wages of $6.80, $5.35, and $3.65, respectively.
40 *Excélsior*, Mexico City, June 25, 1920.
41 The 1920 strike is documented in AGN: Trabajo, Labor Inspector's Report, 211/11, 213/13; AGENL: Trabajo – Conciliación y Arbitraje, 1/7; Bowman, July 30, 1920, SD 812.504/225; Paco Ignacio Taibo II, "La gran huelga de 1920 en Monterrey," *Cuadernos de cultura obrera* 4 (Monterrey, 1981).

him to "exhort [the strike leaders], for the good of the nation, to do every-thing possible to avoid the exodus." How many workers followed remains uncertain. But the rash of local newspaper stories on the hardships faced by immigrants suggests that the loss of *regiomontano* workers remained a local concern.[42] Meanwhile, in a final effort to sustain the walkout, the Monterrey unionists traveled to the CROM's national convention to appeal for strike funds and propose a nationwide solidarity strike. They would depart empty handed. But the ensuing debate divided the CROM leadership and several key railway unions broke from the federation for its refusal of support.[43] The debacle certainly explains the subsequent disdain that Monterrey unionists would hold toward the Mexico City–based CROM into the mid-1920s.

Now lacking the funds to sustain nearly 4,000 idled workers, union leaders decided to risk unfavorable settlements and ordered a return to work. The industrialists held firm in their refusal to bargain with "outside" union representatives. They settled separately with union workers at each plant. The companies also maintained their prerogative to adjust their labor forces in conformity with economic conditions. ASARCO's machinists thus saw their previous work-sharing schemes rescinded by management. Skilled workers subsequently labored under one-month contracts at all metal plants. The strike achieved new and lasting concessions, including 60 percent wage hikes and the extension of medical benefits to families. ASARCO even agreed to recognize shop-floor grievance committees to be established by its workers. But the 1920 strike marked a zenith in the metal workers' capacity to act collectively. The changing nature of the labor market and the companies' own antiunion strategies would diminish their organizational unity. Monterrey's steel and smelter workers would not renew their ties of solidarity until the mid-1930s.

Indeed, throughout the city, union rights grew elusive as shortages of skilled labor became a bygone relic. Records of the state employment office highlight the trend. In early 1921, the labor placement agency filled only 37 of 1,121 requests for foremen, mechanics, and carpenters. One year later it counted 2,500 job seekers on its registers. The interval saw mines close throughout the North and mass layoffs in the Gulf Coast oil fields. Workers in the latter industry received rail passes to Monterrey.[44] They certainly found little relief. "This district," it was reported, "has been suffering from a general economic depression of the most severe character. . . . [A]pproximately half the laborers of Monterrey are out of

---

42 For hardship tales and reports filed by Mexican consular officials in San Antonio and Chicago see *El Porvenir*, Mar. 3, 1919, Sep. 4, 1920, Jan. 8, Aug. 18, 1922, Mar. 12, 1923, May 17, June 22, 1924, June 10, Nov. 8, 1926.

43 Taibo, "La gran huelga," 19.

44 AGN: Trabajo, 285/6, 313/5–9; AGENL: Trabajo – Asociaciones y Sindicatos, 4/77.

work, prices continue [to be] high . . . and there is no relief in sight." Things got worse. The United States Consul reported a 50 percent rise in food costs and rents. Seven months later he found that "unemployment grows more alarming as winter approaches and to this is attributed a wave of thievery with which the police are unable to cope." A longtime American business traveler found the economic situation worse than any time in memory, "even during the worst period of the revolution."[45] It was under these conditions that unions suffered setbacks and government authorities rescinded their begrudging tolerance of strikes.

The industrialists parlayed the crisis into their own collective resistance to both unionism and state intervention in their industries. The fear of losing skilled workers was no longer a concern. Indeed, ASARCO punitively dismissed five union leaders months after the 1920 strike. The labor court system offered workers no respite because the employers refused to recognize its authority. As Monterrey's unionists protested to the governor, workers hoped to see the tribunal function efficiently. But they added that, "it is well known by all revolutionaries that the Capitalists are the ones who refuse to comply with the Ideals of the Revolution. . . . We trust that you will make sure that the revolutionary principles are respected."[46] Their hopes would be dashed. By 1921, the revolutionary government's own preoccupation with the economic crisis led it to quell labor militancy. Early that year workers struck Monterrey's Peñoles smelter in sympathy with Coahuila coal miners employed by the same American firm. The governor ordered cavalry troops to break their pickets as the company fired the strikers and contracted replacements.[47] Even the railroaders' strategic bargaining power failed them in a bid to win union recognition from the government-run National Railways. Federal authorities firmly repressed a subsequent strike that became an issue of authority for President Obregón ("Either the workers rule or I rule!"). The national strike became particularly violent in the Monterrey shops where officials had sit-down strikers jailed, locked union workers out, and contracted "free" workers from as far as Sonora and Mexico City. Sabotaged tracks and violence against strikebreakers prompted a military occupation of Monterrey's shops and rail stations. In the end, both the strikers and many replacement workers kept their jobs.[48] But the struggle left many local unionists embittered toward a government that they had expected to uphold their understanding of "revolutionary principles." The

45 Bowman, May 7, Jul. 11, Nov. 15, 1920, SD 812.50/83, 92, 94.

46 Federación de Sociedades Gremials Ferrocarrileras to Gov. Porfirio González, July 9, 1920, AGENL: Trabajo – Conciliación y Arbitraje, 1/7.

47 The local Mexican Mining, Smelting, and Refining Company sold its old Smelter #2 to the North American mineral giant in the late 1910s. *El Porvenir*, Dec. 14–15, 1920, Jan. 9, 1921.

48 *El Porvenir*, Feb. 23, Mar. 1–4, 10, 14–16, 1921.

jubilation and militancy that accompanied the 1917 passage of Article 123 thus waned by the early 1920s. Monterrey's skilled workers increasingly forsook their union rights to preserve their jobs.

The postwar depression limited the metal workers' capacity to press the industrialists on the issue of job security. But the specter of unemployment did not diminish their will to employ direct action to defend their prerogatives. The steel workers demonstrated this in late 1922, when a minor dispute sparked a five-week strike that transformed industrial relations at the mill.[49] The conflict began innocently enough. In mid-September a supervisor leveled eight-day suspensions against two furnace workers who damaged a boiler. Several days later, 150 of their workmates walked out in protest because management refused to reduce the suspensions by half. Their department supervisor therefore rescinded the furnace workers' contracts and began hiring replacements. The strike then spread to the rolling mill and machine shops. Meanwhile, the Federation of Railroad Brotherhoods filed a protest with the labor board on the steel workers' behalf. They demanded the workers' reinstatement with lost wages, union recognition, and the establishment of shop committees to handle such grievances. The company held out. "One cannot conceive," one official said, "how a group of conscientious and hardworking men would resolve to lose 5,000 pesos a day because two of their workmates lost 100 pesos during a four-day suspension." The plant's director blamed the strike on "outside influences" and refused to negotiate "the impossible demands imposed by elements foreign to this enterprise." By early October, the strike had paralyzed steel production.

In the meantime, the company began hiring 800 strikebreakers and used its access to the press to arouse public opposition to the strikers. Industrial patriotism and paternal benevolence highlighted the discourse. A press release published in local and Mexico City newspapers warned the public that the mill "will close its workshops if the strikers do not solve their problems." Company stockholders would therefore be forced "to deliver the national enterprise into foreign hands." The Fundidora exalted its role "in sustaining thousands of Mexican workers and serving as a school where many competent and useful men had been forged." In an interview with Monterrey's *El Porvenir*, the mill's German supervisor, Meliton Ulmer, outlined how the Fundidora "has always been concerned with the material, moral, and intellectual well-being of its more than 2,000 workers." He described the mill's company housing, its school, and the recreational facilities provided for "our boys." Finally, Ulmer proclaimed his company's "willingness to

49 Unless indicated otherwise, this account of the 1922 steel strike is from AGN: Trabajo 444/10; *El Porvenir*, Sep. 20–Oct. 25, 1922; Flores, *Burguesía, militares y movimiento obrero*, 238–45.

satisfy the constitutional aspirations of the working classes."[50] The industrialists' use of the local and Mexico City press to trumpet the dangers of unionism and publicize their own benevolence became standard practice in Monterrey.

The Fundidora strike endured five weeks. Mexico's national railway workers' union donated the strike funds that helped sustain more than 1,000 striking steel workers. Picket-line violence broke out early on as strikers and "free workers" went at it with clubs and machetes. The municipal government then conceded to the Fundidora's petition and ordered police to protect the strikebreakers' "constitutional right to work."[51] The unionists demanded that the mayor call off the cops. By permitting them to "act as company representatives," they pleaded, the city was "shouting to the scabs that the doors of the Fundidora are open to all who wish to work." The mayor held firm. By the third week of the strike, an uneasy peace settled outside the mill as police protected plant gates from what the local press referred to as the union's "Red Guards." An estimated 840 nonunion workers, foremen, and new hires sustained minimal production levels. Some would remain in the mill for the strike's duration. Back outside, strike leaders made a point of riding the streetcars and jitney buses that passed by the plant to persuade nonunion workers to respect their pickets. Even Monterrey's staunchly probusiness daily alluded to the expressions of public sympathy seen at downtown strike rallies. Indeed, as the strike entered its fourth week, nonunion workers were "leaving their jobs out of loyalty to their comrades."[52]

Nuevo León's labor board convened daily throughout the conflict. Early into the strike, the steel workers dropped their demands for lost wages and union recognition. They pledged to return to work under the terms set forth in Article 123's strike clause, which mandated the reinstatement of striking workers into positions taken by strikebreakers. The conflict became a question of seniority. But management upheld its "obligation to award those [workers] who provided their services during the strike." The company's recalcitrance perhaps explains President Obregón's order that the governor remain neutral. Indeed, strike leaders ordered workers to resume their aggressive picketing when the negotiations stalled. An overwhelmed police force stood by as the strikers prevented replacement workers from entering the plant. Roving pickets blocked the rail lines into the mill and thwarted the company's attempt to bring in 200 strikebreakers by train. One month into the strike, some 3,000 steel workers and their sympathizers rallied before the state capital. Departing downtown, the workers began a

50 *Excélsior*, Oct. 4, 1922; *El Porvenir*, Sep. 21, Oct. 4, 1922.
51 AGN: Dirección General del Gobierno (hereafter DGG), D.2.84.41, 7/40.
52 *El Porvenir*, Oct. 11, 1922.

two-mile march to the steel mill, where the unionists promised to "remove the scabs by force." But when the strikers reached the plant, they discovered the police marshaled across the road in a "firing line." They dispersed without incident. But picket-line violence between unionists and "free workers" intensified the next day.[53]

From Mexico City, Fundidora officials criticized the authorities' failure to protect the strikebreakers and threatened to close the mill. Indeed, rumors of the mill's "imminent closure" dominated local headlines throughout the conflict. An alarmed press castigated the strikers for "doing little honor to the composure with which popular classes in this region know how to act." Their actions not only "harm those of the same class," but they "are not in line with the education, traditions, and discipline of the regiomontano worker." Editors also lamented the image that the strike created of Mexican labor relations at a time when the nation needed foreign capital investments. They therefore demanded government intervention to defend the "free workers' legal and just right to work." The nonunion workers also protested the state's failure to protect them from "sabotage" and "violence." Indeed, workers inside the plant even staged their own one-day stoppage "in defense of our constitutional rights." After five weeks, the mounting violence in Monterrey finally prompted government intervention. Labor Department officials arrived at Monterrey accompanied by their newfound collaborators in the CROM. To the strikers' dismay, one of the Mexico City labor leaders upheld the government's "obligation to help and protect the 'free workers'." Meeting with the federal labor inspector, local union leaders expressed their members' fears of losing "their intermediary places" in the mill's occupational hierarchies. The mill's management initially defended its "freedom to assign workers where we see fit."[54] But federal officials forged a compromise, and all except the furnace workers regained their lost jobs. Supervisors agreed to rehire the workers who started the conflict only when new positions opened in their department.

The longest strike up to that point in Monterrey's history thus ended, and the steel mill resumed operations with union and nonunion workers alike. The press lauded mill director Adolfo Prieto for "for retying the friendly and cordial bonds that unify the company and it workers." But as we shall later see, supervisors swiftly violated the strike accord and retaliated against union workers. Conflicts therefore simmered in several mill departments throughout the following year. Whereas management regained the upper hand as a result of the settlement, the steel workers secured lasting concessions. Company administrators subsequently recognized and signed contracts with the very unions and union leaders who played key roles as

---

53 *El Porvenir*, Oct. 20, 1922.
54 AGN: Trabajo, 444/10.

strike organizers. The machinists, rollers, and structural iron workers all won separate contracts establishing job security, higher wages, and new production bonuses for the mill's most skilled workmen. The Fundidora also agreed to institute shop committees in each of the plant's twenty departments. While union membership stagnated at the mill, company managers never attempted to eliminate unionism per se. The strike's relative success, if measured by its duration, demonstrated the Fundidora's need to negotiate a consensual relation with its skilled union workers. Management therefore courted the loyalty of the strike's leaders, who subsequently performed an important role in disciplining the rank and file. The end of the strike also marked the beginning of a new era of labor relations at the Fundidora and other major local industries. The industrial strife inspired the development of company paternalism in Monterrey.

3
Work, Gender, and Paternalism at the Cuauhtémoc Brewery

Since the 1920s, Monterrey's captains of industry have been renowned for their systems of company paternalism. Be they hagiographic or critical, histories of these industrialists largely assume that paternalism produced disciplined, quiescent, and malleable labor forces.[1] These studies largely define paternalism in terms of the nonwage incentives proffered to workers. But those welfare benefits underpinned a specific system of social relations between workers and their employers – workplace encounters punctuated by benevolence, patriarchy, and personalism. While other employers in Mexico offered nonwage benefits to their workers, none did so with greater enthusiasm, resources, and self-promotional panache than the pillars of *regiomontano* industry. Monterrey's largest companies offered the incentives for all the usual reasons: to retain workers, to foster deference and loyalty, and to prevent the intrusion of government and organized labor into their factories. They employed crafty lawyers and outright intimidation to combat unionism as well. And they publicized their benevolence to purchase political capital and enhance their civic prestige. But the industrialists also shared, judging by their words and deeds, a sincere and heartfelt concern for their workers' well-being. Moreover, decades later, the workers who retired from these companies continued to express their own reverential gratitude toward Monterrey's pioneers of paternalism.

The systems of paternalism practiced in Monterrey paralleled those introduced elsewhere in the industrial world.[2] But the Monterrey elite devised

---

1 Among the classic works of hagiography are Nemesio García, *Una industria en marcha* (Mexico City, 1955) and Saldaña, *Apuntes históricos*; critical counterpoints include Máximo de León Garza, *Monterrey: Un vistazo a sus entrañas* (Monterrey, 1968) and Nuncio, *El Grupo Monterrey*, 122–58. Academic scholars posit similar conclusions: Saragoza, *The Monterrey Elite*, 89–93 and Mora-Torres, *The Making of the Mexican Border*, 246–54.

2 Studies that informed the analysis herein include Douglas Flamming, *Creating the Modern South: Millhands and Managers in Dalton, Georgia, 1884–1984* (Chapel Hill, 1992); Patrick Joyce, *Work, Society, and Politics: The Culture of the Factory in Later Victorian England* (New Brunswick, 1981); Walter Licht, "Fringe Benefits: A Review Essay on the American Workplace," *International Labor and Working-Class History*, 53 (1998), 164–78; Andrea Tone, *The Business of Benevolence: Industrial*

54

their managerial strategies within a unique context – that of revolutionary Mexico. Indeed, we shall see that it was the labor militancy inspired by the revolution that prompted the industrialists to expand the welfare benefits established before 1910 and extend them to all full-time workers. Furthermore, not only did Mexico's new constitution establish the basis for state interventionism; it also legislated the groundwork for mass unionization. In contrast to the United States, where the consolidation of welfare capitalism abetted a decline in union activity, paternalism's appearance in Monterrey paralleled the emergence of the strongest organized labor movement in 1920s Latin America. Unionism made some solid inroads in other industrial centers of Mexico. But not in Monterrey. The *regiomontano* workers largely forsook their right to union representation because paternalism provided a modicum of security that proved particularly appealing after the hardships of the 1910s.

Finally, Monterrey's style of paternalism assumed an unusual cast relative to those in other regions of the world. The North American model inspired the *regiomontano* industrialists. But the locals did not simply lay a Yankee blueprint upon their corporate labor policies. Rather than hire a battery of university-educated personnel specialists to administer company paternalism, the *regiomontanos* channeled fringe benefits through cooperative societies run jointly by workers and management. Paternalism thus built upon working-class traditions of mutual aid and tapped into labor's historic aspirations of self-improvement. Indeed workers themselves played an active and innovative role in its development. This chapter examines the first and most enduring of those cooperatives, the brewery's Cuauhtémoc Society. To the extent that paternalism was designed to blunt unionism, it succeeded at Cuauhtémoc because the peculiarities of the brewing industry conspired on behalf of the company's open-shop philosophy. The brewery thus serves as our point of departure because deference became and remained the predominant pattern of behavior among the Cuauhtémoc operatives.

The Pioneers of Paternalism

Despite countless national precedents, Monterrey's businesspeople have long portrayed themselves as Mexico's pioneers of industrial paternalism, progressive industrialists whose corporate labor policies anticipated the social reforms instituted by government policymakers.[3] Contemporary civic

Paternalism in Progressive America (Ithaca, 1997); and Gerald Zahavi, *Workers, Managers, and Welfare Capitalism: The Shoeworkers and Tanners of Endicott Johnson, 1890–1950* (Urbana, 1988).

3 Prerevolutionary examples are found in French, *A Peaceful and Working People*, 51–55; García Díaz, *Un pueblo del porfiriato*; Tony Morgan, "Proletarians, Politicos, and Patriarchs," in William Beezley, et al.,

boosters and several generations of scholars have done much to bolster their claims.[4] No company more assiduously cultivated its image as a benevolent employer than the Cuauhtémoc Brewery. In an industry where a company's success depends as much upon the quality of its product as its marketing skills, Cuauhtémoc parlayed paternalism into a basic ingredient of its promotional recipe. Its company literature ascribes the brewery's economic success to the owners' "constant preoccupation with the workers' well-being." A business history commissioned by the firm attributes this benevolence to Cuauhtémoc's perception of its operatives as more than "just another commodity. Each worker is an essential collaborator in the business and thus worthy of respect." A company history written by veteran workers in 1930 asserts that industrial benevolence reflected the "progressive spirit" of the brewery's founders. The Garza Sadas not only built a company that "liberated" Mexico from its historic dependence on foreign imports. By doing so they offered "gainful employment and always demonstrated a profound concern for elevating the workers' cultural level."[5] The appreciation expressed by such loyal workers reflected a widespread rank-and-file attitude. But what inspired their employers' paternalism? And how does one explain the timing of its development?

We saw earlier that an incipient form of paternalism emerged with industrialization itself. In addition to competitive wage rates, the city's industrialists offered fringe benefits to recruit and retain the skilled immigrant workers needed to launch operations. However, industrial paternalism developed as an institutionalized system of labor relations after the revolution, when Monterrey's foreign workers had been largely displaced. The system therefore drew inspiration from sources additional to skilled labor scarcity. The industrialists, their historians, and contemporary boosters cite various ideological inspirations – from patriotic benevolence to Bismarckian and North American models of paternalism – to explain this development. However, that most commonly advanced is social Catholicism, the Vatican's nineteenth-century response to European labor radicalism.[6] This papal advocacy of humanized capitalism was championed by Mexican clergymen in the early 1900s. Catholic doctrine undoubtedly shaped industrial

eds. *Rituals of Rule, Rituals of Resistance: Public Celebrations and Popular Culture in Mexico* (Wilmington, 1994), 151–171.

4 For the Cuauhtémoc Brewery's precedent-setting labor policies, see *El Porvenir*, Apr. 18, 1920; *Excélsior*, Feb. 2, 1936; García, *Una industria en marcha*, 69–75; Saragoza, *The Monterrey Elite*, 90–91.

5 Cuauhtémoc Brewery, *Cien años son un buen tiempo* (Monterrey, 1990), 27; Salvador Novo, *Crónica regiomontana: Breve historia de un gran esfuerzo* (Monterrey, 1965), 17; Gerónimo Dávalos, et al., *Cuarenta años son un buen tiempo* (Monterrey, 1930), 52.

6 Nuncio, *El grupo Monterrey*, 145–58; Saragoza, *The Monterrey Elite*, 90–93; Mora-Torres, *The Making of the Mexican Border*, 247–48.

relations in places like Guadalajara – where employers, priests, and workers organized joint opposition to "red" unionism – or Mexico City, where religion pervaded many industrial workplaces.[7] But Christianity's impact on traditionally secular northern Mexico is dubious. Indeed, Catholic unions never appeared in Monterrey. Moreover, during the 1920s, the revolutionary government's anticlerical policies elicited a mute response in Monterrey, where local businesspeople became ardent supports of Church-baiting governor Aaron Saénz. Former brewery worker Manuel Carranza thus recalls of the period that "the priests were always on the side of the employers. But in those days, they didn't have the influence to carry out their [antiunion] propaganda [in Monterrey]."[8] Significantly, the conservative Catholicism with which Monterrey is often identified did not emerge publicly until the 1930s, when the local elite began promoting it as an ideological antidote to the government's policies of "revolutionary nationalism."

Today the brewery's promotional literature cites Christian doctrine as the inspiration for company paternalism. But that system's architect, Luis G. Sada, admitted to North American influences, notably an apprenticeship in Chicago, where his father sent him in 1906 to learn firsthand the technical and supervisory aspects of brewing. Back in Monterrey, the younger Sada assumed direction of the brewery's daily operations. Then, during the revolutionary upheaval of the 1910s, he and other local elites returned to the United States, where several studied business and engineering at the University of Michigan and M.I.T. Sada's biographer later acknowledged that "the ample knowledge about labor acquired abroad during the ill-fated days of exile" inspired the brewery's subsequent managerial policies.[9] Moreover, since the late nineteenth century, Monterrey's industrialists had socialized with American administrators from the local ASARCO plant, including the Guggenheim brothers. They and the subsequent director of the mineral concern's Mexican operations, William Morse, helped pioneer welfare capitalism in the United States, where some 2,500 firms had adopted such corporate labor policies by the 1910s. The Fundidora, for its part, would send representatives to scout the welfare benefits system engineered by Republic Steel in Cleveland.[10] Meanwhile, *Actividad*,

---

7 Jean Meyer, *La Cristiada* (3 vols., Mexico, 1974); Lear, *Workers, Neighbors, and Citizens*, 92–95.

8 Carranza interview; for the noted absence of "clerical" sentiments into the 1930s, see Zapata Novoa, *Tercos y triunfadores*, 47.

9 Antonio L. Rodgríguez, *Homenajes* (Monterrey, 1954), 11 (quoted); El Norte, *Constructores de Monterrey* (Monterrey, 1945), 153–54; Saragoza, *The Monterrey Elite*, 143–44.

10 O'Connor, *The Guggenheims*, 97–98, 337–38; Tone, *The Business of Benevolence*, 2; AHFM: Cooperativa Acero, 153/2. The Fundidora also propagated that other tenet of American industrialism, scientific management. During the 1920s, they published Frederick Taylor's work in Spanish and distributed it to such proponents of industrial capitalism as President Calles. Adolfo Prieto to Calles, July 2, 1928, AGN: Presidentes – Obregón-Calles (hereafter O-C) 728-C-56.

the monthly publication of Monterrey's Chamber of Commerce, regularly published articles translated from American business journals. Thus while Catholicism later permeated and lent sanction to paternalism in Monterrey, the North American model served as the primary source of local inspiration. Company paternalism thenceforth acquired a "nationalistic twist." Monterrey's influential businesspeople soon touted *their* model as the most efficient means of achieving the labor-capital harmony that would foster Mexico's economic progress.[11]

The ideological factors do not in themselves explain the timing of paternalism's development or the unusual cast it assumed in Monterrey. Company paternalism was a tactical response to militant unionism and fears of government regulation. Government labor policy had evolved in dramatic fashion during the 1910s. The federal inspectors who staffed the Labor Department eagerly embraced their role as official mediators and counselors to workers. Moreover, the government openly courted the support of organized labor, having patronized the CROM's founding convention in nearby Saltillo. We shall see that a similar government–labor alliance evolved in Monterrey as well, where union activists pressured authorities to legislate meaningful labor laws. Meanwhile, the unprecedented industrial strife of the later 1910s demonstrated how the 1917 Constitution established new standards of labor rights that those activists understood quite well. The Cuauhtémoc Brewery's system of industrial paternalism dates to this moment when Mexico's industrial capital first experienced widespread labor unrest.

The brewery itself experienced no explosions of working-class militancy akin to the metal workers' strikes. But the company was by no means immune from labor disputes. In the mid-1910s, inflationary pressures led local factory workers to petition the federal authorities for wage hikes. Responding to a government decree, the brewery's directors pledged themselves to a 50 percent salary increase. They never complied with the settlement. When their workers protested to the government, Cuauhtémoc's owners threatened to close the brewery, leaving hundreds of workers unemployed. President Carranza ordered local authorities to seize the factory. Two days later, the company announced its willingness to "humbly concede to the workers' demands." The concession did not preclude the brewery operatives from embracing another product of the revolution, the right to organize. In 1917, an unknown number of operatives organized the Free Alliance of Cuauhtémoc Brewery Workers. The company fired the union's leaders. Months later, management responded to the employees' apparent longing for organization. In 1918, twenty-two veteran workers joined with Luis G. Sada to constitute the Socieded Cuauhtémoc y FAMOSA

11 Saragoza, *The Monterrey Elite*, 140–44.

(SCYF).[12] Initially established as a savings cooperative, the Cuauhtémoc Society would administer all aspects of industrial paternalism, from education and healthcare to recreation and publications. It also organized the cultural programs designed to integrate workers, managers, and their kin into Cuauhtémoc's extended family. Cooperatives thereafter became the principle vehicle through which Monterrey's industrialists channeled nonwage benefits to their workers.

Historians date the formation of Mexico's earliest cooperative societies to the mid-nineteenth century. They evolved from the *cajas de ahorro* (communal savings banks) first established by Spanish immigrants. By the 1890s, artisans and middle-class professionals had organized dozens of savings, consumer, and building cooperatives in Mexico's urban centers. Cooperatives received the sanctioning of government officials and the Church hierarchy, which promoted them as part of a broader program of Catholic social action. The Mexican business community also lauded cooperatives as an acceptable means of improving working-class living standards. Its leading journal praised British precedents, where "workers saved millions rather than squander their earnings in taverns and gambling joints, destroying their families and corrupting their spirits." Cooperatives not only appealed to the elite's taste for European culture. They provided workers with a safe and viable alternative to that most unacceptable of Old World imports, socialism. Reform-minded businesspeople thus endorsed cooperatives in a language that would soon be familiar to Monterrey's workers: "Don't look for happiness in the destruction of order, for you will be the first to perish in the ruins. Your happiness depends on yourselves. Learn to moderate your desires and restrain your passions. Learn to economize, to save, and you will possess an infallible means of improving your own moral, intellectual, and material conditions."[13]

After the revolution, social reformers, moderate labor leaders, and government officials all promoted cooperatives as an alternative to militant unionism. Francisco Loria, a railroad engineer, trade unionist, and author of a guide to *cooperativismo* recognized that squalid working-class living conditions opened dangerous inroads to "radical communists." Cooperatives, he advocated, would restore the "social balance" lost during the Porfiriato, when the "centralization of wealth" left Mexico's working classes "illiterate, indolent, and vice-ridden." The cooperatives would help "resolve the anxiety and discomfort caused by [labor's] unsatisfied needs." Loria

---

12 Flores, *Burguesía, militares y movimiento obrero*, 147–48; Rojas, "Poder político," 137; *Trabajo y Ahorro*, Apr. 23, 1993. Fábricas Monterrey (FAMOSA) is Cuauhtémoc's subsidiary packaging plant.

13 Rosendo Rojas Coria, *Tratado del cooperativismo en Mexico* (Mexico City, 1982 [1952]), 310–15; Marjorie Ruth Clark, *Organized Labor in Mexico* (Chapel Hill, 1934), 89; *El Economista Mexicano*, Nov. 9, 1901 (quoted).

himself spent the 1910s organizing dozens of consumer cooperatives within Mexico's railroad unions, including the Monterrey locals. In the view of such activists, unionization ideally provided the basis for self-help rather than collective protest. Cooperatives were thus meant to "counteract the excesses of irresponsible labor leaders."[14] During the 1920s, the federal government propagated the benefits of cooperatives. The secretary of public education published 50,000 manuals that offered organizational advice and promoted *cooperativismo* as a means of "making workers into their own bosses."[15] On the issue of cooperatives, then, the Mexican government reached common ground with the Monterrey industrialists. Both the state and business leaders perceived them as an acceptable means of shaping the kind of morally, culturally, and physically fit proletariat demanded by a nation upon the brink of modernity. More importantly, by building upon prerevolutionary working-class tradition, the company-sponsored cooperatives appealed to workers as well.

A unique feature of paternalism in Monterrey, organizations like the Cuauhtémoc Society marked the intersection of working-class tradition, employer benevolence, and elite resistance to unionism. According to company literature, the brewery's Luis G. Sada gained his knowledge of the workers' "means of thinking and eagerness to improve themselves" through his association with the plant's mechanics and foremen.[16] In prerevolutionary Monterrey, such workers had organized dozens of mutual-aid societies. Those of the brewery founded their own Sociedad Mutualista Cuauhtémoc in 1898. Perhaps the best endowed were those established by immigrants. The Centro Español and the American Beneficence and Recreation Society helped procure work for newcomers and unemployed immigrants. They also strived to improve their members' "physical, intellectual, and moral" character through athletic clubs, reading rooms, and popular theater.[17] As precursors to the company-based cooperatives organized after the revolution, these societies brought together both industrial workers and white-collar professionals. Moreover, as we saw earlier, the workers' avid promotion of and participation in night classes and vocational schools testified to a culture of self-improvement within Monterrey's working-class community. Company paternalism would tap into and build upon these historic aspirations. But private employers were not alone in responding to these desires.

14 Francisco Loria, *Sociedades cooperativas: El cooperativismo como elemento de libertad y progreso* (Mexico City, 1927 [1918]), 8–10, 30–31; Rojas, *Tratado del cooperativismo*, 421.

15 Secretaría de Educación Pública, *La historia de las sociedades cooperativas*, (Mexico City, 1925); Joaquín Ramírez Cabañas, *La sociedad cooperativa en México* (Mexico City, 1936), 27. By 1935, 470 agricultural, savings, and consumer cooperatives had been officially registered with the government under the General Law on Cooperative Societies.

16 *Trabajo y Ahorro*, Apr. 23, 1993.

17 AGENL: Trabajo – Associaciones y Sindicatos, 1906–1912, 2/184, 2/444.

During and after the revolution, Monterrey's workers replicated the national transition from mutual-aid societies to unionism. Their sustained commitment to cooperative societies represents an overlooked point of continuity within that process. Beginning in 1912, the city's railroad unions organized savings and consumer cooperatives within their locals. As the self-perceived vanguard of organized labor, the railroaders encouraged the governor to distribute cooperative propaganda to other unions in the state. Organized labor did not perceive unionism and cooperatives as mutually exclusive forms of working-class organization. Indeed unionists often advocated cooperatives as a means of maintaining working-class independence. But in Monterrey labor activists certainly recognized their tactical deployment by antiunion employers.[18] By the 1930s militants were discouraging workers from enlisting in company-sponsored cooperatives. In the meantime, Monterrey's industrialists, the state, *and* many workers reached common ground on the issue of cooperatives. For the latter, the well-financed company cooperatives offered genuine rewards that outweighed the risks of labor activism. Thus while Mexican labor made its postrevolutionary transition from mutual-aid to "resistance" societies, workers in the nation's industrial capital learned to forsake unions in favor of company-sponsored cooperatives. The particular form that industrial paternalism assumed at the brewery, where the company channeled nonwage benefits through a cooperative society, would be replicated by Monterrey's other large employers. The Cuauhtémoc Society became an exemplary model of *cooperativismo*, lauded by one proponent for its sound administration and the enthusiasm displayed by its members.[19] Indeed, as part of a labor relations system designed to stymie militant unionism and promote company loyalty, no cooperative enjoyed greater long-term success than the SCYF, which survived into the twenty-first century.

The Cuauhtémoc Society

Whereas the revolution inspired the birth of industrial paternalism in Monterrey, the city's systems of welfare capitalism evolved gradually. They departed from prerevolutionary precedents not only in the expanded scope of benefits but in their extension to the families of all full-time workers regardless of skill. Moreover, despite their common genealogies, the paternalistic

18 Rojas, *Tratado del cooperativismo*, 417; Confederación de Sociedades Obreras Ferrocarrileras to Governor González, Dec. 28, 1920, AGENL: Trabajo – Associaciones y Sindicatos, 4; Alan Derickson, *Workers' Health, Workers' Democracy: The Western Miners' Struggle, 1891–1925* (Ithaca, 1988), 22–25, finds that hard-rock miners organized consumer cooperatives to resist company welfare schemes, which they perceived as a paternalistic strategy to assert control over their lives.

19 Rojas, *Tratado del cooperativismo*, 413.

practices designed by Monterrey's industrialists assumed distinct forms that reflected the contrasting managerial philosophies of the companies' directors. Referring to Mexican political tradition, former workers and managers distinguish the brewery's local owners as "conservatives" relative to the "liberals" who administered the steel mill from their Mexico City headquarters.[20] Cuauhtémoc's owners exemplified the northern Mexicans' begrudging contempt for central government authority. Their antistatism dated to the earliest years of revolutionary violence. Recall that the Garza Sada family's financial ties to counterrevolutionary forces led rebel leaders to sequester the brewery during the mid-1910s. In the 1920s, the continued threat of state intervention – in the form of tax levees, forced loans, and temperance reform – further sharpened their business conservatism.[21] The government's fluctuating support of organized labor sharpened their indignity as well. Cuauhtémoc would therefore refine its managerial policies in rhythm with the ebbs and flows of government labor policy in an ongoing effort to shield its workers from unionization.

Cuauhtémoc's directors viewed and treated their workers as children in need of benevolent protection and paternal guidance, a social outlook not inconsistent with nineteenth-century conservative thought and practice. Ideally, industrial paternalism forged rank-and-file loyalty toward the company by making the workers feel as part of a family. The system's success depended upon its ability to minimize the social distance between the factory operatives and their bosses. Along those lines, the brewery crafted a distinctly personalized style of paternalism, one more reminiscent of rural patron–client relations than the bureaucratized welfare capitalism practiced in the United States by the 1920s. The brewery's personal style of management – manifested clearly in its hiring policies – reflected the firm's status as a family-owned and operated business. Cuauhtémoc and its subsidiaries filled top administrative posts with family members educated in the United States. Moreover, during the 1920s and 1930s, the Garza Sadas designed the most selective policies of labor recruitment in Monterrey.

The hiring practices marked both a defensive response to unionism and the benevolent face of paternalism. Admitting that a single wage earner could not satisfy a family's needs, Luis G. Sada advocated the employment of multiple family members.[22] Alejandro Monsiváis and his brother secured jobs at the brewery upon the recommendations of their two sisters. The father of Apolonio López brought him to work at the age of twelve. When

---

20 Interviews with Manuel González Caballero, June 30, 1995 and Juan Manuel Elizondo (with Raúl Rubio Cano), Apr. 9, 1996.
21 Flores, *Burguesía, militares y movimiento obrero*, 85–87, 147–48, 208–15; Saragoza, *The Monterrey Elite*, 105–09, 122–23.
22 Rodríguez, *Homenajes*, 37.

the father of María de Jesús Oviedo passed away, the plant superintendent hired María, her brother, and her two sisters. In other cases, Cuauhtémoc hired the widows of deceased workers. Cuauhtémoc also recruited entire families from the countryside, particularly from Santiago, a region south of Monterrey whose residents take pride in their "non-conflictive" character. Decades later, local union activists perceived the hiring of rural Mexicans as a strategy to shape a quiescent and loyal labor force. But unionists understood the appeal of factory work for rural migrants. As one recalled, "they used to bring in those kind of people, country people, you know, who came to work here and well frankly what they earned was pretty good because they weren't accustomed to earning salaries or anything. . . . They handled them pretty well in the sense of convincing them that, as they say, the company is the goose that lays the golden egg, that sustains them, that gives them everything they need to live, so they have what they have, so that their family is well off." The preferential hiring practices restructured the composition of the labor force during the 1920s, when the brewery's workforce grew from 600 to 1,200 operatives.[23]

The hiring policy explains the significant numbers of rural migrants and, especially, women on Cuauhtémoc's payroll. Indeed, the proportion of female workers increased from 15 to 40 percent during the 1920s, a phenomenal figure for a historically male-dominated industry. Monterrey's textile and food-processing companies followed the national trend and employed high percentages of female workers. But Cuauhtémoc was the only Mexican brewery to hire women.[24] Their experience at the brewery manifested and reinforced the gender ideologies then prevalent in Mexico. The process began on the production lines, where occupational segregation became the rule. Nearly all female operatives worked in the plant's bottling and packaging divisions. Men supervised the departments and the women earned lower wages than male coworkers employed alongside them. Indeed, females earned on average 40 percent less than male employees.[25] Management also saw employment at the brewery as a temporary stage in a young woman's life, for company policy required women to retire upon marriage. The brewery's educational and cultural programs therefore served as a finishing school meant to prepare them for the future, preferably as wives and mothers of Cuauhtémoc employees. So in the case of female operatives, company paternalism did not aspire to cultivate a well-trained, permanent labor force.

23 Interviews with Alejandro Monsiváis, Dec. 11, 1995, Apolonio López, Dec. 11, 1995, María de Jesús Oviedo, May 23, 1996, and Manual Carranza (quoted). Cuauhtémoc sales increased from 11.6 to 23.2 million liters between 1924 and 1929, during which time the brewery's share of the Mexican market increased from 22.2 to 32.2 percent. (Haber, *Industry and Underdevelopment*, 163.)

24 Employment and wages figures for Mexican brewing in AGN: DT, Estadística 280/3, 436/3.

25 In 1926, Cuauhtémoc's female operatives earned an average wage of $1.67 while men earned $2.84. AGN: DT, Labor Inspector's Report, 1100/5.

Precisely why the brewery hired on so many women remains unstated in the archival record. But certain male workers believed they understood the reasoning behind the policy. Manuel Carranza later said of the female operative that "she is a harder worker, in other words, they produce more than male workers, and they are more constant in their work." Moreover, he went on, "The woman is more easily convinced and women are always more docile." Antonio López agreed, relating the historic absence of militancy among the brewery workers to women's presence at the plant.[26] Many male workers believed in the unitary character of the urban working class and perceived the hiring of both women and country folk as an antiunion ploy to deter class unity. However, we shall see that the short-lived development of union activism at Cuauhtémoc cut across gender lines, just as the practices of paternalism appealed to male and female operatives alike. Moreover, as management rightly asserted, the firm's hiring policies satisfied a working-class reliance on family labor, a means of survival common to both rural and urban Mexico. Finally, by hiring the kin of trusted employees, Cuauhtémoc limited its own dependence on workers of troublesome backgrounds. Along those lines, the company began subcontracting skilled labor on a part-time basis. The company paid such tradespeople less than the full-time workers they replaced.[27] It also excluded them from the welfare benefits of company paternalism. The policy would not go unchallenged. But it reflected the industry's limited reliance on skilled labor. Their contractual status also facilitated the dismissal of the kind of skilled workers more likely to carry union cards in Monterrey.

Over time, Cuauhtémoc would further refine its hiring policies and attempt to regulate the operatives' lives beyond the factory gates. This policy of vigilance began with the cooperative's administration. Its official history highlights the agency of a "Group of 22" workers who provided the "longing and initiative" to organize the Cuauhtémoc Society. However, Luis G. Sada and his administrative cohorts oversaw all aspects of company paternalism. Brewery workers elected delegates to the cooperative's board of directors. But the SCYF's statues, written by Sada, granted management the right to appoint three of six board members and to approve all decisions made by the cooperative's benefits and cultural affairs commissions.[28] This managerial control neither dampened the operatives' enthusiastic participation in the SCYF nor elicited a rebuke from the workers themselves.

---

26 Carranza and López interviews.
27 Between 1921 and 1926, when the total workforce doubled, Cuauhtémoc eliminated 47 percent of its mechanics and 60 percent of its electricians. Wages for those skilled positions fell by 25 to 30 percent during the same period. By the mid-1920s, some 40 percent of male workers and 30 percent of female operatives were contract laborers. AGN: DT, Estadística, 280/3 (1921) & 1100/5 (1926).
28 Dávalos, et al., *Cuarenta años*, 52; *Trabajo y Ahorro*, Apr. 23, 1993.

Indeed, throughout the 1920s, rank-and-file members elected an activist core of veteran mechanics, office personnel, and department supervisors to the cooperative's board.

The SCYF's biannual elections themselves generated much fanfare and politicking on the operatives' behalf. The electoral process lent a certain legitimacy to the ideal of a worker-controlled cooperative. But it also promoted more important objectives. The internal elections, the monthly assemblies, and weekly dues all led workers to perceive the cooperative as a union. The inauguration of new officers also provided the occasion to promote the SCYF's respectable status within local society. Cuauhtémoc's owners attended the ceremonies in the company of local political and military authorities. As with other recreational and cultural activities – from baseball games to monthly fiestas – the inaugural festivities received extensive coverage in the local press.[29] Most importantly, their common membership in the cooperative helped bridge the social and economic gap between production workers, office clerks, and supervisory personnel. The collaborative project underscored the company's policy of blurring social boundaries between blue- and white-collar employees. Whereas Mexican labor law differentiated *obreros* (blue-collar workers) and *empleados* (white-collar employees), company discourse categorized all Cuauhtémoc employees as *trabajadores* (working people), portraying each as a "stockholder" in the privately held firm. The SCYF's newly elected presidents, be they mechanics or office clerks, thus used their inaugural addresses to reaffirm the "reigning unity" between "workers" and *oficinistas*.[30]

As respected members of the Cuauhtémoc family, SCYF activists employed the cooperative's resources to shape the social and political outlooks of the members. The SCYF's biweekly magazine, *Work and Savings*, promoted the cooperative's reigning motto: "To stimulate savings and promote the love of work." It provided a forum for the plant's worker–poets, reported weekend baseball results, and offered homemaking advice to the workers' wives. Editorials promised operatives a share in the company's prosperity in exchange for their steady attendance and disciplined work. The magazine also articulated the owners' conservative politics. Looking back on the 1930s, Manual Carranza recalled that, "The brewery had its great ideologues and spent a lot of money, still spends great sums of money, on their anti-union, anti-revolutionary ideology, the philosophy they use to convince the workers that the company is the goose that lays the golden

---

29 See for example *El Porvenir*, Aug. 9, 1926.
30 *Trabajo y Ahorro*, Apr. 13, 1929. After the 1930s, factory operatives were distinguished from the office and managerial workers by the term *sindicalizados* (unionized employees), for they alone would belong to Cuauhtémoc's company union. Interview with Luis Alfonso Cavazos, SCYF Director of Social Affairs, Feb. 8, 1996.

eggs. Frankly, they tried to brainwash you soon as you entered [into employment]."[31] While all oral history testimony comes laden with subsequent experience, Carranza's past as a Communist Party member and ardent union supporter makes his an astute but particulary critical view of Cuauhtémoc's labor policies. Yet even workers like Carranza, whom Cuauhtémoc fired during a 1938 organizing drive, read *Work and Savings*, attracted by its sharp photographs and weekly summaries of the social and cultural life of the brewery.[32]

The Mexican government, its labor laws, and the labor movement all received their due criticism in the pages of *Work and Savings*. Editors blamed Mexico's bloated federal bureaucracy (*empleomanía*) for the poverty of a nation rich in natural resources. Locally, they leveled corruption charges against Monterrey's labor-dominated government of the mid-1920s. Finally, they blamed Mexican labor law as the cause of industrial unrest and countered union leaders' "radical" claims that the working class created Mexico's wealth. As one editor lamented, "It is erroneous to speak of those who work with their hands as if they were the only genuine 'workers'." By drawing legal distinctions between production and salaried workers, the labor law directly contradicted Cuauhtémoc's own efforts to level distinctions between salaried employees and factory operatives. But at times, *Work and Savings*'s white-collar editors betrayed their own class prejudices. They associated the "poor preparation of the men of the workshops" with the alleged capacity of "demagogic leaders to incite their passions." However, they also believed that the "constant atrophying of the workers' intellectual faculties," itself a product of manual labor, would be corrected by the SCYF's educational programs. SCYF directors thus endeavored to "help the worker understand his rights and duties and thereby avoid falling prisoner to professional [labor] leaders."[33]

A range of contemporary observers shared these beliefs about the presumed malleability of Mexico's working class. For some, the assumption explained the labor movement's failure to achieve the democratic aspirations that had inspired working people to support Madero's revolution. One American diplomat thus attributed the "political tyranny known as Syndicalism" to workers' alleged "timidity, unassertiveness, and obedience . . . [to] imposed leadership." A decade later, his successor would perceive Mexican "laborers" as "incapable of thinking . . . docile . . . [and] but pawns of the leaders." Such portrayals of Latin America's popular classes had long been widespread in North America. But a good many elite and middle-class Mexicans shared the perceptions and expressed equal concern

31 Carranza interview.
32 Monsiváis and Oviedo interviews.
33 *Trabajo y Ahorro*, Jan., Sep. 15, 1923; Mar. 13, Aug. 21, 1926; Apr. 4, 1933; Sep. 7, 1935.

about the causes of what came to be known as *liderismo*, or union bossism. A railway inspector thus explained a 1927 strike by reminding his superiors that "it is well known that the working masses are easily influenced and that agitators take advantage of this."[34] Even labor militancy could be dismissed as a result of rank-and-file deference to manipulative union bosses. Company paternalism built upon both these assumptions about workers. Local employers believed that the more veteran, independent-minded, *regiomontano* workers were immune from the appeals of union agitators. The industrialists therefore relied upon the more experienced employees to assist in their paternalistic project and thereby shield the vulnerable rural migrants and malleable young workers from "professional labor leaders."

In the meantime, *Work and Saving's* editors provided their blue-collar readership with constructive alternatives to Monterrey's world of organized labor. They lauded such "Mexican Heroes" as former president Porfirio Díaz for his promotion of national peace and unity. They counseled workers to orient their own efforts not toward the destructive ends of unionism but the positive fruits of civic activism. The column "I Am *Regiomontano*" counseled workers to participate in neighborhood improvement projects, to consume locally manufactured products, and to cooperate "in the abolition of all revolutionary movements."[35] They also offered advice from Samuel Smiles, the Scottish inspirational writer who earned international acclaim for his best-selling self-improvement guides, *Character* (1871), *Thrift* (1875), and *Duty* (1880). His translated essays delivered an upbeat message that hard work, discipline, and high moral standards would guarantee individual success. Workers who bothered to read these essays discovered lessons to be applied to contemporary Mexico. "No laws, however stringent, can make the idle industrious, the thriftless provident, or the drunken sober," Smiles advised. "Such reforms can only be effected by means of individual action, economy, and self-denial; by better habits, rather than greater rights."[36] Thus did *Work and Savings* promote its namesake virtues of hard work and thrift.

To what extent did the brewery workers subscribe to the political views propagated by the company ideologues? To the extent that actions manifested beliefs, the Cuauhtémoc Society achieved mixed results during the early years of its existence. What appears to be a minority of workers readily embraced the rights bequeathed by the 1917 Constitution. But

34 Dawson, Mexico City, Mar. 14, 1924, SD 812.504/556; Bowman, Mexico City, Feb. 14, 1936, SD 812.504/1576; Inspector Especial Roberto Cruz, Monterrey, to National Railways, Mexico City, Feb. 2, 1927 in Centro de Estudios del Movimiento Obrero y Socialista (CEMOS).

35 *Trabajo y Ahorro*, Sep. 15, 1923, Sep. 22, 1928.

36 *Trabajo y Ahorro*, Apr. 13, 1929; the quote is from Smile's *Self-Help* (1859); see also Tim Travers, *Samuel Smiles and the Victorian Work Ethic* (New York, 1987).

many more seemed to perceive their and the company's interests as common if not intertwined. They certainly shared their employer's sense of "business patriotism." In a book written to commemorate Cuauhtémoc's fortieth anniversary, eight veteran operatives employed since the 1890s expressed their pride in the company's Mexican ownership. They lauded its use of patriotic imagery rather than European-sounding labels to market its product. And they commended their employers' endeavors to morally and culturally elevate the Mexican proletariat. In accord with Cuauhtémoc's philosophy, they also perceived themselves as "stockholders" in the firm rather than mere wage laborers.[37] As the 1920s progressed, workers came to share their bosses' mistrust of both the government and organized labor, whose common promotion of temperance threatened the brewery's prosperity.

By the 1920s, most high-ranking political authorities advocated temperance reform as a means of uplifting the morality and enhancing the productivity of Mexico's working classes. The brewery responded with public relations campaigns meant to convince the state, consumers, and its workers that beer was a "nutritious" beverage and a "healthy" alternative to hard liquor. *Work and Savings* devoted its sporadic "Beer is Good for You" column to the issue. For the public, Cuauhtémoc promoted its Carta Blanca label as "the best beer for the home." A 1924 promotion, for instance, encouraged consumers to "drink it at midday, with dinner, and before going to bed ... the kids can drink it, too." Given these benefits, Mexican brewers lobbied the government to lower taxes and place their product "within reach of our popular classes."[38] Others who spoke for the working class drew no distinction between malted and distilled beverages. Temperance campaigns played a prominent role in organized labor's own promotion of working-class self-improvement. In 1922, their lobbying efforts paid off when Nuevo León's Congress passed a Sunday dry law, thus prohibiting beer sales on the one day when *regiomontano* workers most avidly consumed Monterrey's famous product.[39] In response, the SCYF mobilized hundreds of Cuauhtémoc workers and their families to march on the state capital. Joined by the industrialists and tavern owners, the workers protested that the dry law threatened their jobs and the livelihood of their families. The governor failed to convince the state congress to abolish the law. But the reform went unenforced in Monterrey's 355 cantinas, prompting street demonstrations by local unionists. Labor leaders also protested directly to President Obregón, volunteering their services to enforce compliance

---

37 Dávilos, et al., *Cuarenta años*, 11. I borrow the term "business patriotism" from Saragoza, *The Monterrey Elite*, 7.

38 *El Porvenir*, June 3, 1924; Convención de Cerveceros Mexicanos to President Calles, July 6, 1925, AGN: Presidentes, 205-C-169.

39 Rojas, "Poder Político," 138–39; *El Porvenir*, July, 17, 1922.

with "this justified restriction on vice." Nuevo León's Congress ultimately reformed the decree and exempted beer from its statutes, a compromise that certainly pleased more local workers than the Cuauhtémoc operatives alone.[40]

Eighteen months later the Cuauhtémoc Society again mobilized its members in defiance of organized labor. This time, however, the conflict pitted the SCYF against fellow brewery workers. In May 1924, word reached management that its operatives had organized their own Cuauhtémoc Brewery Workers Union. The unionists had yet to demand recognition or press demands when the company answered with a swift and unambiguous statement of its union policy. Within a week, the unionists later testified, the company began "its work of hostility, espionage, and persecution." Police first arrested two union leaders on what seemed to be trumped-up charges of beer theft. The company then dismissed forty-two other known union members over the next three weeks. The origins, size, and composition of the union remain unclear. Its members perhaps came from the 30 percent of workers who had yet to enlist in the Cuauhtémoc Society. The union emerged in the packaging department and garnered sympathy from female operatives. Indeed, as the men who led the union boasted to authorities, "we should point out that our movement includes a feminine contingent acting in union with the [male] workers."[41]

The punitive dismissals would provoke the first and only strike recorded in Cuauhtémoc's history. Nuevo León's governor extended his verbal support to the union workers and ordered the brewery to rehire the dismissed operatives. Management refused. Within two hours, the union was picketing the plant. They demanded the reinstallation of all union members and freedom for their two incarcerated leaders. As picketing workers and community supporters surrounded the brewery, SCYF activists once again mobilized the rank and file to march on the capital in protest. They also telegraphed President Obregón that "outside elements have attempted to impede our right to work through a scandalous use of force." The president approved the use of troops to disperse the pickets when a local military authority confirmed that "a minority of unhappy workers [had] closed the factory."[42] The strikers were thus dispersed and work resumed. In the end, government mediators convinced the brewery to rehire all striking workers except nine union leaders. In what became a commonplace strategy, the

---

40 *El Porvenir*, July 18, 1922; Federación Regional de Sociedades Obreras to President Obregón, Jan. 7, 1923, AGN: Presidentes, 407-M-13; Rojas, "Poder político," 140–41.
41 Federación General Obrera de Nuevo León to President Alvaro Obregón, June 28, 1924, AGN:DT 726/7.
42 Sociedad Cuauhtémoc y FAMOSA to President Obregón, June 23, 1924, and General José Cavazos to Obregón, June 24, 1924, AGN: Presidents, 811-C-165.

brewery rid itself of the troublemakers by paying them severance wages in accordance with the law. For the second time in six years, the brewery's directors had resisted an organizing drive by punitively dismissing the movement's leaders. In 1918, the conflict resulted in the formal establishment of company paternalism. In 1924, the most apparent product of that system, the Cuauhtémoc Society, mobilized its members to provide popular sanction to the company's antiunion campaign. Shortly thereafter, the company made membership in the cooperative a mandatory term of employment for all full-time workers.

"They Helped All The Workers"

For a nominal monthly fee, the cooperative provided its members with welfare benefits whose range grew as the 1920s progressed. The nonwage incentives began with free beer. Cuauhtémoc rewarded its employees with one glass for lunch and another after work, a practice customary to the industry. Other benefits would be replicated by the steel mill, the smelter, and the glassworks. A hallmark of the cooperative societies was their subsidized commissaries. These company-financed consumer cooperatives evolved over the years from purveyors of bulk foodstuffs to veritable general stores. The brewery then expanded the educational opportunities offered its workers and their families, adding evening literacy classes for adults and college scholarships for students from the company school. The SCYF also launched a program to make workers into property owners. Operating under the slogan "To each worker his own home," the company awarded ten furnished, wood-frame houses annually to its employees. Some received their "chalets" through holiday raffles. SCYF directors nominated other recipients for their "seniority, perseverance, and good service." By 1930, some ninety homes had been constructed in Colonia Cuauhtémoc, an inner-city barrio of brewery workers that would host 1,300 such dwellings by the 1960s. Workers could also subscribe to life and medical insurance and, in the mid-1920s, Cuauhtémoc opened its own clinic with a special wing "for illnesses proper to the ladies."[43] The brewery thus made substantial nonwage benefits available to its workers, the majority of whom earned subsistence wages. The constitution theoretically obligated large employers to provide most of these benefits. But few companies complied and the government rarely enforced a labor code that remained a blueprint for the future.

Employment at the brewery also demanded the workers' mandatory participation in the SCYF's hallmark program, the savings plan. *Work and Savings* presented illustrated covers, editorials, moral parables, and even

---

43 Dávilos, et al., *Cuerenta años*, 33; *Trabajo y Ahorro*, Feb., Mar. 1923, Mar. 20, 1926, July 16, 1927, Nov. 25, 1933; AGN: DT 1100/5; Novo, *Crónica*, 13.

cartoons to both justify the policy and inculcate the workers into the culture of thrift. The editors reminded the operatives of the tumultuous revolutionary past and the need to safeguard one's family from an uncertain future. They exhorted workers to "accumulate capital" so that "you too can be your own Judge and Boss." Company ideologues also equated the ability to save with one's manliness: "He who has the will to conquer his vices, work hard, and SAVE, can say loudly and with pride: I am a big man (*Yo soy muy hombre*)."[44] In practice, the SCYF's directors determined the percentage of each worker's wage packet to be deposited each week. In a further testimony to Cuauhtémoc's style of paternalism, the operatives went before the Savings and Withdrawal Commission to request the right to retire their "capital." They could do so only for "urgent demands": medical care, burials, and home purchases. Workers could not retire their savings for "a night on the town, luxuries, or similarly unjustified expenses." Alejandro Monsiváis recalls going before the commission on many occasions during his forty-two year career: "You had to explain your motives to them, things like home improvements. It wasn't easy. One went to them and [said], 'I want a withdrawal,' and [they demanded], 'why do you want it?'" Workers occasionally protested these "interrogations." But in the long run the savings plan succeeded and many veteran operatives parlayed their earnings into home ownership.[45] We shall see how the seasonal nature of the brewing industry conditioned this positive response to the imposition of thrift.

Workers did not accept all welfare benefits with the enthusiasm that the company had hoped and foreseen. The operatives adjusted to the incentives gradually, due either to their unfamiliarity or a calculated fear of extending their dependence on Cuauhtémoc. Many members initially forsook shopping at the commissary, purchasing insurance, or visiting company doctors. Instead, they sustained customary patterns of consumption and survival. They bought goods on credit from neighborhood shops or the itinerant Lebanese and Italian merchants common to the city's working-class districts.[46] The SCYF therefore expanded the commissary's product line and pioneered a home-delivery service to enhance its appeal. Company officials also seemed perplexed because when workers or their families fell ill, they opted for home remedies brought from the countryside or a visit to Monterrey's ubiquitous *curanderos* (healers). *Work and Savings* attempted to convince workers of the company health system's benefits and exhorted them

44 *Trabajo y Ahorro*, June, Aug. 1921, Jan. 16, 1926, Nov. 25, 1933, May 26, 1934, Nov. 21, 1936.
45 Monsiváis interview; *Trabajo y Ahorro*, June 1922, Jan. 24, Mar. 20, 1926; worker complaints in AGENL: JCA 48/1383. During a period when employment levels remained steady, collective savings climbed considerably : $157,000 in 1930, $230,000 in 1935, and $700,000 in 1940. *Trabajo y Ahorro*, Apr. 23, 1993.
46 Nathan, May 29, 1932, SD 812.5011/25.

to purchase medical insurance. Parables recounted hardship tales of workers losing their savings due to a sudden family illness. Editors also penned
diatribes against the *curanderos*. Such "charlatan healers," they suggested,
were unable to cure illness since "they lack all knowledge of the science
and art of healing . . . [and] are motivated by nothing more than profit."
On the other hand, workers who subscribed to the health plan could visit
the company's "honorable and competent doctors."[47] Thus as the decade
progressed, the cooperative society successfully introduced workers to new
patterns of consumption, modern medicine, and the culture of savings for
which *regiomontanos* are renowned. While the SCYF's need to advertise such
services suggests an early apprehension, retired workers all came to express
great pride in the benefits they eventually enjoyed.

From the outset, the brewery workers eagerly embraced the cultural activities organized by the SCYF. The leisure activities offered something for
everyone. The men from the office frequented the SCYF's billiard hall and
reading room. Their blue-collar counterparts preferred bicycle races and
baseball. Occasionally, some brave *oficinistas* squared off against the "boys
from the workshops" in the boxing ring.[48] Women sang in the SCYF's
glee club. Females operatives also became the exclusive members of the
"Artistic Squad," a dance troupe that practiced each afternoon for their
monthly performances at company fiestas. SCYF officials even offered full-
time employment to attractive young women who joined the squad. Female
employees also participated in SCYF-sponsored athletics. They particularly
relished the opportunity to compete in tennis against their social superiors, the well-to-do girls from a "neighborhood" they recall as "Country
Club." As Estela Padilla proudly remembered, "They were all from money,
and sometimes we even beat them!"[49] Meanwhile, workers of all ages attended the company night school. The SCYF promised to make illiterate
workers read in three months' time. Others took courses in the industrial
arts, leatherwork, and English. Their cooking and sewing classes prepared
women workers for a domestic future as wives and mothers. Then early
on weekend mornings, the brewery operatives gathered with families and
workmates at Cuauhtémoc Park to cheer on their "starting nine" baseball
players against rival factory teams. During the fall, the company staged bar-
becues, where they pressed fresh sugar cane juice for the kids as the women
prepared the caramel-and-pecan candies (*glorias*) typical of the region. These
hugely popular events – an inner-city reproduction of Nuevo León's countryside culture – certainly appealed to the migrants and introduced their
children to the traditions of rural life. Meanwhile, thousands of workers

47 *Trabajo y Ahorro*, Mar. 17, 1931, July 30, 1927.
48 *El Porvenir*, Mar. 27, 1926; *Trabajo y Ahorro*, Sep. 16, 1927.
49 Interview with Estela Padilla, Nov. 20, 1995.

and family members gathered at the end of each month for the company fiestas staged at Cuauhtémoc Hall.

The cultural events reinforced the ties developed between workers and managers on the shop floor. When the day shift closed, white-collar employees taught the night classes promoted by the SCYF. Female operatives from the bottling department, for example, took a special interest in the English course taught by their popular supervisor, Juan Botello. Other managers coached and played on the SCYF's athletic teams. Department supervisors also organized excursions to local swimming holes or hiking expeditions in the nearby mountains for workers in their departments. The daily intimacy developed between operatives and managers on the shop floor and baseball field extended to the neighborhoods surrounding the brewery as well. Both workers and managers inhabited the *colonias* developed there during the 1920s and 1930s. Neighborhood residents elected supervisors of the bottling department and repair shop as presidents of their community improvement boards. The brewery offered its company facilities for the festivals the boards sponsored to raise funds for paving, curbs, and street lights.[50] Such endeavors extended paternalism beyond the factory gates, elevating the managers' prestige and respect among the operatives.

The personalism that characterized Cuauhtémoc's style of paternalism also percolated down to the factory floor. Surprise appearances by the firm's top administrators enhanced the family-like atmosphere at the brewery. The owners visited the plant frequently, saluting the operatives, lending a hand, and inquiring about their families. The director's visits left a lasting impression on María de Jesús Oviedo. The former bottling-line worker recalled how "he would come in, greeting us, slapping us on the back, and shouting 'keep at it, girls!' (*ándale muchachas*) . . . That's how he treated us, coming to see us work and helping us out."[51] Plant supervisor Luis G. Sada mingled with the operatives on a daily basis. By one operative's account, Sada's appearance could evoke "a frenzied enthusiasm among all the workers. . . . [He] animated us without muttering a single word." And when Sada spoke, "we obey his orders because we know that whatever he tells us is for our own well-being."[52] Such explicitly deferential attitudes were perhaps exceptional. But for many workers these displays of personalism reinforced the company's benevolence. Furthermore, the intimacy between workers and managers was not simply a top-down proposal. The brewery operatives often honored their supervisors with watches on their birthdays and staged festive receptions to celebrate their return from vacations. For

50 *Trabajo y Ahorro*, Sep. 16, 1927; Archivo Municipal de Monterrey: Juntas de Mejoras Materiales, 1927, 4/3; *El Porvenir*, Aug. 9, 1926.
51 Oviedo interview.
52 *Trabajo y Ahorro*, Sep. 4, 1926.

the SCYF's directors, such displays of reciprocity testified to the "harmony that exists between workers and supervisors in every department."[53]

In Monterrey, the limits of paternalism manifested themselves first and foremost on the shop floor. Nonwage benefits could not humanize all aspects of industrial capitalism. Thus at the steel mill, smelter, and glassworks, issues of workplace safety and abusive foremen undermined the promises of paternalism. These factors proved minimal in the brewing industry. The daily work regime itself, one characterized by relatively light tasks and a cool atmosphere during Monterrey's scorching summers conspired in favor of congeniality rather than tension between workers and their supervisors. By local standards, beer production presented minor dangers. Workers who cleaned bottles and barrels or labored in the cellars and ice house suffered exposure to fumes, dust, dampness, and cold. Joint management–worker shop committees ostensibly handled the daily grievances and disciplinary problems that invariably arose. Moreover, company policy invited workers to seek out their supervisors to resolve problems arising in the workplace or the home.[54] Cuauhtémoc also encouraged individual workers to suggest means of improving working conditions, rewarding their proposals with considerable ten-to fifteen-peso bonuses. Most concerned workplace safety issues. One operative earned the Industrious Worker Award for her innovative plan to remove broken bottles from the conveyor belt. Another proved her industriousness by proposing that a "respectable person" watch over the restroom to prevent fellow workers "from going there and wasting time."[55] Most importantly, workplace relations remained congenial because the brewery's foremen did not generate the indignity fostered by their aggressive, demanding, and abusive counterparts in other local factories.

In further contrast to the steel mill and glassworks, with their well-defined hierarchy of job categories and pay schedules, the question of occupational mobility rarely arose for most brewery workers. The majority of operatives worked at relatively unskilled jobs on the bottling line, packaging floor, and loading docks. The nature of the brewing industry and the preponderance of women employed by Cuauhtémoc thus lent it a reputation as a place of light, emasculated work and limited opportunities. Cuauhtémoc employed relatively few tradespeople on a full-time basis. The company farmed out the hiring of many skilled positions – welders, sheet metalworkers, building tradesmen – to a smattering of in-house labor contractors. Hundreds of laborers and haulers thus vied for relatively few but high-paying positions as mechanics, maintenance men, and foremen.

53 *Trabajo y Ahorro*, Aug. 21, 1926, Jan. 14, 1927, July 17, 1932, Jan. 11, 1936.
54 Carranza interview.
55 *Trabajo y Ahorro*, July 27, 1935, Dec. 24, 1936; Padilla interview.

Indeed, youngsters seeking to learn a trade shunned offers to work at the brewery for the opportunity to hone their skills, accumulate seniority, and earn higher wages in such fascinating industries as steel and glass.[56] They considered Cuauhtémoc as a place to work a summertime stint while awaiting their chance to enter what were considered to be more prestigious worlds of work.

The seasonal character of the brewing industry further conditioned the seeming aversion shared by local working-class youth toward Cuauhtémoc. To this day, Cuauhtémoc's unspoken secret remains the yearly layoffs that plague the brewing industry. In northern Mexico, the swelling summertime demand for cold beer produces a season of intense output at Cuauhtémoc. The arrival of cooler weather signals the coming wintertime of slack production and layoffs. All workers experienced the adverse consequences of a seasonal demand. The brewery's part-timers felt it first. As management eliminated shifts and shortened the work week, contract laborers received their pink slips and promises of springtime employment. While working conditions rarely fostered shop-floor antagonisms, charges of favoritism indeed erupted over the issue of layoffs and promotions.[57] With full-time status came a greater sense of security. But even veteran workers suffered the seasonal downturns. They saw summertimes of double shifts and overtime reduced to three-day weeks and menial tasks. Thus for those awaiting a move up Cuauhtémoc's limited occupational ladder, the benefits of paternalism provided an important supplement to unskilled wages. This proved especially true for the female operatives.

While local women discovered plentiful opportunities as retail clerks or domestics, Mexico's industrial capital offered them limited manufacturing jobs. The city's large metallurgical plants, small workshops, and the building trades remained exclusively male domains. Indeed, while economic growth created thousands of new factory jobs for women in the 1920s, their presence declined from 18 to 13 percent of the manufacturing workforce. By the end of the decade, Cuauhtémoc alone employed nearly 20 percent of the female factory workers in Monterrey.[58] The brewery thus stood as a beacon for young women seeking the opportunities derived from wage labor. For some, that meant the possibility of contributing to the family budget, as both their parents and the company expected. For others, steady work translated into a degree of freedom from parental authority and the chance to postpone their eventual role as head of their own household. The chance to work for a nationally renowned company – one that offered

---

56 Interviews with Luis Monzón (Monterrey Glassworks), Mar. 18, 1996 and Dionisio Aguilar (Monterrey Glassworks), Mar. 20, 1996.
57 AGENL: JCA 66/2049; Oviedo interview.
58 Secretaría de la Economía Nacional, *Quinto censo de la población*, 22.

women relatively high wages and welfare benefits as well – proved a mighty attraction in Monterrey.

Since the female operatives enjoyed limited opportunities elsewhere, the issue of job security was of paramount importance for them. Company managers parlayed the situation into a means of courting the women's loyalty, offering them entry into the ranks of full-time employment and the benefits derived therefrom. Those included not only the perks of paternalism but the right to be last in line when the inevitable seasonal layoffs arrived. For female workers, relegated to the plant's occupationally homogeneous bottling and packaging departments, the possibilities of advancement were limited. A few made the exceptional move from factory operative to office clerk. Men monopolized the supervisory positions. Most women thus portray their promotion to full-time status as a watershed in their working careers. Estela Padilla earned her full-time position when she accepted a supervisor's offer to join the SCYF's dance squad. She harks back on that day when "I achieved my career" with a celebratory clap of her hands. María de Jesus Oviedo remembered that, "We really struggled (*batallamos*) to get full-time work." Clasping her hands with a sigh of relief, she still recalls the moment her foreman "came to the *máquina* where I was working and he says, María de Jesus, from now on you'll be a full-time employee, we won't be suspending you anymore."[59] In exchange for this sense of security, Cuauhtémoc earned their loyalty and work discipline. Moreover, while some men relate the women's presence to their presumed docility, they are also quick to recognize them as harder and more dependable workers.[60] The women agree.

The female operatives, especially those who remained single and working, came to perceive themselves as "the cement of the factory." By the 1930s, they dominated the brewery's bottling and packaging departments. On the shop floor, men supervised their labor, maintained the machinery, and, recalled one bottling line worker, "generally stood around with their arms crossed."[61] Teenage boys, paid wages that equaled the women's, labored as haulers. But the women handled the plant's most arduous tasks. Cleaning bottles, placing them on the conveyor belt, and packing full bottles into passing cartons were repetitive and stressful jobs. Cuts, bruises, and calloused hands distinguished them as working women. The brewery's labeling and bottle-capping machines posed constant hazards to wearied workers. Furthermore, it was in these departments where heightened summertime demand translated most directly into longer shifts and quickened

---

59 Padilla and Oviedo interviews.
60 Carranza interview.
61 This account of women's brewery work based on Medrano, Oviedo, and Padilla interviews, and accident reports in AMM: Accidentes, 1926, 6/7.

production rates. "That's why they say that we were the cement of the factory," María de Jesús Oviedo asserted, "and it's true, more of us worked there than [men] . . . and we raised that factory through our own efforts and by overcoming many dangers."[62]

Those dangers ranged from broken glass on the conveyor belt to returning home through dark city streets after a night shift. One former operative remembered when she and a workmate were chased home by soldiers from the nearby barracks. "Who knows what intentions they had," she wondered with a hint of näivete. "Maybe they wanted to rob us." When asked, one former worker contended that the risks of work did not extend to the realm of sexual harassment, as was often the case in power-laden factory settings where females labored under male supervision. Of course, such a response could be an assertion meant to convey a sense of respectability as much as one that describes life in the factory. Other workers recall that sexual encounters did transpire since, as one retiree asserted, "temptation does not lack wherever there are men and women." Moreover, while women heard rumors of supervisors demanding favors in exchange for full-time jobs, official company policy held that displays of sexual affection were grounds for suspension.[63]

The personalism that characterized relations with their supervisors did not translate into the women's passive acquiescence in their shop-floor status. Indeed, they chafed at their "female wages," surpassed as they were by those of men who performed less rigorous labor. "At the least we worked like men, *more* than men," María de Jesus later asserted. Returning to the brewery years later, she saw that mechanization had rendered her old job obsolete, a process that led to the elimination of female employment by the 1970s. "Now," she points out, "they just stand there, watching the bottles, pushing buttons, but we, no, we were always "Go, Go, Go!" "We worked *harder*," she concludes with a sense of indignity, "we worked harder and they paid us less." But Estela Padilla and her female workmates silenced their protests, for "if you didn't watch yourself on the job, you'd end up in the streets, and that's where you remained because they instructed all the other factories not to give you work. . . . That's why if you didn't take care, you would lose everything."[64] Like their male counterparts, the women believed that a punitive dismissal earned one a place on the local blacklist.

Today, the brewery's former female operatives derive immense pride from the role they played in the formative years of a pillar of *regiomontano* industry, a sense of dignity that balances the gender inequalities they experienced,

62 Oviedo and Carranza interviews.
63 López, Medrano, and Oviedo interviews.
64 Oviedo and Padilla interviews.

and that they recollected only upon questioning. Indeed, during their testimonies, they universally and spontaneously emphasize the "family-like"
atmosphere and "camaraderie" discovered at Cuauhtémoc.[65] Their hard-
earned wages won them the economic independence to treat their friends to
dinner, to enjoy the cinema, or even to solicit the services of local practition-
ers of witchcraft (*brujería*), who would cast hexes on their enemies. Others
spent their earnings on the latest fashions available in Monterrey. Indeed,
photos of the operatives gathered on their countryside excursions portray
them dressed resplendently as young Mexican flappers.[66] Many therefore
never practiced María de Jesús Oviedo's philosophy that "you should hand
[your wages] over to your parents." Indeed, she recalls, "the [widowed]
mothers who worked there complained about that a lot." Unlike her workmates, María de Jesús "married the brewery." As the youngest in a family
of women, she earned the responsibility of supporting herself and a widowed mother on her salary alone. She thus forsook marriage and obligatory
retirement from Cuauhtémoc, working double shifts when the rent came
due.[67] But María de Jesús proved the exception. For in the end, most female operatives perceived brewery work less as a career than a moment of
transition. Even more so than the men, the SCYF's night school, dance
troupes, and tennis teams provided them cultural diversions enjoyed by
few women of their class in Monterrey. Furthermore, Cuauhtémoc offered
them the chance to earn spending money, contribute to the family budget, and perhaps meet their future spouse. Indeed, many young women
sought work at the brewery with that very opportunity and future in
mind.[68]

The marriage of two workers was an occasion to reaffirm the intimacy of
the Cuauhtémoc family. Many workers – from young female operatives to
veteran foremen – met their spouses at the brewery. While marriage marked
the end of the women's careers, the occasion prompted their workmates to
stage grand celebrations. Workers in the bottling and packaging departments organized retirement parties and showers for future brides nearly
every month. In 1926, Ismael Prado requested the hand of María de los
Angeles Oviedo after meeting the young operative in the brewery's bottling
department. Prior to retiring, María's fellow operatives offered her a bridal
shower in the cooperative's cultural center. On the eve of their wedding,
the couple joined 300 fellow bottling-line workers for a prenuptial picnic
in Cuauhtémoc Gardens, a park adjacent to the brewery. After the couple exchanged vows in the SCYF's assembly hall, the brewery's cofounder,

65 Oviedo and Padilla interviews.
66 *Trabajo y Ahorro*, Sep. 16, 1927.
67 Oviedo interview.
68 Oviedo and Medrano interviews.

Fransisco G. Sada himself, feted the newlyweds with a toast and an inspirational poem prepared especially for the occasion.[69]

With the operatives' marriage, the young women's parents perhaps lost an important contribution to the family budget. But as brewery workers' wives, the former operatives retained the benefits of company paternalism. Their new families enjoyed subsidized foodstuffs and health coverage. The benefits alleviated the responsibility of maintaining the household economy on a single wage-earner's salary. The brewery astutely reached out to these former workers beyond the factory gates. *Work and Savings* addressed the workers' wives by devoting "The Woman's Section" to their "unrecognized and underappreciated domestic chores." Acknowledging that "for her there is no eight-hour day," the column offered advice on childcare, hygiene, and affordable vacations and published model family budgets, which included not only a savings quota ("for when there is no work") but three monthly outings to the cinema as well. In tacit recognition of women's gendered roles as consumers, the editors encouraged the male operatives to entrust their wives or mothers with their earnings, as "they were better prepared to handle the money." This, the editors noted, was the proper means of ensuring the family's happiness "in this, our radio age."[70] The retired women also participated in the brewery's cultural and recreational affairs. They returned frequently to Cuauhtémoc, taking their children to the company school, shopping at the commissary, and attending the monthly dances and Mother's Day celebrations sponsored by the SCYF. The brewery's style of paternalism integrated all of the workers' dependents into the system. By doing so, they gave the operatives' wives an incentive to pressure their husbands into safekeeping their jobs. The extension of paternalism into the workers' homes thus made Cuauhtémoc's an extended family.

The brewery's practices of paternalism provided the operatives and their families with the material and cultural means to realize their own aspirations to social security and self-improvement. While workers learned to embrace the benefits in a gradual and piecemeal fashion, they actively embraced the system's cultural components. They did so because the cooperative society, the baseball leagues, and the countryside excursions built upon prerevolutionary customs, traditions, and practices of mutual aid and popular culture. In this sense, Cuauhtémoc's style of paternalism – and the workers' reception of its practices – made it indistinguishable from other local systems. What made the brewery unique was the workers' mandatory participation in the SCYF, a policy that reflected the owners' distinct managerial philosophy. But the brewery operatives did not perceive the obligatory SCYF membership as an infringement upon their independence. Indeed, membership

69 *Trabajo y Ahorro*, Jan. 15, 1927.
70 *Trabajo y Ahorro*, Mar., Apr. 1923, July 17, 1932, Aug. 11, 1934.

was a privilege. It not only granted one access to the company's extensive fringe benefits. It marked a cherished entry into the ranks of full-time employment. Workers even came to accept the mandatory savings plan that reduced their take-home pay. Antonio López recalled that, "if it wasn't for [the plan] we would have drunk our earnings away, we never would have saved anything." The industry's seasonality also conditioned the workers' reception. The occasional layoff taught the values of savings, for, as Estela Padilla later recalled, "you could be suspended at any moment, when you least expected it." She therefore praised the SCYF "for making us save."[71] Managers learned to parlay the circumstances into a means of courting rank-and-file deference.

However, for most workers, their loyalty toward the company became more genuine and less a feigned and calculated response to fears of unemployment. While operatives like Apolonio López recognized the practices of paternalism as a means "to call us to order," they shared a common appreciation towards the company.[72] Workers manifested their gratitude through the fiestas staged to honor their supervisors and in scores of letters to *Work and Savings*. Many noted how the company's welfare policies alleviated the hardships faced by working-class families. A group of women from the bottling department simply lauded Cuauhtémoc for "enlightening our culture." They emphasized the company's athletic and educational programs, heaping special praise upon the scholarships offered their children and the instructors who taught the SCYF's night classes. "Noooo," López recalled in his distinctly *norteño* accent, "I believe that there is no other factory that teaches their workers so much, they gave us classes in *everything*.... [T]hey helped all the workers who wanted to study." Consistent with the values of many blue-collar *regiomontanos* of their generation, López and his wife reserved special praise for the company scholarships that sent their children to college. As she remembered, "A worker who wanted to give a good education to his children could not do so [alone], and I wanted them in college." Their children then returned the favor to Cuauhtémoc. A daughter who attended the University of Texas worked for ten years as a company doctor, while their son studied business and found employment in Cuauhtémoc's personnel department.[73] The voices we hear are those of workers who stayed on at the brewery until they retired. They are therefore a minority of those hired by Cuauhtémoc after the revolution. Their families benefited most from company paternalism, their pension checks sustain them economically, and they continue to fill their leisure hours with

---

71 López and Padilla interviews.

72 López interview.

73 *Trabajo y Ahorro*, Jan. 16 and 24, Mar. 6, 1924, June 19, Aug. 21, 1926, Feb. 19, 1927; López interview.

visits to the Cuauhtémoc Society. Their unique family histories thus shape their collective memories of the past. But their experiences and testimony manifest the success of Cuauhtémoc paternalism, for these were the very workers whom its practices endeavored to make.

For the Cuauhtémoc operatives, be they urban women or male migrants from the countryside, the practices of paternalism helped alleviate the harsh realities of the market while providing the workers with the facilities to realize their own aspirations of self-improvement. During the 1920s, paternalism bred what Patrick Joyce defines as an "affective" form of deference, one that rested more on a base of benevolence and less upon a real or promised threat of coercion.[74] Some operatives, like those fired during the ill-fated organizing drive of 1924, experienced the company's antiunionism in bold relief. The company's swift response to the union taught a lesson to other workers. Nonetheless, we shall later see that the seemingly loyal workers of the 1920s would not maintain a passive acquiescence to the gendered hierarchies that defined shop-floor relations at the brewery. Underneath their public manifestations of deference, the operatives would construct and nurture a culture of resistance toward what they considered shared injustices, from wage differentials in the bottling department to the company's denial of fringe benefits to the tradespeople hired on contract. Come the 1930s, when the local political tides shifted in favor of collective action, a militant minority of Cuauhtémoc workers would challenge these gendered hierarchies and practices of exclusion, forcing the company to once again revise its managerial strategies.

74 Joyce, *Work, Society, and Politics*, 93.

4

Making Steel and Forging Men at the Fundidora

In 1926, during a commemorative speech to honor the Fundidora steel mill's twenty-fifth anniversary, Director Adolfo Prieto made the ambitious declaration that, "From these workshops and schools will emerge the genuine aristocracy of the national proletariat."[1] Echoing the ideals of Mexico's revolutionary government, the company adopted the task of "forging the fatherland" by shaping its "men of steel" into exemplary workers and model citizens. The steel workers were to embrace these patriotic ideals. They came to perceive their work as more than the exchange of labor for wages. Steel production assumed the aura of a patriotic mission because, in their minds, no industry played a more significant role in Mexico's economic reconstruction than Monterrey steel. The Fundidora and its employees proudly acclaimed the steel they produced as an "element of peace," for it would serve "Mexico's progress and its inhabitants' well-being" rather than wartime exigencies.[2] With the products of the steel workers' labor, the nation would build the railroads, bridges, schools, and factories symbolic of the new Mexico. From this sense of mission – and the dangers they faced in the mill – a distinct culture of work, patriotism, and masculinity developed among the steel workers. A popular *corrido* sung at the Fundidora even eulogized colleagues who lost their lives in the workplace for having "died for the homeland." The peculiarities of steel making thus led the Fundidora workers to distinguish themselves – and to be perceived locally – as a "caste apart."[3]

Like the Cuauhtémoc Brewery, the steel mill earned local renown during the 1920s for the welfare benefits extended to its workers. Both systems of paternalism shared prerevolutionary antecedents and both companies employed paternalism to shape hard-working, loyal, and disciplined labor forces. But paternalism assumed a peculiar cast and produced a distinct outcome at the steel mill. Consistent with their "liberal" managerial

1 *Colectividad* (company magazine), Nov. 17, 1926.
2 González Caballero, *La Maestranza*, 6, 24.
3 *Corrido* in "Memorias de Acero: Fundidora, 1900–1986", *El Diario de Monterrey*, May 9, 1996; interview with Luis Monzón (Vidriera Monterrey), Mar. 20, 1996.

philosophy, the Fundidora's directors never attempted to repress unionism. Instead, they negotiated the loyalty of the one-time union militants who led the strikes of 1918, 1920, and 1922. Those unionists and other veteran workers subsequently played active roles in the integration of their workmates and their kin into a common company culture known as the Great Steel Family. By the mid-1920s, labor militancy waned as company paternalism promised workers the modicum of security to which they aspired after years of revolutionary upheaval. Moreover, in further contrast to the brewery, the steel mill granted its workers the independence to subscribe to welfare benefits as they pleased. The Fundidora channeled its resources less into "social control" and more into the making of a well-trained, physically fit work force, one that could meet the daily challenges and rigors of steel making. Finally, whereas the brewery's more personalized style of paternalism percolated down to the production lines, welfare capitalism met its limits in the steel mill's furnaces and workshops. Shop-floor abuses cut against the benevolent grains of paternalism. Still, the nature of work and the practices of paternalism forged a sense of community among steel workers of diverse backgrounds.

Negotiating Industrial Peace

Industrial paternalism developed in a gradual and piecemeal fashion at the Fundidora, where labor unrest continued into the mid-1920s. The protracted strikes that followed the armed revolution had revealed the steel workers' collective embracement of their constitutional rights and the potential militancy of the plant's union tradesmen. While a minority of workers carried union cards, they proved their capacity to mobilize the mill's nonunion laborers. Moreover, the steel industry depended mightily upon these skilled craftsmen for whom union membership was a cherished right and mark of respectability. The company thus courted their loyalty, especially the well-organized machinists and rollers who led the 1922 strike. Management recognized their unions and acquiesced in their demand to establish shop committees that would mediate the sort of grievances that had fueled labor unrest. Having played an active role in that strike's conclusion, the state helped to broker a lasting resolution. The outbreak of peace saw the revolutionary government launch a program of national reconstruction to build a new Mexico upon the ruins of the old regime. Monterrey steel performed an integral role in its mission. Determined to stimulate national industrial development, modernize the nation's infrastructure, and lessen its dependence on foreign imports, the central government awarded the Fundidora lucrative contracts for steel rails and structural iron. Mexico City thus sought a durable industrial peace at the mill and dispatched a federal labor inspector to mediate a final settlement. He faced a difficult task.

The months following the 1922 strike witnessed a protracted struggle between unionists, former strikebreakers, and management. Two related issues obstructed a peaceful labor settlement: the unchecked authority of department supervisors and their poststrike reprisals against unionists. In a key concession, management agreed to establish joint worker–management shop committees (*comités de ajuste*). The committees would handle workplace grievances, allocate promotions, and mediate layoffs. Their presence would ostensibly democratize shop-floor relations by checking the unilateral authority once conferred on supervisors and foremen. Management's demand that each committee include an equal number of union and "free" (nonunion) workers met staunch resistance. The Machinists Union refused to recognize the strikebreakers' right to serve on the machine shop's committee. The federal labor inspector backed the union once he learned that the department counted only two nonunion workers among its 152 full-time operatives. The same issue proved more problematic in the rolling mill, a union stronghold where supervisors balked at relinquishing their authority. They refused to cooperate with shop stewards elected by the Rollers Union and persistently harassed the strike leaders employed in their department. In the strike's aftermath, some unionists lost their jobs to "free" workers and suffered the indignity of being reassigned to lower-grade positions. The union rollers therefore walked out, another general strike threatened the mill, and the state intervened once again. The federal labor inspector convinced the unionists to accept the right of nonunion workers to sit on the shop committees. Management then acquiesced to the union demand's for greater shop-floor democracy. The supervisors, it was agreed, would subsequently consult the committees on such contentious issues as job assignments, promotions, and layoffs.[4]

Political upheaval soon tested the accord. In late 1923, the military rebellion of General Adolfo de la Huerta diverted the federal government's limited resources, forcing it to suspend purchases of Monterrey steel. The fighting's disruption of regional transportation also interrupted the mill's access to raw materials. The Fundidora ordered an emergency curtailment of operations.[5] Workers learned of the suspension, effective immediately, upon receiving their paychecks one Saturday in late 1923. Fearing a strike, the commander of the regional military garrison demanded an explanation from company officials. Plant director Meliton Ulmer responded that "despite the sharp decline in orders the mill had attempted to maintain production for the benefit of the workers." But the crisis necessitated the suspension,

---

4 Federal labor inspector Juan Sánchez de Tagle's reports in AGN: DT 444/10 and 678/8.
5 Governor Ramiro Támez to Secretario de Industria, Comercio y Trabajo, Dec. 19, 1923; Federación Regional de Sociedades Obreras to President Obregón, Dec. 22, 1923, AGN:DT, 686/6. *El Porvenir*, Dec. 18, 1923–Jan. 8, 1924.

"which the workers understood and accepted perfectly well."[6] The workers' response suggested otherwise.

On Christmas Day, 1923, thousands of steel workers and their supporters marched before the state capital to protest the "unjustified suspension of 2,000 brother workers."[7] Fearing an escalation of the conflict, the governor wired Mexico City and requested federal intervention to force the company to resume full production. Meanwhile, pickets appeared once again at the Fundidora. Unionists declared their intention to shut the mill down unless the company retained all operatives through work-sharing schemes. Supervisors convened with the Machinists and Rollers Union leaders and agreed to resume limited production in their departments. The well-organized and equally militant structural iron workers won similar concessions. The furnaces would remain idle until market conditions improved. Indeed, Ulmer noted, the furnace worker had not even joined the protests, "for they know and identify with this customary system."

The company also provided the suspended workers with a measure of security not enjoyed before 1923. To demonstrate its "concern for the workers who depend upon it," the Fundidora announced a series of nonwage benefits that would introduce all operatives to industrial paternalism.[8] During the production stoppage, workers retained access to company medical benefits. Management also enlisted delegates from the plant's shop committees to visit idled laborers in their homes and extend interest-free loans to those in need. Finally, in response to local food shortages, the Fundidora opened a commissary and extended workers credit to purchase essential commodities at below-market costs. The benefits ostensibly ensured the workers' return to the steel mill after the layoffs. But the incentives also remained in effect subsequent to the crisis. Thus did a five-year period of sporadic labor unrest draw to a close and a new era of industrial paternalism dawn.

In contrast to the birth of company paternalism at the Cuauhtémoc Brewery, the Fundidora never forced its workers to abandon their right to union representation. Indeed, management remained, by Meliton Ulmer's account, "completely distanced from the workers' social affairs" and recognized their "absolute freedom to organize themselves in any way they please." A minority of steel workers remained members of the trade union locals first organized by Monterrey's railroaders.[9] It appears that the workers' organizational ties remained nominal, as the company refused

---

6 Unless indicated otherwise, details on the 1923–24 conflict in Fundidora Monterrey to Secretario de Industria, Jan. 15, 1924, AGENL: Trabajo – Conciliación y Arbitraje, 3.

7 *El Porvenir*, Jan. 3, 1924.

8 *El Porvenir*, Jan. 9, 1924.

9 Meliton Ulmer to Gobernación, May 23, 1923, AGN:DGG 2.331.8 (16)/ 32-A/34; union membership in AGN: DT, Associations, 916/6.

to negotiate with unions directed by outsiders. For that reason, Dionisio Palacios recalled, many union militants left the mill and migrated to the United States.[10] Management did, however, negotiate with the mill's machinists, rollers, and structural iron workers. These "local" unions, as they became known at the mill, were composed exclusively of steel workers. In exchange for promises of job security and preferential production contracts, these skilled workers helped instill discipline on the shop floor and steered younger workers away from the militants who led Monterrey's organized labor movement. Similar department-based unions emerged in other sectors of the mill as the decade progressed.

The steel mill's machinists exemplified this transition from militant to collaborative unionism. The machinists were the most active organizers of the 1918–22 steel strikes. They were the ones who pressured management to institute shop committees and work-sharing schemes in 1923. Thereafter, the machinists, rollers, and structural iron workers enjoyed better wage schedules and production bonuses than their counterparts in other departments.[11] Management courted the loyalty of these workers with further, nonwage benefits. For example, the machinists received a paid holiday in honor of their union's founding. In 1928, they celebrated its sixth anniversary with daytime tours of the local brewery and glassworks. That evening, management sponsored a dinner for the operatives, attended by leading company officials.[12] Unlike their counterparts at the brewery's Cuauhtémoc Society, veteran steel workers did not harbor antigovernment sentiments. On the contrary, they championed the policies of Mexico's revolutionary government. In 1925, they put their politics on display by helping to organize the festivities honoring President Calles's visit to the mill. Lauding Calles as "the father of national reconstruction," the foundry workers rewarded his "highly patriotic work" by unveiling a bronze bust of the president as a workers' mariachi band serenaded him with revolutionary ballads.[13] Like so many of Calles's cohorts, these skilled steel workers belonged to Masonic lodges, promoted temperance, and supported anticlericalism. In line with government labor policy, they also believed in the patriotic duty of unions to promote industrial peace. Indeed leaders of the Machinists and Rollers Unions served as worker delegates to the state's labor arbitration board. By 1929, they were running candidates to the board in opposition to their old allies, Monterrey's railroaders. The railwaymen,

10 Interview with Dionisio Palacios, Mar. 13, 1996.

11 By 1926, the 160 workers in the machine shops earned an average daily base wage of $4.12 while 325 operatives employed in the rolling mills earned $3.43. The average wage at the mill was $2.37, but relatively few workers enjoyed the production bonuses earned by skilled tradesmen. AHFM: *Informe*, 1927.

12 *Colectividad*, Oct. 1928.

13 Workers cited in González Caballero, *La Maestranza*, 29–32; *El Porvenir*, Apr. 19, 1925.

they argued, "are unfamiliar with our [work] environment and therefore inadequately qualified to understand our conflicts."[14] These steel workers had come to echo the reasoning employed by their bosses a decade earlier.

Labor militancy declined dramatically as the 1920s progressed, a period when steel production stabilized and the labor force grew from a monthly average of 1,500 to 2,400 by the decade's close.[15] The Fundidora thus remained a small-scale steel operation by North American standards. However, set against the dramatic backdrop of Monterrey's Saddle Mountain, the Fundidora's immense chimneys acted as a beacon drawing hundreds of potential workers to the nation's most renowned industry. They came with the hope of learning the art of steel making and thereby earn some of the highest wages in industrial Mexico. Who were the steel workers? The Fundidora's workforce reflected the industry's diverse labor demands as well as the socially constructed notion that steel making was men's work.[16] They were former farm laborers, village artisans, and industrial workers from the cities and mining camps of northern Mexico. Many entered the mill as teenagers. During the 1920s, 60 percent of the steel workers hailed from Nuevo León. The native sons worked alongside migrants from contiguous states and a smattering of workers from Mexico City and San Antonio, Texas. By the decade's close, nearly half were local city kids. They entered the mill with a solid future ahead. Many were steel workers' sons who graduated from the company school and then studied vocational arts at Monterrey's Obregón Industrial School, which opened in the 1920s just blocks from the mill's gates. In contrast to the rural migrants, who often remained common laborers, the young *regiomontanos* started as apprentices, learned skill trades, and then entered into the mill's graded occupational hierarchy.

Despite their diverse origins, few if any of these workers arrived to the mill trained in the art of steel making. The mill's workshops and night schools thus served the purpose envisaged by Adolfo Prieto, as vocational training grounds for the making of the "genuine aristocracy of the national proletariat." In honor of that status, the Fundidora became known locally as the "Maestranza," the great school where aspirant workers mastered their trades through education and experience. The workers' vocational skills, personal connections to the plant's foremen, and capacity to endure the rigors of steel making determined their job assignments and longevity in the mill. Those who stayed on saw their wages climb an average of

---

14 Unión de Maquinistas, Forjadores y Similares to Governor Sáenz, Jan. 7, 1929, AGN: DGG 2.331.8 (16)/32-A/26.

15 AGN: DT, Accidentes, 1923–1929.

16 The following collective profile of 772 steel workers is based on AGN: DT – Accidentes, 1925–29, 888/4, 901/6, 1033/2, 1033/4, 1294/1, 1558/2, 1829/1, 1833/2; AGENL: Industria, Comercio y Trabajo, 1930, boxes 3–5. The several dozen young women who labored as machine operators had been displaced from company payrolls by the end of the 1920s.

25 percent during the late 1920s. Indeed, federally financed public works projects made the years between 1926 and 1930 the most prosperous to that point in the Fundidora's history.[17] The issues that fueled the strikes of the early 1920s waned and many workers realized their aspirations of occupational mobility. Moreover, the material perquisites of paternalism provided these workers and their families with a modicum of security that supplemented their wages. But Don Adolfo's ambition of working-class transformation was not only a vocational endeavor; it included a project of cultural engineering as well. The cultural practices of paternalism integrated these workers of diverse social backgrounds into what the company promoted as the Gran Familia Acero, the Great Steel Family.

La Gran Familia Acero

The steel mill replicated the welfare benefits and cultural programs pioneered by the brewery. But the process evolved more gradually. In further contrast to Cuauhtémoc, the steel workers subscribed voluntarily to the system, and the worker societies through which benefits were channeled retained a degree of autonomy from the company throughout the 1920s. These contrasts reflected distinct corporate cultures and managerial philosophies. While the brewery parlayed its system of paternalism into a means of inculcating the owners' "antirevolutionary" politics among the operatives, the Fundidora's administrators earned a reputation locally and among their own workers as "liberals." Their distinct political outlooks reflected the backgrounds of these corporate executives. Few of the Fundidora's leading managers were *regiomontanos*. In fact, despite his nationalist posturing, company director Adolfo Prieto was himself a Spaniard. Residing in Mexico City, the company's top executives did not share the *norteños'* contempt for central government authority. After all, they depended upon that state as the principal consumer of Monterrey steel. The Fundidora thus accommodated its policies to the shifting political tides of revolutionary Mexico. In one symbolic display of these practices of accommodation, company engineers developed the idea of transforming the nation's Legislative Palace, a Porfirian project interrupted by the civil war, into today's Monument to the Revolution.[18]

17 Wages and production figures in AHFM: *Informes*, 1925–1929; Haber, *Industry and Underdevelopment*, 164–65.

18 Completed with Monterrey steel, the memorial in downtown Mexico City contains the remains of such revolutionary heroes as Madero, Villa, and Cárdenas. While a study of these distinct business cultures and their effects on labor relations awaits its historian, a starting place would be Saragoza, *The Monterrey Elite*, 69–70 and Nora Hamilton, *The Limits of State Autonomy* (Princeton, 1982); on the Monument to the Revolution, see González Cabellero, *La Mestranza*, 49–52.

The steel mill's system of industrial paternalism built upon the company's initial dependence on skilled foreign labor. The need to house the foreigners and their families gave birth to the mill's own company village, Colonia Acero. The original Steel Town, built on plant grounds, consisted of a cluster of single-family homes and the three-story Hotel Acero. The company town prospered and grew during the 1920s, as the workforce expanded and native workers replaced the foreign recruits. Just months before the 1922 steel strike, company officials purchased land from a nearby hacienda to expand Colonia Acero. There, the Fundidora would construct "comfortable and hygienic housing," a new school, and recreational facilities for the operatives. The company portrayed its endeavor as part of its "long-term concern for the workers' material, moral, and intellectual well-being." More practical concerns also motivated the proposal. Low-rent company housing helped retain the workers whose prized skills were also sought by other local industries. Furthermore, in the early 1920s, the steel mill remained some two miles from Monterrey's working-class barrios. The company demanded a core of mechanics, machinists, and boilermakers on hand in case their expertise was needed during a night-shift emergency.[19] While housing represented a privilege, it came with obligations.

By 1922, Colonia Acero had become a source of pride for its inhabitants, the company, and the city itself. In addition to the hotel, the company town would house upward of 600 residents in 96 two-and three-bedroom stone-masonry homes. The workers and their families enjoyed private patios, potable tap water, and electricity. In 1931, the company installed toilets, sinks, and showers in the workers' homes, real luxuries by Mexican working-class standards.[20] Along the neighborhood's paved streets stood a post office, a movie house, and a bakery. Residents of Steel Town established their own Agricultural Society on company land north of the village. There, the workers cultivated garden plots, while full-time farm laborers raised livestock, harvested crops, and operated a dairy. Meanwhile, the Acero School became the largest in the state and the first to offer instruction through the seventh grade. The company provided the sons and daughters of steel workers with free books, medical services, and scholarships to the national polytechnic university in Mexico City. By the end of the 1920s, sons of steel workers were returning from their studies as company engineers. Colonia Acero thus met the daily needs of these skilled

19 Meliton Ulmer to Governor Ramiro Támez, Sep. 15, 1922, AGENL: Industria, Comercio y Trabajo, 3; interviews with González Caballero and Gabriel Cárdenas Coronado, June 18, 2001.

20 AGN:DT, Labor Inspecto's Reports, 1922, 444/10; 1938, AGN: Departamento Autónomo del Trabajo (DAT), 351/14; Fundidora Monterrey to Instalaciones Sanitarias, March 30, 1931, AHFM, 162/1.

steel workers and their families. Indeed, despite its proximity to the loud, smoke-belching mill, Steel Town's pleasant gardens, plaza, and walking paths were said to "attract even the elegant people of Monterrey."[21]

The steel mill also offered welfare benefits to workers residing away from Colonia Acero. All full-time workers and their families enjoyed access to company doctors and medical facilities. The company operated a subsidized commissary to provide workers with basic foodstuffs. Like the brewery, the steel mill promoted thrift among its employees, albeit with minimal success. Indeed, while few workers guarded their earnings in the company's savings plan, the Fundidora's interest-free loan program proved one of its most popular. All workers, from administrators to common laborers, took advantage of the plan. The loans helped them survive sudden emergencies or just improve their lot. Their formal requests illuminate the economic gulf that separated the steel workers. At the high end of the scale, one finds workers borrowing for the "urgent" purchase of an automobile battery or to acquire land for a home. But the majority of workers who borrowed from the company, over 75 percent, earned less than $3.00 daily. They requested loans to attend to a brother's illness, to bury a daughter, to purchase the children's school supplies, or to simply cover the costs of "basic necessities." Migrants borrowed to send money to their families back home. However, the most common loan request cited the need to cover medical expenses, a testimony to the dangers of steel work and the limits to the company's medical services.[22] The loan program enhanced the workers' economic security, allowing them to forsake the loan sharks who gathered at local factory gates throughout the city.[23]

Securing a loan required a worker to maintain a cordial relationship with his shop-floor superiors. Requests arrived at the desk of the personnel manager with a letter from a supervisor testifying to the worker's character. In a typical example, a bricklayer's boss noted the hopeful borrower's five years of service, during which time the worker had "always been more than punctual and consistent in his labor." The foreman thus considered that he would "faithfully comply with this '*compromiso*'." Frank Bassett, the American supervisor of the blast furnace, noted of one employee requesting a loan, "he is one of our best foreman, very steady and reliable ... worthy of this assistance." Others testified to their subordinates' "good conduct," "consistency," and "competency."[24] Not all workers faithfully complied with their

---

21 AHFM: Escuela 'Adolfo Prieto,' 151; González Cabellero, *La Maestranza*, 20; AGN: DT, Labor Inspector's Report, 1923, 598/5; *El Porvenir*, Apr. 12, 1926 (quotation).

22 AHFM: Comprobantes de Caja, Nov.–Dec. 1920 (#8), Nov. 1925 (#17), May 1927 (#65).

23 Allegedly of "Arab" descent, the loan sharks' "usurious" practices received much negative commentary in the local press. By the mid-1930s, the loan sharks became the target of police sweeps. See *El Porvenir*, Sep. 5, 1935, Nov. 22, 1938.

24 AHFM: Comprobantes de Caja, Nov. 1925 (#17).

obligations. In 1931, the company hired a lawyer to track down workers who "mocked the [company's] good faith" by borrowing and departing Monterrey. In an effort to curtail the abuses, the company demanded that two of any borrower's workmates cosign the loans. They were then expected to cover an unpaid debt "out of a laudable spirit of *compañerismo* (comradeship)."[25]

Throughout the 1920s, the veteran workers and department supervisors who resided in Steel Town remained the primary beneficiaries of industrial paternalism. They were the ones upon whom the company depended most and whose loyalty management courted. They lived in company housing, sent their children to Acero School, and shopped at the commissary. The skilled workers were relatively affluent, aspired to respectability, and sought to instill their values among their younger workmates. Like the Fundidora's directors, they also sought to reform their workmates' culture as a means of promoting the "intellectual and moral elevation" of the country.[26] Their activities began in 1923 with the founding of the "Acero" Recreational Society (Recreativa Acero). Initially, the Recreativa conformed to the cultural aspirations of its original 300 members, the mill's older, better-educated, and urbanized tradesmen and supervisors. The Fundidora's directors noted with pride that "the workers themselves" organized and managed the society. The company simply financed the programs through which their workers' could realize their own longings for self-improvement. The Recreativa's social hall, fronting the plaza in Colonia Acero, included a billiards room, a barber shop, and an exposition hall to display the products of the steel workers' labor. The society had its own library, to which the company donated such eclectic titles as *The Encyclopedia of Mechanics*, *The Life of Henry Ford*, and *Will the United States Take Over Baja California?* Recreativa members performed in the company band, staged theatrical events, and edited company publications.[27] From the outset, the Recreativa's directors – mainly skilled tradesmen, supervisors, and teachers from Acero School – used the organization as a vehicle to promote company loyalty and shape the workers' outlooks.

While their objectives served the company's interests, they acted out of a genuine and somewhat pretentious concern for their fellow Fundidora employees. The Recreativa's slick monthly magazine, *Colectividad*, illuminates that project and the people who administered it, how they perceived themselves, and how they proposed to reshape their fellow workers' lifestyles into their own image of respectability. "All of the articles published in the pages of *Colectividad*," they set forth, "have been directed especially towards our companions in the workshops." It was among these workers that "we

25 *Colectividad*, Nov. 7, 1931.
26 *El Porvenir*, Apr. 17, 1926.
27 *Colectividad*, July 1926, July 1927, Aug. 1929; *El Porvenir*, Feb. 2, 1925, Apr. 17, 1926.

hope to infiltrate sound ideas in order to reach our goal, which is none other than banishing our customs, many of which are highly destructive." These erstwhile reformers exalted the manliness of steel production. But they also sought to abolish other aspects of machismo. As one Recreativa founder recalled of the 1920s, "the guy who could drink a lot of booze (*vino*) and keep a couple women (*viejas*) on the side was considered a big man."[28] *Colectividad* therefore offered its readers advice on the dangers of drink and the wonders of thrift. "It is not a question of higher salaries or militant unions," editors counseled, "it is one of economizing, of morals." "What good does a lot of money serve a worker," they asked, "if he wastes it hanging out in cantinas and, as an inevitable consequence of his vices, finds it necessary to spend it at the pharmacy?" Unlike their counterparts at the brewery, the editors of *Colectividad* did not bemoan unionism per se. Rather they promoted the mill's local unions because, by the end of the 1920s, the mill's unionists no longer condoned "the unjust, radical ambitions that had created so many difficulties in other regions of the country." Instead, they "look[ed] to create an ambiance of morality within their unions and societies," promoting "anti-alcohol campaigns . . . [and] the honor of complying with [one's] working obligations."[29]

Class harmony, work discipline, and self-improvement were all articulated on "The Worker's Page." Notably absent from the pages of *Colectividad* were the languages of revolution and constitutional rights that bolstered the steel workers' strikes less than a decade earlier. While workers read little about revolutionary politics, the editors did condemn "those [labor] struggles caused by utopian beliefs, whose disastrous effects we have already experienced." They instead advocated that "Labor and Capital must never be separated, since neither can survive without the other . . . [and] because they have been, are today, and always will be the basis of Progress among all civilized Peoples." An article entitled "Bosses and Subalterns" declared that the "animosity" workers felt toward their foremen was, "in most cases," unjustified. As workers were reminded, "If a subaltern complies faithfully with his duties, his Boss will never be forced to treat him improperly."[30]

Veteran workers received special attention as exemplary laborers whose perseverance and mastery of their trades won the respect of their supervisors. "Don Panchito" González had his leg "crushed by a locomotive in our very workshops." Despite the crippling accident, González continued to "conscientiously carry out his duty," never missing a day of work.[31] As a young man, Flavio Galindo rose from an apprenticeship to become

28 *Colectividad*, Apr. 1928; González Caballero interview.
29 *Colectividad*, Aug. 1926, July 1928, Jan. 1930.
30 *Colectividad*, Feb. 1927.
31 Ibid., Feb. 1926, June 1928.

supervisor of the foundry. By the 1920s, he served on the city council, conducted the Acero Band, and excelled as an athlete. Veterans like Galindo, who ascended to positions once held by foreign recruits, embodied the essence of the respectable steel worker, "buying good books, taking classes, [and] perfecting themselves in their labor." Yet even exemplary workers could stray from the path of respectability. Galindo earned legendary status among his workmates during a fiesta to honor the foundry's twenty-fifth anniversary. Apparently forsaking the Recreativa's promotion of temperance, he "had a little beer" and then drunkenly exhorted his workmates "not to lose hope, that the entire Fundidora will one day be in Mexican hands." His speech did not go over well with the company's European-born administrators, who demoted Galindo for his outburst of patriotism.[32]

The Recreativa's reading room, theatrical productions, and Explorers' Club mainly appealed to Steel Town residents. The society's directors thus expanded the scope of their endeavors to integrate all operatives and their kin into the Great Steel Family. Thursday evening concerts by the company band drew workers and their families back to Plaza Acero. On weekends, they returned for movies or baseball games at Acero Park. Bimonthly parties staged in Monterrey's Independence Theater, a locale more accessible than Steel Town, drew upward of 2,000 workers and their families. The Recreativa also staged outdoor movies and bull fights in nearby Guadalupe, the hard-scrabble suburb across the river from the mill.[33] Adolfo Prieto's visits from Mexico City prompted extravagant ceremonies as well. "Don Adolfo," as the workers affectionately knew the company director, returned frequently to the "bosom" of the Great Steel Family, visiting the school and workshops and joining the festivities. The workers, of course, understood the company's motives. Dionisio Palacios, who entered the mill as a fourteen-year-old in 1924, recalled these affairs as a means of "making the workers happy and endeavoring to put our vices to one side." He perceived the Recreativa's cultural activities "as a way of forming an honest family" of steel workers and managers. By the early 1930s, Palacios remembered, "nearly everyone from the Fundididora was a member [of the Recreativa]." As one of the society's founders later recalled, the events staged by the Recreativa filled an important void in a city that offered "absolutely no cultural diversions" except hundreds of cantinas, brothels, and unlicensed *pulquerías*.[34]

32 Ibid., July 1926, Jan. 1930, Dec. 1925; Galindo incident recalled by Antonia Quiroga during March 26, 1996, interview.

33 *El Porvenir*, Apr. 3, 1926; *Colectividad*, July 1926, Apr. 1930; *CYPSA* (company magazine), Dec. 19, 1931, Aug. 20, 1932.

34 Palacios and González Cabellero interviews. Palacios added that many workers joined "because they wanted only to go to the parties."

Company athletics served as the most important means by which the Recreativa attempted to inculcate company loyalty and a "wholesome lifestyle" (*cultura sana*) among the workers. During the 1920s, civic boosters lauded the "moral influence of modern sports" with a near utopian zeal. Company-sponsored athletics would ostensibly "increase labor efficiency," "garner the operative's sincere loyalty," and divert workers from dangerous vices.[35] The Recreativa's directors explicitly promoted sports as an alternative to the cantina lifestyle. "It is preferable that the worker spends his free hours in the sports field," *Colectividad* proclaimed, "exercising and enjoying himself honestly." Otherwise, the editors warned, workers would be "going to the cantina to waste the money earned so arduously during the week, money that could be used to provide a little happiness for [their] parents, wives, or children."[36] Guided by these ideals, the company donated the land and construction materials used by Recreativa members to build a multipurpose sports facility, Acero Park. Constructed by workers on the weekends, the complex included a 400-meter track, basketball and volleyball courts, and a baseball field complete with locker rooms and grandstand seating for 1,000 spectators. The steel workers soon earned local renown as the finest athletes in Monterrey, a city whose inhabitants retain a reputation as Mexico's most ardent and enthusiastic sports fans.

No sport in Monterrey attracted more participants, fans, or local press coverage than baseball. The state of Nuevo León proudly proclaims itself as Mexico's "cradle of baseball." On the fourth of July, 1884, American railroad workers allegedly organized the first game just outside the city. They thereafter popularized baseball among Mexican workers. By the 1920s, the *regiomontano* industrialists patronized the game zealously. While soccer remained "little known in Monterrey," baseball was a "game that turned half of the city crazy." Every major factory fielded its own "starting nine" team in the city's industrial league. The companies took the contests seriously, recruiting worker–ballplayers from Cuba, Texas, and from rival factories, the latter earning considerable promotions to switch their allegiances.[37] Each Sunday morning from spring through fall, brewery, glass, steel, and smelter workers represented their workmates in games played before thousands in Acero and Cuauhtémoc Parks. Local all-star teams also took the field against regional rivals from Saltillo, Torreón, and Texas. Boosters thus promoted the "king of sports" as means of reinforcing the *regiomontanos'* "sincere identification with their native soil." Within a city of baseball fanatics, the residents of Steel Town earned special renown.[38] Each of the mill's

35 *El Porvenir*, Sep. 16, 1922, Jan. 28, 1924.
36 *Colectividad*, Feb. 15, 1926.
37 *El Porvenir*, Sep. 18, 1922; González Cabellero interview.
38 *El Sol*, Oct. 11, 1932; *El Porvenir*, Oct 16, 1922, Nov. 4, 1926.

departments fielded its own team. The company also promoted Monterrey's pastime among the Acero School students, who excelled like their fathers. Indeed, come the mid-1950s, a founding member of the Recreativa would coach the sons of steel workers to victory in two of the first Little League World Series in the United States.[39] However, while the workers embraced the "healthy and happy sporting life" promoted by paternalism, they never adopted to temperance. As Jesús García later recalled, he and his workmates came to see baseball and a postgame beer "as our two favorite sports."[40]

By the late 1920s, the Fundidora took steps to formalize its system of welfare capitalism. In 1928, the company established its own Cooperativa Acero to administer the fringe benefits already offered to steel workers, from the subsidized food commissary to the savings and loan plan. Adolfo Prieto promoted it as a self-sufficient entity to be administered by and for the workers. While Prieto drafted the Cooperativa's statutes, he submitted them to the plant's shop committees for their own revisions.[41] Workers in each department then elected delegates to the cooperative's board of directors. Such dedicated workers soon earned praise for the sacrifices made on behalf of others: "As good workers, as real go-getters (*luchadores*), they are always looking out for their workmates' well-being and for the future of those who depend on them."[42] The workers who oversaw the cooperative subscribed wholeheartedly to their employer's vision of an autonomous cooperative. Upon formally requesting a $15,000 "loan" in startup capital, the steel workers expressed their wish "to some day become economically independent . . . as our most vehement desire is to not to be a burden for the company." They even proposed to contract their own physicians rather than depend on company doctors. However, while the workers' took Prieto's promotion of workers' control seriously, he privately cautioned the mill's Monterrey director to "guard over the nascent society's development with . . . paternal affection."[43]

The Cooperativa Acero launched formal operations with great fanfare. Nuevo León's governor, Aarón Sáenz, inaugurated the cooperative building as the newest edition to Steel Town. However, despite the potential benefits of a Cooperativa membership – the low prices and availability of credit – only 700 of some 2,400 steel workers had joined by the early 1930s.[44] The rest preserved their family's customary practices of buying on credit from neighborhood merchants. Some did so to explicitly uphold their

39 *El Porvenir*, May 20, 1935; González Caballero interview.
40 *Colectividad*, Feb. 4, 1931; interview with Jesús García Martínez, Nov. 15, 1995.
41 Adolfo Prieto to Meliton Ulmer, Apr. 2, 1928, AHFM: Cooperativa Acero, 153/1.
42 *Triunfaremos*, June 27, 1931.
43 *Colectividad*, Feb. 4, 1931; Prieto to Ulmer, Sep. 28, 1928: AHFM: Cooperativa Acero, 153/2.
44 *Colectividad*, May 1930, Feb. 4, 1931.

independence from the company and from what they considered to be a
tienda de raya, a reference to the infamous company stores of prerevolutionary
Mexico.[45] Therefore, two years after the Cooperativa's founding, Prieto com-
menced a campaign to enhance paternalism's appeal. In 1931, the Fundidora
streamlined its benefits programs into a single entity, Consumption and Social Welfare "Acero" (CYPSA), and placed them under the direction of a
full-time administrator. Months after assuming his post, CYPSA's director sent a representative to scout the company welfare plan at Republic
Steel in Cleveland. Then, in an ambitious effort to attract subscribers, he
announced an array of new fringe benefits: life insurance, pension plans,
a maternity hospital, and additional housing developments. Meanwhile,
the cooperative expanded its scope of operations to include more than
300 goods, from American food products to work clothes to cigarettes.[46]
The program proved a success. Over the next eighteen months, nearly
the entire work force joined the CYPSA program. But their change of
perspective seemed to owe less to the enhanced benefits than the harsh
realities of the market; for an economic depression and the layoffs that
ensued inspired rank-and-file steel workers to embrace the benefits of
paternalism.

The Limits of Paternalism

The mill's consolidation of industrial paternalism reflected Monterrey's
changing political climate as much as the company's concern for its workers'
welfare. CYPSA's founding transpired just months before the government
passed the 1931 Federal Labor Law. The new labor code promised stricter
compliance with workers' constitutional rights. We shall later see that its
passage coincided with the onset of the Great Depression and a resurgence
of militant unionism in Monterrey, much of it led by Communist Party labor activists. The developments did not pass unnoticed by the Fundidora's
directors. It was in this context that they hired Manuel Barragán to direct the company's welfare programs. The son of a wealthy *regiomontano*
family, Barragán returned from Mexico City where he had spent the later
1920s editing the influential, conservative daily, *Excélsior*. With Barragán's
arrival emerged two new company publications, the monthly *CYPSA*
and the optimistically titled weekly, *Triunfaremos* (We Will Triumph).
The moralizing cultural eclecticism that had defined the old *Colectividad*
lost ground to front-page editorials on the wonders of Taylorism, the
dangers of communism, and Monterrey steel's contribution to an economic revival. Company ideologues warned the steel workers to act with

---

45 Interviews with Palacios, Castañeda, and Salvador Solís Daniel, Nov. 14, 1995.
46 AHFM: Cooperativa Acero, 151/4, 153/2; *Triunfaremos*, July 4, 1931.

caution, "as the present epoch is contagious with the deviated mentalities of [those] who go about perverting and corrupting mens' hearts." Articles culled from the red-baiting pages of *Excélsior* preached ominous warnings, to those steel workers who read them, of a coming "dictatorship of the proletariat."[47] The reporting proved consistent with the rightward drift of a Mexican government that had launched a repressive assault on the sort of communist labor militants then making inroads in Monterrey's factories.

The steel mill's union leaders heard the warnings as well. By then, several of those former militants had emerged at the vanguard of local working-class opposition to "red" union organizers. These veteran steel workers shared the fervid anticommunism preached by Barragán. They thus acted to assert greater control over the rank and file. In 1930, they unified the mill's department-based unions as the Federación de Sindicatos del Acero (hereafter the Steel Unions). The Steel Unions fell under the direction of union leaders from the machine shops and rolling mills, especially Pancho Guzmán and Rosendo Ocañas. Ocañas and Guzmán were by then popular figures throughout the sprawling steel works. Ocañas, an assistant mechanic and local *"regiomontano* bohemian," earned acclaim as the "Bard of Steel" for his considerable literary talents.[48] Both were outstanding orators with close ties to the National Revolutionary Party's political machine. Indeed, Guzmán served as a state congressman during the 1920s. These qualities led workers who were young at the time to later recall such unionists as "natural leaders." They, in turn, proudly reminded the ranks of their own status as "workers from the shops." They promised to uphold what was by then becoming a *regiomontano* tradition of independence from Mexico's national labor federations. By their judgment these Mexico City–based unions were colonized by middle-class opportunists and communist radicals. In contrast to such "professional [labor] leaders moved by a spirit of agitation," the Steel Unions would not impose "exaggerated demands" upon the company.[49] These veteran steel workers thus practiced their own project of class harmony, genuinely believing that industrial peace rather than collective action was in the best interest of both workers and the company.

In late 1931, the Steel Unions negotiated the workers' first collective contract. Negotiations transpired just as the Great Depression made its first impact on local steel production, which would fall more than 50 percent below its record 1929 levels.[50] Nonetheless, the union, its leaders, and the contract all received lavish praise in the company press. While the

47 *CYPSA*, June 18 and 25, July 30, Aug. 20, 1932.
48 González Caballero, *La Maestranza*, 35–36.
49 *CYPSA*, Nov. 28, 1931; Palacios interview.
50 Nathan, Aug. 31, 1931, Jan. 30, 1932, SD 812.00 NL/14, 27.

mill had already begun suspending workers, union leaders claimed that "a spirit of cooperation and harmony reigned throughout the meetings." "There was no fundamental reason for disagreements or controversies," a company spokesman agreed. Rosendo Ocañas even added that the contract guaranteed workers "benefits superior to those stipulated by law." Another union official cited this as a testament "to the good will and honest judgment of the plant's director." He then crowed that Monterrey's local unions, concerned only with their respective industries, "had once again proven their lofty stature . . . and demonstrated ideals more advanced than those found in other regions of the country."[51]

Here was the increasingly ubiquitous language of company unionism, one that countered the emergence of radical labor activism through appeals to the workers' regional identity. The Communist Party press labeled the Sindicatos del Acero a "white union," as Mexicans referred to management-friendly unions.[52] Monterrey's industrialists in fact organized company unions during this period to ward off the increased threat of independent union organizing. But the collaborative drift of the Steel Unions resulted from the agency of its leaders, veteran workers who were both anticommunist and pragmatic. The deepening economic crisis and the government's crackdown on strike activity made militant unionism a risky venture in the early 1930s. While the Steel Unions' leaders acted within this context, their seeming complacency lent credence to later rank-and-file charges that they "sold out" to management. The contract awarded the workers no benefits beyond those won as a result of the strikes of 1918–22. The contract did, however, enhance the Steel Union's power. It established the closed shop, giving the union the capacity to dismiss dissident workers, and extended union leaders the right to appoint delegates to the shop committees. All shop stewards, the contract stipulated, would have five years' seniority; none could receive counseling from "outside" union representatives. Most importantly, all decisions settled by the committees – from layoffs to promotions – would be "final and obligatory," a shrewd means of circumventing the authority of the state's labor court system.[53]

The economic crisis tested company paternalism and the Steel Unions' leaders. Late in 1931 the Fundidora began suspending operations on a departmental basis. The process continued into mid-1932, a year when iron and steel production fell to less than half of the mill's record 1929 output. While many operatives continued working two- or three-day weeks, others received ten-week suspension notices. The new labor code required

---

51 *CYPSA*, November 28, 1931.
52 *El Machete*, Mexico City, May 1, 1932.
53 Contrato Colectivo: Compañía Fundidora de Monterrey y Federación de Sindicatos del Acero, December 1, 1931, AGENL: Trabajo – Conciliación y Arbitraje, 3.

government authorization of layoffs. The steel mill astutely circumvented state intervention by channeling the suspensions through the shop committees. The process did not transpire without resistance. Collective protest emerged most dramatically in the plant's structural iron department. The iron workers were among the Fundidora's most specialized tradesmen, designing and manufacturing construction profiles according to engineering specifications. They were also the only union workers to remain independent of the Steel Unions. Not only did the iron workers disavow the collective contract, they were associated with the communist faction of organized labor. They suffered the consequences of the mounting economic crisis early because the Fundidora could not stockpile the made-to-order products of their labor. The iron workers therefore acquiesced to a ten-week work suspension in late 1931. But they rebelled when the Steel Unions agreed to a managerial request to extend their suspensions indefinitely.

The iron workers filed a claim with the government arbitration board. Their "red" allies inundated the governor's office with letters of sympathy while street protestors rallied opposition to layoffs at Monterrey's largest employer. The iron workers themselves launched a hunger strike in the halls of the state capital, thereby pressuring the state to address their case. The labor board ordered the workers' reinstatement because the company failed to petition for the right to suspend them. But authorities also upheld the binding nature of the Steel Unions' collective contract. The iron workers therefore sustained their protest to defend their trade union autonomy. Their resistance collapsed as work suspensions spread to other departments. Faced with bleak prospects of securing employment elsewhere, the majority of the department's 134 workers returned to work, a logical response to an economic crisis whose relatively short-lived impact on Mexico was by no means foreseeable in 1932. In the end, some three dozen dissidents held out, finally accepting severance pay rather than return to the steel mill.[54] The iron workers' struggle marked the only collective resistance to the layoffs.

Indeed, the steel mill remained relatively tranquil during a period that witnessed escalating worker protest in Monterrey and elsewhere. The layoffs generated minimal protest because in return for signing "voluntary separation" waivers, the company offered suspended workers a verbal promise of rehiring, emergency loans, and extended credit at the consumer cooperative. By the close of 1932, 2,221 steel workers, nearly the entire workforce, had joined the Cooperativa Acero. The same year saw the

---

54 Iron worker strike in AGENL: JCA 11/377; AGENL: Trabajo – Conciliación y Arbitraje, 3/12; *El Machete*, Apr. 10, 1932.

distribution of $20,650 in interest-free loans.[55] The Great Depression thus led the steel workers to embrace the company's welfare benefits program. These nonwage incentives provided the steel workers with a sense of collective security during a time of great uncertainty. Moreover, the economy soon conspired on behalf of a quick resolution to the crisis. Public works projects and industrial protectionism reflated the economy and stimulated demand for Monterrey steel.[56] In late 1932, the mill began calling the workers back. True to the company's patriotic spirit, Fundidora director Prieto reminded them that the plant's return to full capacity would quickly stimulate the regional economy, restoring jobs to miners and railroaders as well. He also announced the firm's intentions to launch the manufacturing of iron tubing and barbed wire, further promoting Mexico's economic independence. The Fundidora's recovery transcended his expectations. By 1934 the steel mill registered new production and sales records.[57]

In contrast to the United States, where the Depression's prolonged effects led companies to cut welfare benefits, the crisis proved relatively short-lived in Monterrey.[58] For the families of steel workers, the availability of credit and loans from the cooperative alleviated the collective hardships of the time. The crisis thus tested the efficacy of Fundidora paternalism, enhancing its appeal to a broader strata of the workforce. Much like their counterparts at the Cuauhtémoc Brewery, the steel workers embraced the company's recreational activities early on. Only after 1932, however, did the welfare program appeal widely to workers who resided outside of Steel Town. Increasingly, workers began enlisting in the company's pension and life insurance plans, shopping at the Cooperativa Acero, and sending their children to Acero School. Indeed, enrollment at the company school increased dramatically after the mid-1920s, climbing from 500 students to more than 1,200 a decade later. The higher enrollment reflected not only the city's improved transportation system but also the development of working-class neighborhoods on the mill's periphery. By the 1930s, then, both workers and their families came to rely on the mill for more than just steady work and wages. Many families, especially those with fathers and sons at the mill, could thereby lead a comfortable lifestyle by the standards of working-class Monterrey. Furthermore, the cultural practices of paternalism – from baseball to fiestas to the company school – helped create a broader sense of community within the Great Steel Family. For the workers, those cultural practices enhanced the bonds established through

---

55 AHFM: Póliza de Caja, 1932, no. 50 and Cooperativa Acero, 153/2; *CYSPA*, Feb. 25, 1933.
56 Enrique Cárdenas, *La industrialización mexicana durante la gran depresión* (Mexico City, 1987), 55–59.
57 Prieto in *CYSPA*, Oct. 7, 1932; Nathan, Apr. 29, 1933, SD 812.00 NL/43; AHFM, *Informe*, 1935.
58 Flamming, *Creating the Modern South*, 188–98; Lizabeth Cohen, *Making a New Deal: Industrial Workers in Chicago, 1919–1939* (New York, 1990), 213–49.

the daily rigors of steel production. But it was there, in the furnaces and workshops, where paternalism met its limits.

Steel workers braved considerable dangers in the mill. Mandatory accident reports filed with the Labor Department reflect the scope and severity of the occupational hazards they faced.[59] Falling objects, unprotected machinery, and the constant movement of railcars injured and occasionally killed workers. They also died from severe burns, electrocutions, and falls. Much as in mining communities, families living near the mill feared the unexpected mid-shift cry of the Fundidora's well-known whistle because it most always signaled a severe accident. Moreover, official accident reports do not account for the silent dangers that workers faced through prolonged exposure to gases, metallic dusts, and asbestos.[60] Each department produced its own peculiar risks. In the furnaces, workers faced debilitating heat and explosions of molten metal as it spilled from the kettles and struck the wet ground. Accidents here could prove fatal. The most notorious incident cost seventeen workers their lives. But workers in the rolling mills faced the most persistent risks. Hookers who caught heated steel bars and guided them through the rollers were often struck by runaway slabs. Others were thrown onto the rolling beds by the force of passing steel. One rolling mill veteran later recalled the challenge: "Don't think that just anyone [can work the rollers], because in the first place you must have a lot of experience and then you must have courage, that's right, because many people feared that red-hot steel."[61] They did so for good reason. By the early 1930s, fully 60 percent of the steel workers each year suffered an injury that required medical treatment. Those accidents translated into an average of ten days lost per incident. Accidents thus proved costly for the company, not only in terms of lost productivity, but compensation packages as well.[62]

The Fundidora therefore launched a well-publicized Campaign Against Accidents, promoting it as the first of its kind in Mexico. CYPSA published safety tips in the company press and hired a local artist to paint graphic warnings throughout the mill.[63] For the steel workers, however, a wide gulf separated the company's claims to high safety standards from everyday practice. Department supervisors often failed to implement rudimentary

---

59 AGN: DT, 1923–1929; AGENL: Industria, Comercio y Trabajo, 1930, 3–5.

60 Sandra Arenal, *Fundidora, diéz años después* (Monterrey, 1996), 94–97.

61 Castañeda interview.

62 As compensation, the company provided medical treatment and 50 percent of the worker's wages, spending a monthly average of $5,563 in the early 1930s. The compensation proved insufficient, however, as nearly all workers returned to the mill well before their prescribed period of treatment had concluded. AGENL: Industria, Comercio y Trabajo, 1930, boxes 3–5.

63 González Caballero, *La maestranza*, 81–84; AHFM: Comprobantes de Caja, Oct. 1929, no. 75; *CYPSA*, Jan. 1 and July 2, 1932.

precautions. In the foundry, where the operatives cast molds with such volatile metals as copper and bronze, the supervisor persistently rejected demands for protective goggles until a young worker lost an eye to molten metal. Basic provisions like work boots became widespread only in the 1930s. Indeed, workers recall the 1920s as the "time of *huaraches*," a reference to the tire-soled sandals then worn commonly by working-class Mexicans. Other workers blamed the high accident rates on the fact that the workers' wages were tied directly to tonnage output, an effective means of driving the crews harder during peak production periods.[64] The accidents themselves proved less damaging to labor relations than the means by which the company handled them. Protests filed with federal labor inspectors during the mid-1920s suggest a company practice of dismissing incapacitated workers, granting them their legal severance pay, but "not a single cent" for their occupational injuries.[65] Even when compensation came, many workers found it inadequate. The steel mill continued to compensate workers in accordance with the state's 1906 Accident Law. Injured workers thus received half rather than the federally stipulated 75 percent of their wages. Nonetheless, the fact that the Fundidora even compensated the workers distinguished the company from others in a city where employers brazenly violated labor laws well into the 1920s.

Workers chafed at these infringements on their rights. But they also accepted the risks as an integral part of the culture of steel work. Many later spoke of and displayed their scars and crippled limbs with a pride and stoicism reminiscent of veterans of war. Indeed, the daily rigors of labor in the furnaces, foundry, and rolling mills, where the operatives worked in tightly coordinated crews and collectively faced the dangers of steel making, sealed a camaraderie that itself helped compensate for the perceived abuses of the company. In the end, an operative's safety depended mightily on the vigilance of his workmates. Those workmates often donated part of their own earnings to mutually assist an injured colleague during his time of convalescence.[66] The steel workers also compensated for the plant's high accident rate and their seeming powerlessness in the face of danger through black humor. Dionisio Palacios, the worker who lost an eye in the foundry, thus earned the nickname "El Ciego," The Blind One. Meanwhile, a popular ballad composed by a steel worker referred to colleagues killed in the mill

64 Interviews with Palacios, Gerónimo Contreras, Dec. 5, 1996, and Rafael Reyna, May 22, 1996.

65 Jesús Carranza to Secretaría de Industria, Comercio y Trabajo, Nov. 12, 1924 in AGN: DT 736.

66 The company promoted such mutual aid by deducting the donations from the workers' paychecks. See AHFM: Comprobantes de Caja, 1927, #65–68; AGENL: JCA, 1930, 6/228.

as having "died for the homeland."[67] The steel workers thus parlayed their exposure to danger into a source of manliness and patriotic pride, lasting traits of their collective identity.

While the practices of paternalism could never compensate for the dangers of steel making – as the workers understood – other aspects of shop-floor life vividly exposed the limits of company welfare. Indeed, as with all forms of paternalism, the mill's benevolent concern for its workers' welfare often masked the flipside of the paternalistic coin, one tarnished by favoritism and coercion. The plant's shop committees never met their ostensible goal of democratizing shop-floor relations. Controlled by the same men who directed the Steel Unions, they became sources of patronage rather than mechanisms for the equitable assignment of jobs, overtime, and promotions. Often, ties of family, cronyism, or a hefty bribe determined one's occupational mobility. Furthermore, among a cast of equals, it was often the "most flattering" (*barbero*) who won the advancement. Indeed, Antonio Quiroga recalled a fellow foundry worker awarding his boss with a used car in return for a prized promotion. Giving the prevailing job grades of the time, an occupational hierarchy marked by sharp wage differentials, the move from third- to second-category tradesmen could double an operative's earnings for a task that proved no more demanding than that from which he had ascended.[68] Favoritism bred demands for seniority rights and, ultimately, aspirations for a more democratic union.

Workers also chafed at the "arrogant and despotic" manner of the plant's foremen. Dionisio Palacios entered the mill's foundry as a fourteen-year-old. While his testimony betrays a heartfelt loyalty to the steel mill, he later remembered that, "frankly when I entered in 1924 the abuses leveled by the company against the workers were severe." In particular, he recalled the power wielded by the foremen, who retained control over hiring and firing into the 1930s.[69] The foremen's reputation for cruelty persisted ten years later, when the mill hired Rafael Reyna as an apprentice machinist. The workers still regarded many of their shop-floor bosses with fear. Some foremen earned unsavory reputations for physically abusing young laborers, especially migrants from the countryside. They arbitrarily fired workers for committing minor infractions or erring in their work. Reyna even recalled workers voluntarily laying down their tools and leaving the plant rather than suffer a foreman's wrath. The foremen were a diverse crew. Some were veteran workers who had ascended from the operatives' ranks and treated

67 Palacios interview; "Memorias del Acero: Fundidora, 1900–1986," *El Diario de Monterrey*, May 9, 1996.
68 Quiroga interview; 1931 wage scales in Nathan, Dec. 1, 1931, SD 812.5041/48.
69 Palacios interview.

their subordinates with dignity and respect. A few still belonged to militant trade unions, a status that often earned them a good deal of harassment and intimidation.[70] But these were exceptions. For the workers who suffered their abuses, the typically overbearing foremen served as a reminder that the promises of paternalism did not extend to the shop floor.

Lastly, the mediating channels of government arbitration boards offered little reprieve. The steel workers enjoyed few means of legally challenging managerial authority prior to the 1930s. While the 1917 Constitution theoretically protected them, Palacios recalled that most workers "knew nothing about laws." Individual workers who did understand their rights generally shunned protest for fear of retribution. Palacios learned why. In 1929, he filed a claim for legal compensation after losing an eye to a foundry accident. Arriving to the labor board's office in the state capital, he encountered the mill's chief legal counsel, then serving as interim governor. The high-placed lawyer reminded Palacios of the company "watchword": workers who "do not protest and settle with the company stay on the job." But should a worker appeal to the labor board, the company "immediately looked for a way to throw you out." Why was the law rendered ineffective? "The principal reason," Palacios believed, "was because one had no means of defense; you see . . . there was a lack of organization." "By yourself you could only do so much against a well-prepared company, one with *money*," he emphasized.[71]

The company dismissed troublesome workers with relative ease. Most commonly, supervisors coached workers to instigate fights with dissident operatives, thus creating legal grounds for a punitive discharge. In other cases, the steel mill simply fired workers and gave them their "time," the severance pay required by law. Not surprisingly, workers at Monterrey's largest employer left few cases archived in the labor board files of the 1920s. We shall see in the next chapter that such practices were not unique to the steel mill. Neither was the widespread belief among operatives that a blacklist circulated among Monterrey's leading industrialists. The steel workers' collective contract finally sealed their inability to protest to the government labor authorities. All worker grievances would be settled internally by the very shop committees that company had agreed to recognize after the 1922 strike. Indeed, for fear of undermining the competency and legitimacy of these committees, Nuevo León's labor board refused to overturn their decisions.[72]

These conditions bred a generalized sense of powerlessness among the steel workers. Looking back to the period, Dionisio Palacios recalled that,

70 Reyna interview; Unión Internacional de Forjadores to Governor Sáenz, Oct. 7, 1929, AGENL: Correspondencia nacional de gobernadores, 11/26.
71 Palacios interview.
72 AGENL: JCA 11/375, 11/377.

"in order to keep one's job . . . we had to conform ourselves to whatever the bosses said. . . . [S]tated simply, the worker had no protection." "There was," his colleague Antonio Quiroga remembered, "nothing one could do." Indeed, for Quiroga, nothing chafed more than the restrictions imposed by their supervisors on their right to protest without fear of retribution.[73] In the end, the workers' collective desire for job security – a feeling bred by the hardships of revolutionary upheaval and the labor unrest that followed – conditioned their willingness to protest managerial authority. As the 1920s progressed, they earned higher wages, greater opportunities for mobility, and expanded welfare benefits for their families. Why then do retired steel workers highlight these abusive conditions in their oral testimony? Perhaps because this legacy of powerlessness buttressed later struggles to organize and defend a strong union that effectively redressed their grievances. Indeed, the workers later blamed the ineffective leadership of the Steel Unions – rather than the company itself – for the shop-floor abuses. Nonetheless, the steel mill's system of employee representation schooled workers in the arts of negotiation and leadership. By the early 1930s, former militants had come to accept the Steel Unions as the only viable means of pressing demands upon the company. But as that decade progressed and the ship of Mexico's revolutionary state assumed a more radical tack, the steel workers would test the company's above-cited policy that its workers enjoyed the "freedom to organize themselves in any way they please."

Through its company schools, its welfare benefits, and its athletic programs, the Fundidora sought to create a physically fit and well-trained work force, one that prided itself on its contribution to national reconstruction. By the early 1930s, the Maestranza's schools and workshops had indeed produced one of Mexico's most specialized workforces, the "genuine aristocracy of the national proletariat." Mexico's railroad and oil workers would have disputed the claim. But the steel workers' own testimony indeed betrays a sense of hard-earned superiority. While the affronts to their dignity cut across the benevolent grains of paternalism, the shop-floor conflicts never undercut their loyalty toward a company in which the steel workers took great pride. The experience of work and paternalism created a common company culture that endured for generations. Aurelio Arenas, one of seventy family members who labored at the mill, later considered the Fundidora as "an expansion of the family: we respected the older workers, they were like fathers to us, showing us where to go and what we should do and how best to achieve it." As mill workers, they all discovered "great solidarity in work and in leisure, through the dangers we faced and through our struggles as well." Combined with the daily rigors and shared grievances produced

73 Palacios and Quiroga interviews.

by shop-floor life, their common integration into the Great Steel Family created a sense of community among workers of diverse social backgrounds. Thus did Dionisio Palacios later reminisce that, "in spite of certain abuses, we had a great deal of affection for the Fundidora. . . . [W]e saw ourselves as one big family."[74]

74 Aurelio Arenas interview in Arenal, ed., *Fundidora*, 181; Palacios interview.

5
The Democratic Principles of Our Revolution

Labor Movements and Labor Law in the 1920s

Historians of industrial paternalism long focused attention upon the places where the system achieved its greatest results: the semirural textile mill villages and the isolated company towns of the industrializing world, places where employers enjoyed a greater capacity than urban industrialists to regulate their workers' lives. As Patrick Joyce concludes in his seminal study of British labor, "What made paternalism so effective was the employer's capacity for defining and thus delimiting the social outlook of the workforce."[1] The traditional view of southern (U.S.) mill villages held that the beneficiaries of paternalism remained shielded from the world of organized labor and the political cultures upon which unionism rested. When labor organizers did arrive, local elites could mobilize antiunion resistance by portraying unionists as outsiders intent upon unraveling the social fabric that wove the lives of workers and managers together. Workers in company towns, of course, fashioned countless means of negotiating their loyalties with paternalistic employers. And paternalism itself could foster working-class solidarities that bolstered militant struggles for union recognition.[2] Consistent with the Monterrey case, scholars have also compared how welfare capitalism's scope and reception may differ in an urban environment. While many urban workers lived in relatively insulated inner-city communities dominated by a single employer, they were nonetheless exposed to political cultures and organized labor movements that challenged the paternalistic pretension of their employers.[3] Furthermore, the

1 Joyce, *Work, Society, and Politics*, xxi.
2 Mary Lethert Wingerd, "Rethinking Paternalism: Power and Parochialism in a Southern Mill Village," *Journal of American History* 83:3 (1996), 872–902; Zahavi, *Workers, Managers, and Welfare Capitalism*; Flamming, *Creating the Modern South*; John Gaventa, *Power and Powerlessness: Quiescence and Rebellion in an Appalachian Valley* (Urbana, 1982); Blair B. Kling, "Paternalism and Indian Labor: The Tata Iron and Steel Company of Jamshedpur," *International Labor and Working-Class History* 53 (1998), 69–87.
3 Peter Winn, *Weavers of Revolution: The Yarur Cotton Workers and Chile's Road to Socialism* (New York, 1986); Cohen, *Making a New Deal*; Elisabetta Benenati, "Americanism and Paternalism: Managers and Workers in Twentieth-Century Italy," *International Labor and Working-Class History* 53 (1998), 5–26.

very practices of paternalism could diverge within a single urban neighborhood and industry – and produce strikingly different results – as a history
of Chicago meat packing demonstrates.[4]

Such was the case in "Mexico's Chicago," too. There, the employers' practices and the workers' reception of paternalism differed markedly between
the Cuauhtémoc Brewery and the Fundidora Steel Mill. Moreover, as on
Chicago's South Side or the working-class barrios of Turin and Santiago,
the dynamic urban setting of Monterrey provided workers with cultural and
political alternatives to those promoted by their paternalistic employers. In
the aftermath of the armed revolution, Monterrey's captains of industry
were challenged by local citizens who contested their "antirevolutionary"
politics and corporate labor practices. Throughout the 1920s, these radical
labor activists developed their own discursive and cultural practices to keep
the promises of the revolution alive in the memories of Monterrey's workers.
They also pressured political authorities to defend workers' constitutional
rights, lobbying the government to implement and enforce an effective
state labor code.

Monterrey's industrial elite therefore did not restrict their efforts to shape
their workers' worldview to the private realm of the workplace. Through
their control of the city's radio and press, they endeavored to fashion the way
regiomontanos of all classes perceived themselves as a community. They also
broadcast their paternalistic benevolence to a local and national audience to
booster their civic prestige and purchase political capital. This public face
of benevolence camouflaged paternalism's coercive underside. The labor reforms ushered in by the revolution complicated but never stymied many
employers' drive to keep unions out of their factories. Indeed, from organized
labor's perspective, the 1920s were years of disappointment as the industrialists both resisted the labor law and subverted it to their own ends. Counseled by a battery of corporate lawyers, they shrewdly shielded their workers
from organized labor and then, in the early 1930s, established the company
unions for which Monterrey holds renown. Thus consistent with findings
elsewhere in Latin America, their experience with the law "produced simul-
taneously in working class labor activists both deep bitterness and cynicism
and an unprecedented hopefulness and utopian militancy."[5] Labor activists
learned that the shifting political tides of revolutionary Mexico could offer both beneficial openings and stinging setbacks, making direct action

4 Paul Street, "The Swift Difference: Workers, Managers, Militants, and Welfare Capitalism in
  Chicago's Stockyards, 1917–1942," in Shelton Stromquist and Marvin Bergman, eds., *Unionizing
  the Jungles: Labor and Community in the Twentieth Century Meatpacking Industry* (Iowa City, 1997),
  16–50.
5 John D. French, "Drowning in Laws But Starving (For Justice?): Brazilian Labor Law and the Workers'
  Quest to Realize the Imaginary," *Political Power and Social Theory* 12 (1998), 184.

a viable alternative to the bureaucratic channels of labor law. They would carry that lesson into the 1930s.

Cultured Workers, Progressive Employers

With the gradual achievement of political stability in the 1920s came a restoration of the economic dynamism, urban growth, and civic pride that characterized prerevolutionary Monterrey. Local chroniclers later lamented the "parade of governors and mayors" who passed through political office. But Nuevo León's unpredictable political tides – the status quo by contemporary Mexican standards – proved a limited obstacle to renewed modernization. Henry Ford struck a blow to local pride by selecting Mexico City to host the automaker's first Mexican plant. So the *regiomontanos* forged ahead with capital of their own. Even during the uncertain days of the armed revolution, their "deep-rooted *regiomontano* business spirit" inspired a new generation of industrialists to open factories. By the early 1920s, they produced mattresses, furniture, mirrors, and cement for what promised to be an expansive domestic market. Established industries rebounded as well. The Cuauhtémoc Brewery launched its own malt and packaging subsidiaries. Monterrey Glassworks added crystal and plate glass divisions to its Vidriera bottle plant.[6] Meanwhile, the city's building trades boomed; the railroad stations bustled with freight cars, migrant workers, and tourists from Texas; and a network of new regional highways shortened travel times between Monterrey, cities like Saltillo and Torreón, and the Texas border towns. As local boosters could proudly boast, this regional dynamism contrasted mightily with the national economic scene. For after an early export-led revival, Mexico's economy sank after 1926 into a recessionary spiral that would blunt the sharp edge of the Great Depression. By 1929, workplace modernization and economic stagnation caused employment to fall in Mexico's first big industries – the railways, mines, textile mills, and then oil. Many of those workers ended up in Monterrey, where the number of factory, transport, and construction workers more than doubled (to 29,000). The "Sultan of the North" thus lived up to its new moniker during a decade when government policymakers equated "revolution" with "reconstruction."[7]

The return to full production schedules at the factories also brought unexpected returns that plague the city to this very day – pollution and housing shortages. With round-the-clock smelting and steel making, the

---

6 Mendirichaga, *Los cuatro tiempos*, 335–56; Saldaña, *Episodios contémporaneos* (Monterrey, 1955), 12–19; César Morado Macías, *Concesiones: La política de fomento industrial, 1868–1940* (Monterrey, 1991), 3–21.

7 Jean Meyer, "Revolution and Reconstruction in the 1920s," in Leslie Bethell, ed. *Mexico Since Independence* (Cambridge, 1991), 220–27.

smokestacks and mountains symbolic of Monterrey conspired to wreak environmental havoc. Farmers from the northern outskirts protested to the governor that "arsenic vapor emanating from the [ASARCO] smelter here in the suburbs" had "poisoned" their lands and killed off the livestock "that constitutes the basis of our work and lives." In the eastside neighborhoods abutting the Peñoles smelter a journalist reported that "a night never passes without one noticing the unbreathable air, even with the doors and windows hermetically sealed."[8] On some mornings, *regiomontanos* awoke to find their canaries dead and laundry blackened with soot. Angry citizens registered hundreds of protests with city hall. In 1927, the mayor finally lashed out at the culprits when Peñoles failed to follow ASARCO's lead and install the antipollutant devices ordered by the city. Not only had the American firm "paid *not a single cent* in tax contributions" since its concession expired in 1910; the city also had to support the "widows and orphans of workers killed due to a lack of modern hygiene and work procedures" at the smelter. A company lawyer retorted that the pollution "was a nuisance, but in no way harmful's to one's health." It was the "just price" paid for the 900 jobs Peñoles provided and, he reminded the mayor, "in many cities of the United States, like Chicago, the authorities tolerate these problems in virtue of the benefits provided by industry."[9] After a half-hearted threat to move its operations elsewhere, the American firm installed the environmental safeguards. Industrial pollution remained a burden suffered by all *regiomontanos*. But the protests marked a rare instance when the public and Monterrey's probusiness press awoke to the negative consequences of heavy industry.

Meanwhile, industrial renewal sustained the flood of migrants from the farms and mining towns of northern Mexico. The demographic expansion swelled the population beyond 130,000 inhabitants, boosting Monterrey past Puebla as Mexico's third largest city. The newcomers strained an inadequate housing stock. Overcrowding grew severe, slums like Little Matehuala expanded, and shantytowns mushroomed along the railway lines and riverbanks. Rents skyrocketed an estimated 50 percent during the early 1920s. As elsewhere in urban Mexico, a militant tenants union led mainly by local women pressured state authorities to intervene. As the decade progressed, private builders and government agencies developed new working-class *colonias* of wood frame dwellings and "California-style" bungalows upon the former pasture lands abutting the city's industrial districts.[10]

8 AGENL: Correspondencia Local de Gobernadores, 1919, 4/48; *El Porvenir*, Oct. 15, 1923.
9 *El Porvenir*, May 26, 1927; AGN: DGG 2.331.8 (16)/32-A/1.
10 *El Porvenir*, July 1, 1921, Dec. 5, 1923, May 26, 1927; AGN: DT, Statistics, 245/1 (1922) and 369/2 (1923); for tenant activism in Mexico, see also Andrew Grant Wood, *Revolution in the Street: Women, Workers, and Urban Protest in Veracruz, 1870–1927* (Wilmington, 2001).

The industrialists, meanwhile, moved their families to higher ground, constructing sumptuous mansions on Obispado Hill. From their summit, they enjoyed cool summertime breezes, cleaner air, and a commanding view of the bustling industrial flatlands below.

Down there, where belching smokestacks punctuated the landscape, the rhythm of everyday life accelerated. Concrete replaced cobblestones on Monterrey's major thoroughfares. The first traffic lights appeared to accommodate the arrival of automobiles and jitney buses, which sped past bicyclists, mule-powered carts, and tramways on crowded city streets. Monterrey's once-tranquil sidewalks and plazas now teemed with vendors hawking lemonade, lottery tickets, and the latest news. The newly christened Madero Boulevard became a center of popular diversions, a site to which workers, their families, and teenagers flocked to eat, visit the cinema, or flirt with the opposite sex. Dozens of new theaters, arenas, and dance halls opened as well, offering workers access to a mass culture of American and Mexican movies, jazz music, boxing, and bullfights.[11] Life thus went on in the "Sultan of the North," as Monterrey's boosters began promoting the industrial city. As the years passed and life returned to normal, the industrial strife and radical promises ushered in by the revolution receded in the minds of many – albeit not all – *regiomontanos*.

By some accounts, the hopes and uncertainties borne by revolution receded quickly. One contemporary later claimed that, "one finds almost no reference to the Revolution in its immediate aftermath, not even in the political literature. Almost no one spoke of [it]."[12] The American consuls seconded his assessment. In 1920, one diplomat characterized the *regiomontanos* as a people "tired of revolutions." At the decade's close a successor reported that, "The people of Monterrey will accept almost anything in federal politics as long as it does not interfere with the stability of the manufacturing industries . . . or the satisfactory relations now existing between labor and employers." Nuevo León's political authorities viewed class harmony and industrial prosperity as interrelated processes. Indeed, immediately after the revolution's close, they had courted Henry Ford with economic incentives and the promise of a labor peace exceptional by Mexican standards.[13] Later in the decade, Governor Aarón Sáenz explained that, "our labor relations . . . without doubt the best in the Republic . . . owe principally to the culture of the workers and the progressive spirit of Nuevo

11 Alfonso Ayala Duarte, *Músicos y música popular en Monterrey, 1900–1940*, (Monterrey, 1998), 91–143; José P. Saldaña, *Monterrey de 1920 a 1930 con la tónica de "el elemento sano"* (Monterrey, 1967).

12 Vizcaya Canales, *Los orígines de la industrialización*, 142.

13 First consul cited in Saragoza, *The Monterrey Elite*, 120; Balch, Dec. 20, 1929, SD 812.00 NL/3; Governor Zambrano to Henry Ford, Aug. 6, 1918, AGENL: Industria y Comercio, 2/11; *El Porvenir*, Dec. 2, 1923.

León's employers." Sáenz admitted that industrial relations "may have been lightly and fleetingly disturbed [after the revolution]." But this resulted from "outside elements underhandedly stirring up the disputes." By the late 1920s, "the reigning harmony between workers and businessmen" marked the point of departure for "the constant growth of new industries, the development of existing ones . . . and, most importantly, steady work [for all]." By Sáenz's account, local industrial prosperity translated into the highest working-class living standards in Mexico. Furthermore, the renowned "regiomontano business spirit helped confront and resolve" the economic ill's of the entire republic.[14] Political dignitaries, industrialists, and a good many unionists persistently echoed this discourse of class harmony and industrial patriotism.

Many observers agreed with what they heard. When the editor of *The Nation* visited the steel mill during his mid-decade tour of Mexico he found the operatives to be "fully satisfied with conditions there." "True," he observed, "[the Fundidora] has done everything for its workers – gardens, schools, sports fields, a model dairy – but in other cases benevolence alone has proved far from successful." The American therefore credited the steel mill's moderate union leaders for a state of industrial peace that contrasted markedly with what he witnessed in the central and Gulf Coast states.[15] Only the sharp ear heard a false note in the serenade of industrial boosterism. The Mexican left saw through the benevolent facade of paternalism to its more coercive underside. Upon returning to his hometown in 1927, communist labor organizer Valentín Campa found that "the industrial workers were very repressed." He recalled that, "both the steel mill and the Garza Sada's factories were already using advanced Yankee methods to obstruct unionism. The few truly independent unions were weak, except for the railroad brotherhoods."[16] Organized labor blamed its relative weakness on the state government's failure to enforce the labor law, which became the "laughing stock" of the city's industrialists.[17] Not until the 1930s, however, would political rulers in Mexico City agree publicly. In the meantime, they devoted their limited resources less to social reform and more to economic reconstruction and the cultural uplift of the Mexican masses. Mexico's new ruling class found developments in Monterrey much to their approval.

Education played an early and key role in the revolutionary projects of economic development and cultural engineering. Nuevo León's authorities

14 AGENL: *Informe del Gobernador Aarón Sáenz, 1927–1928*, 13; *Informe . . . Sáenz, 1928/29*, 19.
15 Ernest Gruening, *Mexico and its Heritage* (New York, 1928), 354.
16 Valentín Campa, *Mi testimonio: memorias de un comunista mexicano* (Mexico City, 1978), 39.
17 Federación Regional de Sociedades Obreras to President Obregón, Jan. 7, 1923, AGN: Presidentes 407-M-13.

distinguished their state for the scope and success of its public education system. Census figures backed their claims. Between 1921 and 1930, Monterrey's literacy rate climbed from 59 to 77 percent, among the highest rates in the relatively literate North.[18] The city's expanding public school system was as much a product of the revolution as Nuevo León's long-term commitment to industrialization. As we saw earlier, local authorities coupled youth education to a vocational night school program geared toward the "urgent need to make expert workers . . . for this essentially industrial city." First-year enrollment exceeded 700 worker-students and, by 1926, more than 2,000 men and women attended evening classes in the "mechanical arts and trades."[19] Two years later, local industrialists helped finance the costs of the new Escuela Industrial Obregón, the sprawling vocational school that covered three city blocks between the steel mill and the glassworks. As Governor Sáenz proclaimed at the school's inauguration, "Monterrey's industries will no longer face the difficult job of instructing their own workers in the tasks with which they are entrusted [nor the need] to bring in competent personnel from abroad to initiate new industries."[20] Public schools did not simply respond to the industrialists' demand for skilled labor. As elsewhere in Mexico, they served to transform working-class culture. Local authorities offered to "help the men of our workshops and factories by converting them from illiterates into conscious citizens who know how to read, write, and count with the same agility as students from schools for the rich."[21] Despite the rhetoric, the public schools represented more than a top-down cultural engineering project. They marked a wedding of elite interests and popular demand for vocational training.

Monterrey's largest employers also earned good grades for their systems of industrial paternalism. Their corporate labor policies neatly complimented the cultural project conceived by the "Sonoran Dynasty" government of the 1920s. Like their fellow northerners who ran that government, the *regiomontano* industrialists endeavored to shape their workers into hardworking, clean-living, and productive citizens. They constructed hygienic housing, promoted "modern" sports, and trained their operatives in the industrial arts. They also extended their efforts into company schools. In addition to athletics and vocational training, the steel mill's Escuela Acero offered bathing facilities, provided regular medical exams, and even developed a savings plan for its employees' children. The political and intellectual

---

18 AGN: DT, Statistics, 1919, 166/2; Secretaría de la Economía Nacional, *Quinto censo de la población*, 47–48.
19 AGENL: *Informe del Gobernador Juan M. García, 1921*, 18; *Informe del Gobernador Jerónimo Siller, 1926–1927*, 16–17.
20 AGENL: *Informe del Gobernador Aarón Sáenz, 1928–1929*, xi–xiii, 132.
21 AGENL: *Informe del Gobernador Jerónimo Siller, 1926–1927*, 16–17.

elite of the nation regarded such endeavors as modern, patriotic, and worthy of official support. During one 1924 visit the secretary of education, José Vasconcelos, praised paternalism and hailed Monterrey as the ideal model for the future of urban Mexico.[22] By the end of the decade the government itself had begun to replicate the *regiomontanos'* corporate practices, from the sponsorship of athletic leagues to the development of worker housing. Meanwhile, the local elite's assiduous boosterism carried the message of harmony and progress to all who would listen, from the local middle and working classes to the corridors of power in Mexico City.

The industrialists understood well that benevolence was not only good for business. It became an effective means to accumulate political capital as well. Along those lines, the city's leading employers developed a host of civic and philanthropic activities. The Fundidora, for instance, generated significant local fanfare when it donated and erected one hundred "elegant light poles" along Madero Boulevard. Cuauhtémoc supported community improvement projects in the neighborhood surrounding the brewery. Both companies also sponsored parades and regional expositions, hosted visiting presidential dignitaries, and offered the use of their facilities for athletic events and the annual Fall Fair. The women of the prominent Garza Sada family did their part as well, raising funds for the Red Cross, sponsoring toy drives for poor children, and patronizing the fine arts.[23] Such endeavors elevated the industrial elite's status in local society.

Throughout the 1920s, the press played a key role in shaping the perceptions that literate *regiomontanos* shared of themselves and their city. As part of their broader effort to promote class harmony, Monterrey's industrial elite portrayed hard work, thrift, and industriousness as traits shared by *regiomontanos* of all socioeconomic backgrounds. Civic and political leaders persistently reminded local citizens that their city was Mexico's preeminent industrial center. It was a city where all citizens, regardless of their economic status, claimed working-class origins, from the well-heeled elites to politicians courting the labor vote. Local boosters promoted the benefits of industry and the dignity of work during civic celebrations. Monterrey's annual Fall Fair mixed baseball and rodeos with tours of the Obregón Industrial School and local factories.[24] Visitors to the exhibition halls marveled at the products of local workers' labor, from expertly crafted brews to hand-blown glassware to precision valves. Tours of the brewery and steel mill became mandatory itinerary for presidential visitors. The dignity of manual labor was promoted ceaselessly, while the bearer of rough and calloused

---

22 Escuela Acero in AGN: DT, 1923, 598/5; Vasconcelos speech in *El Porvenir*, June 5, 1924.
23 AGENL: *Informe del Gobernador Juan M. García, 1921*; *El Porvenir*, May 7, 1923, July 8, 1926; Saragoza, *The Monterrey Elite*, 136–37, 145–47.
24 *El Sol*, Monterrey, Oct. 1, 1932.

hands could display them with pride. The mainstream press also addressed issues they deemed "important to the workingmen," whom the editors considered "a vital part of our readership." They thus mixed articles on the mechanical arts with stories on "the truth about the socialist doctrine." Workers who read them learned that "Carlos" Marx, the famous "salon socialist," came from the "well-accommodated middle class" and never knew "the experience of manual labor."[25]

Monterrey's leading daily, *El Porvenir*, betrayed the industrialists' vision of a postrevolutionary future of order and progress. Its editors appropriately launched the 1920s with the first of many reports on Monterrey's "Great Industries." They found it "just and natural" to inaugurate the series with the Cuauhtémoc Brewery, by then a "seal of pride for the entire [northern] frontier."[26] The report, "There Have Never Been Strikes at the Brewery," established a blueprint for local industrial boosterism. Readers were reminded of Cuauhtémoc's local ownership and the threat posed to the company – and thus Monterrey's economy – by government taxation. The article then outlined the industry's role in "the moral and intellectual development of society." The brewery provided employment to 1,500 local workers. The daily work regime "tempered the character and sharpened the faculties" of its employees. Steady wages and paternalistic benefits "assured the family's well-being." In the editors' view, "the operatives have always been content with the wages they enjoy and the treatment they receive." The brewery thus stood as a pillar of class harmony in a city just recovering from its first bout of industrial strife. Indeed, the boosters triumphed, "the [brewery] workers have not even lent an ear to the agitators who come to Monterrey." Through their promotion of employer benevolence, the boosters hoped to keep the agitators away for years to come.

Five years later, when the 1922 steel workers' strike seemed a distant memory, *El Porvenir* could present the Fundidora in a similar light. A new series, "Monterrey: Industrial and Industrious," outlined Monterrey steel's contribution to national reconstruction. It then enumerated a list of nonwage incentives that the company's altruism had inspired. "The great regiomontano business has not only satisfied the workers' aspirations but has showered [benefits] upon them . . . due not to the pressures of the workers, but spontaneously, anticipating their every demand." This became the dominant discourse on industry and labor. Monterrey's progressive employers forecasted their workers' needs. They revised their managerial strategies accordingly. Their benevolence then set the standard for other industrialists and Mexican labor legislators as well. For the steel workers, that

25 *El Porvenir*, Feb. 2, 1919.
26 *El Porvenir*, Apr. 16–18, 1920.

meant free housing, schools, medical treatment, and so forth. Furthermore, working conditions at the mill "[left] nothing to be desired," matching "the most advanced industries in the United States or Europe." The system produced visible results, *El Porvenir* concluded, for the steel workers "are no longer simply dispersed and anonymous entities. They now constitute a by all means respectable nucleus within this city's laboring class." Labor militance thus gave way to working-class respectability. For many *regiomontanos*, the press's persistent correlation between industrial strife and the designs of outside agitators made sense, for militancy ran against the respectable grains of local working-class culture. *El Porvenir*'s self-censorship of local conflicts and sensational, front-page reporting of labor violence elsewhere drove the point home succinctly.[27]

The Democratic Principles of Our Revolution

Throughout the 1920s, organized labor contested the elite's efforts to shape popular thought and action through their practices of paternalism and control of the local media. While lacking privileged access to the press and radio, which they regarded as key weapons in the industrialists' antiunion arsenal, local labor militants broadcast their message through pamphlets, labor rallies, and popular theater. They attracted large and captive audiences of workers during the Sunday afternoon street meetings they staged on bustling Madero Boulevard.[28] Activists used such impromptu forms of propaganda to speak their languages of class, revolution, and constitutionalism to an audience that included both local workers and the government officials whom they expected to defend labor's rights. While their politics contrasted markedly, the *regiomontano* labor militants also shared a common regional identity with their more conservative opponents, the activist workers who organized cooperative societies and led the Steel Unions. Indeed, militants distinguished themselves as exemplary *regiomontano* workers as well.

Since before the revolution, civic boosters had lauded the region's working classes for being industrious, hard working, and orderly. Contemporary visitors often agreed. A decade after the armed insurgency, one "outside observer" who visited the steel mill noted of Monterrey that, "Its workers, in general, are not like those of other regions of the country. The regiomontano workers read, study, and stay on top of the events that stir the nation."[29] Another Mexican visitor, a "southern journalist," toured the city's working-class districts and concluded that "a different rooster crows up here." He

27 *El Porvenir*, Apr. 12, 1926.
28 Palacios interview; Campa, *Mi testimonio*, 40.
29 *CYPSA*, Feb. 20, 1932.

lauded the *regiomontanos* for their "steady work . . . clean homes . . . [and] money in their savings accounts." He found them "dressed like the '*gente de razón*' and, what's more, living like [the middle class] rather than animals drunk on mezcal." For those reasons, workers could "have as much right as the captains of industry to figure among the upright creators of regiomontano prosperity."[30] Retired union militants themselves distinguish the local proletariat for being "more cultured" than workers elsewhere. From their point of view, the assertion reflects nothing more than the pride and dignity they derived from their superior levels of skill and education.[31]

But as we saw in earlier chapters the activist workers who edited company magazines derived political implications from the regionalist discourse. Regionalism promoted class harmony. Much like the industrialists, blue-collar *regiomontanos* focused their lives on work and family, finding little time or sympathy for the destructive ideas promoted by "outside agitators." As company ideologues at the steel mill reminded the operatives, "their love of work is a common virtue among those who wear the regiomontano seal." Most importantly, "among our workers there does not exist the unjust radical ambitions that have created so many difficulties in other regions of the country."[32] Labor relations in Monterrey were in fact stable and harmonious by the standards of 1920s Mexico. The city never experienced the battles for supremacy that generated fatal labor violence between Catholic, communist, and progovernment unions in Puebla, Tampico, and Guadalajara.[33] Those tragic conflicts had much less to do with "radical ambitions" than political power, personal ambition, and religious passion. But their absence from Monterrey reflected a level of industrial peace that was as much a byproduct of paternalism as the influential role of those workers who steered the rank and file away from militant unionism.

The railwaymen, artisans, and metal workers who dominated the city's principal labor central manifested their own acceptance of a regional working-class identity. These militants prided themselves for their northern heritage, their level of culture, and the order with which they conducted their affairs. But they did so in a manner that contested mainstream definitions of working-class respectability. During the 1921 national railroad strike, for instance, unionists coupled their own notions of "honor" to respect for union pickets. Over the following years they would reward those who displayed a "spirit of struggle" during that strike with special

30 Cited by Saldaña, *Constuctores de Monterrey*, 117.
31 Castañeda interview.
32 *Colectividad*, July 27, 1930.
33 Gregory Crider, "Material Struggles: Workers' Strategies during the Institutionalization of the Revolution in Atlixco, Puebla, Mexico," (Ph.D. diss., University of Wisconsin, 1996); Santiago, "Huasteca Crude"; Barry Carr, *El movimiento obrero y la política en México, 1910–1929* (Mexico City, 1974), 194–212.

diplomas upon their retirement.[34] In the mid-1920s, these homegrown radicals wrote to President Obregón to protest "countless violations of the democratic principles of our revolution." They enumerated such "arbitrary acts" as the punitive dismissal of union organizers at the city's smelters, steel mill, and brewery. Contesting elite assertions to the reign of class harmony, they characterized local "managers, foremen, and servants of Capital . . . [as] the hateful enemies of the working class." "All of our efforts to realize the emancipation of our tyrannized class via legal channels have been exhausted," they warned. The failure to address these grievances "will carry grave consequences, even though we must honestly proclaim that the organized worker of the North is conscious of his actions, just, law abiding, and orderly."[35] These were the voices of the very trade unionists who allied with Monterrey's steel workers to protest the abrogation of their constitutional rights during the labor unrest of 1918–22. But as the 1920s progressed the former militants who led the Steel Unions articulated a vision of the revolution's meaning contrary to that of their former allies. Despite their common embracement of a regional identity, these politically active workers forged competing means of reaching a common end: the right to speak on behalf of Monterrey's working class.

One can only wonder what Adolfo Prieto meant when he proclaimed his ambition to shape his employees at the steel mill into the "genuine aristocracy of the national proletariat." But a core of blue-collar *regiomontanos* – be they militant railwaymen or moderate steel workers – manifested certain characteristics once ascribed by British historians to a "labor aristocracy."[36] They were literate, politically active, and relatively affluent masters of their trades who aspired to respectability within local society. These men enjoyed relative security of employment, dressed well, owned their own homes, and earned the admiration of fellow workers. The railway unionist Valentín Campa, for example, earned the respect of his "semiliterate" workmates for the mere fact that he finished secondary school while they attended "three to four years at best." In the neighborhoods that blossomed around

34 *El Porvenir*, Feb. 27, 1921, Apr. 15, 1926.

35 Federación Regional de las Sociedades Obreras to President Obregón, Jan. 7, 1923, AGN: Presidentes, 407-M-13.

36 In the traditional historiographical view, the labor aristocracy theory held that a "cult of respectability" among skilled tradespeople served to divide labor and smother the presumed radicalism of the nineteenth-century British working class. As the debate evolved, historians argued that workers who fit the aristocratic mold could prove as likely to collaborate with employers as to spearhead radical labor politics. Their respectability thus "consisted essentially in the way they lived" rather than in their political dispositions. See Eric Hobsbawm, *Labouring Men* (London, 1964), 272–315; John Foster, *Class Struggle and the Industrial Revolution* (London, 1974), esp. 203–50; Neville Kirk, *The Growth of Working-Class Reformism in Mid-Victorian Britain* (Urbana, 1984); Stuart Macintyre, *Little Moscows: Communism and Working-Class Militancy in Interwar Britain* (London, 1980), esp. 82–89 (quoted above).

the steel mill, skilled craftsmen merited their own prestige for being the first Mexicans to master their trades. Such workers' success on the baseball field and talent as musicians further enhanced their reputations within their communities. So did their positions as leaders of cooperative societies or trade unions. Skilled *regiomontano* tradesmen also played visible roles in civic society. Many hobnobbed with local merchants in Monterrey's Masonic lodges. They often shared the stage with the local dignitaries during visits by Mexican presidents or the opening of regional expositions. And several served in political office at the municipal, state, and federal levels.[37] The role of these activist workers within *regiomontano* society earned them respect among their younger or lesser-skilled peers, be they sons of Monterrey or recent migrants. That is why employers like Prieto pinned their hopes of moral improvement on these labor aristocrats.

Whether they acted in collaboration with or in opposition to the industrialists, Monterrey's activist workers employed their influence to broadcast their competing visions and values to other blue-collar *regiomontanos*. In the sense articulated by an Italian contemporary, the socialist activist and theorist Antonio Gramsci, they operated as *"dirigentes intelectuales,"* providing shop-floor and community leadership to the working class. They drew upon languages from both the Porfirian past and the revolutionary present to fashion the new political discourses used to mobilize workers into distinct forms of collective action.[38] They could do so because they possessed better education, organizing experience, oratorical skills, or simply a greater ambition to assume the risks inherent to activism. Many did so to fight for social justice. Others were motivated by opportunism, seeing union leadership as a means of escaping factory labor for a political career within the new ruling party or the expanding government bureaucracy. Their capacity to organize, direct, and articulate the grievances and aspirations of fellow workers owed to the trust, respect, or even fear they engendered among their workmates. Monterrey's labor activists were not cast in a singular functional mold. As we saw in previous chapters, such veteran workers at the steel mill and brewery discovered allies among white-collar workers, collaborated in the practices of paternalism, and effectively steered their workmates away from the world of organized labor. But they would be challenged by workmates in the ranks and by a growing community of organized labor activists who contested workers' loyalty to their employers.

---

37 *El Porvenir*, June 9, 1926; González Caballero, *La Maestranza*, 29–36; Campa, *Mi testimonio*, 13–26; Gabrial Cárdenas-Coronado, "'Los Labores' en los 1920s" in Celso Garza Guajardo, ed., *Historia de nuestros barrios* (Monterrey, 1995); González Caballero interview.

38 Antonio Gramsci, *Selections from the Prison Notebooks*, eds. Quintin Hoare and Geoffrey Nowell Smith (New York, 1971), 93; this argument also builds upon Steve Feierman, *Peasant Intellectuals: Anthropology and History in Tanzania* (Madison, 1990).

Organized labor suffered more setbacks than success in the 1920s and early 1930s. But the movement persisted, remained vibrant in the public sphere, and nurtured a culture of resistance to the paternalistic pretensions of the industrial elite and their working-class allies.

The Working Class Has Its Own Heroes

One product of the revolution from which Monterrey's industrialists could not shield their workers was May Day, Mexico's official labor holiday since 1918. A brief analysis of Labor Day festivities illuminates the factional divides among the city's activist workers and the competing discourses they fashioned over the course of the 1920s. The festivities surrounding May Day followed a standard pattern, albeit one with important variations as the decade progressed.[39] A worker on horseback headed each year's parade, bearing the imposing red-and-black flag of labor solidarity. Behind him rode a finely attired pack of bicyclists, followed in turn by the local Musicians' Union performing renditions of the "Himno Internacional." Then came union workers, numbering up to 10,000, marching silently through the narrow streets of downtown Monterrey. The city's railroad workers dominated newspaper reports and photos of the events. Nattily dressed in coat, tie, and fedora, they proudly fell in line behind the standard bearers of their respective craft unions. Following the railroaders marched metal workers, factory operatives, and artisans dressed in traditional proletarian garb: *overols* and baggy workers' caps. Equally conspicuous were the Working Women's Resistance League and members of the city's Tenants Union, whose female activists dressed resplendently in bright red blouses and flowing black skirts. Socialist students, teachers, and other middle-class *regiomontanos* active or sympathetic with the labor movement turned out as well.

Above the procession sailed banners identifying the marchers' affiliations or proclaiming more fiery slogans: "Labor unions are the bulwark of the honorable worker"; "Justice is neither purchased nor begged for on the knees"; "Eternal hatred towards the Yankee Bourgeoisie." The marches passed by the state capital, where government dignitaries saluted Monterrey's workers from the balcony above. The parades often passed by the United States Consulate as well. There, workers paused to hear activists promote different forms of solidarity with American labor, from boycotts of imports lacking the union label to warnings against the labor contractors who would arrive to Monterrey to recruit Mexican strikebreakers. On other occasions, activists organized solidarity rallies for imprisoned American labor leaders. In 1927, they turned out to protest the coming execution of Sacco and Vanzetti, the

39 The following account is based on *El Porvenir*, May 2, 1919, May 2, 1923, May 2, 1924, May 2, 1926.

Italian-born anarchists who had lived in their midst but a decade before.[40] The daytime events concluded with speeches at Monterrey's Alameda Park, where speakers addressed issues more immediate to local workers, from the need of stricter enforcement of labor laws to demands for rent control. In the evening, workers and their families gathered in local theaters for the customary *velada*, the literary-musical events that journalist John Reed once described as "the conventional and respectable way of celebrating anything [in Mexico]." The workers' custom of closing the day with a salutary discharge of their pistols elicited reprimands from the press ("the day's only disorder"). But local editors generally lauded the "orderly and peaceful" festivities as "a demonstration of the already traditional culture of the regiomontano laborites."[41]

The organizers of the May Day festivities articulated a discourse of international labor solidarity as a means of promoting workers' sense of class identity. Addressing a 1924 rally, one speaker thus admonished the gathering to teach their children of the "martyred workers ... who made our extraordinary history." The younger generations would thereby appreciate "that the working class has its own heroes just like those taught in the schools to instill love for the fatherland."[42] During the keynote address at that evening's *velada*, a railway shop worker recounted the struggle for the eight-hour day in the United States. The movement that May Day honors culminated in 1886 with a general strike, widespread urban violence, and the arrest and execution of eight Chicago anarchists for their alleged role in the bombing deaths of seven police officers. Another speaker thus followed with a poem, "The Chicago Gallows," to honor those "eight sacrificial martyrs who bequeathed to the worker his daily rest." On May Day in Monterrey, names like Parsons, Fischer, and Schweib received more discursive attention than Juárez or Madero. Indeed, the names of the martyred anarchists arguably enjoyed wider recognition in "Mexico's Chicago" than in its North American namesake. As the decade progressed, these evocations of international labor solidarity masked the local activists' division into the progovernment and radical factions evident elsewhere in Mexico.

Meanwhile, the most consequential division among Monterrey's activist workers developed between the city's militant unionists and their upstart rivals from the cooperative societies. The differences manifested themselves on multiple fronts. The militants perceived Mexican society as one torn by class struggle and the language of class soaked their written and spoken texts. They also advocated temperance reform and stronger labor legislation. On the other side, organizations like the Cuauhtémoc Society preached

40 *El Porvenir*, Aug. 22, 1922; Campa, *Mi testimonio*, 40.
41 John Reed, *Insurgent Mexico* (New York, 1983; 1914), 11; *El Porvenir*, May 2, 1923.
42 *El Porvenir*, May 2, 1924.

class harmony and orchestrated resistance to dry laws. They found allies among the most moderate of railwaymen, the Conductors Union. While the conductors considered themselves "the nerve center of the railroads," they remained independent from Mexico's federation of railway unions. Indeed, they persistently refused to back strikes by Monterrey shop workers "because we lack neither discipline nor love for the homeland."[43] The conductors shared their perspective with the brewery workers in a 1923 letter to the Cuauhtémoc Society. While organized labor was lobbying the state to strengthen and enforce labor legislation, the conductors argued that "first comes duty, then come the rights." Among those duties was the patriotic support of national reconstruction. They therefore condemned "unjust petitions and violent strikes" as an obstacle to "the progress of industry and commerce." Furthermore, the conductors pledged to "disavow flags of any color except those of our beloved national banner" and concluded that, "the best proof that we can give of our culture, is the respect that we share towards our ally, Capital."[44] Monterrey's more conservative labor activists thus countered the language of class and revolution with both patriotic and regionalist discourses to mobilize rank-and-file workers against militant unions.

The polarization of Monterrey's working-class associations had crystallized in 1927. Parallel events to commemorate labor's holiday exemplified the division. The city's leading newspapers sponsored one celebration in Cuauhtémoc Park on the Saturday preceding May Day, which inconveniently fell on a working Monday. The festivities attracted 10,000 *regiomontanos*, "representing," the sponsors boasted, "all the city's social classes." The region's leading industrialists, politicians, and military authorities attended, mingling with managers, operatives, and their families. Baseball games, patriotic speeches, and class harmony were the order of the day. The event's organizers gloated that "not a single discordant note was sounded on this great day in the world of labor."[45] Two days later, on the evening of May 1, Monterrey's trade unionists gathered at the Mechanics Union assembly hall. Posters announcing the event juxtaposed it to the past weekend's festivities: "It is our duty to energetically protest the outrages suffered by the Working Class, and more so than ever now that the eternal mystifiers are attempting to diminish the true meaning of Labor Day through their illicit alliance with Capital."[46] The fact that the event transpired during the 1927 railroad strike added a solemn and militant flavor to the proceedings.

43 *El Porvenir*, Dec. 25, 1920, Mar. 3, 1923.
44 Unión de Conductores, Maquinistas, Garroteros y Fogoneros to Sociedad Cuauhtémoc in *Trabajo y Ahorro*, Oct. 15, 1923.
45 *El Sol*, May 2, 1927; *El Porvenir*, May 2, 1926; *Trabajo y Ahorro*, May 7, 1927.
46 AMM: Asociaciones y Sindicatos, 1927.

Indeed, the evening began with an appropriate social drama, "Love and the Strike," performed by the "Martyrs of Chicago" theater troupe. The railroaders' strike committee concluded the night with an update on the increasingly violent labor dispute. The strike carried crucial implications because since the turn of the century, the city's railroaders had largely defined the institutional parameters of organized labor in Monterrey.

Railroad Workers and Unionism in Monterrey

The historiography of Mexican labor during the 1920s largely follows the conflictive rise and precipitous fall of the nation's first major labor federation, the Regional Confederation of Mexican Workers (CROM).[47] Whether they adopt a national or regional focus, scholars analyze the contestation for power between the Mexico City-based CROM and its erstwhile challengers in the capital and the provinces. The federal government saw in the labor central an ally in its struggle to centralize political power and check labor disputes so as to promote economic development. CROM leaders assisted that endeavor by promoting cooperation and responsibility as the essence of its moderate style of unionism. Through this tactical alliance, the CROM secured key political posts for its leaders, often won significant concessions for its affiliated workers, and became the most politically influential labor central in Latin America. But the legendary corruption of the CROM leadership and the gangsterism and strike breaking it used against its rivals tended to discredit the labor central's legitimacy in the minds of many workers. As regional labor studies advance, the CROM's provincial weakness relative to its political muscle in Mexico City becomes increasingly apparent.[48] That fragility was clear by 1928, when the CROM went into rapid decline after President Calles stripped it of his government's patronage. The labor central's ephemeral presence in Monterrey exemplifies the trend.

Local unionists had mistrusted the CROM leadership since the time the labor central failed to support the metal workers' strikes in 1920 and 1922. By mid-decade, the CROM's limited inroads in Monterrey had waned considerably. In 1926, as the labor central reached its apogee in Mexico, one Monterrey textile local complained that CROM officials responded "with much nervousness and little action" when the mill fired its leaders.[49] Within a year, the CROM had been eclipsed in Monterrey by its rivals on the left.

47 Carr, *El movimiento obrero*, 127–265; José Rivera Castro, *La clase obrera en la historia de México: En la presidencia de Plutarco Elías Calles* (Mexico City, 1983); Meyer, "Mexico in the 1920s," 227–32.
48 See Jaime Tamayo and Patricia Valles, eds., *Anarquismo, socialismo, y sindicalismo en las regiones* (Guadalajara, 1993).
49 Sindicato de Obreros y Obreras "La Fama" to CROM, Mar. 26, 1926, AGENL: Trabajo – Conciliación y Arbitraje, 2/31.

These self-described "anarcho-communists" employed the soap box and printing press to rally working-class opposition to both the CROM and the Calles government. One flyer that appeared on local streets charged that, "Yesterday's revolutionaries have become today's dictators." It decried Calles and his CROM allies for "serving as the guardians" of foreign capital and corrupting the ideals of the revolution. As another broadsheet protested, "In the times of the Porfirian dictatorship, the people were tyrannized in the name of the comfortable classes; now tyranny acts in the name of freedom and the people." For the anarcho-communists, the most powerful force behind the subversion of revolutionary dreams remained "the four letters symbolic of working-class treason: C-R-O-M." Indeed, workers in those days fashioned a new meaning for the acronym: "Calles Roba al Obrero Mexicano" (Calles Robs the Mexican Worker).[50] The great railroad strike of 1926–27 would drive a factional spike between militants tied to the Mexican Communist Party and the CROMistas whose survival depended upon government patronage. The split between communist and progovernment activists endured for decades.

The railroaders shaped the early trajectory of the Mexican labor movement. In Nuevo León, where some 3,000 linemen, shop workers, and station clerks resided, they spearheaded organized labor from the 1890s to the 1930s. To what does the predominance of the railroad workers within the union movement owe? As in other industrializing societies, their sector was the first to undergo large-scale unionization, a project largely completed by the close of the revolution. The mobile nature of their trade allowed the railroaders to spread the gospel of unionism to other industries, notably mining. Moreover skilled union railwaymen were often recruited by other industries, from Gulf Coast oil refineries to the factories of Monterrey. Thus did local craft unions first organized in Monterrey's railway shops draw membership from local smelters, the steel mill, and the building trades.[51] Subsequently, the meeting hall of the Unión de Mécanicos Mexicanos served as the political and cultural center of the labor movement. The role played by Monterrey's railroaders in the steel and smelter strikes of 1918–22 revealed another characteristic of these workers: their self-perception as natural leaders of the Mexican working class. Indeed, the statutes of the Confederation of Transport and Communication Workers established "the economic and moral improvement of all Mexican workers" as a key objective.[52] They

---

50 Such antigovernment propaganda was brought to the attention of authorities in Mexico City: AGN: Presidents, 407-L-27. Dionisio Palacios recalled another play on the CROM acronym: "Como Roba Oro Morones," or "See how [CROM leader] Morones steals our money."

51 Santiago, "Huasteca Crude," ch. 6; Campa, *Mi testimonio*, 38–42.

52 Marcelo N. Rodea, "La huelga de 1926–27" in Centro de Estudios del Movimiento Obrero y Socialista, *Cuatro sindicatos de industria* (Sinaloa, 1988), 23–24.

would accomplish the task through union activism and political action. Not coincidentally, no other local industry produced so many noteworthy labor activists, many of whom went on to national prominence.

The railroad strike of 1926–27 marked a watershed not only for the development of railroad unionism but the entire labor movement in Monterrey. The struggle's political consequences and the legal implications of its settlement thus deserve brief attention. The national strike began as a protest against layoffs at the National Railways shops. It led to labor violence throughout Mexico as CROM strikebreakers replaced independent union workers, unionists sabotaged the lines, and hundreds of federal troops occupied key railroad shops and stations. Government officials justified their actions by blaming the conflict on Communists and foreign radicals "whose actions in no way reflect the workers' true feelings." For our purposes, the events surrounding the strike are less important than its consequences.[53] The breaking of the strike instilled in union leaders the idea of superceding their craft divisions by organizing an industrywide union of railway workers. In Monterrey, government repression and the commitment displayed by communist militants during the strike also helped attract many railroaders into the fledgling Mexican Communist Party (PCM). Their militant stance – coupled with CROM strike breaking – earned the Communists' reputation for honesty and integrity. The Monterrey branch subsequently grew into one of the party's strongholds of blue-collar support due to the railroaders' integration of other workers into the PCM.[54]

For many local activists, the strike discredited the progovernment CROM once and for all. One name in particular went down in the collective memory of local militants as a traitor to their struggle, that of a young CROM bureaucrat then employed by the secretary of industry: Vicente Lombardo Toledano. This would have important implications in the 1930s, when Lombardo ascended to the leadership of Mexico's principal labor federation. By then, Monterrey's railway workers would still harbor a keen distrust of the man they regarded as a government strikebreaker. The 1927 railroad strike also led to another development of long-term consequence. In the conflict's aftermath, the Mexican Supreme Court struck down the secretary of industry's right to intervene and declare the strike illegal because CROM officials dominated the government ministry. In response, the CROM's national leaders, notably Lombardo, worked with the Calles government to create a federal labor board with jurisdictional status over industries that operated under federal concessions. The ruling set an important precedent because it removed the railroad, mining, oil,

53 Rodea, "La huelga," 14; for the strike's development in Monterrey see AGENL: Trabajo – Conciliación y Arbitraje, 2/24.
54 Campa, *Mi testimonio*, 34–39.

and metallurgical industries from the oversight of state labor boards and placed them under federal jurisdiction. The ruling thus held implications for Monterrey's steel and smelter workers, as we shall later see. As expected, the new federal labor board declared the railroaders' strike illegal and thereby permitted thousands of CROM strikebreakers to be hired. For Monterey's communist railroaders and their allies on the labor left, the decision at once justified and hardened their aversion to government intervention in industrial disputes. The consequences became evident in the late 1920s, when local unionists increasingly abandoned political alliances and the bureaucratic channels of government labor mediation in favor of direct action. They did so because, by the end of the decade, the very labor code that these working-class activists had lobbied the state to write would be subverted by the shrewd legal maneuvering of Monterrey's industrial elite.

The Freedom to Work

The 1920s proved to be lean years for unionism in Monterrey. This was especially so given the union effervescence of the 1910s and in comparison to national trends. Sectors that became well organized elsewhere – like printing, electric and streetcar workers – remained nonunion in Monterrey. Even Nuevo León's textile workers, organized since the early 1910s, saw their unions broken through intimidation and attrition during the following decade. What caused the organizational decline and weakness of labor during the 1920s? Why did the achievements of the 1910s prove so ephemeral? One indication lies in the emergence of industrial paternalism. But not all workers simply abandoned their union rights for fringe benefits. Thus while the steel mill courted the loyalty of its trade unionists, most industrialists adhered to the policies of the Cuauhtémoc Brewery. That company stifled a 1924 organizing drive by firing dozens of activists. One year earlier, Monterrey Glassworks had suffocated its own labor problems by discharging more than sixty union members.[55] Employers no longer faced shortages of skilled labor. Indeed, throughout the 1920s, the local labor market was "inundated by thousands of workers from Tampico and other parts of the Republic . . . attracted by Monterrey's [economic] boom."[56] Moreover, from organized labor's perspective, punitive dismissals struck fear in union organizers and demonstrated the limits to Mexican labor law. Guided by an initial determination to work through legal channels, Monterrey's labor activists attempted to overcome these more coercive antiunion strategies

---

55 AGN: DT, 650/10; 1923 glass strike in Chapter 7.
56 Migration from Tampico to Monterrey in AGN: Trabajo, 1921, 285/6, 313/5–9; AGENL: *Informe de Gobernador Aarón Sáenz, 1928–1929*, xix, 109 (quoted).

by forging alliances with Nuevo León's new political elite. Political action initially succeeded in pressuring local authorities to first implement, then strengthen and enforce a state labor code. By law, that labor code would satisfy the guidelines set out in Mexico's 1917 Constitution.

Assessing Mexican labor in the late 1920s, Marjorie Ruth Clark explained the gulf separating the country's advanced labor legislation from workplace reality. Workers benefitted from Article 123 "only as far as they have been able, through their own strength or through political intrigue . . . to secure enforcement of the laws." This American visitor understood that the 1917 Constitution did less to culminate a labor reform movement than to begin a new phase, the struggle to enforce compliance. She saw that, "It took the workers a very short time to realize that legal rights meant nothing if the government in power was determined not to grant such rights."[57] During the 1920s, Monterrey's working class never developed the degree of political clout captured by the workers of Veracruz, Puebla, or Tampico. Come election time, local politicos certainly courted the labor vote. In industrial Monterrey, a candidate's avowed working-class origins proved as important as one's status as a veteran of the revolution. But most politicians' populist posturing – "I, too, am the humble son of workers" – masked their real social backgrounds as sons of prominent local families.[58]

Local activists organized dozens of political parties during the decade. But outfits like the Defenders of the Proletariat, the Railroaders' Party, and the Worker-Peasant Socialist Party collapsed after each electoral season. Moreover, in the 1920s, the urban working-class vote proved less influential in statewide elections than a patronage network based in the countryside. Victory depended more upon a party's skills in the arts of electoral fraud than its capacity to articulate a program or mobilize the popular vote. The perennial charges of stolen ballots, jailed opponents, and coerced votes – confirmed by federal election observers – forced the Supreme Court to decide most electoral contests in Nuevo León.[59] Furthermore, the constant turnover of state and municipal officials inhibited labor's ability to cultivate reliable political allies. The same held true for the industrialists. They chafed at their inability to restore the political hegemony enjoyed before the revolution, when Governor Reyes bestowed lucrative tax concessions, checked labor activity, and lobbied their interests in Mexico City. But this dispersal of power did not result in a decline of managerial authority. Rather, political instability inhibited the establishment of a viable labor code and the mechanisms to enforce it.

---

57 Clark, *Organized Labor in Mexico*, 45, 53.
58 General Jerónimo Siller cited in *El Porvenir*, July 7, 1925; see also Governor Nicéforo Zambrano in *El Porvenir*, May 6, 1919.
59 AGN: Presidentes, 243-N2-G-2; AGN: DGG 2.331 D.L. (16) 103–108.

The authors of the 1917 Constitution bequeathed the responsibility of enforcing labor's rights to local authorities. Article 123's lead-off clause gave each state the ambiguous duty to design a labor code that conformed to both constitutional principles as well as "local conditions." Within months of its passage, union leaders in Monterrey were petitioning Congress to legislate such a labor law.[60] Six years passed before Nuevo León codified Article 123, the last of Mexico's more industrialized states to do so. The labor arbitration board that first convened in 1918 functioned sporadically thereafter, meeting at the governor's discretion to resolve industrial disputes. The nominal rights of greatest interest to workers – protection from punitive dismissals and occupational safety laws – became effective only gradually. Initial compliance with the law came through direct pressure by workers. The steel workers, for instance, won the eight-hour day and overtime pay – a significant achievement in that industry – during the 1918 strike. But their victory did not establish a pattern. Four years later, the federal government was still sending circulars to local industrialists begging their compliance with the basic precept of revolutionary labor law.[61]

Organized labor brought these shortcomings to the President Obregón's attention. They protested that, "All of our efforts [to promote reform] within legal channels have been useless, because neither the state's executive nor legislative powers will attend to our demands."[62] Under pressure from labor, the state did establish a permanent arbitration board in late 1922. But the labor court heard only thirty individual claims in 1923, arising mainly from punitive firings. A backlog of cases piled up as employer and government representatives alike failed to appear for hearings. Moreover, the board lacked formal operational statutes and binding authority. It thus remained, from labor's perspective, "a ridiculed barrel of laughs for the industrialists . . . who neither respect it nor accept its decrees."[63] Nuevo León was not unique in having an ineffective labor board. In a series of rulings during the early 1920s, Mexico's Supreme Court refused to permit such tribunals the right to effect binding settlements. In 1924, however, the court reversed its position and sanctioned the right of state legislators to grant the boards the binding authority they needed to be effective.[64]

---

60 Rojas, "Poder político," 108.
61 *El Porvenir*, Sep. 24, 1922; by way of comparison, U.S. Steel dropped the twelve-hour day in 1923 but offered no compensation for overtime (Cohen, *Making a New Deal*, 187).
62 Federación Regional de Sociedades Obreras (FRSO) to President Obregón, Jan. 7, 1923, AGN: Presidentes, 407-M-13.
63 *El Porvenir*, Aug. 16, 1922, Mar. 12, 1923, Dec. 21, 1923; AGENL: Trabajo – Conciliación y Arbitraje, 1/1; FRSO to Obregón, AGN: Presidentes, 407-M-13 (quoted).
64 Graciela Bensusán, "Construcción y desarrollo del derecho laboral," in *El obrero mexicano, Vol. 4: El derecho laboral*, ed., Pablo González Casanova (Mexico City, 1978), 9–72; Kevin Middlebrook, *The Paradox of Revolution: Labor, the State, and Authoritarianism in Mexico* (Baltimore, 1995), 58.

For organized labor in Monterrey, relief seemed to arrive with Governor Porfirio González. In late 1923, the Supreme Court awarded the revolutionary veteran a controversial electoral victory over Aarón Sáenz, the candidate backed by the industrial elite. The industrialists came to despise González. Their antipathy dated to his first stint as governor, in 1920, when the general attempted to coerce a $100,000 loan from wealthy *regiomontanos*. By mid-decade, his corrupt ways had assumed legendary status. According to the opposition, he skimmed tax revenues, murdered opponents, and oversaw smuggling and banditry rings during "his triumphal march to tyranny."[65] González thus acted like many military men who became governors during the 1920s. He used his office to enrich himself, satisfy his retainers, and stay in power. He did so with more ambition and venality than most. One foreign observer labeled him "probably the most dishonest governor in [Mexico's] twenty-eight states." From the outset, however, organized labor found an ally in González. His tenure coincided with the elections of several leftist labor militants to political office.[66] In his first act as governor, González outraged the industrialists by appointing his congressional labor allies to a committee charged with codifying a state labor code. They swiftly established a permanent labor mediation board with binding authority. Other clauses of Nuevo León's labor law set a minimum wage, sanctioned the right to strike, and to the further dismay of local business leaders, prohibited the employment of strikebreakers.[67]

A lawyer representing the steel mill protested the legislation to federal authorities. Since "a labor leader formulated the project," he claimed, the law "did not balance the rights of workers and employers," as the framers of the constitution intended. Rather, he went on, "one sees in it a marked hostility to capital, [which is] harmful to all." He protested the short time frame (five days) within which the labor board would hear and decide a case and the binding authority of its settlements. The lawyer complained that the tribunals would base their decisions upon "conscience, reason, and fairness" (as the constitution established), rather than legal precedent. Most alarming to the industrialists was the prohibition against strikebreakers. Not only did this deny labor the "freedom to work," itself a constitutional right; the decree would "hand the control of industry over to the workers . . . [which is] not an unfounded fear."[68] For this corporate lawyer, the 1922 Fundidora strike confirmed his concern. The role played by strikebreakers in the

---

65 Jerónimo Siller to President Calles, Dec. 16, 1925, AGN: Presidentes 243-N2-G-2.

66 Gruening, *Mexico and Its Heritage*, 468; Saragoza, *The Monterrey Elite*, 122–24; *El Porvenir*, Jan. 7, 1924.

67 "Ley Constitucional que Establece la Junta Central de Conciliación y Arbitraje," Jan. 24, 1924 in AGENL: Industria, Comercio y Trabajo, box 3.

68 Manuel González Garza to Secretary of Industry, Commerce, and Labor, Mar. 27, 1924, AGN: DT 813/4.

weakening of that movement two years earlier certainly influenced the clause's inclusion in the new state labor law.

Elite fears would be quickly if not so quietly dispelled. In mid-1925, a congressional opposition bloc organized a coup against González. They named an interim governor and constituted a rebel government in a local hotel. For several days thereafter, political gangs traded gunfire on downtown streets. González retained power, briefly. For the political street fighting coincided with President Calles's visit to Monterrey. The occasion was the marriage of his son, Plutarco Junior, to the sister of Aarón Sáenz, who was by then Mexico's secretary of foreign relations. The local elite feted the president with tours of their factories and lavish gifts for the newlyweds. The industrialists and Sáenz also used the occasion to lobby for Governor González's removal. Two months later, Calles ordered the corrupt general's ouster. In 1927, Sáenz himself won the governorship of Nuevo León with the enthusiastic endorsement of Monterrey's industrialists. This key player in the federal government promised to voice their concerns in Mexico City. To further ensure regional political stability in northeastern Mexico, President Calles assigned General Juan Andrew Almazán to command the region's military garrison. Much like Sáenz, Almazán soon became a "mainstay of elite social life." From the industrialists' perspective, "the long-awaited days of [prerevolutionary governor] Bernardo Reyes seemed at hand."[69]

Governor Sáenz did not disappoint. He shared the *regiomontano* elite's entrepreneurial spirit. In the revolution's aftermath, the Nuevo León sugar baron became a construction magnate. His company, Urban Development, Inc. (FYUSA), reaped great profits by winning public works contracts in Mexico City and Monterrey. During his tenure, FYUSA paved the streets, built new schools, and doggedly resisted its workers' right to organize. Immediately after his inauguration, Sáenz lifted state taxes on beer and commissioned a group of local businesspeople to rework the tax structure. To spark regional industrial growth, Sáenz also renewed the prerevolutionary system of tax concessions and incentives for both new developments and plant expansions.[70] But Sáenz did not only concern himself with his and the industrialists' prosperity. Unlike his fellow Nuevo León businessmen, he harbored no disdain for central government authority. In fact, as a rising star within that government, he embodied it.

69 *El Porvenir*, July 7–25, 1925; Saragoza, *The Monterrey Elite*, 124, 132–34 (quoted). Almazán would use his decade-long tenure in Monterrey to build an economic empire based on the highway construction and tourism industries.

70 Saragoza, *The Monterrey Elite*, 124–25; AGENL: *Informe del Gobernador Aarón Sáenz, 1928–1929*, 13; Sáenz's political career and his capacity to parlay his government connections into fabulous wealth are recounted by Nora Hamilton, *The Limits of State Autonomy: Post-Revolutionary Mexico* (Princeton, 1982), 87–90.

Since the end of the revolution, Sáenz had risen from the general staff of the Constitutionalist army to become a Nuevo León congressman, ambassador to Brazil, and secretary of foreign affairs. As part of President Calles's inner circle, he would be entrusted with the construction of the new National Revolutionary Party's political machine in Nuevo León.[71] He thus balanced the promotion of economic development with policies intended to win a measure of popular support for the ruling party. It was his government, for example, that inaugurated the Obregón Industrial School, much to the delight of Monterrey's unionists. As a Protestant and "enemy of the clergy," he also applied the government's anticlerical policies in Nuevo León, banishing a number of priests and giving the city's primary labor central the right to use one shuttered church as a union hall. But the very policy that sparked a civil war in west-central Mexico barely caused a ripple in more secular Monterrey. Religion played little discernible part in the locals' sense of regional identity. Nor did the Church dominate the social and cultural life of the city to the extent it did in other regions of Mexico.[72] Finally, local political authorities did not adopt the central government's policy of sponsoring trade unionism as it did in other regions. What Sáenz did promise the city's workers, however, was that under his watch the state's labor arbitration board would serve "eagerly, effectively . . . [and] impartially" to enforce their constitutional rights.[73]

The Spirit of the Constitution

Historians of Monterrey have suggested that a labor arbitration board meant to protect workers' interests served instead "as a key mechanism for controlling labor." Yet as one scholar of Mexican labor rightly asserts, "virtually nothing is known about the impact of these state-level labor codes" on industrial relations or organized labor.[74] As one of the few states to open its labor board archives to scholarly inquiry, Nuevo León offers a case study in how astute industrialists revised their managerial strategies as the government's capacity and willingness to regulate industrial relations increased. No other clause of the Mexican labor law provoked greater ire than that which limited employers' capacity to dismiss workers as a basic managerial prerogative. The law stipulated that an unjustly dismissed worker be either

71 On the 1927, 1928, and 1929 elections, during which the Calles-Sáenz political machine was consolidated in Nuevo León, see AGN: DGG 2.331 D.L. (16) 103–108.

72 Campa, *Mi testimonio*, 40; for the limited institutional presence of the Church or lay Catholic organizations in Nuevo León, see the figures in Jennie Purnell, *Popular Movements and State Formation in Revolutionary Mexico: The Agraristas and Cristeros of Michoacán* (Durham, NC, 1999), 92–98.

73 AGENL: *Informe del Gobernador Aarón Sáenz, 1927–1928*, 14.

74 Saragoza, *The Monterrey Elite*, 131; Middlebrook, *The Paradox of Revolution*, 344, fn. 24.

reinstated or rewarded severance equal to at least three months' wages. Management abhorred the measure for two reasons. They feared that the promise of job security would undermine labor discipline. It would also, they believed, limit their ability to discharge workers during economic downturns.[75]

But the same law provided employers with the very means to legally discharge troublesome workers, especially union activists. They paid for the privilege. But with their deep pockets, Monterrey's industrialists preferred severance pay to independent unions. In 1923, for example, Monterrey Glassworks squelched an organizing drive by firing and indemnifying more than sixty union sympathizers. A few examples sufficed. The workers learned that in exchange for union activism they would simply "get their time," as former operatives refer to the indemnities. Workers thus weighed the right to union representation against their desire for job security. Indeed, laid-off workers often preferred letters of good service to the short-term benefits of severance pay.[76] Union organizers recognized this unintended consequence of the law. In mid-1925, a national labor official protested "this fraudulent use of Article 123" to Nuevo León's governor. Citing the case of a Monterrey printer, he claimed that employers used the law to fire union sympathizers and charged that "this procedure contradicts the true spirit of the Constitution." Furthermore, he criticized the local labor authorities' failure to properly interpret the law. As the clause on arbitrary dismissals stated, he emphasized, "it remains the *worker's choice*" to accept indemnity or elect reinstatement. And so it did. But a Supreme Court ruling permitted employers to refuse a worker's reinstatement, and they invariably opted to do so. Not until 1936 would a more prolabor court briefly overturn the ruling.[77]

Local employers also channeled punitive dismissals through shop committees like those pioneered locally by the steel mill. With joint worker-management representation, these *comités de ajuste* ideally settled conflicts arising from departmental promotions, temporary layoffs, work-rule violations, or other issues "that the company places under their consideration." Nearly two-thirds of the steel workers' collective contract outlined the functioning of these "specialized labor boards." The statutes explicitly stipulated that neither union or nonunion workers could protest workplace grievances to government labor authorities. Moreover, resolutions handed down by the factory committees were binding and beyond the overriding

75 Bensusán, "Construcción y desarrollo del derecho laboral," 17.
76 Palacios interview; AGENL: JCA 2/4; AGENL: Trabajo – Conciliación y Arbitraje, 1923, 1.
77 Armando Morales, Secretario del Exterior de la CROM to Governor Porfirio González, June 27, 1925, AGENL: Trabajo – Conciliación y Arbitraje, 1/24; Mario de la Cueva, *Derecho mexicano del trabajo* I, (Mexico City, 1967), 259.

sanction of the state labor board.[78] As we saw earlier, the shop committees did management's dirty work by firing workers or sanctioning layoffs in such a way that cleared the company of future legal responsibility. Thus the grievance committees first demanded by workers were accepted by employers and subverted to opposing ends. In the United States, labor management journals were then praising the virtues of these "employee representation plans" that large companies ingeniously referred to as "industrial democracy."[79] However, rather than democratize shop-floor relations in Monterrey, the committees became vehicles to eliminate dissent. Individual workers consistently challenged the factory commissions' authority to supercede the labor law. But for fear of undermining the commissions' legitimacy, labor authorities refused to overturn their decisions until the 1930s.[80]

When Monterrey's workers did file complaints with the labor courts, they fared far less successfully than their counterparts elsewhere. During 1925–26, Mexico's labor boards arbitrated a striking 89 percent of 9,167 cases on workers' behalf. In Nuevo León, on the other hand, labor won 45 percent of the cases decided by arbitration during the period. Local workers fared even worse over the next three years, winning only 32 percent of ninety-four arbitration hearings. Nearly 66 percent of those cases involved unjustified dismissals, with the recovery of back wages and accident compensation accounting for another 15 percent. The figures suggest why Monterrey's workers placed little confidence in the labor board. Indeed, during the six years after the board's 1924 inauguration, local workers filed an average of only eighty-six claims per year, or less than 2 percent of the protests registered nationwide. That was a remarkably low figure for a city of nearly 20,000 industrial workers.[81]

How do we explain the discrepancy between the local and national figures? Governor Sáenz ascribed the "scarcity of cases" to "the harmony that reigns between workers and employers." Perhaps the labor board, composed of responsible worker representatives, disinterested businesspeople, and a neutral government mediator, functioned as impartially as authorities claimed. Workers, after all, provided their employers with such justifiable reasons for dismissal as absenteeism, fighting, drunkenness, or insubordination. Furthermore, the high number of claims and labor's lopsided success rate outside Monterrey reflected organized labor's exceptional

78 Collective contract in AGENL: Trabajo – Conciliación y Arbitraje, 3.

79 Cohen, *Making a New Deal*, 171–74.

80 Factory commission statutes from the Fundidora and Troqueles y Esmaltes chinaware (a subsidiary of Monterrey Glassworks) in AGN: DT 678/8, AGENL: JCA 22/624. On the sanctioning of the commission's authority see AGENL: JCA 11/375.

81 Nuevo León's statistics in AGENL: Informes de Gobernadores, 1923–1929; national figures in Gruening, *Mexico and Its Heritage*, 378.

political influence in other states. In Veracruz, for example, Gruening cited the antibusiness bias of the arbitration court to prove that "labor's coercive power [was] great." After speaking with workers and managers in Monterrey, he described the local labor board as "fair and without bias."[82] Monterrey industrialists also possessed key advantages and developed astute strategies to undermine or evade the system.

During the 1920s, labor faced a formidable adversary in the well-trained corporate lawyers who represented Monterrey's industrial elite and quickly discovered loopholes in the law. Union leaders in fact accused managers of capitalizing on workers' presumed ignorance of the labor code. One activist at the Peñoles smelter thus complained to the governor that, "[The personnel director] knows well that the workers have never been to college to study Laws, many do not even read." But, he pointed out, they did "understand what is just and unjust."[83] Even smaller employers lacking the industrialists' resources fashioned weapons of resistance. They delayed labor court proceedings for months by simply ignoring petitions to appear before the tribunal. They reneged on conciliatory agreements and they refused to pay indemnities awarded workers by the arbitration board.[84] While labor authorities could and did threaten to seize the employers' property – an action that generated quick results – the tactic still forced workers to wait months for their compensation. Finally, employers increasingly resisted unfavorable decisions by appealing the labor board's settlements to district judges. Indeed, one governor cited such recourse to judicial review to explain the low level of cases settled on workers' behalf in Nuevo León.[85]

Elsewhere in Mexico, the naming of the government's delegate to the tripartite labor court became politically charged affairs. That was because the state's representative generally cast the deciding vote that determined a board's tilt in favor of management or labor.[86] In Nuevo León, on the other hand, the issue generated little controversy. Early in the labor board's existence, both labor and business leaders had protested what they considered to be partial appointments.[87] But the early protests proved exceptional. It was

82 AGENL: *Informe del Gobernador Aarón Sáenz, 1927–1928*, 13; Gruening, *Mexico and Its Heritage*, 354–55, 380–81.
83 Sindicato de Trabajadores Metalúrgicos de la Fundicion #2 to Governor Sáenz, Dec. 28, 1929, AGENL: Trabajo – Conciliación y Arbitraje, 2/30. This protest responded to the smelter's strategy of reducing workers to one-day schedules rather than lay them off and pay them severance.
84 AGENL: JCA, 1929, 3/71; AGENL: Trabajo – Conciliación y Arbitraje, 1923, box 1.
85 AGENL: *Informe del Gobernador Jerónimo Siller, 1925–1926*, 7.
86 See for example Leticia Gamboa Ojeda, "La CROM en Puebla y el movimiento obrero textil en los años 20," Centro de Estudios de Movimientos Obreros y Sociales, *Historia del Movimiento Obrero II* (Puebla, 1984), 33–67.
87 *El Porvenir*, June 27, 1924, July 24–25, 1925.

the election of labor delegates that generated the greatest dissension. By the late 1920s, the city's primary labor central lost its capacity to appoint its members to Nuevo León's arbitration board. The big railwaymen's unions were now under federal jurisdiction, just as the memberships of the co-operative societies and the Steel Unions grew. Organized labor protested their rivals' presence on the labor board as "a direct assault on the principles of the revolution." The militants erroneously charged that "citizens without any connection to the laboring class come along acting like they're the workers' representatives." Said delegates could not "impartially defend labor," because their "mutual-aid societies" were "directly subordinated to the employers' opinions."[88] The protests elicited no reply. For not only did such figures as Governor Sáenz and President Calles recognize the cooperatives as a respectable form of worker association; the cooperatives themselves represented far more workers than the city's trade unions.

Labor activists drew a valuable political lesson from what they perceived as the labor law's failure to deliver on its promises. As the 1920s progressed, many unionists came to regard direct action as a more effective means of defending workers' interests than the dubious channels of state mediation. Throughout Latin America, the anarcho-syndicalist tradition of employing the strike to effect workplace change persisted well after the advent of corporatist labor laws that established the government as mediator of industrial conflicts.[89] In Mexico, the revolution and pressure from below led to the earliest crystallization of this legal framework for labor relations. Workers quickly embraced the hope that the law would establish rules of fairness and a standards of justice. But they also saw the loopholes that left the law open to evasion and subterfuge. Union militants would therefore learn to combine legal and direct action. Monterrey's leading proponents of the latter strategy – both anarchists and then the communists who superceded them on the labor left – promoted direct action as much for ideological as practical reasons. They shared a common mistrust of the revolutionary government and disdained its allies in the CROM. Their experiences of state mediation – the failed organizing drives at the glassworks and brewery, the railway strike of 1926–27 – reinforced their philosophy of direct action. So did the glacial proceedings of the labor board. At the same time, some industrialists abandoned their early suspicions about the state's role as a labor arbitrator. They came to understand that unauthorized wildcat

88 Federación Regional de Sociedades Obreras to Governor Sáenz, June 12, 1929, AGENL: Correspondencia Local del Gobernador, 9/5.
89 For the well-researched case of how both Brazilian workers and employers responded to the corporatist labor law see French, "Drowning in Laws," and John D. French, *The Brazilian Workers' ABC: Class Conflict and Alliances in São Paulo* (Chapel Hill, 1991), 85–88, 169–74, 309–10.

strikes were legal grounds for the permanent replacement of troublesome workers.

An increasingly typical scenario thus developed at Monterrey's "El Fénix" match factory. Militants struck the plant when the owner refused to promote a union apprentice to a recently opened position.[90] Dismayed by the unionists' intractable resolve, the manager suggested government arbitration. The unionists balked. As they protested, "Our affairs having nothing to do with the government, much less with the labor board. We are the only ones capable of settling this case with you because we don't want to lose time waiting for justice." Fifty-five union workers – men and women – struck the factory. When police drove their pickets from company gates, the strikers regrouped across the street. They remained there for three weeks as managers and nonunion workers attempted to maintain production. But other forms of direct action hampered their efforts. According to a manager's later testimony before the labor board, union operatives had removed machinery components and hid them throughout the plant before their walkout. Once production resumed, the company's delivery trucks suffered numerous tire punctures on the surrounding streets. Handbills soon appeared around town calling for "all workers and the general public" to boycott "El Fénix" matches as "a charitable contribution towards those of us who suffer Capital's intransigence." The sabotage and boycott prompted government intervention. Siding with the company, the labor court declared the strike illicit for the union's failure to petition for the right to strike and the "violence" employed by the strikers. The match factory rescinded the union's collective contract and hired permanent replacement workers. Thus did one of the clearest achievement's of working-class political activism – the enactment of a state labor code – prove a bitter disappointment from organized labor's point of view. That is why workers proved no more enthusiastic than employers when the government abolished dozens of state labor laws and replaced them with a uniform code, the 1931 Federal Labor Law.

These People Will Never Be Capable of Defending Us

The federalization of Mexico's labor law had been a recurrent proposal since the mid-1920s. By codifying Article 123, the law's framers hoped to end its intermittent and uneven enforcement at the state and municipal levels, where some ninety laws had been decreed since 1917.[91] For progressives

---

90 AGENL: JCA 1/7. For analogous cases of direct action involving the city's tramway operators and local furniture workers see AGENL: JCA 1/12 and *El Porvenir*, Apr. 1–4, 1925.

91 Unless indicated otherwise, the following discussion of the 1931 Federal Labor Law is based upon Bensusán, "Construcción y desarrollo del derecho laboral"; Saragoza, *The Monterrey Elite*, 155–69; Middlebrook, *The Paradox of Revolution*, 56–58; and Arnaldo Córdova, *La clase obrera en la historia de México: en una época de crisis (1928–1934)* (Mexico, 1980), 48–54.

within the new National Revolutionary Party, the law would ensure effective worker rights. The party's right wing perhaps saw in the law a means of exerting control over workers after the fall of the CROM and the consequent rise of the labor left. Moreover, a uniform labor code established the conditions for industrial stability. Many business leaders had initially supported the idea – if not the final outcome – for that very reason. Labor peace became a paramount concern as the Great Depression's effects grew increasingly visible in Mexico. Indeed, after months of debate the national executive rushed the Federal Labor Law's 600 clauses through Congress in less than three weeks in mid-1931. By then, both Monterrey's industrialists and local communist activists would share a common disdain for the state's newfound powers of labor mediation.

The Communists had considered Mexican labor law to be a deceitful ploy to "deceive and oppress" workers since the early 1920s. They regarded the new labor code as a vehicle for the state's "domination of the proletariat."[92] The law indeed established the government's authority to legally certify unions. It also granted labor authorities the right to award collective contracts but established no fixed regulations for union representation elections. Employers remained free to sign a collective contract with a union of their choice. Rivals who could claim greater rank-and-file support were then forced to petition the labor courts to win collective bargaining rights. The Communists also feared that the law's regulation of the right to strike would undermine collective action. They argued that it "restrict[ed] the rights and freedoms of workers" by authorizing the labor boards to determine a strike's legality, just as Nuevo León's original law had done. In radical circles, the labor code thus earned notoriety as the "Fascist Labor Law," a tool of the corporatist state to control labor and thus satisfy the ambitions of the probusiness legislators who authored the code. By mid-1931, local Communists would be protesting the law as vehemently in the streets as the city's industrialists were in the press.[93]

Regiomontano businessmen quickly and vociferously established themselves at the vanguard of organized capital's well-orchestrated resistance to the law. Ironically, the industrial elite opposed the same clauses of the labor code as their radical adversaries, albeit to opposing ends. They feared that the law's planks on union recognition would impose "compulsory unions" upon their factories. The industrialists also argued that the broad and ambivalent conditions under which workers could strike virtually ensured an outbreak

92 See the PCM paper *Vida Nueva*, Dec. 25, 1920, which quotes a line from their hymn of labor solidarity, "La Internacional": "La ley nos engaña y nos oprime"; David Siqueiros quoted in Bensusán, "Construcción y desarrollo del derecho laboral," 17.
93 *El Porvenir*, May 28, 1931.

of labor unrest. Finally, the onset of the Depression heightened their concern regarding the law's restrictions on management's right to suspend workers, cut wages, or even close their factories without government authorization. But the law passed and Monterrey's industrialists lost their most visible battle to date against central government authority. Nonetheless, the process of resistance strengthened the *regiomontanos'* organizational ties amongst themselves and to other Mexican businesspeople. One product of the labor law debates, the founding of the Mexican Employers' Confederation (COPARMEX), became the most enduring example of this new corporate solidarity. Led by none other than the Cuauhtémoc Brewery's Luis G. Sada, this national employers' association became the primary vehicle through which the Monterrey businessmen would organize resistance to an increasingly interventionist state. The COPARMEX also became a medium in which the *regiomontanos* broadcasted their innovative managerial strategies to their class cohorts. Luis G. Sada was soon touring the country to share his philosophy on company paternalism with fellow industrialists.[94] Meanwhile, back in Monterrey, the industrial elite busily engineered the newest response to federal labor legislation: the organization of company unions.

Just as Monterrey's industrialists foresaw and feared, the Federal Labor Law's passage unleashed a bout of union organizing in local factories.[95] Union organizers drafted statutes, enlisted rank-and-file support, and registered their unions with the labor board. With union certification they scored the right to negotiate a collective contract. But the industrialists just as often beat them to the punch. The union certification process took several weeks. In the meantime, labor authorities were required to notify employers of their workers' petition. Thus forewarned, the industrialists organized their office clerks, foremen, and loyal workers into company unions, padding the membership rolls with white-collar employees. The process transpired during 1932, the worst year in what proved to be a relatively short-lived economic depression in Mexico. At the time, the future appeared uncertain if not grim. Many factories were reducing operations to survive the hard times. Militants attempted to appeal to workers by advocating the need for independent unions to resist layoffs and wage cuts. Company unions, on the other hand, bolstered their ranks by promising steady work or threatening punitive dismissals to frightened workers. Under these circumstances, these so-called "white" unions soon proliferated in Monterrey. Some faced significant resistance from militant workers; others emerged unchallenged.

---

94 Saldaña, *Constructores de Monterrey*, 152–54.
95 The following is based on dozens of protests filed by union workers before Nuevo León's labor board in AGENL: JCA 1931–32, 3–10.

The process transpired smoothly at the city's largest plants, notably the Cuauhtémoc Brewery and the Fundidora Steel Works. Weeks after the labor law's passage, veteran workers and foremen at the brewery organized the Cuauhtémoc Workers' Union. The development passed unnoticed by most operatives. Indeed, many former workers do even not recall the union's existence during the 1930s. They regarded the Cuauhtémoc Society as their union because it acted like one: collecting dues, holding assemblies, and administering fringe benefits.[96] The steel workers learned immediately when their department-based unions amalgamated as the Federated Steel Unions. As related above, the union, its leaders, and the collective contract received lavish praise in the company press. Negotiated in two days, the contract guaranteed the employees "benefits superior to those stipulated by law." Union officials could then crow that Monterrey's workers "had once again proven their lofty stature, demonstrating ideals more advanced than those found in other regions of the country." They would also make the premature claim that, "the Labor Code has not produced the multiple problems that it seems to have created in other parts of the Republic, where the businessmen's lack of foresight, or better yet, exaggerated demands by workers and . . . the agitation of professional leaders has placed not a few industries on the verge of extinction."[97] The discourse of regionalism was thereafter employed to legitimize the company unions and celebrate their independence from Mexico's "red" labor centrals. Indeed, veteran steel workers soon spearheaded the formation of the Independent Unions of Nuevo León, a federation of company unions that astutely adopted their moniker as a badge of autonomy from organized labor.

Company unions were not new to Mexico. What made those of Monterrey unique was their pervasiveness and their persistence into the twenty-first century. "White" unions were hardly confined to Monterrey's largest industries, where workers forsook the right of union representation for the benefits of paternalism. Owners of small factories, bakeries, hotels, and bus companies all emulated the city's leading industrialists. These employers organized company unions less as a precautionary antiunion tactic and more in response to a militant union's emergence. Some remained ignorant of in-plant organizing drives until an "outside" union representative arrived at management's doors to bargain on labor's behalf.[98] It was thus in these smaller plants – whose owners could not afford or simply refused to develop company paternalism – where a decade-long struggle between "red" and "white" unions first transpired. The earlier militance in these factories perhaps owed to the presence of skilled union workers whose loyalty could

---

96 López, Monsiváis, and Medrano interviews.

97 *CYPSA*, Nov. 28, 1931.

98 See Unión de Mecánicos Mexicanos vs. Fábrica de Cerillos "El Fénix," AGENL: JCA 8/321.

not be purchased by the higher wages and fringe benefits offered by larger enterprises. Despite the obstacle, two factors worked to the employers' advantage: the onset of an economic crisis and the complicity of Nuevo León's labor board. During the early 1930s, company unionists served as labor delegates on the board entrusted with union certification. They used their positions to thwart the militants' attempts to make inroads in local plants. The following two cases illuminate the issues at stake and management's role in these early battles for union supremacy.

In February 1932, workers at Monterrey's Cementos Mexicanos (CEMEX) plant organized the CEMEX Workers Union and registered with the labor board.[99] They recruited sufficient rank-and-file support to claim majority status. Managers responded immediately. They enlisted loyal workers, clerks, and supervisors and founded the CEMEX Workers and Employees Union, a company union whose membership included not only production workers but the salaried employees distinguished in Mexican labor law as *empleados de confianza*. The company then bolstered the union's membership by recruiting new workers and enlisting them in the organization. The fact that the cement company could hire during the crisis reflected CEMEX's unique position as a supplier to the public works projects meant to alleviate growing unemployment. Such government contracts would help CEMEX to one day become the largest cement company in the Americas. Meanwhile, management launched a typical strategy of intimidation to bolster the company union. Obeying the guidelines established in the Federal Labor Law, CEMEX petitioned authorities for the right to reduce operations to alleviate overproduction. Although a federal labor inspector found the plant's inventories to be "extremely low," the state labor board acquiesced to their petition. Management then ordered the plant's shop committees to readjust the workforce.

Headed by the same company loyalists who directed the "white" union, the committees suspended the contracts of some militant unionists. Others saw their workloads reduced to one or two days weekly. The militants protested their alleged harassment to authorities. Their petition noted that the new recruits continued working three- to four-day weeks despite their limited seniority. They also argued that the CEMEX Workers and Employees Union failed to meet the legal definition of a union. Its leaders included the foremen, the time checker, and security guards. "As one can see," they asserted, "these people will never be capable of defending [workers] or representing us honorably before the company, due to the nature of their jobs, and for fear of being fired." In the end, the labor board registered both unions but awarded the collective contract to the loyalists. Their first organizing drive thus thwarted, many militant cement

99 Sindicato de Trabajadores de CEMEX vs. Cementos Mexicanos, AGENL: JCA 5/266.

workers swallowed their pride and joined the company union. This became a common strategy. The "reds" would then employ the organizational structure of the company union to defend rank-and-file interests, awaiting a more opportune moment to again challenge the legal status of the "white" union.

Another case from the period highlights not only the tactics of intimidation employed by managers but also the gendered belief that union activism was a male prerogative.[100] During the first week of 1932, workers organized a union at Monterrey's "La Industrial" Pasta and Cookie Factory. Two weeks later, the company signed a collective contract with a newly formed company union. Again, the labor board recognized both unions but awarded the contract to the "white" union after the company proved that a majority of the plant's 204 workers had signed the collective contract. The militants declared this a fraud. They charged that plant director Enrique Santos locked eighty-six female operatives in the plant and forced them to sign the contract. But the militants continued to resist efforts by the "Santos Union" to enlist them in its ranks. One operative, Josefina Díaz, received an invitation to attend the company union's meetings. The letter asked her why she chose to remain "distanced from her friends." Did she not "love the company?" What "ambiguous ambitions" motivated her to follow the "Judases" who directed the militant union?

Díaz penned a response that succinctly and sarcastically outlined why some workers resisted company unions. She remained "distanced from the pompously titled 'Union'," she began, "because I understand perfectly well that it has been formed and sustained by the owners . . . in order to snatch away the rights granted to workers by the Federal Labor Law." She noted that the union always met within the factory under the owner's vigilance. Díaz also pointed out that the union's contract "facilitated the owners' ability to fire workers and suppress wages [in violation of] the Law." For that reason, "would not the union's motto 'Justice, Harmony, and Progress' be better [stated] as 'Injustice, Servitude, and Retreat'?" As regarded her view of the company, she considered "that my love for myself and my class are of greater value than the miserable crumb of bread with which my surrender would be awarded." "I prefer to obtain what belongs to me by law," Díaz continued, "rather than [accept] the handouts that offend my dignity." She quickly dismissed the charges against the militant union's leaders, whom she considered "honorable and dignified men." "Who do you guys believe really deserves the title of Judas," she

---

100 Unless indicated otherwise the following case appears in Sindicato de Obreros, Obreras, y Empleados "La Industrial" vs. Fábrica de Galletas y Pastas "La Industrial," AGENL: JCA 5/278, 8/317, 9/338.

queried, "he who demands what is his by Law, or the one who sells himself out along with his class brothers and sisters?" She concluded that "my
ambitions are clear: that I be treated like a working woman . . . and not like
a slave."

Militants like Josefina Díaz suffered reprisals for resisting the company
union. As one fellow union leader wrote to the governor, "the owners
consider it a crime that we have not joined up with the foremen and
the 'confidential' employees to nullify the labor law." He described the
"employer offensive" that began as soon as they constituted their union.
First, the company threatened punitive dismissals to all who "resisted their
pretensions." Then came the poor treatment, the punitive demotions, and
excessive demands from the foremen. Finally, their workloads were reduced
to one or two days weekly, while the company hired on replacements. This
way, one manager informed them, "hunger will eliminate your rebellious-
ness." The company, for its part, consistently argued that, "since some time
ago, [the unionists] have been tools of professional agitators." But as the
weeks passed, the union successfully represented its members – and in
some cases all workers – before the labor tribunal. Their protests forced
the company to restore the female operatives' wages, which the company
had cut by 25 percent without the labor authorities' consent. The labor
board also demanded the payment of back wages to workers who suffered
reduced hours. In a final ruling on the case, labor authorities ordered the
company to reinstate the punitively dismissed union sympathizers – except for Josefina Díaz.[101] The plant manager, Santos, had fired the young
operative upon reading her scathing response to his union's "invitation."
The company's lawyer claimed that Díaz's letter was "harmful to its interests" – justifiable cause for a discharge – even though she directed her
remarks to the company union. The labor board's government-appointed official disagreed. He found that Díaz's response was "justifiable from a moral
standpoint." However, he concluded that "given her sex, she should have
avoided [writing the protest], since among her union *compañeros* there were
males who could have assumed the responsibility."[102] Josefina Díaz's defense
of her dignity treaded upon prevalent ideas of acceptable gender roles. She
thus lost her job while labor organizing in Monterrey remained the men's
responsibility.

The words of Josefina Díaz indicate that labor's understanding of the
"democratic principles" of the revolution remained alive in the collective
memory of many workers. For Díaz and her comrades, those principles sanctioned a struggle to secure their right to organize and to resist the "handouts"
that affronted their dignity and honor as a class. They demanded what was

101 AGENL: JCA 12 and 13.
102 AGENL: JCA 8/317.

their's by law and insisted upon contractual guarantees. Josefina Díaz challenged the status quo on two fronts, as a militant unionist and as a woman. While nearly 3,000 females labored in local industry by 1930, few passed through the halls of the labor courts and fewer still appeared on union committees. That proved consistent with the experience of most male workers. Women also played a negligible role in the brewery's Cuauhtémoc Society, despite their appreciable presence on the company payroll. But they refused to conform to their male coworkers' belief in their presumed docility. Nor did their presence in the labor force deter working-class unity. What the Josefina Díaz case illuminates is how the bureaucrats who manned Mexican legal institutions attempted to prescribe gendered boundaries around the world of organized labor, just as women were denied the "effective suffrage" that the revolution once promised. Indeed, the law, the workplace, and the home all became sites where women's gender roles were constructed and reaffirmed. Women like Josefina Díaz therefore asserted their own class identities to challenge these discriminatory barriers to activism. They faced a difficult struggle. For as we shall see, Monterrey's male workers, be they champions of "red" or "white" unionism, increasingly developed a masculine discourse of manly independence to sanction their competing forms of activism.

As a union militant, Josefina Díaz spoke the language of those activists who struggled to put the promises of the revolution into practice. Led by Monterrey's railroaders, they explicitly challenged the hegemonic pretensions of the Monterrey elite, who employed corporate welfare, shrewd legal maneuvering, and their control of the media to "diminish the true meaning" of the revolution. The radicals countered by fashioning a discourse of class and constitutionalism to neutralize the cross-class appeals of regionalism. But these militant trade unionists were but one faction of a diverse cast of labor activists speaking on behalf of Monterrey's workers. Equally prominent were their rivals within the cooperative societies or the Steel Unions, workers who shared their employers' commitment to class harmony and industrial progress.

While Monterrey's activist workers embraced a common regional identity, they derived distinct meanings from the shared cultural values of dignity and respectability. Many encouraged rank-and-file workers to place their "duty" above "rights." Their militant rivals promoted the struggle for union representation as a defense of their honor. The industrialists' capacity to quell unionism meant that the voices of the radical dissenters remained more conspicuous in the public sphere than in the factories of the Monterrey elite. But just as historians conceive of Mexico's revolution as a three-decade process of struggle and negotiation, so too was the construction of an enduring organized labor movement a long-term project. The revolution established the political and legal parameters upon which that movement would build. The widespread militance of the late 1910s gave way to significant setbacks during the 1920s, a time when the government proved to be less "revolutionary" than many activists in Monterrey had expected. But their inability to secure union recognition did not entail a total defeat. Labor militants persevered in their project – educating, organizing, and preparing for a time when they could put their vision of the "democratic principles" of the revolution into practice. Their moment would come in the 1930s.

6

Every Class Has Its Leaders

ASARCO, The Great Depression, and Popular Protest in Monterrey

Early on the morning of May 24, 1932 – just as social unrest reached its peak in Depression-era Monterrey – 240 workers barricaded themselves inside the ASARCO smelter. As news of their sit-down strike spread, hundreds of strike supporters gathered outside the plant's gates. Present were the smeltermen's wives and children, unemployed workers, and residents of the surrounding neighborhood. ASARCO's workers struck as they did – in defiant violation of the labor law – to force management to sign a collective contract with their union. The action culminated a violent season of labor protests and hunger marches in the streets of Monterrey. As an alarmed public would have read in the press, Communists directed both the demonstrations and the ASARCO union. The sit-down strikers held firm as authorities beseeched them to exit the smelter. Late in the afternoon, the president ordered federal troops and mounted police to the scene. Faced with the threat of military intervention, the workers exited from the smelter. As they did, a skirmish broke out between police and union sympathizers. The ensuing melee left one worker dead and dozens of men, women, and children injured. Further protests were silenced by a military occupation of downtown Monterrey. The ASARCO strike ended in tragic defeat. But it symbolized a visible transformation of working-class attitudes and behavior in the industrial regions of Mexico.

Ambivalence defined the state of Mexican labor in the early 1930s, as new actors sought to capitalize on the void created by the decline of the CROM. While Mexico City labor bosses rebuilt their alliance with influential politicians, a new kind of union movement was emerging in the provinces. Spearheaded by communist labor organizers, it was more radical in its politics and more militant in its practices. It therefore elicited a swift and repressive response from authorities facing an economic crisis and popular protest. The federal government had veered to the right during the late 1920s. Mexico broke diplomatic relations with the Soviet Union, outlawed the Mexican Communist Party (PCM), and imprisoned its activists at the notorious Islas Marías penal colony. While ardent anti-Communists ran the government in Mexico City, communist organizers scattered to the provinces and helped organize unions. Histories of the party focus less on this grass-roots activism and more on its sectarian politics.[1] That sectarianism certainly mattered. At the national level, the PCM adhered rigidly to its attacks on the "bourgeois government," its "fascist" labor law, and its "servile alliance with American imperialism." But the Communists combined this political agenda with aggressive workplace organizing, especially in heavy industry and the export sectors. The strategy would result in the conspicuous presence of Communist-led unions in industries dominated by foreign capital, including mining, smelting, and oil. The Communists federated these geographically dispersed unions in their own labor central, the Mexican Confederation of Trade Union Unity (CSUM). Two *regiomontano* railroaders – Valentín Campa and Cruz Contreras – sat on the CSUM's executive committee. They made sure to include their hometown on the party's agenda.

Northern industrial cities like Monterrey and Tampico hosted "old and important branches" of the PCM. Activists therefore looked to "penetrate" basic industries in these relative strongholds early on. Local organizers were exhorted to "participate actively in all struggles for immediate working-class demands . . . [and] to be always on the front line of all conflicts, strikes, and mass actions." Party strategists were particularly keen on integrating activists into "reformist unions" to win rank-and-file trust "through a constant defense of their interests."[2] At ASARCO, communist union leaders challenged company health and safety policies, defended workers against abusive foremen, and mobilized community resistance to layoffs. The company's harassment of these popular union leaders in turn galvanized rank-and-file sympathy for their strategies of defiance. The means by which communist union leaders earned rank-and-file respect deserves attention, for such worker–activists soon made inroads at the steel mill and glassworks as well. As a result, Monterrey became one of the few cities in Mexico where the party established a solid working-class membership, one that persisted well after the PCM's nationwide decline in the early 1940s.[3] Furthermore, the ASARCO case demonstrates precisely why company paternalism met its limits on the shop floor. There is where the workers' desire for a strong and militant union was born.

---

1 Barry Carr, *Marxism and Communism in Twentieth Century Mexico* (Lincoln, 1992); Anatoli Shulgovski, *México en la encrucijada de su historia* (Mexico City, 1968), 21–90; for a first-hand account of one young militant's experiences in the party, see José Revueltas, *Los días terrenales* (Mexico City, 1979).

2 *El Machete* (PCM publication), Oct. 30, Dec. 10, 1931; May 1, 1932; Campa, *Mi testimonio*, 57.

3 Carr, *Marxism and Communism*, 52, 79; their persistence is well documented in Records of Foreign Service Posts of the Department of State, Monterrey Consulate, National Archives Washington (NAW RG 84), Confidential Records, 1936–1949, (boxes 3, 8), where consular officials provide intelligence on individual activists, factory and neighborhood "cells," and members' occupations.

Foreign Capital on Mexican Soil

Throughout Mexico, the Great Depression gave birth to a working-class insurgency that continued into the later 1930s. Labor protest escalated dramatically in Monterrey. Annual claims filed with the labor court jumped from an average of 74 (1923–29) to 338 (1930–32). But these were largely individual acts of resistance rather than collective action.[4] Local strikes became conspicuous only when an economic recovery and shifting political tides made collective action more feasible. How does one then explain the early militance of the smelter workers? And why did their experience generate a culture of solidarity in the community surrounding the plant? One answer lies in ASARCO's relation to the global economy. The smelter felt the consequences of the Depression earlier and more profoundly than any local industry. Monterrey's steel mill, brewery, and glassworks all manufactured products for the domestic market. During the worst moments of the crisis, these companies restricted the length and severity of layoffs through stockpiling and work-sharing schemes. The nature of smelting and ASARCO's direct link to foreign markets precluded such options. But these structural factors do not in themselves explain the militancy of the smelter workers much less the public sympathy generated by their plight. Other peculiarities of the company, from its foreign ownership, to its handling of the economic crisis, to its relation with the government set the context for the 1932 sit-down strike.

The American Smelting and Refining Company was by then Mexico's largest private employer, owner of five smelters and dozens of mines. The company's managers were therefore adept at handling industrial disputes. In Monterrey, ASARCO managers had responded to the protracted labor conflicts of the late 1910s and early 1920s much as their counterparts at the steel mill. They begrudgingly recognized craft unions representing their most skilled and prized operatives, the mechanics and furnacemen who led the early walkouts. The resurgence of the Mexican mining industry then conspired on behalf of industrial peace. From 1923 to 1930, ASARCO's 1,000 workers enjoyed a level of job security unprecedented since the onset of revolution. Moreover, as an early pioneer of welfare capitalism in the United States, ASARCO exported its system of fringe benefits to Mexico early on. The benefits of paternalism – the medical services, company school, the housing, and a consumer cooperative – provided an important supplement to the smelter workers' hard-earned wages. Indeed, during the 1920s, ASARCO earned a reputation as "the best employer in Mexico," a portrayal

---

4 AGENL: *Informes de gobernadores*, 1929–1933. For Mexico, see Marcos Tonatiuh Aguila M., "Trends in Mexican Labor Conflicts, 1927–1931," *Economía, teoría y práctica* 4 (1994), 85–101.

presented by an otherwise caustic critic of the company.[5] But ASARCO's status as a foreign enterprise imposed certain limits on its practices of paternalism.

Unlike the steel mill or brewery, ASARCO could not parlay working-class patriotism into a means of fostering the workers' pride in their employer. The smeltermen labored on behalf of Mexico's largest foreign enterprises, a company whose profits enriched its stockholders far more than Mexican workers. For those workers who missed the point, there were plenty of local radicals ready to remind them. However, in contrast to prerevolutionary Mexico, when the unequal treatment of foreign and native-born workers fueled labor disputes at the smelter, the 1920s witnessed a noteworthy decline in ethnic antagonisms. Mexicans had largely displaced Americans by then. While ethnic tensions no longer defined labor relations, they nonetheless complicated them. Confusion often reigned on the shop floor due to poor communications between native workers and their American supervisors. The latter still spoke little if any Spanish. One foreman gave orders to his workers by hand signals, growing angry and punishing operatives who failed to respond promptly.[6] But only eight of the smelter's twenty-three foremen were foreigners and, as we shall see, Mexican foremen proved as abusive as the foreigners they replaced. Thus by the 1930s, only one aspect of the Americans' presence really aggravated the Mexican smeltermen: their occupation of high-paying jobs for which native-born workers were qualified. ASARCO continued to employ several dozen foreigners not only as managers and foremen, but as skilled tradesmen as well. As unionists reminded federal labor authorities, the Americans "have long surpassed their intended duty of training Mexican workers."[7]

ASARCO cultivated its own unique relationship with government officials. In Monterrey, the smelter's personnel director, Rex Keep, socialized frequently with the city's police chief. Union leaders saw Colonel Cejudo enjoying ASARCO's recreational facilities with frequency. Indeed, they later charged that the company "holds the keys to the police department and the local penitentiary through Colonel Cejudo, whom Mr. Keep orders about between sets of tennis."[8] But as the unionists understood, company policy took shape in New York and Mexico City, where ASARCO

5 O'Connor, *The Guggenheims*, 338; for the benefits provided ASARCO mine workers in Chihuahua and Coahuila see French, *A Peaceful and Working People*, 51–55, and Juan Luis Sariego, *Enclaves y minerales en el Norte de México* (Mexico City, 1988), 100–08.

6 Sindicato de Obreros Productores de la ASARCO to Labor Dept., AGN: Junta Federal de Conciliación y Arbitraje (JFCA), 215/931–222.

7 AGN: Departamento Autónomo del Trabajo (DAT), 364/7.

8 ASARCO strike committee propaganda in Nathan, June 1, 1932, SD 812.504/298.

employed its own Mexican lawyers to work with the bureaucrats who regulated their industry. The Calles government established federal oversight of the mining-metallurgical industry in 1927. But the company had long before learned to shape its policies in accordance with Mexico's shifting political and legal tides, aware that its foreign status subjected ASARCO to the scrutinizing eye of federal authorities and a wary public.[9] After 1931, the Federal Labor Law permitted employers to cut wages, dismiss workers, or suspend production only with the consent of government labor authorities. The Depression's immediate impact on mineral prices forced ASARCO to adapt to these legal parameters. By doing so scrupulously, ASARCO proved exceptional by local standards. As the crisis percolated down into Monterrey's manufacturing sector, employers like the steel mill tried to evade these legal impediments to layoffs by acting through company unions. But two exceptional and related features of the ASARCO smelter – its jurisdictional status and the presence of a militant union – foreclosed the option of legal evasion.

ASARCO made no apparent effort to organize a company union. Since the early 1920s, the American firm had publicly recognized and apparently accepted its workers' right to organize. Both independent and CROM-affiliated unions represented workers at ASARCO's other Mexican smelters and many of its mines.[10] Moreover, evidence suggests that many of its Monterrey workers arrived at the plant with industrial experience and union backgrounds. While migrants comprised a significant part of all local workforces, more than 40 percent of the smeltermen came from San Luis Potosí, where ASARCO operated two smelters and several of its largest Mexican mines. The higher wages offered at ASARCO-Monterrey, the urban environment, and family migration networks certainly lured some of these *potosinos* to the local smelter.[11] There, during the 1920s, ASARCO had negotiated collective contracts with its mechanics, furnacemen, and carpenters. But the majority of workers remained unorganized. This was consistent with ASARCO labor policy in the United States, where the company worked closely with more conservative craft unions to resist the inroads of a leftist industrial union, the Mine, Mill, and Smelter Workers. ASARCO soon confronted a similar dilemma in Monterrey when communist activists organized the smelter's laborers and skilled operatives into a single union.

ASARCO's jurisdictional status facilitated their union drive. As a company under federal jurisdiction, the smelter received frequent visits from

9 O'Connor, *The Guggenheims*, 88–96, 326–37; Marvin D. Bernstein, *The Mexican Mining Industry, 1890–1950* (New York, 1964), 144–57.
10 AGN: JFCA, 198/930-1393; AGN: Presidentes, Obregon-Calles 407-A-16.
11 Collective profile of 500 smelter workers from AGN: DT, Accidentes, 1925–29; wage differentials in Monterrey and San Luis Potosí in AGN: DT, Labor Inspector's Reports, 1926, 1100/1, 1130/20.

an inspector sent out by the Department of Labor. These federal labor inspectors counseled workers on their legal rights, distributed antialcohol propaganda, and apparently helped organize unions. At ASARCO, the inspector advised the workers throughout the unionization process. In mid-1930, he also mediated the negotiation of a collective contract between union delegates and ASARCO officials in Mexico City. By all accounts, the meeting transpired amicably.[12] At least two-thirds of the plant's 400 full-time workers joined the ASARCO Production Workers Union. At the time of the union's founding, it appears that neither the labor inspector nor the company knew of the union's affiliation with the communist labor central, the CSUM. The union's prestige grew quickly thereafter. Neither ASARCO's federal jurisdiction nor the union's resistance limited the company's ability to suspend production, restructure the work regime, and dismiss more than 70 percent of its workers over the next two years. ASARCO's response to the Depression would foster the sort of rank-and-file discontent and solidarity that the Communists found "favorable to the party's development."[13]

Shop-Floor Activism

The crisis depressed the Mexican mining industry faster and more profoundly than any sector of the economy. Between 1929, a year of prosperity, and 1932, national production of silver, lead, and zinc declined by an average of 50 percent.[14] These were the metals processed at ASARCO-Monterrey and exported to Europe and the United States. Beginning in mid-1930, ASARCO petitioned federal authorities for permission to launch a series of work stoppages. Government officials conceded repeatedly to their petitions. Mexico's secretary of industry supported the stoppages (*paros técnicos*) as the only means of preserving jobs in an industry battered by the fall in mineral prices and the threat of bankruptcies. He also supported the company's plan to rationalize the mining and smelting industries to guarantee their long-run competitiveness.[15] In mid-1930, the federal government sanctioned a ninety-day shutdown of the ASARCO smelter. The suspension generated immediate hardships. But the workers apparently understood the rationale. There were no recorded protests. However, when the company resumed production three months later it did so minus

---

12 AGN: DT, Labor Inspector's Report, 1930, 1882/17.
13 O'Connor, *The Guggenheims*, 335–36; *El Machete*, Dec. 10, 1931.
14 Institito Nacional de Estadística, Geografía e Informática (INEGI), *Estadísticas históricas de México*, Vol. 2 (Mexico, 1994), 543.
15 ASARCO to Junta Regional de Conciliación y Arbitraje, Jan. 7, 1931, AGN: JFCA, 210/931-90; Luis León in Secretaría de Industria, Comercio y Trabajo, *Boletín Semanal* #51 (1930), AGENL: Industria, Comercio y Trabajo, 2.

500 contract laborers and two dozen full-time workers, paring the labor force in half.[16]

While the union could do little to resist the government rulings, its leaders did challenge ASARCO's past and present violations of the workers' legal rights. Over the following weeks, union leaders filed dozens of protests with labor authorities. They demanded the company's prompt payment of back-logged accident compensation claims. They insisted that ASARCO indemnify all dismissed workers. And they brought the government's attention to the eviction of workers from company housing. The federal labor inspector intervened and brokered a settlement. Management extended housing rights to all dismissed workers for two months. For others, they waived rents during the temporary stoppages. ASARCO further agreed to compensate workers injured over the preceding three years according to new guidelines established by federal law. Finally, upon reviewing the union's petition, a federal labor court ordered ASARCO to pay legal severance to all laid-off workers.[17] But as the crisis deepened, managers held firm to their historic contention that the nature of metallurgy required them to "increase or diminish the number of workers from time to time . . . as a consequence of irregular mineral shipments, shortages, and so forth." Unlike the late 1910s, when the same issue fueled persistent conflicts at the plant, ASARCO now compromised with union demands. They paid severance to dismissed workers. And, upon the union's insistence, managers preserved a few more jobs by instituting work-sharing schemes.[18]

Union activists further bolstered their reputations by championing the rank and file's oldest grievances, those related to workplace health and safety issues. The smelting industry earned notoriety as one of the most hazardous known to workers. Smeltermen were exposed to unguarded machinery, the constant movement of ore cars, and molten metal.[19] These were the visible risks. The workers' greatest enemies were the fumes and dust that made lead poisoning a peril faced by all operatives. Furthermore, the constant exposure to extreme heat, a threat compounded by Monterrey's long, hot summers, weakened workers whose wages afforded them poor diets. Fainting spells were common at ASARCO. Moreover, subsistence wages made the seven-day week a customary and accepted practice into

---

16 AGENL: Huelga ASARCO.

17 AGN: DT, Labor Inspector's Report, 1930, 1882; AGN: JFCA, 229/931-587.

18 AGN: JFCA 240/931-932. In this case, the union protested when ASARCO dismissed eight refinery workers, pressuring the company to instead place sixteen workers on three-day weekly schedules.

19 For specific accidents at ASARCO-Monterrey see AGN: Trabajo – Accidentes, 1923–28; on industry-wide hazards see O'Connor, *The Guggenheims*, 315–18 and Derickson, *Workers' Health, Workers' Democracy*, 35–36, 53–55.

the 1930s. As one Monterrey smelterman lamented to labor authorities, "Due to our [economic] needs, we sacrifice our health at the altars of labor." Some lost their lives, as lead poisoning could take a worker after only six months on the job. Before the Federal Labor Law became widely effective, workers received minimal compensation for such occupational hazards. At ASARCO, families of deceased workers received the equivalent of one month's wages, minus burial and medical expenses.[20]

The unionists protested the company's ongoing transgressions of accident compensation laws. They demanded that injured workers receive full wages – rather than the customary 50 percent – to prevent their return to the smelter before they recovered. The union also began contracting its own physicians to counter the perceived complicity of company doctors, whom the operatives mistrusted. Union activists also challenged work rules that permitted foremen to arbitrarily reassign workers to tasks for which they lacked proper training. They achieved some notable results. Their protests, for instance, led the company to compensate workers for accident claims filed even before the union's founding.[21] On the shop floor, however, ASARCO supervisors denied such mundane requests as protective work apparel. As the claims mounted so did management's harassment of union leaders. In early 1930, a supervisor denied a union demand to provide safety shoes for the refinery workers, many of whom still labored in a style of working-class sandals (*huaraches*). Union officials turned to the federal labor inspector, who agreed to tour the smelter with union leader Juan Guerra. Shortly thereafter, ASARCO punished Guerra with a seven-day suspension because he had abandoned his work station without the foreman's consent. That provoked the union's first threat of collective action: a series of four-hour slowdowns during each shift. The company reconsidered its position, reinstated Guerra, and provided work boots to the smeltermen.[22]

After months of reduced but steady production, the work stoppages began anew in 1931. They came with little warning and limited notification. After each *paro técnico*, the firm called fewer workers back, reducing their numbers to less than 300 of the original 1,000 operatives by 1932. Moreover, the stoppages coincided with the arrival of North American technicians charged with increasing the forty-year-old smelter's efficiency. As a result, ASARCO installed new machinery during the temporary closures. They also engineered a series of rationalization schemes and speed ups that soon

---

20 Workers' diets, fainting spells, and quote from AGENL: JCA, 1928 2/27; fatal effects of lead poisoning in *El Porvenir*, Apr. 4, 1926; workers' compensation and the seven-day week in AGN: Presidentes, 407-A-16 and AGN: JFCA 248/931-1101.
21 AGENL: Huelga ASARCO; AGENL: JCA 2/29; AGN: JFCA, 229/931-567.
22 AGN: JFCA, 196/930-1347.

enabled the plant to surpass its earlier production figures. During one stoppage, mechanized ore crushers were introduced to the milling department. When twenty-four hand millers returned to work they found themselves reassigned to new and lower-paying jobs. The mechanization demonstrated how archaic the production process had remained. But the new technology and its means of introduction fueled shop-floor rancor. Indeed, the union protested that only two years before, an ASARCO foreman had "played the role of deceitful contractor (*enganchador*)" and recruited the millers from the Peñoles smelter with "better guarantees of security." In the cupelling room, where metals were separated with chemical solvents and high-temperature oxidation, workers protested when the supervisor breached a custom by which each furnaceman received one full-time assistant. One lost his job for refusing to labor unassisted in this "rough and unhealthy" department.[23]

The most pronounced conflicts developed in the antimony refinery, where speed ups and the harassment of union leaders caused tensions to escalate. One foreman demoted Simón Múñoz for tardiness after the union president labored for six consecutive months without missing a day. Múñoz had arrived ten minutes late. Moreover, the refinery's union stewards consistently intervened on the workers' behalf but supervisors refused to recognize shop committees as stipulated by the collective contract.[24] Thus did union officials inform the federal labor inspector, in rather understated fashion, that relations with management "were growing distant."[25] The circumstances owed less to the work stoppages and more to the rationalization schemes and persistent harassment of unionists. Those reprisals would backfire on the company. The intimidation did less to instill fear among the smeltermen than to galvanize rank-and-file sympathy for the activists, the men in whom the workers now invested their trust for having defended rank-and-file interests. In the meantime, the conflicts at ASARCO soon converged with another product of the Depression, the unemployed workers' movement.

Extremist Social Doctrines

The Great Depression battered economies throughout the Americas, with lasting social and political consequences. But the crisis proved relatively brief and produced fewer hardships in Mexico. Having a vast population of subsistence farmers and their families alleviated the effects. Moreover, the generation who lived through the Depression suffered less than they had during the armed revolution. Remarkably few former workers even recall

23 AGN: JFCA, 210/931-88, 215/931-243.
24 AGN: JFCA, 217/931-278, 198/930-1384, 215/931-222.
25 AGN: JFCA, 202/930-1487.

the crisis when asked to recollect its impact.[26] Nonetheless, like other
Mexican cities or industries linked to global markets, Monterrey indeed
experienced the Depression, however sudden its arrival and short-lived its
effects. While Mexico's economy slid into gradual recession by the later
1920s, industrial Monterrey experienced a relative boom. The local steel
mill, smelters, and brewery all produced at record levels in 1929. In late
1930, the governor reported that "the country's economic situation has
not caused a serious imbalance in the [local] labor market." He related the
circumstances to "the good judgment of the industrialists, [who] managed
to keep their operatives employed in construction and repair projects."
The United States consul seconded the governor's optimistic outlook in
mid-1931. He reported that "the Monterrey district, while undergoing a
period of depression, is without any real distress, even among the lower
classes." But the Depression's impact on regional mining was profound.
Bonanza turned to bust in northern Mexican mine camps and closures soon
displaced half the industry's 90,000 workers.[27]

The collapse of mining echoed immediately in Monterrey, and not only
at the smelters. By the late 1920s, authorities were already reporting
an accelerated influx of migrants from northern mining states as well as
the Gulf Coast oil fields. Commerce and transport also tied Monterrey
to these regions. Local merchant houses and manufacturers of consumer
goods – from beer to overalls to hardware – suffered the contraction of the
miners' and oil workers' purchasing power. So, too, did their clerks and
workers. Likewise, in mid-1931, the National Railways suspended 1,000
local employees, an effect not only of the crisis but a government program to restructure the state-controlled railroad company.[28] A mounting
unemployment problem was compounded by the influx of Mexican immigrants deported from the United States. As many as 500,000 *repatriados*
returned to their homeland in the early 1930s. Each month, thousands arrived in Monterrey by train and auto from the Texas border. Many were
farm laborers. But thousands returned with industrial skills. One train
carried a contingent of steel workers from Chicago. Another arrived with
1,050 passengers from Detroit.[29] While the majority continued on home,
many single men remained in Monterrey, one of the few Mexican cities

---

26 Interviews with Dionisio Aguilar, Mar. 20, 1996, Palacios, and Quiroga.
27 AGENL: *Informe del Gobernador Francisco Cárdenas, 1931–1932*, 5; Nathan, Apr. 1, 1931, SD 812.00,
    NL/9 (quoted); Marcos T. Aguila Medina, "The Great Depression and the Origins of Cardenismo:
    The Case of the Mining Sector and its Workers, 1927–1940," (Ph.D. diss., The University of Texas,
    1997), 60–110.
28 AGENL: *Informe del Gobernador Aarón Sáenz, 1928–1929*, 109; *El Porvenir*, Mar. 1 and 30, 1931.
29 *El Porvenir*, Mar. 7, 1931; *El Sol*, July 16, 1932; *Colectividad*, Dec. 3, 1932; AGENL: *Informe del
    Gobernador Francisco Cárdenas, 1931–1932*; Camille Guerin-González, *Mexican Workers and American
    Dreams* (New Brunswick, 1994), 100–08.

where they could ply their vocational skills. Thus in reports coinciding with the idling of several large factories and layoffs at the steel mill and smelters, the United States consul grimly observed "much misery among [Nuevo León's] urban and rural lower classes." By 1932, reports of suicides became alarmingly common while the homeless grew conspicuous on the streets of Monterrey.[30]

Civic boosters responded to the crisis with a curiously upbeat message of hope. Some newspapers simply informed readers who certainly saw otherwise that "there appears to be no crisis." The steel mill's magazine suggested the same to its workers, even as the company's Gran Cine Acero offered movie tickets at "crisis prices." The business press now embraced the opportunity to put its regional chauvinism on display. Editors pondered why other regions were not prospering like Monterrey: "Could it be that the opiate of apathy puts the inhabitants of those states to sleep, or that their governments hinder economic development?" "As a model to be imitated," they boasted, "we present Monterrey, where industry thrives in spite of the crisis and where optimism abounds in these days of privation." In an effort to lift Mexico's spirits as well as its economy, local business leaders launched their own "Buy Mexican" campaign. The nationalistic endeavor, they believed, should disprove critics of their "Americanized" (*Yankados*) ways. The Fundidora's press thus applauded how "these men of unbreakable faith, prototypes of the go-getter Norteño . . . have initiated a campaign to promote national products, a cry of true patriotism that will echo in every corner of the nation."[31] Much like the revolution or government labor policies, the economic crisis became just another obstacle to be conquered by the *regiomontano* elite. But civic boosterism offered little in the way of material relief.

Government policymakers did respond when demands for public assistance grew louder. Inspired by their own "disinterested motives," local ruling party officials established the Committee for the Unemployed that "integrated honorable laboring elements into diverse activities in the region." A state employment office hired "thousands of workers" for brief stints on highway construction crews. Others were sent to the strawberry fields of neighboring San Luis Potosí. The lucky ones stayed home, building new schools, paving streets in once-neglected neighborhoods, and refurbishing the city's parks and plazas. Local authorities also took measures to alleviate the problems caused by repatriation, allocating free rail passes to the arrivals' home states. But some remained behind and joined a growing

---

30 *El Machete*, Apr. 15, 1931; Nathan, Aug. 31, Oct. 31, 1931, SD 812.00 NL/14, 22 (quoted). By February 1932, *El Porvenir* was reporting three suicides per week.

31 *El Porvenir*, Mar. 30, 1931; *CYPSA*, Feb. 20, 1932; *Actividad*, May 1932 in Zapata Novoa, *Tercos y Triunfadores*, 41.

number of restive workers on Monterrey's streets. Indeed, as the governor later observed, "the situation created by [unemployment] proved favorable to the development of extremist social doctrines."[32]

Various organizations spoke on behalf of destitute workers. The Monterrey Unemployed Council, an association of neighborhood relief committees, demanded government action to offset "the misery that the capitalist class has thrown upon the shoulders of all workers." The council sought direct relief through soup kitchens, public shelters, and free rent for the unemployed. They also demanded that the government seize and operate shuttered factories, as authorities would do in several other states. Unbeknownst to local officials, Communist Party activists were also organizing idled workers, including newly arrived "deportados," in several northern cities. In Monterrey, they spearheaded the Union of Unemployed Workers, which echoed the PCM's call for a national social security system. Local leaders threatened direct action as well. They warned that, "If the workers of Nuevo León have not yet given their unanimous cry of protest, that is only because our culture does not permit it."[33] By mid-1931, their street protests had grown in size and scope. When word spread that a new American-owned celluloid plant had begun training operatives, hundreds of desperate job seekers crowded the factory's gates. Police dispersed the crowd when demands for work gave way to broken windows. The government soon ordered police to remove all "subversive propaganda" from public spaces. But they permitted the protests to continue because most remained "orderly."[34]

Tensions at ASARCO added to those on the streets. The smelter conflict escalated in February 1932 when a federal labor court authorized another three-week stoppage.[35] The announcement stunned the operatives. In less than two years, 70 percent of their workmates had been laid off. Rumors also circulated that ASARCO planned to close the smelter and concentrate operations at its Chihuahua plant. In a hastily convened assembly, the workers agreed to seize the plant should the company proceed with the stoppage. Communist Party activists had by then established the sit-down strike, or "taking the factories," as a strategy of protest.[36] The governor ordered the unionists to appeal the suspension through legal channels. If

32 *El Sol*, May 28, July 6, and Aug. 6, 1932; AGENL: *Informe del Gobernador Francisco Cárdenas, 1931–1932*, 3–6.
33 Consejo de Desocupados de Monterrey to Governor Cárdenas, Jan. 21, 1932, AGENL: Trabajo – Asuntos Laborales, 2/17; *El Machete*, May 1, 1932; Sindicato de Obreros sin Trabajo to Cárdenas, Oct. 29, 1930, AGENL: Trabajo – Asociaciones y Sindicatos, 7/120.
34 *El Porvenir*, May 26, 1931, Feb. 2 and 8, 1932.
35 Unless indicated otherwise, the following account is from *El Porvenir*, Feb. 23–29, 1932 and *El Machete*, Mar. 20, 1932.
36 Campa, *Mi testimonio*, 55.

not, he promised, federal troops would be deployed. Union officials rejected government mediation and went directly to management. Citing their commitment to "respect the will of the ranks," union leaders demanded that all operatives receive guarantees to be rehired and full salaries during the shutdown. The company balked and the workers refused to exit the smelter. Frightened by the "threatening attitude" of union leaders, the plant manager hastily telephoned Police Chief Cejudo. The smelter workers dispersed peacefully when Colonel Cejudo arrived. Police nonetheless arrested several union leaders for "verbally abusing the authorities." They would remain in jail for weeks.

Meanwhile, in downtown Monterrey, protestors had gathered in front of the smeltermen's union local on busy Madero Boulevard. The ASARCO workers shared the office with the Union of Unemployed Workers. For months, communist activists had staged street protests, organized a hunger march to Mexico City, and pressured authorities to provide relief to idled workers. In their speeches and propaganda, they persistently portrayed relations between the "imperialist company" and "its lapdog, the government" as a real and symbolic cause of local working-class misery. One American reported that ASARCO's union leaders "always took a prominent part in public demonstrations, shouting against the 'Gringo Company'." As he pointed out, "The fact that this was the only local plant operating under an American name helped to arouse prejudice in [the workers'] favor."[37] The showdown at the smelter transpired on the "National Day of Protest Against Unemployment." Organized by Communists throughout Mexico, the movement registered its largest turnout in Monterrey, where thousands of demonstrators marched on the state capital. There, they heard orators speak on a range of issues, from local layoffs to global imperialism. The protestors then departed, crowding through downtown streets before spilling out onto Madero Boulevard in front of the smeltermen's union local. Upon arrival, they learned the news about ASARCO: The company had again discharged its workers, the smeltermen resisted, and union leaders were arrested while exiting the premises.

The protest grew unruly. As mounted police converged on the scene, the demonstrators began stoning the nearby offices of the city's largest furniture manufacturer. Owned by Joel Rocha, a leading activist among the Monterrey elite, the company had recently shuttered the plant. A police lieutenant trotted into the crowd and pleaded for peace. He was showered with rocks. As he retreated, a knife-wielding protestor lunged at the officer, throwing him from his horse. The officer and his adversary fell to the ground, a struggle ensued, and police fired over the panicked crowd. The would-be assailant, a local worker named Leonides López, sprung to his feet, turned,

37 *El Machete*, Mar. 20, 1932; Nathan, June 1, 1932, SD 812.504/1298.

and charged another officer. He fell from his mount as López drove the knife into his shoulder. The officer's colleagues shot López dead and the protestors dispersed.

The violent turn of events alarmed Monterrey's authorities, who pondered the demise of the once peaceful protest movement. They soon found an answer at the offices of the ASARCO Production Workers Union. There, state police agents discovered documents linking the ASARCO unionists and the Union of Unemployed Workers to the PCM. Within days it was reported that federal police were on the trail of "Communist agitators" in Monterrey. The governor ordered police guards posted at local factory gates to prevent "outside elements from approaching the workers." The state stepped up its public works projects and began dispersing demonstrators by hiring them on to highway construction crews outside the city. The private sector launched its own relief campaign as well. Organized by the brewery's Luis G. Sada, Monterrey's industrialists developed a charitable fund to finance further public works projects. They also opened a soup kitchen at a local Masonic hall and noticeably stepped up the "Buy Mexican" campaign. The Communists considered this response from the chamber of commerce as a small victory for their struggle to defend the unemployed.[38]

Three weeks later, ASARCO complied with the labor court's ruling and resumed operations on schedule. For its workers, however, communist assertions that the labor law and the government in Mexico City served foreign interests rang increasingly true. In contrast to federal authorities, Nuevo León's labor board aggressively minimized unemployment by wielding its right to keep factories running. Powerful industrialists like the furniture magnet Joel Rocha thus proved somewhat exceptional. Throughout the crisis, the United States consul would comment upon how this "enforced production" and "stringent enforcement of the labor law" prevented layoffs in local industry.[39] So, also, did worker protest promote the policy. In April 1932, the steel mill laid off its structural iron workers. Local activists mobilized to protest layoffs at the city's largest employer. The iron workers themselves staged a hunger strike in the halls of the state capital. Authorities responded swiftly. The state labor board, under whose jurisdiction the steel mill still fell, ordered their rehiring because the company had failed to attain authorization for the suspensions.[40] However, as employees of an industry regulated by a Mexico City labor court, the smeltermen did not wield the steel workers' leverage. Their livelihood remained in the hands of distant bureaucrats who seemed immune from popular pressures.

---

38 *El Porvenir*, Mar. 1–2, 9, and 17, 1932; *El Machete*, Mar. 20, 1932.
39 Nathan, Mar. 31, 1932, Jan. 31, 1933, SD 812.00 NL/14, 40.
40 AGENL: Trabajo – Conciliación y Arbitraje, 3/7; AGENL: JCA 11/377.

The Spirit of the Law

No sooner had ASARCO resumed production when news arrived that the company's Mexico City lawyers were petitioning for another work stoppage. One month later, federal authorities approved ASARCO's proposal to operate the smelter on a twenty-day on, ten-day off schedule.[41] The plan would remain effective indefinitely and, as the union quickly protested, entailed a 33 percent wage cut for the remaining workers. Moreover, the earlier production changes allowed ASARCO to surpass during the first twenty-day stint what the smelter previously produced in an entire month. As union leaders later charged, "The imposed rationalization allowed the company to increase its profit margins while our workers grow impoverished."[42] In this context, their collective contract came due for renegotiation. ASARCO rejected all but four clauses in the union's proposal. Eleven of these clauses dealt with health and safety issues, from the workers' right to consult independent physicians to stronger accident compensation plans. Another clause forbid further rationalization plans and speed ups without union consultation. The company also rejected demands for the closed shop and seniority rights, prerogatives enjoyed by few Mexican unions at the time.[43] ASARCO offered an alternative contract. But union leaders refused to alter their proposal without rank-and-file consent. They therefore requested a three-day recess. What the plant superintendent considered to be "friendly discussions" adjourned at six in the evening. At seven the following morning, word reached his office that workers "were rioting in the plant, having chained the gates shut, refusing exit to the foremen, and threatening acts of sabotage should the company solicit [police] intervention." The smeltermen had taken the factory.

Despite the alarmist tone, ASARCO undoubtedly foresaw the action. As the United States Consul reported at the time, the Communist Party press "has long been agitating in regard to a strike" at the smelter.[44] Indeed, on May 9, ten days before contract negotiations even began, union leaders had announced their intentions in a circular issued to all communist-affiliated unions in Mexico. They requested strike funds and sympathy demonstrations to call the nation's attention to events transpiring in Monterrey. Union officials portrayed their movement as a struggle against the "Ley Fascista

---

41 *El Porvenir*, Mar. 21, 1932, Apr. 21–27, 1932.

42 Unless indicated otherwise, the following section is based upon the extensive labor court documentation in the file AGENL: Huelga ASARCO.

43 Nathan, June 1, 1932, SD 812.504/1298.

44 Nathan, June 1, 1932, SD 812.504/1298. The consul was correct. See *Defensa Proletaria*, Mexico City, May 12, 1931 and *El Machete*, May 20, 1932, where the Monterrey correspondent of the Communist Party organ solicited strike funds for the upcoming "struggle against the imperialist company."

de Trabajo," the labor code that protected "Yankee imperialist companies while workers are cast to misery." As the Communists had argued before its passage, the Federal Labor Law "legalized strikebreaking." Not only did it require advanced notice of such action, a cooling-down period during which the "company could prepare its defense." It also "permitted the government to break strikes by ordering production to resume or by protecting scabs with armed force." The circular promised that the ASARCO strike "would counter the law's effects by harming the company as much as possible." The bulletin recognized the union's disadvantageous position given the economic crisis. But its authors declared themselves "enemies of those who defend the bourgeois theory that workers cannot struggle under these circumstances." Working-class quiescence, the strike leaders argued, "leaves our exploiters with a free hand to reduce us to hunger while demanding maximum production and efforts on our part." They thus pledged that, "Our experience will be a struggle for all workers. And if we triumph, it will be a stimulus, for we will prove it possible to fight and win."[45]

The solidarity displayed by the smelter workers, union and nonunion alike, reflected months of struggle, negotiations, setbacks, and organizing. Hours after the contract negotiations had recessed, union leaders called an emergency assembly. They informed the smelter operatives that all legal and pacific means of defending their rights were exhausted. They then proposed the sit-down strike, to be coordinated by the eleven-man "self-defense units" organized previously in each department. The unionists compared the action to ASARCO's practice of allegedly stopping production without notifying the union. Moreover, they argued, the strike remained their only recourse given the company's relation with the government. The workers elected to strike.

Later that evening, the smeltermen, their families, and local supporters rallied in nearby May Day Plaza. As the rally concluded, secret police moved in and arrested the night's principal speaker, Valentín Campa. The former Monterrey railroader had been in town since his late 1931 release from a Mexico City jail. As the national leader of the communist labor central (CSUM), Campa had drafted the collective contract presented to ASARCO. As one worker later testified, Campa's arrest signified the authorities' desire to "break our will to struggle through police terror." For others, from ASARCO's managers to government officials to the local press, the arrest of this "dangerous communist" confirmed the strike's subsequent portrayal as the work of outside agitators.[46]

---

45 "Circular Numero 1 del Comité de Huelga, Sindicato de Obreros Productores de La American Smelting Refining," May 9, 1932 in AGN: DGG 2.331 (16)/13-A/23.
46 Interview with Albino Reyes in *El Porvenir*, May 26, 1932.

The sit-down strike began much like previous protests at the plant. But it ended on a tragic note.[47] Moreover, unlike the first plant seizure, this one elicited community-wide support. Throughout the morning, the strikers remained in the smelter while the government attempted to negotiate a peaceful settlement. Union leaders declined the federal labor inspector's offer to mediate contract negotiations. As he reported, "The workers would listen to no explanations, alleging that the company had always extorted and deceived them." Union leaders promised to resume work only when the plant manager entered the smelter and signed their collective contract. As an economic incentive, the strike committee extinguished the smelter's furnaces and thereby permitted the kettles to cool and crack. The unionists rejected the inspector's pleas to keep the furnaces lit – as the law stipulated – for, in their words, "we care nothing about the company's losses." Meanwhile, Police Chief Cejudo arrived to the plant. He was immediately surrounded by an unruly crowd of former workers, workers' wives, and their children. He and his men therefore stationed themselves in the company's offices.

By mid-day, news of the strike had spread through Monterrey. Flyers called upon workers "to reinforce our movement . . . for our victory shall be shared by all our class brothers!" The broadsides informed locals of ASARCO's layoffs, rationalization schemes, increased profits, and rejection of the union's contract. Strike leaders even linked their "anti-imperialist struggle" to that of Nicaraguan rebel Augusto Sandino, then waged in an ongoing war to oust the U.S. Marines from Nicaragua. Their handbill further explained that, "As the crisis mounts, our workers grow hungry while the bankers of Wall Street fill their safes with gold. We knew beforehand that the foreign company could count on the authorities' support. It is thus the duty and obligation of all workers to demand the most absolute respect for the strike."[48] Unemployed workers, local activists, and curious citizens converged on the plant. Hearing of these developments, the governor ordered in reinforcements of mounted police. Meanwhile, the labor inspector wired Mexico City, informing his superiors that "workers directed by communist agitators had illegally seized the plant." Late that afternoon, the president ordered federal troops to the smelter.

The commanding officer gave the strikers an ultimatum: Abandon the plant or be removed by force. The workers opted for the peaceful alternative. But as they departed, a melee erupted. Protestors rushed the plant gates. As one witness recounted, "fifty hotheaded women waving union flags" led the resistance. They "encouraged the workers to maintain their attitude of defiance" and showered bottles, stones, and iron fragments on mounted

47 Strike narrative in *El Porvenir*, May 25–26, 1932 and *El Machete*, May 30 and June 10, 1932.
48 Nathan, June 1, 1932, SD 812.504/1298.

police as they attempted to clear the gates. By police accounts, a shot rang out from a nearby rooftop. They therefore responded with "a light volley of bullets." According to the press, a "riot" ensued. Mounted police charged into the crowd as some strikers fled from the plant and others sought cover inside. At least three workers fell wounded to police bullets. One, a shoe-maker by trade, later died of his wounds. Others were struck down by sabers as they were chased through nearby streets. Three women protestors sustained severe injuries and horses trampled upon children trapped in the skirmish. When the violence concluded, the remaining strikers slowly ex-ited the plant. As they emerged, ASARCO's superintendent identified their presumed strike leaders to Colonel Cejudo. Police arrested one dozen work-ers and two representatives of the communist labor central. That evening, federal police kidnaped five strike leaders and transported them to Mexico City. They were held incommunicado for the next three months. But au-thorities did not deport them to the Islas Marías penal colony for "agitating our peaceful workers," as Nuevo León's governor had insisted.[49]

That night, federal troops patrolled the neighborhoods surrounding the smelter, dispersing the protest marches organized by workers and their sympathizers.[50] Several days later, federal police arrested two more strike committee members as they spoke at a rally near the steel mill. The strikers appealed once again for public support. Leaflets announced a demonstration for the following Sunday to demand freedom for imprisoned workers and the dismissal of Police Chief Cejudo. President Ortíz Rubio ordered a full-scale troop mobilization. Early Sunday morning, hundreds of workers converged cautiously on Monterrey's Arco de Independencia. The United States consul reported, with a sense of relief, that the protestors "quicky and quietly dispersed" upon the military's arrival. "Indeed," he observed, "the military forces were such as to appall any demonstrators, for in addition to cavalry and infantry even machine gun troops were brought on the scene. It is believed that no further demonstrations will be attempted for the present."[51]

The strike and its aftermath transcended Monterrey. Workers throughout Mexico heeded the union's earlier call and organized protest demonstrations over the ensuing days. In the northern mining town of Santa Eulalia, work-ers from an ASARCO mine defied their union leaders' orders and marched through the streets to express their solidarity with the smeltermen. Far-ther south, in the state of Veracruz, the Liga Femenil Rosa Luxemburgo protested "the barbaric attitude of Nuevo León's reactionary government." Like the strike in Monterrey, their action elicited a swift and repressive response. In the weeks after the strike, letters of protest arrived at the

49 Francisco Cárdenas to Gobernación, May 24, 1932, AGN.DGG 2.331.8 (16)/13-A-23.
50 *El Porvenir*, May 28, 1932.
51 Nathan, June 6, 1932, SD 812.504/1301.

governor's desk.[52] Their origins reveal the geographical scope and social diversity of the "proletarian family" organized by the Communists: bricklayers from the border towns, miners from the sierra, laborers on southern banana plantations, and Gulf Coast oil workers. One protest letter even arrived from Chicago's Trade Union Unity League. Sympathizers lauded the workers' "heroic movement." Others condemned the "police terror" that followed: the "kidnaping" of ASARCO union leaders, the prohibition of public protest, and the arrest of activists for distributing propaganda. They condemned the Mexican government as "a loyal servant to Yankee imperialism" and characterized the police brutality against "defenseless women and children" as an act "worthy of Porfirian times." In Monterrey, the repression would earn renown as the "ASARCO massacre," a testament less to the number of casualties (one) than the nature of the government's response.

The ASARCO strike remained effective until the labor board convened to determine its legality. The union's lawyer admitted during hearings that the workers had violated the law by striking without proper notification. But he justified their action by noting ASARCO's refusal to address their demands. On this point, the federal labor inspector agreed. ASARCO officials countered that the only issue open to discussion was how "the workers took over the workshops and rioted in the refining plant." They violated the law by "kidnaping" their supervisors, sabotaging machinery, and damaging the furnaces at a cost of $100,000 to the company. ASARCO could thus rescind the workers' contracts and hire replacements. Workers refuted the charge of sabotage. So did an American foreman, who also denied claims that workers abused company personnel, who had in fact hidden when the sit-down strike began. Furthermore, argued the unionists, the government never subjected ASARCO to such "severe punishments" when it violated Mexican labor laws.

Several weeks later, Mexico's secretary of industry completed his review of the hearings. He declared the strike illegal because of the workers' "failure to adhere to the spirit of the law." But he then ordered the immediate reinstatement of all smelter workers with the exception of the strike's leaders. The decision betrayed a widespread belief that a handful of agitators instigated the conflict. In his report to Washington, the United States consul cited "outside assistance and agitation" as one of the "underlying causes of the strike." His remarks echoed those in the local press, which linked the movement to a "dark hand" conspiring to "agitate our workers and provoke a crisis."[53] Indeed, the police cited the organizers' status as "outsiders" to

52 Letters and telegrams in AGENL: Huelga ASARCO; for events in Jalapa, Veracruz see *El Machete*, June 19, 1932.

53 Nathan, June 6, 1932, SD 812.504/1301; *El Porvenir*, 26 May 1932. Another of the "underlying causes" cited by the United States consul was that "the local managers of the plant are not empowered

justify their arrest and "deportation" to Mexico City. This is what police chief Cejudo told Valentín Campa when he ordered the communist labor leader expelled from Nuevo León. Campa replied to Cejudo that he was born in Monterrey – as were the majority of his fellow deportees. He also reminded the police chief that *he* (Cejudo) came from San Luis Potosí.[54] While several union leaders were also migrants from San Luis, like so many of their fellow smeltermen, they all worked at the plant or had labored in local factories after being laid off by ASARCO. More importantly for the rank-and-file workers, the "outside" status of their leaders mattered less than their character as organizers. As one smelter operative thus testified before the labor court, "Every class has its leaders, those who best interpret their interests and confront our struggle's hardships and dangers with courage and determination."

Learning from Defeat

The Great Depression provided the first test to the efficacy of industrial paternalism in Monterrey. In the United States, pioneers of company paternalism dismantled their systems as the Depression deepened. Chafed by this abrogation of their perceived rights, workers fought back with the collective strength of unionism. A sense of community born of paternalism sustained their struggles. A sympathetic state sanctioned their demands.[55] In Monterrey, layoffs, wage cuts, and mass unemployment fueled popular protest. But it remained minimal if not conspicuously absent at the city's leading industries. In earlier chapters we saw how, for the steel workers, paternalism helped alleviate the harsh effects of the market economy. Likewise, at the Cuauhtémoc Brewery, the Depression-era layoffs marked an extended seasonal downturn, an experience to which workers in that industry had grown accustomed. Paternalism provided the workers a modicum of security that reaffirmed their employers' concern for their well-being. Initially, at least, they acquiesced in the formation of company unions, the local industrialists' common response to the 1931 Federal Labor Law.

ASARCO proved exceptional on all these fronts. Unlike the brewery and steel mill, the foreign-owned smelter did not avoid the cost-conscious dismantling of paternalism. Neither did ASARCO aggressively resist when worker–activists launched a union drive in the late 1920s. Finally, no workers felt the effects of the Depression more swiftly and directly than the smeltermen. Union leaders understood the industry's peculiar vulnerability

to act on their own initiative but are obliged to refer matters to their superiors in Mexico City, New York, or elsewhere."

54 Campa, *Mi testimonio*, 82.
55 On company paternalism, the Depression, and the rise of industrial unionism in the United States see Cohen, *Making a New Deal*, 251–89.

to global markets. It was the impersonal means by which ASARCO handled the crisis – and the federal government's seeming complicity – that generated rank-and-file support for a strike that brazenly defied the law. The onset of economic recovery would galvanize rank-and-file sympathy for militant unionism elsewhere. The Communists tapped into popular protest by following the organizational strategies outlined by the party in the early 1930s. Organizers worked within existing company unions and won grass-roots allegiance "through a constant defense of [the workers'] interests."[56] In the case of ASARCO, they achieved that goal by challenging company safety and health policies and defending workers against abusive foremen. The same strategies would earn such militants renown as honest unionists willing to take risks in other factories where similar conditions prevailed.

At ASARCO, smelting operations resumed in late June with 230 former strikers. Meanwhile, local Communists were soon driven off the streets by a "cycle of police terror" that ranged from the arrest of activists distributing flyers to a ban on public demonstrations. They therefore followed the party line and returned to workplace organizing. The Communist Party press considered the ASARCO strike less as a setback than a lesson upon which to build local activism. Activists lauded the solidarity displayed between union and nonunion workers. They celebrated the "the outstanding role played by proletarian women," adding that "they were the most determined ones during the clash with police." Their actions therefore "erased the prejudicial views about the conservatism of working women, especially in Monterrey." The Communists also proclaimed the strike "of capital importance [for having] destroyed completely the theory of social peace in Nuevo León." "Monterrey's proletariat has learned to defend their jobs with vigor," they concluded, while "Monterrey's bourgeoisie has seen that state's paradise of exploitation vanish forever."[57] At the national level, the CSUM continued organizing workers in Mexico's basic industries. Veteran communist activists played key roles in the formation of national industrial unions capable of challenging companies like ASARCO, which operated throughout the republic. In Monterrey, they began by establishing solid inroads in the smelters and railroad shops. The political opening that arrived with the 1934 election of President Lázaro Cárdenas offered even greater opportunities to realize their goals. Then, as militant unionism challenged company unions in Monterrey's leading industries, local activists would evoke the workers' historical memory of the "ASARCO massacre" to juxtapose those times of "reactionary" government with the radical promises of Cardenismo.

56 *El Machete*, Dec. 10, 1931.
57 *El Machete*, June 10 and 20, 1932.

7

Stay with the Company or Go with the Reds

In February 1935, General Lázaro Cárdenas paid his first visit to Monterrey as Mexico's president. Coming just weeks after his inauguration, he passed the brief, twelve-hour stop meeting with the city's most prominent industrialists and labor leaders. The *regiomontanos* expressed some earnest concerns. Strikes had then reached record levels in their hometown. So had claims filed with the state's labor court system. Local politicians had become increasingly troublesome as well, publicly pledging their support of "red" union activists as they challenged the legality of company unions. The industrialists could, nevertheless, reflect upon the positive. Manufacturing thrived as never before. Moreover, labor disputes remained conspicuously absent at such major industries as steel, brewing, glass, and smelting. The businessmen attributed that to the "sensible" leaders who led the Independent Unions of Nuevo León, the city's federation of company unions. They reminded President Cárdenas that these activists were all blue-collar workers who had been "forged within the factories and workshops of Monterrey." They therefore claimed to represent "genuine working-class interests," as opposed to the "false leaders" who used workers to promote their own political ambitions. The industrialists then outlined their paramount concern: the threat posed by Communists to their city's economic prosperity. The president assured them that "communism would not be introduced" to Monterrey.

Cárdenas also met with Pancho Guzmán and Rosendo Ocañas, steel workers speaking on behalf of the Independent Unions. Ocañas reiterated that the white unions were "serious organizations comprised exclusively of working people." And while he certainly knew better, the machinist promised Cárdenas that, "in Nuevo León, labor problems are practically nonexistent, except for those created deliberately by professional agitators."[1] Guzmán and Ocañas were two of Monterrey's most well-known labor activists at the time. They directed the Federated Steel Unions and led the city's dominant labor central. They had both represented workers on the labor arbitration

---

1 *El Porvenir*, Feb. 26, 1935.

board. Guzmán was also serving his second term in Nuevo León's congress. However, their noteworthy role in local labor politics belied their waning popularity among the steel workers they represented. Indeed, ten months after the president's visit, the rank and file ousted their long-time union leaders and voted to join the national Miner-Metalworkers Union. Their union, Local 67, became the most activist union in Monterrey and one of the most influential in Mexico. By affiliating with *los Mineros*, the steel workers forsook the *regiomontanos'* celebrated autonomy from national unions for the promises of Cardenismo.

For working-class Mexicans, the most important of those promises was the government's unambiguous support of their right to unionize. Responding to an unprecedented level of labor protest throughout Mexico, President Lázaro Cárdenas (1934–1940) adopted an aggressively prounion stance that tested the limits of industrial paternalism in Monterrey.[2] His government's labor policy established two basic objectives: the organization of workers into a single labor central, the Confederation of Mexican Workers (CTM), and the negotiation of collective contracts that guaranteed effective compliance with constitutional labor law. It was hoped that working-class unification would end years of interunion conflicts. Labor peace would in turn promote national industrial development, thereby weakening Mexico's historic dependence on foreign capital and imported goods. Cardenista labor policy aspired to broader ends as well. The "revolutionary unions" would become schools for the making of a new Mexican working class – hard working, clean living, and loyal to the ruling party. Yet as so many workers came to believe, a genuine humanism motivated Lázaro Cárdenas. He believed it his patriotic duty and paternalistic obligation to protect workers' rights and improve their families' lives. He did so by defending striking workers and mediating disputes on labor's behalf.

From his government's perspective, Monterrey offered a paradoxical case. As Mexico's preeminent industrial center – and the only one where native capital predominated – the city embodied policymakers' vision of a "Mexicanized" economy with a strong manufacturing base. Moreover, the well-publicized paternalism of Monterrey's largest employers offered blue-collar families a standard of living to which many a Mexican worker aspired. But as a stronghold of company unions, Monterrey stood as a primary obstacle to national working-class unification. The Cardenistas thus faced the same dilemma as previous and succeeding governments: how to balance

---

2 On the Cárdenas regime and its labor policy, see Alan Knight, "Cardenismo: Juggernaut or Jalopy?," *Journal of Latin American Studies* 26 (1994), 73–107; Nora Hamilton, *The Limits of State Autonomy: Post-Revolutionary Mexico* (Princeton, 1982), 143–62; Marcos Tonatiuh Águila M. and Alberto Enríquez Perea, eds., *Perspectivas sobre el Cardenismo: Ensayos sobre economía, trabajo, política y cultura en los años treinta* (Mexico City, 1996).

the state's commitment to economic development with the revolutionary promises of social reform. Seen from the *regiomontanos'* perspective, however, there were no contradictions inherent to Cardenismo. The locals either embraced the government's new labor policy, or they loathed and resisted it. The struggles that ensued drew nationwide attention to Monterrey and did much to shape the outcome of these years of defiance in Mexico.

The Stress of Frenzied Industry

Monterrey industry was thriving when Cárdenas became president. The recovery of mining activity in northern Mexico reverberated in the local factories and merchant houses dependent upon consumers throughout the North. The smelters renewed exports of industrial metals to foreign markets, while public works programs stimulated domestic demand for Monterrey steel and cement. One observer reported the Depression over by early 1934. The following year, sales figures for local industries surpassed 1934 levels by 20 percent.[3] The United States consul predicted a bright future for *regiomontano* industry. He attributed these prospects to two factors: protective tariffs – "privileges taken as a matter of course [by the industrialists]" – and the "excellent character and abundant supply of labor."[4] The Great Depression was by then a distant memory and Monterrey prospered as never before, a testimony to how the *regiomontanos'* "family cohesion, optimism, and other cultural traits" drove them to overcome such obstacles to progress.[5]

The economic rebound cast an upbeat shadow across the "Sultan of the North." Monterrey grew by 50 percent – to 200,000 – during the 1930s. Out-of-state migrants still comprised one-third of the population, a sure sign that the city's renown as a place of opportunity continued to exert a pull on migrants from the North.[6] Travel writers described the thriving, modern, and welcoming lifestyle the newcomers encountered. A writer for a Mexican tourist guide discovered an "opulent and prosperous" city during his 1934 visit. An American found in Monterrey "a homey, hospitable place, noted for its friendly people, its good local government, and its civic pride." But foreign visitors often seemed perplexed by their encounter. An English traveler expressed his surprise when he reached "this Mexican Birmingham." He arrived to a city that "hummed like a gigantic beehive under the stress of its frenzied industry." "One might almost have been in New York," he sensed, "for the bustle and movement . . . in the streets were

3 Nathan, May 29, 1934, SD 812.00 NL/61; Haber, *Industry and Underdevelopment*, 177–80; *El Porvenir*, Jan. 24, 1936.
4 Nathan, Feb. 26, 1936, SD 812.504/1561.
5 Zapata Novoa, *Tercos y Triunfadores*, 23–24.
6 Secretaría de la Economía Nacional, *Sexto Censo de Población, 1940: Nuevo León* (Mexico City, 1943), 37.

completely foreign to Mexico." A writer from the United States concurred. He described Monterrey as "the one Mexican city whose main streets look more modern and more American" than "many cities" in his native land.[7] Some travelers caught a glimpse of the "old Spanish atmosphere" in the city's few cathedrals, the pastel shades of its one-story housing, and its palm-lined plazas with their sparkling fountains. They found in this mix of the Old and New Worlds "a happy blend of the useful and the beautiful, or the material and the spiritual." But after traveling elsewhere in Mexico, most writers found evidence in "the bustle of commerce" and in new neighborhoods reminiscent of the "Los Angeles suburbs" that "the city is becoming more Americanized each day."[8] Indeed, the renewal of economic prosperity soon brought the conspicuous presence of an American staple, the automobile, to one observer's attention. Meanwhile, the arrival of tourists from the United States certainly stoked the optimism of the city's boosters, who took pride in the visitors' views of their modern and progressive hometown. That reputation, it seems, led one traveler to consider Monterrey but a stopping-off point on his journey to "the real Mexico of the south."[9]

Monterrey's working class experienced this unique level of Mexican modernity not only in the "frenzied stress" of industry, but in the rapid development of mass culture. For at least one traveler, the city's "night-clubs and modern movies . . . sports and social life" distinguished it from other regions of Mexico.[10] Relatively few cities then offered blue-collar families greater access to commercial entertainment. Bullfights, circuses, and rodeos all visited the city during the long summer months. So did touring professional baseball teams from both the United States and Cuba. The new Arena Obrero hosted weekly boxing and wrestling matches while Monterrey's cinemas screened the latest American releases. Not surprisingly, one retired steel worker agreed that one of his favorites was *Modern Times*, Charlie Chaplin's satirical commentary on the industrial age. Entrepreneurs courted the patronage of blue-collar customers by offering tickets to such attractions at "popular prices." It was also during this decade that radios became conspicuous in the home and in the cantinas frequented by workers. Operated by the same families that controlled the print media, Monterrey's commercial stations broadcast throughout northern Mexico. What civic boosters lauded as a "modern means of propaganda" became a

7 *Mapa*, Mexico City, Sep. 1933 in Mendirichaga, *Los 4 tiempos*, 365; J.H. Plenn, *Mexico Marches* (Indianapolis, 1939), 274; R.H.K. Marett, *Eye-Witness of Mexico* (New York, 1939), 146–47.

8 Harry Frank and Herbert Lanks, *The Pan American Highway: From the Rio Grande to the Canal Zone* (New York, 1940), 9–10; T. Philip Terry, *Terry's Guide to Mexico* (Boston, 1938), 7; MacKinley Helm, *Journeying Through Mexico* (Boston, 1948), 40; Leonidas Ramsey, *Time Out for Adventure: Let's Go to Mexico* (New York, 1934), 13.

9 Nathan, May 6, 1935, SD 312.00 NL/98; Marett, *Eye-Witness of Mexico*, 146.

10 Frank and Lanks, *The Pan American Highway*, 10.

key component of the local elite's ongoing efforts to influence working-class consumption patterns as well as their social and political outlooks.[11]

Government officials also courted the sympathies of working-class families. The city paved and lighted streets, constructed parks, and built new schools in Monterrey's blue-collar districts. Inner-city slums like Little Matehuala succumbed to a "wave of urbanization." While residents of the infamous shantytown resisted the bulldozers' arrival, the government replaced their dwellings with new working-class housing tracts like Colonia Moderna and Colonia Obrera. These public works projects addressed working-class grievances and aspirations expressed since the early 1920s when housing shortages and flooded streets had plagued their neighborhoods and prevented their children from attending school. Had foreign visitors ventured beyond Monterrey's bustling central district, they would have found that many of the city's poorest working-class families still resided in wooden shacks and raised farm animals on their lots. Indeed, the municipal government's drive to promote tourism led city fathers to level and redevelop several of these "primitive corners of Monterrey" in the mid-1930s.[12] The government's commitment to workers' well-being ideally generated popular support for the National Revolutionary Party (PNR). Along those lines, the Christmas season saw the wives of party officials distribute fruit, candy, and sweaters to working-class children. Government-sponsored street fairs became commonplace in their neighborhoods. The PNR even fielded its own athletic teams and staged well-funded regional sports festivals. To a certain extent, such government initiatives brought benefits reminiscent of company paternalism to additional working-class families. They also paralleled similar government policies meant to secularize and sanitize popular culture elsewhere in Mexico.[13] But workers were not just beneficiaries of the changes taking shape in Monterrey during these years. They were instigators as well.

Monterrey's workers grabbed the opportunities offered by economic recovery and shifting political tides to assert greater control over their lives. The revival of industrial production resulted in a sustained period of labor protest and union drives. Claims filed with the state labor courts escalated annually from an average of 86 (1924–29) to 223 (1933–34) and 762 (1933–34).[14] The causes of protest shifted as well. As the economy rebounded,

11 *El Sol*, July 22 and Oct. 1, 1932, June 19, 1934, Sep. 27, 1935. See also Joy Elizabeth Hayes, *Radio Nation: Communication, Popular Culture, and Nationalism in Mexico, 1920–1950* (Tucson, 2000).

12 *El Porvenir*, Dec. 5, 1923, May 26, 1927, June 1, 1932, Aug. 11, 1934, July 7 and 15, 1936; AGENL: Industria y Comericio, 5.

13 *El Porvenir*, Nov. 8 and 24, Dec. 25, 1934; on the state's cultural policies, see Alan Knight, "Revolutionary Project, Recalcitrant People: Mexico, 1910–1940," in Jamie Rodríguez O., ed., *The Revolutionary Process in Mexico, 1880–1940* (Los Angeles, 1990), 227–63.

14 Labor court figures from AGENL: Informes de Gobernadores, 1924–1935.

demands for back wages and reinstatement were surpassed by struggles for higher pay and collective contracts. These protests reflected workers' new organizational muscle. Unions certified by the state labor board increased their total membership from 4,070 to 11,485 between 1932 and 1934 alone. Those falling under federal jurisdiction represented another 8,344 workers in Nuevo León's textile, smelting, and railroad industries. Thus roughly 68 percent of Nuevo León's 28,893 industrial workers were already unionized when Cárdenas assumed the presidency.[15] For federal labor authorities, then, the unionization of Monterrey's workers posed few problems. Their unification was a different matter.

Unionization developed in the three distinct patterns discernible since the late 1920s. The company unions for which Monterrey earned renown were the most cohesive. United as the Independent Unions of Nuevo León, they represented 50 percent of workers in industries under state jurisdiction. The so-called white unions were not cast in a single mold. While some were merely paper organizations directed by foremen or office workers, those that represented labor in the major industries (steel, glass, cement, beer) assumed highly active roles in the city's labor movement. The Independent Unions' capacity to elect delegates to the state labor board played a paramount role in their struggle to resist internal challenges because the labor tribunal held the key to union certification. For that reason, militants like those at ASARCO made their first substantive inroads in plants under the jurisdiction of the federal labor boards, where both government and labor delegates were hostile to company unions. Opposed to the Independents were Monterrey's *sindicatos revolucionarios*, as their members referred to the "red" unions.[16]

The reds diverged in their leaders' politics and their membership composition. To one side stood unions led by anti-Communists tied to the

---

15 AGENL: *Informe del Gobernador Francisco Cárdenas, 1931–1932*, 17; *El Porvenir*, Dec. 3, 1934; Sindicatos Independientes del Estado de Nuevo León to President Cárdenas, Dec. 8, 1934, AGN: Presidentes 433.1/8; AGN: DAT, 161/2; Secretaría de la Economía Nacional, *Quinto Censo de la Población* (Mexico City, 1934).

16 The etymology of these color-coded union labels remains unclear for the Mexican case, but largely adheres to the white/conservative, red/militant dichotomy used in Europe at the time. In the Mexican context, for example, the paramilitary forces organized by landowners to resist agrarian reform came to be known as "White Guards." Throughout Latin America and Europe, "red" is often applied to regions or cities known as strongholds of radical politics or of outstanding working-class militancy. But Stuart Macintyre notes that "red" has also been employed by opponents of unionism to convince locals of the alien and conspiratorial character of labor militancy, if not to remind them of the atheism, immorality, and dictatorial rule associated with Russian Bolsheviks (*Little Moscows*, 14–15). In the case of Monterrey, the terms "red" and "white" were first applied by the detractors of militant and company unions, respectively. But their widespread currency blunted their negative connotations and workers belonging to such unions readily used the color-coded terms, as well as the "revolutionary" and "independent" labels.

National Revolutionary Party. Their unions largely represented workers in Monterrey's smaller factories (food processing, apparel) and service industries (waiters, taxi drivers, vendors). The Communists, on the other hand, made their earliest inroads in Nuevo León's railroad, smelting, and construction industries. A notable loosening of official anticommunism in 1934 offered them new organizational opportunities. In that context, Communists spearheaded the founding of Mexico's first national industrial unions of railway and mining-metallurgical workers. Political factionalism became and remained a hallmark of the red unions. At times, Monterrey's progovernment and communist activists organized competing labor centrals and waged ceaseless battles for supremacy within local factories. But their common commitment to militant unionism bore fruit. By 1936, their organizing success would allow the reds to challenge their white rivals for control of the local labor courts.

Several overlapping factors explain the surge in popular protest and unionization. The economic recovery provided labor the bargaining power to redress old grievances and press new demands. Moreover, the fanfare that accompanied the passage of the 1931 Federal Labor Law certainly renewed workers' awareness of their legal rights. Equally important were government reforms that increased labor's confidence in the law and improved the labor board's efficiency. The Labor Attorney's Office (*Procuraduría del Trabajo*), a new state agency staffed largely by law students, provided workers free legal counseling and representation before the labor tribunal.[17] In 1933, Nuevo León added a second labor tribunal to handle cases outside the manufacturing sector. The state also began operating the court on a daily rather than a twice-weekly basis. That alleviated the backlogs that had hampered the board during the 1920s. Even the probusiness press, once an ardent foe of the Federal Labor Law, lauded the reforms for establishing the means to resolve disputes without recourse to costly strikes. As one editor noted somewhat prematurely, "Article 123 is no longer an abstract precept subjected to diverse interpretations for lack of regulations." Labor protest also escalated because the courts became more favorably responsive to working-class grievances. In 1933, for example, fewer than 10 percent of 584 claims even reached the arbitration stage. Employers essentially admitted to their Depression-era transgressions and reached conciliation with their workers by reinstating them in their old jobs and paying back wages.[18]

---

17 The *Procuraduría del Trabajo* greatly benefited the day laborers, domestics, and employees of small workshops, the less-educated and poorly paid workers who rarely garnered the attention of the lawyers working with Monterrey's labor centrals. AGENL: Informes de Gobernadores, 1932–1933, 7 and 1933–1934, vii–viii; for 1936 caseload of Labor Attorney's Office see AGENL: JCA 91/2085.
18 *El Porvenir*, Nov. 16, 1935; AGENL: *Informe del Gobernador Pablo Quiroga, 1933–1934*, 12.

But from the viewpoint of red worker–activists, the board's legitimacy remained tainted as long as white unions controlled the appointment of labor delegates to the court. That remained the case into the mid-1930s. In 1934, a foreman at Monterrey Glassworks and the secretary general of the Steel Unions represented workers' interests on the tribunal. The company unionists often served impartially, excusing themselves from hearings involving their workmates.[19] But they more commonly sided with the city's employers, as when they vetoed a minimum wage hike.[20] The Independents' control of the tribunal also made it virtually impossible for militants to challenge the legal status of company unions. The conservative tilt of the labor board soon came under attack not only from organized labor but the government as well.

The Times Have Changed

By 1934, the National Revolutionary Party was already coming under some intense criticism from both the left and the right. Throughout Mexico, embattled conservatives who had long resented the state's anticlerical agenda were further galvanized by the government's decision to adopt a socialist education curriculum for public schools and universities. Meanwhile, a younger generation of Mexicans schooled on the populist promises of the revolution protested the state's official abandonment of its land reform program and its perceived failure to enforce the Mexican labor law. In Nuevo León, Governor Francisco Cárdenas was forced to publicly rebuke charges from his leftist critics that the train of revolution had been derailed in Monterrey. He contended that "the revolutionary program has been implemented in all its breadth" and suggested that "radical critiques" to the contrary came only from the very "professional agitators driven out [of the city] by the workers themselves."[21] But the governor soon lost the confidence of his superiors in Mexico City.

Battered by the Great Depression, charges of corruption, and resistance to its centralization of power, the PNR strove to shore up its popular support and challenge the clout of regional elites. Nuevo León's economic prominence and large working class made the state an early target of these

---

19 The steel worker Pancho Guzmán called in his alternate when Fundidora workers appeared before the board since, he explained in one case, his "economic dependence on the defendant prejudiced his presence." AGENL: JCA 31/888, 34/962.

20 Nuevo León's minimum wage held firm at $1.50 daily after government authorities and organized labor proposed $2.00. The Independents backed the business leaders, arguing that higher wages would cause layoffs and chase potential investors to lower-wage markets in central Mexico. AGENL: *Informe del Gobernador Pablo Quiroga, 1933–1934*, 8; Nathan, Sep. 14, Oct. 3, 1933, SD 812.5041/62, 63.

21 *Excélsior*, Aug. 20, 1933.

designs. Former President Calles, who organized the party and remained Mexico's "Maximum Leader" after leaving office in 1928, appointed his son as Monterrey's mayor and ousted probusiness Governor Cárdenas in 1935.[22] The interim governor, General Pablo Quiroga, judged it his responsibility to take, in his words, "decisive and energetic measures to guarantee respect for workers' rights." Under his tenure, the government provided the labor board with the resources to function efficiently. He also encouraged workers to organize themselves "without compromises or ties to anyone except their *compañeros de clase* (class comrades)." Governor Quiroga opposed company unions and he therefore reformed the labor board's statutes to favor their militant rivals. New stipulations prohibited the election of "confidential employees" (for example, foremen) to the tribunal. The state also began paying salaries to labor representatives, who previously remained on company payrolls, so they "can work with complete independence rather than remain in service to any factory."[23] In a final and decisive action, Governor Quiroga appointed a Monterrey labor lawyer, Teófilo Martínez Pérez, as the board's president. Martínez would oversee several of the most consequential labor conflicts in the city's history, becoming the nemesis of the industrial elite and a hero to many local workers.

As the industrialists long feared, the government now played an increasingly interventionist role in labor relations through its capacity to manipulate the labor law. Martínez demonstrated how during the 1934 elections of delegates to the state labor board. Controversy erupted as soon as the proceedings began. Martínez altered previous voting procedures and decided to base the election's outcome on union membership figures rather than the number of delegates present at the convention. This elicited a futile protest from the Independents, whose delegates outnumbered the reds by a thirty-seven to thirty-six margin. Martínez further angered the white unionists when he certified ballots cast in representation of Nuevo León's 1,200 union cotton pickers. Like their urban counterparts, the rural workers also fell under the labor board's jurisdiction. The legal manoeuver handed a victory to the reds by the slimmest of margins, 5,860–5,625. Leaders of the Independent Unions abandoned the proceedings in protest. In the following weeks, they filed appeals in federal court, staged raucous street demonstrations, and waged an aggressive campaign of protest through front-page manifestos in the local press. They decried the "illegal acts" of Martínez and deplored the rural laborers for being "neither workers nor from Monterrey." The Supreme Court cited legal precedents to justify Martínez's ruling. Nonetheless, Governor Quiroga, shaken by the protests, brokered a settlement. He permitted the Independent Unions to

22 Nathan to State Department, Dec. 26, 1933, SD 812.00 NL/61; Saragoza, *The Monterrey Elite*, 175.
23 AGENL: *Informe del Gobernador Pablo Quiroga, 1933–1934*, 8; *El Porvenir*, Nov. 23, 1934.

appoint their delegates to Group No. 1 of the labor board, which oversaw the manufacturing sector, while the militants sat their representatives on Group No. 2 (rural and service workers).[24]

Quiroga's concession to the Independent Unions reflected political pragmatism at its best. For one thing, Pancho Guzmán, the veteran steel worker who directed the "white" labor central, was also a ruling party activist. Key gubernatorial elections loomed on the horizon. Quiroga thereby mediated a settlement that promised to limit political damage to the ruling party. The labor board elections also transpired in the context of mounting local resistance to state interventionism. The government's attempts to impose its socialist education policies in Monterrey made for an unusual opposition alliance of conservatives and communists. By September 1934 the United States consul witnessed large demonstrations against the constitutional reform. While there, he gathered antigovernment flyers "emanating from Catholic sources" that, "warn parents that their sons will become criminals and their daughters prostitutes under such a system [of education]." Several weeks later parents reportedly pulled their children out of classes when rumors circulated that the letters "P-N-R" were to be "branded" on the students' arms by ruling party fanatics.[25]

But the most intense outcries occurred at the newly opened University of Nuevo León, where students protested the socialist curriculum by barricading themselves in the campus. Authorities ordered troops to disperse the protestors, an intriguing antigovernment coalition of young conservatives and the Revolutionary Student Federation, communist activists who opposed the state's "pseudo-socialist project." Subsequent street demonstrations turned violent when ruling party goons fired on the crowd, killing four protestors, including two union workers. From Mexico City, former President Calles further aroused local indignity by blaming the protests on "the priests and Jew capitalists in Monterrey." "Those industrialists," he went on, "have long enjoyed undue prerogatives, since they know neither how to reciprocate the protection the government has given them nor how to treat their workers."[26] The socialist education policy remained in effect. But Governor Quiroga's resolution of the labor board controversy

24 *El Porvenir*, Dec. 3, 12, and 29, 1934, Jan. 1, 1935; Sindicatos Independientes de Nuevo León to Lázaro Cárdenas, Dec. 8, 1934, AGN: Presidentes, 433.1/8.
25 Nathan, Sep. 20, Oct. 1, 1934, SD 812.00 NL/70, 76.
26 Nathan, Oct. 3, 1934, SD 812.00 NL/ 77; Juan Manuel Elizondo, *Memorias improvisadas: Mi universidad* (Monterrey, 2001), 123–25; *El Porvenir*, Sep. 30, 1934. Calles's "Jew capitalists" remarks reflected either his knowledge of the industrialists' allegedly Sephardic roots or, more likely, the anti-Semitism then as widespread in Mexico as elsewhere. Indeed, the United States consul claimed that the anti-Semitic statement had not been interpreted locally as such, but as a reference to "characteristics which are popularly associated with Jews such as usury, closeness, etc." (Nathan, Oct. 4, 1934, SD 812.00 NL/78).

represented a calculated government effort to rein in the antigovernment sentiments brewing in Monterrey just when General Lázaro Cárdenas assumed the presidency.

Cárdenas's 1934 election had aroused little fervor among Mexican workers. The Six-Year Plan that served as the Cardenista platform indeed promised far-reaching social reforms. But Alan Knight reminds us that "public opinion . . . saw Cárdenas as another puppet [of Calles]," one whose record promised "stability and continuity" and thus "did not inspire support among labour or the independent left."[27] If Monterrey is indicative, workers focused their electoral activism on local politics. Cárdenas thus won handily in Monterrey, as PNR candidates had since the ruling party's 1929 founding. The most important victory from the workers' perspective was not that of Cárdenas but of Francisco Idar, a local railroad brakeman and Liberal Party candidate who won election as federal senator over his ruling-party opponent. Idar became the most heralded working-class politician of his time in Monterrey, one who garnered votes from union and nonunion workers of all political persuasions. His 1938 assassination by ruling party gunmen would further temper local blue-collar distrust of the ruling party.

At the time, the enthusiasm generated by Idar's victory spilled over into Nuevo León's 1935 gubernatorial elections, a key test of the PNR's capacity to win the labor vote in the crucial industrial state. The contest pitted Calles's son, Plutarco Junior, against General Fortunato Zuazua, a local revolutionary hero running under the Liberal Party banner.[28] The United States consul reported that Zuazua's support came from the "better element of town," namely the industrialists who financed his campaign. But some militant labor activists backed Zuazua as well, organizing their own "Red Left" wing of the Liberal Party. For these workers, the Liberals represented less the political vehicle of the rich, as their opponents claimed, than a party with strong local roots. As Dionisio Palacios pointed out, "Benito Juárez was a Liberal too."[29] Working-class sympathy for Zuazua reflected regional pride as well. Calles was not a *regiomontano*, but a Sonoran like his father. Labor's support also expressed a widespread disdain for the ruling party, known locally as the "Party of the Newly Rich" for its corruption and the "parasitic cast of upstart politicos" who ran the local Callista machine. Moreover, as the Railroaders Local No. 19 wrote to Cárdenas, "we have never been with [Calles] nor will we ever be . . . [because] we have known of his anti-revolutionary and anti-worker attitude since [his government broke

27 Alan Knight, "The Rise and Fall of Cardenismo," in Leslie Bethell, ed., *Mexico Since Independence* (Cambridge, 1991), 249–50.
28 1935 gubernatorial race in AGN: DGG 2.331 (16)/277–281.
29 Palacios interview; Campa, *Mi testimonio*, 99.

the 1926–27 railway strike]."[30] Organized labor became the bulwark of the ruling party's political machine in Monterrey. But that outcome would not come easily. Inspired perhaps by a *norteño* spirit of independence, workers of all political stripes commonly resisted the imposition of outside candidates throughout the 1930s. In the meantime, Zuazua carried Monterrey easily. But the PNR claimed a victory that a federal electoral inspector attributed to "voting irregularities" in the countryside. The younger Calles never assumed office, however, as events in Mexico City soon altered the course of Mexican history.

In June 1935, President Cárdenas proved the pundits wrong and broke relations with former President Calles. The split came as strikes engulfed Mexican industry. While Cárdenas inherited the worker protest, his public pronouncements in support of striking workers seemed to galvanize the labor insurgency. Monterrey exemplified the trend. Workers had stricken no less than forty-six plants between August and December 1934 alone, a number that surpassed the previous three years combined. The month following the president's inauguration witnessed an additional fifteen walkouts. Government and business leaders condemned the strikes as politically motivated actions coordinated by "Communist agents" and "professional agitators." Unionists indeed targeted sites rich in political symbolism. Building tradesmen halted work on the Plutarco Elías Calles School when PNR boss and construction magnate Aaron Saénz refused to recognized his own workers' right to organize. Printers also struck the conservative daily *El Porvenir*, while employees walked out at the Casino Monterrey, the social gathering spot of the local elite.[31] The industrialists therefore applauded when Calles chastised the new president for his refusal to rein in labor militancy. In a widely publicized interview, Calles condemned union leaders for "treason," discerned "Communist tendencies" behind the unrest, and demanded the government's suppression of the "entirely unjustified strikes."[32]

Cárdenas held firm against his former mentor and organized labor promptly rallied behind his government. In Monterrey, communist and progovernment unionists forged a United Front against "Callista fascism." In December 1935, Cardenistas shouting "death to Calles" took to the streets, sacked City Hall, and demanded the former president's expulsion from Mexico. A labor leader speaking at an anti-Calles rally exhorted

30 Ala Izquierda Roja del Partido Liberal to Secretaría de Gobernación, Apr. 15, 1935 and Sección No. 19 del Sindicato de Trabajadores Ferrocarrileros to President Lázaro Cárdenas, June 17, 1935, in AGN: DGG 2.331 (16)/277.
31 AGENL: *Informe del Gobernador Morales Sánchez, 1935–1936*, 23; *El Porvenir*, Jan. 19 and 30, June 15, 1935; Nathan, Jan. 31, 1935, SD 812.00 NL/92.
32 On the Calles-Cárdenas conflict see Sariego, *El sindicalismo minero*, 39–40 (quoted); Hamilton, *The Limits of State Autonomy*, 124–28; Alicia Hernández Chávez, *Historia de la Revolución Mexicana: La mecánica cardenista* (Mexico City, 1979), 54–60; Knight, "The Rise and Fall of Cardenismo," 253–55.

workers "to look back and recall the [1932] ASARCO strike, when the government massacred workers. . . . The times have changed and we must now uphold our rights [by supporting President Cárdenas]."[33] Back in the capital, Cárdenas shored up military support, ousted the Callistas from his cabinet, and expelled Calles from Mexico. Right-wing Callismo gave way to a progressive Cardenista coalition. Many old-guard political bosses shifted to the camp of Cardenismo. Some were opportunists; others were dedicated social activists longing for this political opening. Communists bolstered the Cardenista ranks as well. In a timely development, the party concluded its strategy of sectarian resistance and ordered its activists to organize an antifascist, Popular Front coalition with the Cardenistas. Obedient Communists thereafter backed the Cárdenas regime, supported PNR candidates, and forged common ground with ruling-party labor leaders. This Popular Front alliance resulted in the February 1936 founding of the Confederation of Mexican Workers (CTM) and its local affiliate, the Nuevo León Workers Federation (FTNL). In Monterrey, militant workers had by then seized upon the Cardenista opening to challenge company unions. They found sympathy not only in Mexico City but from General Gregorio Morales Sánchez, the interim governor appointed by Cárdenas in mid-1935. Morales, a *regiomontano* who initially "met with the approval of all elements of the population," lost the elite's confidence in late 1935 when he sided with organized labor.[34] Indeed, his brief tenure as governor coincided with several of the most critical industrial conflicts in Monterrey's history. The first emerged at the Fundidora steel mill, where, in early 1936, rank-and-file workers elected to join Mexico's Miner-Metalworker Union.

Neither the Company Nor the Union Wants Workers Who Dissent

The emergence of Local 67 transformed the labor movement and labor politics in Monterrey. Absent the muscle of the steel workers, the Independent Unions lost their capacity to elect their delegates to the state's labor board. It also aroused the concern of local industrialists because the steel workers' affiliation with a national union set a potentially contagious precedent. Why, locals asked, would workers who enjoyed the security of paternalism forsake it for the unchartered waters of revolutionary unionism? Many found a comforting answer in the specter of outside agitation. "PROFESSIONAL LEADERS FROM MEXICO CITY AGITATE THE CONSCIENTIOUS WORKERS OF MONTERREY," read a bold-faced headline announcing the steel workers' decision to oust their long-time

33 *El Porvenir*, June 19, Dec. 12, 1935; Nathan, Dec. 24, 1935, SD 812.00 NL/124.
34 Nathan, Sep. 20, 1935, SD 812.00 NL/117.

union leaders. Those unionists promoted the ideal of outside intervention as well. By their account, the steel workers "went with the reds" due to the false promises of "[union] separatists helped by outside leaders." Notable among the agitators was Miners Union leader Augustín Guzmán, who had ventured to northern Mexico months earlier, leaving a "rash of strikes" in his wake.[35]

These claims still hold widespread currency among many *regiomontanos* due to a study that unequivocally linked Local 67's founding to the sinister and cunning designs of Mexico City radicals. "The action of General Cárdenas was direct," the author asserts. "[The president] himself egged the workers on against the company, a labor sustained by subsequent [presidents], thereby ending definitively the harmony that once existed [at the Fundidora]."[36] Young workers like Rafael Reyna and Antonio Quiroga, who backed the "separatists" at the time, subtly concur by characterizing the union insurgency as *"una cosa política,"* a political struggle beyond their youthful comprehension.[37] Their testimony reflects the nature of a union drive made possible by complex legal battles over union jurisdictions. Moreover, many old-guard leaders of the defeated Steel Unions assumed leadership roles in Local 67. In fact, the "men of steel" would build Local 67 on the organizational ruins of their company union.

Rank-and-file resistance to complacent union leadership preceded the Cárdenas regime. As we saw earlier, the leaders of the Steel Unions were not cut from the same cloth as those of other white unions. Many were veterans of the 1922 strike. Veteran union leaders like Pancho Guzmán and Rosendo Ocañas once enjoyed a measure of respect among their workmates. But they were never elected to their union posts and, by 1936, the means by which the company negotiated their loyalties did little to dispel the charges that they had become allies of management. The Steel Unions they led evolved from the department-based unions established during the mid-1920s. A decade later, skilled machinists like Guzmán and Ocañas continued to play an extraordinary role in the organizational life of the mill. They were the ones who negotiated the steel workers' first collective contract, which became binding for all steel workers regardless of their union affiliation. One worker later remembered that few operatives were familiar with the contract because "Guzmán and Ocañas handled everything."[38]

The layoffs caused by the Great Depression revealed the contract's limitations and implications. It established the closed shop, giving the union the legal right to dismiss dissidents, and extended to union leaders the liberty

35 *El Porvenir*, Jan. 15 and 20, 1936.
36 Juan Zapata Novoa, *La muerte de la Fundidora* (Mexico City, 1989), 32.
37 Quiroga and Reyna interviews.
38 Quiroga interview.

to appoint delegates to the mill's shop committees.[39] Industrial paternalism provided a modicum of security to workers idled by the economic crisis. But the work suspensions did not transpire without resistance. Since the labor code required government authorization of layoffs, the steel mill astutely circumvented state intervention by channeling the suspensions through the shop committees. Collective protest emerged most dramatically among the iron workers, whose resistance forced the company to rehire them. But those skilled tradesmen lost their struggle to defy the collective contract negotiated by the Steel Unions. The iron workers' struggle marked the only collective resistance to the layoffs, which proved to be of a brief, six-month duration. However, the process would inadvertently awake many workers to the nature of their union leadership.

The Fundidora escaped relatively unscathed from the Depression. The late 1932 recharging of the furnaces signaled the renewal of iron and steel production. The mill's recovery transcended expectations. By the mid-1930s the plant's installed capacity utilization reached 80 percent (relative to the 1926–31 average of 49 percent). Company payrolls soon surpassed 3,000 employees as the mill rehired veterans and recruited 800 new workers. Iron production reached the long-anticipated 100,000 ton mark in 1936, a year when workers achieved record steel output and the company, record profits. Indeed, one economic historian concludes that, "what had been one of the most unsuccessful industries in Porfirian Mexico was now one of the most profitable."[40] The success did not pass unnoticed by the workers who proudly achieved the new production records.

Worker protest escalated when production resumed because many workers resented the terms under which they were laid off and then rehired. In the context of increasingly violent labor protest in Monterrey and the labor board's reinstatement of the iron workers, the company had proceeded with caution when laying off other employees. Each operative received one-month severance pay, extended credit at the cooperative, and a promised reinstatement. In return, the workers signed waivers thanking the company for its "voluntary assistance." The statements emphasized that the "separation was arranged by means of the *shop committees*." The workers also agreed with their signature to "absolve [the company] of any future responsibility that may result from my separation."[41] Sensing perhaps that they could do little to resist the layoffs, workers signed the forms without considering the consequences. They soon learned that the waivers relieved the Fundidora of any obligation to rehire them into their previous positions. Workers

---

39 Known in Mexican labor law as the "exclusion clause," the closed shop requires employers to dismiss workers whose union memberships have been rescinded.

40 AHFM: *Informe*, May 11, 1937, 14; Haber, *Industry and Underdevelopment*, 165, 177 (quoted).

41 AHFM: Poliza de Caja no. 46, June 1932.

who demanded seniority recognition lost their old jobs to new recruits. A nine-year veteran in the finishing department refused to return as a "new operative" and filed a protest with labor authorities. He lost his case. Since union leaders had "arranged" the layoffs in accordance with the collective contract, the labor board absolved the company of any wrongdoing.[42] After weeks of idleness and dismal prospects elsewhere, most workers returned to the Fundidora, relieved by the opportunity to work once again. Talk of unionism returned to the shop floor with them.

The union issue had been latent at the steel mill since the early 1930s, when the Steel Unions' affiliates existed in only half of the mill's departments. Workers in other sections maintained nominal ties to "outside" trade unions. For instance, Antonio Quiroga and other workers in the foundry belonged "semi-clandestinely" to the Molders' Union. He recalled that, "We were all youngsters, but we never attracted many recruits due to the other workers' fear." Workers in the blast furnace belonged to the International Forgers' Union. The steel mill made no apparent effort to screen new hires for possible union affiliation. The constant influx of workers and the mill's relative dependence on skilled labor made the task daunting and unreasonable, but easy to remedy should a worker prove troublesome. The workers' backgrounds generated no apparent concern until the early 1930s. Supervisors then began questioning suspected workers about their pasts. A welder in the machine shops, for example, lost his job when his superior discovered his previous membership in the militant ASARCO Production Workers Union.[43] Then, as labor activity escalated, the Steel Unions extended their influence at the mill. By late 1933, they had organized workers in all the plant's fifteen departments, even bringing the resolutely independent iron workers into the fold. Members of autonomous trade unions were soon protesting the intimidation suffered from their supervisors. Militants in the blast furnace complained to local authorities of a campaign of harassment against their members, including union foremen. Unionists there suffered arbitrary dismissals and disciplinary fines for minor transgressions. They also protested that "workers protected by the company deliberately slowed production" so as to minimize their bonuses.[44] The blast furnace became the last department to enter the Steel Unions' fold. The furnacemen would be the first to depart.

Meanwhile, workers increasingly visualized an alternative to their union and the nature of its leadership, a covert form of resistance that preceded and informed their militant opposition. They started with a counterhistory

---

42 AGENL: JCA, 21/610.

43 AGN: JFCA 219/931–358.

44 Unión Internacional de Forjadores to Governor Pablo Quiroga, Oct. 17, 1933, AGENL: Correspondencia Local del Gobernador, 11/26; AGENL: JCA 3/81; AGN: DT, 1882/9.

of labor relations at the mill, a collective critique of the Steel Unions' discursive promotion of cooperation and harmony.[45] The story began with
shop-floor abuses and concluded with the failure of union leaders to defend
workers before management. Foremen were cast as the leading villains for
their "tyrannical" and "despotic" means of driving workers and intimidating dissenters. Salvador Castañeda remembers that "the bosses had always
kicked us around" and that "workers with dignity can only endure that to a
certain point." Moreover, job security remained elusive, wage differentials
vast, and seniority unrecognized. Favoritism bred resentment and inhibited rank-and-file unity. The shop committees, headed by "self-appointed"
delegates, served only to punish or fire dissident workers. Most important,
union leaders "elected themselves" and refused to protect the workers from
these abuses. They were said to have "sold themselves out to the company,"
organizing consensual labor relations in exchange for beneficial production
contracts for workers in their departments. The organization of department-
based unions became, in this transcript of resistance, a ploy to divide the
workers. Guzmán and Ocañas "plotted to unionize us separately, by department, to better control us."[46] Then, with the founding of the Steel Unions,
said leaders bowed to "dictates from management" and signed "imposed
contracts" that legally denied workers their constitutional rights. Apolonio
Belmares thus wrote that "the situation had become intolerable already,
due to the daily abuses against us and the dictatorship [of the union]."
Looking back, former workers remember the 1932 iron workers' struggle
as an opportunity lost, a resistance movement that failed due to an absence
of rank-and-file unity. Later on we shall see that this narrative became the
discursive bedrock upon which union leaders would build rank-and-file
loyalties to Local 67.

These transgressions of power and shop-floor abuses generated a collective
desire for a stronger and more democratic union, a feeling most pronounced
among the furnacemen. They, more than most steel workers, resented the
machinists' control of the Steel Unions. These interdepartmental hostilities

---

45 Unless indicated otherwise, the following derives from interviews with Castañeda, Palacios, Reyna,
and Solís; Apolonio Belmares, "Breve historia de como y porque se formó la Sección 67 el 20 de
Noviembre de 1935." (Unpublished manuscript, 1981, provided to author by Dionisio Palacios.)
For my analysis of the shift from apparent passivity to overt activism, I am indebted to James
Scott's theory on hidden transcripts of resistance, as developed in his *Domination and the Arts of
Resistance: Hidden Transcripts* (New Haven, 1990), 183–84, and employed by Wingert, "Rethinking
Paternalism," 872–74.

46 The notion that the steel workers' identification with their departments and crafts impeded
occupational solidarity is consistent with other Mexican industries. Middlebrook argues this for
the railroad workers, whose own drive to industrial unionism also built upon unsuccessful efforts
to resist Depression-era layoffs. Rank-and-file railroaders embraced industrial unionism for another
reason echoed by the steel workers: their unions' control by cliques of conservative craft workers.
Middlebrook, *The Paradox of Revolution*, 84–85.

reflected the distinct subcultures of work that defined the steel-making process. Workers later ascribed the fact that leaders like Ocañas and Guzmán "didn't like to put up a fight" to their occupations. They were machinists. And, according to Salvador Castañeda, work in the machine shops shaped their "tame" and "laid back" disposition toward management. This rolling mill worker later recalled that "you could fall asleep working in [the machine shops]." Work in the furnaces, on the other hand, was hot, physically exhausting, and fraught with risk. Their occupations made the furnacemen "explosive," "hot-tempered," and therefore "more combative."[47] While other steel workers shared the resentment expressed by the furnacemen, the latter would be the first to act upon their grievances. The labor law provided them a unique opportunity to do so.

The furnacemen launched an insurgency against the union leadership in early 1935. Eight blast furnace workers quit the "white union" in protest of what they considered "illegal" membership dues. Half were veterans of the 1922 steel strike. In his subsequent testimony before the state labor board, the tapper José García protested that "neither the company nor the union wants workers who dissent from their way of thinking." He criticized union leaders for their passive response to abuses at the mill and asserted that the union "is not a revolutionary organization, but one of those known in this country as a white [union]." He complained of union dues "as a kind of interest payment, as if our salaries were a loan." "Naturally," he concluded, "since this is unjust, I remained with no alternative but to renounce the famous union." Armed with the exclusion clause in the collective contract, the union had Garcia and his cohorts discharged from the mill.[48] During the next month, the Steel Unions dismissed nine more dissidents from the blast furnace (several of whom had labored at the mill since 1920). Local labor activists protested these events directly to President Cárdenas. They portrayed the Steel Unions' actions as an effort to "terrorize the workers in order to arrest the disintegration of the white union's ranks."[49] Meanwhile, the furnace workers' lawyer bypassed the state labor board and took his clients' case before federal authorities. He was not the first to attempt the legal manoeuver.

Steel workers began filing grievances with a regional office of the federal labor courts in 1930. They did so to circumvent the local tribunal, where one Steel Union official usually served as a labor delegate. For the next six years, federal officials and company lawyers waged a legal battle over the steel mill's jurisdictional status. A 1927 ruling required the federal boards to arbitrate disputes in the railroad, oil, and mining industries. The decree's

47 Castañena, Elizondo, and Palacios interviews.
48 AGENL: JCA 61/1669.
49 AGN: DAT 376/5.

broad definition of mining – the extraction, storage, and processing of ore into metal – had already placed Monterrey's smelters under federal jurisdiction. But the steel mill presented a quandary. While the law ostensibly assigned several departments (furnaces, foundry, storage patios) to federal jurisdiction, the majority of Fundidora workers manufactured raw iron and steel into new products. Such "transformation" industries fell under the oversight of state labor authorities. The Labor Department recognized this jurisdictional dilemma in a 1930 case involving a blast furnace worker. At the time, a government lawyer argued the need to assert federal oversight of the mill "to establish fixed and definitive norms of judgment" for all steel workers.[50] The company thwarted federal encroachment by appealing the ruling through the Supreme Court.

The issue remained dormant until the furnace workers' insurgency. The jurisdictional dispute then became overtly political, hotly contested, and saturated with long-term implications. By the mid-1930s, a more progressive cast presided over the federal labor board. They demanded the right to hear the furnace workers' case.[51] Opposed to them stood a state labor board seeking to protect the Steel Unions' jurisdiction over the mill. Meanwhile, in Mexico City, a Labor Department with a decidedly radical hue redoubled its efforts to establish federal oversight of one of the country's preeminent industrial enterprises. Leaders of the militant Miner-Metalworkers Union shared the labor authorities' perspective. Founded in 1934, the national industrial union enjoyed organizational jurisdiction over Mexico's mining and smelter workers. Within a year, Miners organizers set their sights on the North. In mid-1935, workers at Monterrey's Peñoles and ASARCO smelters elected to affiliate with the Miners as Locals 64 and 66, respectively.[52] Their new collective contract awarded the ASARCO smelter workers the very demands they had struck for in 1932. The contract doubled base wage rates. It also established the closed shop, seniority recognition, pensions, and full wages for workers recuperating from industrial accidents.[53] Events at the smelters did not pass unnoticed at the steel mill.

The furnacemen's insurgency became generalized in late 1935, led now by dissidents from within the Steel Unions' very leadership.[54] The open-hearth furnace workers declared their autonomy, enlisted the blast furnacemen in their movement, and registered a rival union with the federal labor

50 AGN: DT 1882/9.
51 AGENL: JCA 61/1669.
52 Sariego, *El sindicalismo minero*, 30–38. Local 65 represented the copper miners of Cananea Consolidated in Sonora.
53 Bowman, Mexico City, Jan. 8, 1937, SD 812.5041/107.
54 Local 67's founding narrative is based on Acta Constitutiva de la Sección No. 67 del Sindicato Industrial de Trabajadores Mineros y Metalúrgicos y Similares de la República Mexicana (copy provided to author by Dionisio Palacios).

board. Heading the resistance was Leandro Martínez, a foremen and veteran of the 1922 strike. Another organizer of Local 67 recalled that Martínez had "always distinguished himself for his defiance towards the famous [Steel Unions]."[55] For organizational support, the furnacemen turned to Miners President Augustín Guzmán, then in Monterrey to meet with the local smeltermen. He provided organizational know-how to the steel workers' struggle. In late November, 279 furnace workers convened at the railroaders' union hall and formally declared their affiliation – as Local 67 – to the Miner-Metalworkers Union. In its founding act, Local 67's organizers demanded that their department-based union be decertified. They justified their demand by asserting that the union's leaders, "who insist that this department remain under local jurisdiction, are wrong and only want to ensure that the workers remain passive, with their hands tied, and poorly led, because [the union] has never complied with its original ends." They decried them "for their submission to the company directors" and expressed their aspiration "to achieve our independence." They demanded the right to federal jurisdiction and a new collective contract. They then set out to enlist the other departments into their insurgency.

Rank-and-file support for Local 67 snowballed one week later when the company fired twenty-seven more union militants. Sympathetic workers launched protests downtown to garner support for the movement. They also set up collection boxes outside plant gates to gather funds for the fired workers' families. Dionisio Palacios recalled that, "By then, the entire Fundidora was unified behind the movement." As December passed, large contingents of steel workers gathered outside the mill's gates to hear Miners leader Augustín Guzmán speak. Those in attendance were admittedly attracted less by what he said than "the way in which he expressed himself." "I saw many *great* labor leaders," Palacios emphasized, "but like Augustín Guzmán, noooo, never." He apparently promised the steel workers the same benefits won by the ASARCO smeltermen's Local 66, as the Miners Union sought to standardize such contracts.[56] Meanwhile, the Steel Unions' leadership answered back with appeals to the workers' regional, class, and masculine identities.

In a manifesto published in Monterrey's leading daily, the union's old-guard leaders asserted that "up until now we've maintained our noble attempts to prevent any friction or violent conflicts among the workers ... which we believe demonstrates our class spirit and class consciousness." But they went on that, "the professional agitators who attack the leaders of our organization are all a bunch of scabs and cowards who have never known how to carry out their social obligations, much less have

55 Belmares, "Breve historia," 3.
56 Palacios and Elizondo interviews.

they accomplished what our representatives have, defending the interests placed in their hands with virility and honesty." "The so-called leaders of the Miners Union," they added, "have become known . . . for committing arbitrary acts of violence that in no way mesh with the sincerity and culture of the regiomontano workers." "We repeat," the manifesto concluded, "that if some lamentable and bloody conflict among workers should unfortunately occur, the only ones responsible will be the vile agitators who come along goading and poisoning the consciousness of workers [who] in most cases have lived together intimately in work and brotherhood for twenty or thirty years."[57] Their heartfelt pleas proved futile.

Recognizing the breadth of resistance, the mill's directors acquiesced to representation elections. Exactly what transpired in the Fundidora's Mexico City offices remains unclear. But a Miners Union threat to organize a strike at the mill apparently brought company officials to the bargaining table.[58] It would be the company that formally requested the Labor Department's mediation after Local 67's demand for union elections and a new collective contract. Some 2,000 steel workers gathered in mid-January at a Monterrey theater and unambiguously endorsed Local 67 as their new bargaining agent. Even the conservative press disclaimed the charges of fraud made by the Steel Unions' leaders. As one reporter observed, "A scrupulous count of votes was not even necessary, for a single glance [around the theater] manifested the Miners' superior numbers." Plant managers also admitted to the "general consensus" in support of Local 67. That following Sunday, Miners President Guzmán returned from Mexico City and announced, before a triumphant gathering of steel workers, a government decree that placed the mill under federal jurisdiction.[59] But Nuevo León's state labor board refused to acknowledge the election results and decertify the company union.

Incensed by this rebuff, thousands of workers marched on the state capitol and demanded the ouster of the tribunal's government-appointed president. They instead proposed the return of his predecessor, Teófilo Martínez Pérez, the well-known legal counsel to Monterrey's revolutionary unions. Governor Morales conceded, much to the dismay of many *regiomontanos*. Indeed, the arbitration board's labor delegate resigned in protest. The governor replaced that Independent Union leader with one of his red union rivals. The labor court's composition was thus reversed for the second time in twelve months, now tilting the board in decisive favor of the reds. Indeed, absent the numerical strength of the steel workers, the Independent

57 *El Porvenir*, Jan. 10, 1936.
58 *El Machete*, Jan. 22, 1936. By the late 1990s, neither the union nor the federal labor board had opened the archives that may contain such evidence to public inquiry.
59 *El Porvenir*, Jan. 20–22, 1936. No formal balloting took place.

Unions lost their capacity to elect their people as worker representatives. With the labor and business representatives now divided, the state became the final arbiter of industrial disputes in Nuevo León, performing the role that the industrialists (and many unionists) had long feared. Upon retiring, the labor delegate lamented to a reporter that, "Never in my twenty-three years in the labor movement have I seen a situation so complex and obscure, in which the workers . . . hop incessantly from one union to the next, from a white one to a red one to another of some undetermined color."[60] In its first official act, the reconstituted labor board decertified the Steel Unions.

On May Day, 1936, the Fundidora signed its first collective contract with Local 67. The steel workers secured benefits that surpassed most expectations. The contract boosted wage rates dramatically. Total salaries and production bonuses paid by the mill would triple between 1934 and 1938. In the judgment of Rafael Reyna, then an eighteen-year-old apprentice, "for that reason alone [Local 67] seemed great to us." As we shall later see, the contract also expanded and placed many of the company's welfare programs under union control. Moreover, such paternalistic benefits were now backed by contractual guarantees. Aside from such non-wage incentives, the less tangible rewards proved equally impressive, for, as Antonio Quiroga recalled, "the workers now had the freedom to protest without fear of reprisal."[61] Local 67 democratized shop-floor relations at the mill, an outcome that established rank-and-file loyalty toward an institution that moved to the vanguard of Monterrey's revolutionary union movement.

The complexity of the union struggle explains why young workers correctly perceived it as a "political affair." So, also, does the initial continuity in union leadership. The mill's department-based unions were "absorbed" by Local 67 and most veteran leaders "changed their posture" and joined the revolutionary union.[62] They did so for reasons both principled and pragmatic. Activists like Leandro Martínez appeared to their opponents as opportunists who would parlay union activism into political appointments. Martínez later proved them correct. Other former Steel Union officials had worked within the company union out of their conviction that it represented the only alternative to a nonunion mill. Militancy promised few rewards under the Calles regime. The shifting ideological and political tides that evolved into Cardenismo offered new opportunities. Abetted by the favorable climate of the mid-1930s, workers rebelled against the complacent

60 *El Porvenir*, Jan. 27–30, 1936.
61 Wage figures in AHFM, *Informes, 1935–1939*; collective contract in AGN: DAT 209/4; Reyna and Quiroga interviews.
62 Castañeda interview.

leadership of tradesmen like Pancho Guzmán and Rosendo Ocañas. Their North American counterparts would have been familiar with the process. For they, too, built militant locals upon the institutional ruins of company unions dominated by skilled craftsmen.[63] At the Fundidora, the process made for a relatively smooth transition to revolutionary unionism. As one future leader of Local 67 noted, "there was already a base, there was already leadership among the workers, so they had the experience needed to lead the [new] union."[64]

Guzmán and Ocañas, for their part, genuinely believed that the steel workers' affiliation with the Miners would end years of brotherhood. The opposite proved true. But they displayed their own convictions in the righteousness of their cause by launching a dissidence movement soon after Local 67's triumph. Handbills distributed in the mill called upon workers to "defend their wallets" by resisting the payment of union dues to "opportunists and profiteers." "Wake up comrades," the flyers exhorted, "It is no longer possible that we, who have followed the path of honorable and dignified unionism, can any longer support the exploitation and tyrannical demagoguery of Local 67's leaders." Their resistance attracted less than one hundred supporters. But it convinced the Miners Union to successfully demand the former leaders' dismissals in late 1936.[65] Both had labored at the Fundidora for more than twenty-five years. The steel workers' long-time leaders thus departed the mill rather than acquiesce, as the company did, to the union's new direction. At least one former worker, himself a militant, mourned their departure; for Pancho Guzmán and Rosendo Ocañas had played an integral part in the making of the Great Steel Family.[66]

Management's seeming acquiescence to Local 67 further smoothed the transition to revolutionary unionism. The company's posture, one union leader commented, reflected the owners' "sense of liberalism" as well as its dependence upon the federal government.[67] Pressured by its workers and its main customer, the state, management finally adhered to its traditional philosophy of recognizing employees' "freedom to organize themselves in any way they please." Company directors lamented the decline of the harmonious relation they held with the Steel Unions. In fact one

---

63 The Steel Workers Organizing Committee built its industrial union upon employee representation schemes akin to the Fundidora's Federated Steel Unions. As in Mexico, the organizational skills of the miners' union activists accounted for much of the SWOC's success. See Paul Clark, Peter Gottlieb, and Donald Kennedy, eds., *Forging a Union of Steel: Philip Murray, SWOC, and the United Steelworkers* (Ithaca, 1987).

64 Carranza interview.

65 Augustín Guzmán, SITMMSRM, to José Cantú Estrada, Labor Department, Dec. 30, 1936, AGN: DAT 376/5.

66 Palacios interview.

67 Elizondo interview.

year after signing the collective contract, they complained that, "Relations with our workers, due either to their inexperience, personal ambitions, or contamination by outside elements, have lost much of the cordial and understanding nature that always characterized them." But managers recognized the need to adjust their labor policy to Mexico's shifting political tides. They thus explained to shareholders that Local 67's contract demands were "unavoidable," even "pardonable given the context in which they develop[ed]."[68] While their politics departed, the steel mill's administrators shared a common "developmentalist philosophy" with union leaders. They recognized that it was in the common interest of the union and management to "jointly program the company's future," gearing production schedules and product lines to national economic development. To do so successfully, the company's directors admitted to a union leader and, required "a disciplined and more responsible union," one whose leadership enjoyed genuine rank-and-file support.[69]

Union leaders therefore struck common ground with the company. Both agreed that the steel workers' culture, one defined by an exaggerated machismo forged in the furnaces and workshops, required strong union leadership. Unlike their *regiomontano* counterparts, the Mexico City–based industrialists accepted federal labor policy as the basis of industrial peace and stability.[70] The company's subsequent success proved both sides right. While the steel mill continued setting record production levels, the workers were rewarded with a series of benefits and a generalized sense of liberation for which they subsequently credited President Cárdenas. From those workers' perspective, he – more than their union, the company, or their own actions – became their maker of history. For Monterrey's militant unionists, however, it was the steel workers who had set an example for all to

---

68 AHFM: *Informes*, May 30, 1936, 3–4 and May 11, 1937, 17.

69 Elizondo interview.

70 Two factors account for the Fundidora's unique disposition toward the state relative to the *regiomontano* industrialists. One is the government's role as a purchaser of Monterrey steel. By the mid-1940s, the state-owned railways and public works projects accounted for 46 percent of Fundidora sales. The steel mill's prosperity certainly depended more on government patronage than the local brewing and glass companies. However, state dependency did not correlate directly with employer acquiescence to government labor policy. Monterrey-based Cementos Mexicanos (CEMEX) resisted unionization while profiting handsomely from public works projects. The second factor is the cultural background of the administrators themselves. The Fundidora directors shared the Mexico City–based industrialists' propensity to work with (rather than organize opposition to) the Cárdenas government. While the Monterrey Group forged lobbying alliances with businessmen from cities like San Luis Potosí, Torreón, and Guadalajara, they persistently chastised the *capitalinos* for their complacent stance toward the interventionist state. For these distinct business cultures see Saragoza, *The Monterrey Elite*, and Hamilton, *The Limits of State Autonomy*; on the cement industry see Haber, *Industry and Underdevelopment*, 177; sales figures in AHFM: *Informe*, Mar. 27, 1945.

follow. Indeed, with the emergence of Local 67, revolutionary unionism grew contagious in Monterrey.

Stay on the Company's Side

On the evening of January 10, 1936, dissident unionists at Monterrey Glassworks penned a manifesto and plastered their broadside throughout the sprawling plant. It began: "Monterrey's proletariat celebrates tonight because the Steel Unions abandoned their old ideology and transformed themselves into a revolutionary organization. The bourgeoisie, for their part, grieve. They had not expected that surprise." The militants' communiqué decried the "illegal" existence of company unions in Monterrey, notably the Vidriera's curiously named Red Independent Union, which they described as "white in all senses of the term." As the dissidents reminded their fellow glass workers, the union's leaders never filed grievances, protested layoffs, or pressed for higher wages because "they fear the company's wrath." "They have essentially renounced the freedoms that belong to workers in a democratic country like our own," the militants concluded. They therefore saluted Local 67 as "an example to be followed by Monterrey's entire working class."[71] The militants belonged to a dissident union, the United Glass Workers. The company fired the statement's authors the day after the broadside appeared. One week later, the militants declared themselves to be the plant's majority union, demanded a new collective contract, and called a strike for February 1, 1936. They did so because, by law, a strike would force the government to hold representation elections at the plant.

The labor insurgency at Vidriera Monterrey paralleled that of the steel workers on several fronts, from the nature of rank-and-file grievances to the emergence of dissidence from within the company union. But important variables distinguished the cases. For one thing, rank-and-file glass workers divided on the issue of unionism, an element that added a sense of drama to the looming strike. That distinction built upon and reflected another difference. The Vidriera's owners did not share the Fundidora's vision of their workers' right to union representation. The punitive dismissal of unionists had punctuated the plant's labor history since the early 1920s. The glass workers' 1936 strike led to the historic showdown between President Cárdenas and Monterrey's industrialists, who blamed their labor troubles on state interventionism. That confrontation elevated the union dispute at the glassworks into a labor conflict of nationwide significance, one that has therefore garnered scholarly attention. The glass workers themselves remain conspicuously absent from the standard narrative, which portrays a

---

71 Manifiesto del Sindicato Unico de Trabajadores Vidriera Monterrey, Jan. 10, 1936, in AGENL: JCA, 60/1815.

strike for union recognition as an epic and defining struggle between the revolutionary government and Mexico's most powerful business group.[72] However, the grievances that gave birth to the union struggle predated Cardenismo and the workers themselves ultimately determined the outcome of a conflict that endured for a decade.

By 1936, some thirty years after its founding, Vidriera Monterrey had become one of the largest employers and most modernized industries in the city. Technological innovation and product diversification were the company's hallmarks.[73] Initially a supplier of bottles to the brewery, the plant, its products, and its markets diversified rapidly. By the mid-1920s, Vidriera Monterrey was supplying Mexico's food, beverage, and pharmaceutical industries with bottles produced by automated machinery. In 1928, Belgian workers and engineers constructed a plate glass division at the plant. Then, in the early 1930s, the firm expanded its glass-blowing division by introducing popular consumer products (flasks, water jugs) to a line previously dedicated to more refined tastes (cut glass and crystalware). The Vidriera had nearly monopolized Mexican glass production by the mid-1930s. Meanwhile, its workforce grew from 400 (1926) to 1,600 (1935) employees.[74]

The company's diversified product line mirrored an equally heterogeneous labor force, one subjected to a ceaseless drive to modernize and rationalize production. Since its inception, the Vidriera's owners used mechanization to displace troublesome workers. The Garza Sadas' initial foray into bottle making (1903) concluded when the plant's imported German glassblowers struck to protest contract violations. Six years later, Owens automated bottle machines arrived from the United States. With their arrival came new labor demands. Mechanics repaired and maintained the expensive foreign technology. In a sprawling workshop, molders, pattern-makers, and lathe operators tooled and refurbished the molds that gave each bottle its distinct signature. Back in the bottle room, machine tenders kept the hot molds oiled, generating a pungent smoke that wafted throughout the plant. In another department, five-man teams of Mexican glassblowers crafted crystal vases, pitchers, and glasses. In both departments, temperers and their assistants worked intense thirty-minute shifts, loading and removing bottles and hand-blown products from the tempering ovens.[75]

---

72 See Saragoza, *The Monterrey Elite*, 1–4, 177–85 and Hamilton, *The Limits of State Autonomy*, 145–46, for studies focused upon the industrialists and the state, respectively. See also Hernández Chávez, *La mecánica cardenista*, 64–69; Rosendo Sálazar, *Historia de las luchas proletarias en Mexico, 1923–46* (Mexico City, 1956), 181–83; Shulgovski, *Mexico en la encrucijada*, 278–79.

73 Roberto G. Sada, *Ensayos sobre la historia de una industria* (Monterrey, 1988), 60–63; Haber, *Industry and Underdevelopment*, 89–91.

74 AGN: DT, Labor Inspector's Report, 1926, 1540/1; *El Porvenir*, May 28, 1935.

75 Luis Lauro Garza H., *Cristal quebrado* (Mexico City, 1988), 94–149.

Behind the scenes, dozens of furnacemen mixed and fired the lime, sand, and soda that arrived each day to the plant's loading docks. Hidden away in the basement, more than one hundred women and men worked under the direction of a Czech artisan decorating and engraving the crystal and cut glass. Other young women and boys packaged their products for shipment. As at the steel mill, each department had its own subculture of work, some defined by idle banter and tranquility, others by intense heat, smoke, and noise. Unlike, its sister company, the Cuauhtémoc Brewery, the glassworks required hundreds of skilled and specialized workers.

Labor relations at Monterrey Glassworks followed a familiar local pattern, albeit with certain peculiarities. While the same clan of industrialists owned the brewery and the glassworks, they developed distinct practices of paternalism. The differences began in their hiring policies. Prior to 1936, Monterrey Glassworks did not attempt to shield itself from unionism through selective labor recruitment. Foremen short of hands simply drew them from a daily supply of casual laborers and migrants gathered at the plant's gates. As one recruit later recalled, "Back in those days, you just went to the factory and asked [for work]."[76] Dionisio Aguilar's story demonstrates the desperation with which many of the plant's unskilled workers endured their early years at the plant. His first job collecting broken glass earned him just enough — seventy-five centavos daily — to feed himself. He thus slept on the streets. The layoffs that came with the Great Depression led him back to his farm town in southern Nuevo León, where he worked in a carpentry shop. There, he earned room and board – but no wages. Prompted by the passage of the Federal Labor Law, he finally demanded just compensation. The owner's refusal provoked a return to Monterrey and the Vidriera. The plant hired some 800 new workers in the years after the Depression. Aguilar worked alongside many young migrants like himself, who "came from everywhere. . . . [T]hey were nearly all illiterates, but they were good workers." Those who persevered, dedicated themselves to learning a trade, and stayed out of trouble would see their hard work rewarded with a skilled position in what they all considered a fascinating industry.

The Vidriera earned a reputation among *regiomontano* youth as a company that offered excellent opportunities for advancement. Many from the surrounding neighborhoods followed their father and brothers into the plant, drawn by the possibilities of learning a unique trade or by their relatives' own pride in being glass workers. As a young boy, Juan Montes Orozco turned down a job at the brewery to await one at the Vidriera. He remembered that, "The brewery was nothing but light and easy work and I wanted to learn things, acquire a trade, [and] work with my hands."[77] Orozco learned

76 Interview with Dionisio Aguilar, Mar. 20, 1996.
77 Interview with Juan Montes Orozco, Apr. 26, 1996.

that glass production demanded a variety of skills both generalized and peculiar to the industry. Many trades, notably that of glass blower, were handed down at the plant. Youngsters learned the craft by watching and learning from sympathetic veterans willing to share the secrets of the craft. The development of a first-grade blower required six years.[78] The highly mechanized departments of plate glass and automated bottle production demanded mechanics, machinists, patternmakers, and lathe operators. The company discovered such workers at the nearby Obregón Industrial School. They also sent recruiters to the railroad shops, a mere two blocks from the plant, luring workers away with higher wages and seemingly unconcerned by the railroaders' union traditions. Many of those not recruited directly from the shops were themselves sons of railroaders.[79] Notably, several former railroad workers became leaders of the United Glass Workers Union.

Their organizing drive was not the first. The glass workers organized their first union in 1923. The company responded by dismissing five dozen unionists under the pretext of introducing new machinery that required "steady and disciplined operatives." As management explained to labor authorities at the time, "The workers who attend these machines must show up daily and on time because high production machinery cannot stop its march to wait for the personnel."[80] The government intervened to prevent a strike at the plant. However, rather than reinstate the unionists, the labor board supported the company's desire to rid themselves of the troublemakers with severance packages. The measure became a common practice at Monterrey Glassworks. Indeed, six years later, another organizing drive met a similar fate. It, too, transpired during a "modernization" phase.[81] As the company's labor force expanded, its dependence on skilled labor made it difficult to avoid the recruitment of workers with union backgrounds or sympathies. Therefore, as the militants fired in 1923 protested, the Vidriera "organized a company-controlled cooperative society to resist independent unionism."[82] The Vidriera Recreation and Savings Society became the company's vehicle of paternalism.

On the surface, the Vidriera's practices of paternalism paralleled those at its sister company, the Cuauhtémoc Brewery. The glassworks offered its employees similar nonwage benefits. A well-honed company culture, centered on sports and fiestas, a consumer and savings cooperative, and countryside excursions would all appeal to the workers and their families.[83]

---

78 Orozco interview.

79 Interviews with Luis Monzón, May 8, 1996 and Ricardo Correa, Mar. 20, 1996.

80 AGN: DT 650/10.

81 AGN: DT 791/7; AGENL: JCA 2/4.

82 AGN: DT 650/10.

83 *El Porvenir*, Jan. 28, 1924; interviews with Linda and Angel Rodríguez, Apr. 25, 1996 and María and Ricardo Correa, Mar. 20, 1996.

The owners skillfully cultivated an image of themselves as both beneficent and humble, mixing with their operatives just as their cousins did with the brewery workers. Plant Director Adrián Sada, for example, arrived to work each morning in a horse-drawn carriage, dressed modishly in a white suit and a riding hat. The eccentric industrialist then strolled through the plant's hot, noisy, and oil-stained workshops, picking up trash and chatting up the workers. What struck them as truly odd, one recalled, was Sada's practice of passing the lunch hour with groups of laborers – "eating our humble bean tacos" – rather than return to his mansion on Obispado Hill. "Even though he was one of the big shots," one long-time employee asserted, Sada "was very conscientious of the workers." Linda Rodríguez remembered of the owners that they "always treated the people very well, the Vidriera always concerned itself with their [workers'] well-being." Moreover, "in those days the chief bosses knew all the workers and they all got along well." "Those days" refers to a period before the company became one of Mexico's largest multinationals, when corporate offices were still located on plant grounds. At the time, the presence of the Vidriera's owners at the plant impressed the operatives, who came to respect the Garza Sadas as "humane and just" employers.[84]

Two key differences marked the paternalisms developed at the brewery and glassworks. For one thing, the Vidriera's style of welfare capitalism never translated into intimate shop-floor labor relations. As we shall see, aggressive foremen heightened anxieties among laborers subjected to dangerous working conditions. Notably, Dionisio Aguilar recalled the owners' disposition to remain "aloof from labor affairs," entrusting their subordinates with the daily management of the plant's hard-driven workers. Furthermore, unlike the brewery, membership in the Vidriera Recreation and Savings Society was not (yet) an obligatory term of employment. A minority of workers, mainly foremen, veteran mechanics, and office clerks, belonged to and administered the cooperative during the 1920s. Perhaps for that reason, the militants who entered the plant overtly resisted the programs, not only forsaking participation in company culture but denigrating the system of paternalism as an affront to the workers' dignity. As Ricardo Correa recalled with a hint of curiosity, "The reds always told us not to accept gifts from the company. . . . These were people who opposed all aspects of the Vidriera, even the company doing you favors."[85] As union militants had asserted since 1923, company-sponsored cooperatives simply masked the firm's antiunion policy.

Paternalism did not stifle unionism at Monterrey Glassworks. Sporadic organizing drives and conflicts developed throughout the 1920s. Soon after

84 Aguilar, Correa, and Linda Rodríguez interviews.
85 Correa interview.

management learned of the nascent 1929 organizing drive, they fired the organization's ringleaders. Months later, company loyalists led by a Spanish technician organized a company union composed initially of foremen and office workers. The Vidriera Workers' Union therefore predated the Federal Labor Law.[86] As such, it did not merely exist as an inert body meant to satisfy legal requirements. Rather company unionists established a strong and intimidating presence in all departments through their control of the plant's shop committees, a prerogative won in the first collective contract. By 1934, the Vidriera Workers Union and its 900 members had fallen under the direction of a tough and imposing former mechanic, Nicolás Martínez. Martínez, ostensibly employed as Vidriera Director Roberto G. Sada's body-guard, stashed a Thompson machine gun in his car and prided himself on his reputation as a tough guy. He surrounded himself with like-minded foremen and workers. Violence remained more of a looming presence than a reality at the Vidriera until after the 1936 strike, when interunion conflicts were occasionally waged with pistols.[87] In the meantime, active opposition to the Vidriera Workers Union escalated in 1934. By then, Monterrey Glassworks was booming, operating three shifts, and reaping handsome profits. In a context of stagnant wages, increasingly tense shop-floor relations, and company violations of the labor law, militant workers mounted their first challenge to the company union.

At the time, the union drive was portrayed by the company as the work of outside organizers. The idea of outside manipulation makes former workers chuckle. Linda Rodríguez, who never supported the militants, nonetheless recognized the shop-floor roots of the conflict: "Naturally, they used to say that it was people from outside, that everyone was fine at the plant. But that's not how it was. They were workers discontented with the wages, the foremen, this or that. Some of [the dissidents] got together, organized, and then came the strike." Most workers, it is true, initially stood on the sideline, watching what they perceived as a highly partisan, factional dispute waged after working hours. The union issue "was always outside the Vidriera," Rodríguez added, "it wasn't really part of factory life. . . . [N]ooo, everything was fine at the factory back in those days, there were two syndicates but there was one really nice union, because you have to realize that the people were seen as a family at that time, the union question was like, well, as if there were two political parties."[88] Others concurred that union politics rarely interceded on the shop floor. Workers like Ricardo Correa recall only that the two unions defined their positions by color: "The whites agreed with whatever the company said. . . . [T]he reds did not." Pressured by his older

86 AGENL: JCA 2/4; AGENL: Trabajo – Sindicatos y Asociaciones, 7/28.
87 Interview with Antonio Martínez Chapa, Apr. 29, 1936; *El Porvenir*, Feb. 2, 1936.
88 Linda Rodríguez interview.

brother, a foreman, Correa became and remained a member of the white union, although his true interests lay elsewhere. "I always preferred sports," he recalled years later.

As a seemingly disinterested observer, his views may reflect those of other workers who remained aloof rather than take up a life of activism. But he certainly came to understand the distinction between the rival unions at the plant. The militant union was "the one they organized out on the streets." When queried further on their distinguishing characteristics, Correa replied that, "they called them the reds because they were rebels, they initiated strikes, they were always getting on the company, doing petitions and work stoppages." Moreover, "they used to get angry, they were always demanding a lot of things, they were very demanding, that's [another reason] why they called them reds." As for the whites, "we were in favor of the company; we never spoke poorly of the company [while] they always talked shit about the company in the cantinas." It was in those neighborhood bars where the reds "always came around and hassled us . . . because we didn't want to be in their union." But, Correa strongly emphasized that many "were *really* good guys, they were just on the other side, you know."[89] The lapse of time and his fifty-year membership in the white union apparently erased his memory of how intense the union rivalry became.

The reds first challenged the whites in 1934, when some 200 militants put down their tools and demanded a collective contract separate from the one negotiated by the company union. Management responded unambiguously. They shut down the machinery and ordered the foremen to mobilize loyal workers to march on the mayor's home in protest. The following day, the labor board convened to arbitrate the dispute. At a time when the Independent Unions still controlled the appointment of labor delegates, they allied with the business representative to veto the government appointee's support of the militants.[90] The labor board thus upheld the company union's status as the operatives' legal bargaining agent. The dissident movement seemingly ended as swiftly as it began. The Vidriera therefore agreed to the labor court's order to reinstate the militants, certainly guided by record purchasing orders. As if to disprove the militants' claims that the organization collaborated with management, the loyalists rechristened themselves the Red Independent Union. The curious name betrayed subsequent developments. Several communist militants soon joined the organization in an attempt to reform it from within. Others, meanwhile, maintained the rival

---

89 Correa interview.
90 Teófilo Martínez Pérez was then serving his first stint as president of the labor board. The company union charged him with supporting the dissidents, as he had previously served as the red union's legal counsel. *El Porvenir*, Apr. 14, Nov. 16 and Dec. 30, 1934; Nathan, Nov. 14, 1934, SD 812.00 NL/85; AGENL: Trabajo – Conciliación y Arbitraje, 3/23.

United Glass Workers Union despite a good deal of harassment from the foremen.

An increasingly effective labor law limited the Vidriera's usual practice of simply dismissing dissident workers. They therefore attempted to stifle the organizing drive by offering handsome severance packages to the militants, only one of whom accepted.[91] The company modified its collective contract with the Red Independent Union one week later. The new contract raised the base wage above the legal minimum (to $2.00), extended paid vacations, and, the local press added, "conceded other prerogatives not even granted by law."[92] New contract clauses also strengthened the company union. One established the closed shop for all new hires. Another, the exclusion clause, permitted the union to fire dissident workers, a right upheld after a challenge in the local labor court.[93] The contract also guaranteed preferential treatment for union members during production slowdowns. The company thus negotiated rank-and-file support for the union through a combination of material concessions and the threat of legal reprisals.

Contrary to the Vidriera's public relations campaign in the press, the company neither superseded nor complied faithfully with all aspects of the Federal Labor Law. Workers employed in the Vidriera's glass-blowing department suffered significant infringements upon their legal rights. In June 1935, management violated the law by reducing production in the department without the labor board's authorization. The company temporarily suspended the contracts of 174 workers, most of whom belonged to the "red" union.[94] Of greater long-term concern to the 900 workers in the glass-blowing and tempering divisions was the Vidriera's persistent refusal to recognize their rights regarding occupational illnesses. These workers faced grave and often invisible health risks due to their constant exposure to the excessive heat and arsenic fumes released by the glass furnaces. Protests filed by stricken workers attest to the brutal and often fatal perils to which they subjected themselves on a daily basis.[95] The glass workers later credited that shared danger for the comradeship they developed with their workmates. However, at the time, management's refusal to legally compensate them bred resentment toward the white union and conniving company doctors.

---

91 AGENL: JCA 50/1452.

92 Contrato Colectivo, Vidriera Monterrey, S.A./Sindicato Rojo Independiente, Jan. 23, 1935, AGENL: Trabajo – JCA 66/2025; *El Porvenir*, May 28, 1935.

93 In rendering its mid-1935 ruling, the board argued that internal union issues were beyond its jurisdiction and that the exclusion clause was "amply authorized" by federal labor law (AGENL: JCA 44/1258).

94 AGENL: JCA 127/3656.

95 AGENL: JCA 45/1289, 50/1935, 56/1628, 57/1743, 70/2129.

The physicians testified on their employers' behalf before the labor board, denying the work-related nature of accidents and illnesses, especially tuberculosis. The fatal disease spread rapidly among the glass blowers during the early 1930s.[96] Company lawyers argued that workers contracted the disease outside the plant, where it was in fact widespread at the time. Contagious workers most likely spread tuberculosis to their workmates as soon as they handed them the blowpipe. The glass blowers therefore believed it to be an occupational illness. However, faced with the burden of proof and unable to afford independent physicians, they mostly accepted indemnity payments after waiving the Vidriera of future legal responsibilities. Workers who challenged this practice before the labor board lost their cases against the company. Rather than defend their members, the Red Independent Union arranged the dismissals. Union officials even applied the exclusion clause against one worker who publicly protested its failure to back his claims against the company.[97] The red unionists stepped in to defend these workers before the labor courts. In a process analogous to the ASARCO smelter case, they earned reputations for integrity, as leaders willing to risk their jobs in defense of their fellow workers.

The respect earned by the militants for defending the workers' health rights did not result in a rank-and-file willingness to sign union cards. The foremen did the job for them. While the owners' visits to the shop floor impressed the workers, their intermediaries undermined the company's pretensions to benevolence. Dionisio Aguilar pointed out that, "The foremen were the cause of all the problems, not the company, they were personal issues." The operatives recognized that the foremen's tough, demanding demeanor earned them their jobs to begin with. Supervisors recruited the foremen from the "roughest workers on the floor." Juan Montes Orozco recalled that they were "simply bullies; they had no skills." Indeed, Aguilar noted, "they were not even foremen; they were overseers (*capataces*), completely Porfirian. . . . That's why the strikes came, for that very reason, because of the foremen's poor treatment of the workers. That is why unions were formed."[98]

Recalling the years before the 1936 strike, Aguilar commented that "we went through some really harsh times. . . . [T]hey were always on our backs." "Quite often the foreman would give an order," he remembered, "and one would be working on it, and then he would give another, before you were even done, and you would say 'hold on, let me finish' " "And just like *that*,"

96 AGENL: JCA 37/1103, 46/1305, 64/1964. Tuberculosis generated the greatest controversy because Mexican labor law recognized the disease as an occupational illness only in the mining, meat packing, and healthcare industries.
97 AGENL: JCA 57/1236, 44/1258.
98 Aguilar and Orozco interviews.

Aguilar signaled with a stern snap of his fingers, "they were taking away points." The point system infuriated the glass workers. Steady attendance, surpassing production quotas, and volunteering for overtime earned workers points, and thus bonuses. The points could evaporate quickly. As one worker later testified to the labor court, foremen subtracted them "for the most minor of circumstances," from shoddy work to questioning orders to unauthorized trips to the restroom.[99] "Black points" not only reduced bonus pay. They could prompt one's dismissal as well. Foremen also punished workers with suspensions or reassignments to the most degrading of tasks, crushing recyclable glass for minimum wages. Anxiety thus ran high, but workers enjoyed no formal recourse. The shop committees, which administered the point system, were appointed by, answered to, and defended the company union. As one company engineer later admitted, "In those days the worker had neither a voice nor a vote. The worker was just a worker, and the foreman was the foreman, he hired people, he fired people, and he gave orders."[100] The actions of the union militants therefore made an impact on the rank and file. Their militance was especially welcomed in the most dangerous departments, where earnings were tied most directly to production quotas. It would be the glass-blowing and tempering crews who found the ideal of a strong union most appealing. By risking their jobs, even challenging the foremen to fights, the militants made impressions on already disgruntled and frustrated workers.[101]

The militants further bolstered opposition to the Red Independent Union by criticizing its failure to improve workers' living standards. While company publicists boasted of the Vidriera's extensive benefits, base wages remained only fifty centavos above the state's minimum, a subsistence wage at best. Moreover, it was no secret in Monterrey that the company was thriving by 1935. Even the United States consul later reported that, "a reasonable increase in wages could readily have been granted."[102] Living standards thus earned particular attention in the United Glass Workers' 1936 manifesto. As the dissidents reminded their workmates: "If we examine the situation of Monterrey's workers we will arrive to the inevitable conclusion that, despite the decadent bonanza that the bourgeoisie wail about, the workers live the existence of pariahs. Anyone who denies this should take the bother to pass through our barrios and visit our homes, if that is what you even call those miserable shacks." "And this," they concluded, "is what Monterrey prides itself on?"[103] The authors of this

99 Aguilar interview; AGENL: JCA 49/1417, 57/1763.
100 Monzón interview.
101 For shop-floor brawls between militants and foremen see AGENL: JCA 49/1417, 57/1763.
102 Nathan, Feb. 26, 1936, SD 812.504/1561.
103 AGENL: JCA 60/185.

manifesto – the same one that celebrated the steel workers' insurgency –
quickly lost their jobs. Their firing broadened dissent within the Red Independent Union itself. Several union officials broke ranks and joined the
United Glass Workers Union. The militants then demanded representation
elections and announced their intent to strike on February 1, 1936. The
strike call obligated the state to mediate the dispute by staging representation elections. It would also force the rank and file to leave the sidelines
and enter the politically charged game of unionism.

The Vidriera now took decisive measures to secure rank-and-file support
for the company union as soon as the militants announced their coming
strike. As workers later charged before the labor court, the company relied on coercion, ideological persuasion, and material incentives to restore
rank-and-file loyalty and instill fear in those who sympathized with the
reds. Management fired all members of the strike committee. Then, according to one militant, the foremen "dedicated themselves body and soul
to sabotaging [the union drive]." They forced workers to sign loyalty oaths,
pledging their opposition to the strike. "Don't throw yourselves into an
adventure," one foreman warned, "stay on the company's side. If you persist
with your ideas, you'll be run out of the factory." The personnel manager called individual workers into his office and repeated these threats.[104]
Company officials also paid visits to workers' homes to warn their wives
of the dangers posed by militant unionism. The Vidriera then coupled the
campaign of fear with an incentive. Allegedly conceding to the company
union's petition, management called the workers to a special meeting to
announce "the new deal": Seventh Day Pay. A then neglected clause in the
Mexican labor code, the measure awarded workers a paid day of rest on
Sunday. This national precedent entailed an across-the-board, 17 percent
wage hike. The following day, the Red Independent Union signed its name
to a half-page advertisement in the local daily to boast of this "proof of our
effective action. . . . We invite our detractors to demonstrate the benefits
that they have won on behalf of the laboring classes." The company clearly
understood the precarious balance of union forces within the plant. Even
the loyalists later recognized that many of the militants had "emerged from
the very heart of this [company] union."[105]

The company further attempted to dissuade their workers from supporting the militant union through its privileged access to the media. Local
radio stations broadcasted antiunion messages that linked the union conflict to the arrival of communist agitators from Mexico City. The *regiomontano*
business leaders' friends at the conservative national daily *Excélsior* alerted
the entire nation to events transpiring at the glassworks. The looming

104 AGENL: JCA 58/1788.
105 *El Porvenir*, Jan. 21, 1936; AGENL: JCA 58/1788.

strike and representation elections thereby focused the country's attention on Monterrey. Organized labor rightly perceived the Vidriera conflict as a unique opportunity to secure a victory against Mexico's most powerful clan of industrialists. Monterrey's militant unionists, lacking access to the media, thereby organized raucous demonstrations on the streets surrounding the plant. They, too, reminded the glass workers of the weighty significance of the coming elections.[106] The rank-and-file workers, however, probably perceived their vote in more parochial terms. The labor conflict, after all, predated the emergence of Cardenismo. The strike call merely forced them off the sidelines and permitted them to choose the road that best represented their interests: "[S]tay on the company's side" or go with the reds and their militant union. In the meantime, Monterrey's industrial elite were plotting their own strategy of resistance, one that precipitated a showdown with President Cárdenas.

106 *Excélsior*, Feb. 2, 1936.

8

State Your Position!

Conservatives, Communists, and Cardenismo

Workers were not the only *regiomontanos* taking to the streets in 1936. The industrialists voiced their agenda in the public sphere as well. And the sudden mobilization of well-to-do *regiomontanos* proved far more conspicuous then the labor rallies to which Monterrey had grown accustomed. That, of course, was the businessmen's intent: to reaffirm their social prominence and rally the locals to their cause. While their industries boomed, their political fortunes had tumbled. They rightly perceived a broad, cross-class challenge to their local power from militant unionists, their middle-class allies, and political authorities in Mexico City. Moreover, the business leaders' once agreeable allies in Nuevo León's government now endorsed organized labor. Most important, they had seemingly lost control over their own workers. They therefore refined their strategies of resistance. Six months prior to the Vidriera strike, Monterrey's industrialists and merchants had organized their own "united front against the labor element."[1] They used their influence over the Mexican media to enlist nationwide support for their struggle against unionism, one that built upon a red-baiting, patriotic discourse that would resonate at home and in provincial Mexico as well. They then integrated thousands of local supporters into a social movement meant to defend the *regiomontano* way of life from the threat of an intrusive federal government.

This conservative defiance exemplified the "multifaceted and sophisticated ... 1930s Right" analyzed by John Sherman. Sherman's seminal study emphasizes why Mexico's urban middle classes emerged as a social base of resistance to the revolutionary government. But workers also joined in a crusade that "transcended class lines."[2] The Monterrey elite and their local allies proved particularly effective at engineering the kind of mass mobilizations later associated with the ruling party and its control of organized labor and peasants. The industrialists would incorporate workers into

---

1 Nathan, Apr. 24, 1935, SD 812.4045/211.
2 John W. Sherman, *The Mexican Right: The End of Revolutionary Reform, 1929–1940* (Westport, CT, 1997), xiii.

their movement by propagating a discourse to which blue-collar *regiomon-tanos* had grown accustomed, one that appealed to their regional, patriotic, and gender identities. Their movement – and the response it generated – underscored the extent to which Cardenismo polarized Monterrey. It also galvanized a national campaign of urban resistance to federal government policy, one that pressured the ruling party to conclude the most radical phase of the Mexican Revolution.

Factory Whistles Were Silenced

Despite their origins in the city's factories, the issues that polarized Monterrey in 1936 reflected national and global developments. The parallels did not pass unnoticed by locals. In the United States, protracted and often violent union struggles divided communities. Events there received sensational, front-page coverage in the Monterrey press.[3] So did events in Spain, which locals were "closely following." The Spanish Civil War became a rallying point for *regiomontanos* of rival political persuasions. The ongoing struggle between Franco's Nationalists and the Republican government mirrored their domestic loathing or embracement of the Cárdenas regime, which placed its support for the leftist republic at the heart of Mexican foreign policy. Indeed, one report indicated that "conservative thinking citizens" believed that a Republican defeat by the Fascist rebels would "moderate Cárdenas policies."[4] Closer to home, active membership in the Mexican Communist Party reached its apogee in the late 1930s. Popular Front strategy insisted that party members – be they students, teachers, agrarian radicals, or militant unionists – throw their support behind Cárdenas to resist *la reacción*, as Mexican conservatives became known collectively. The president did little to dispel the Communists' belief in his radical credentials. His programs of socialist education, land reform, and revolutionary unionism emboldened his supporters. But they scandalized and then galvanized a heterogenous opposition. The country's fascists, conservative Catholics, and embattled business classes saw in the Cárdenas government either the embodiment or the victim of an insidious Mexican bolshevism. The lines were thus drawn between the forces of "revolution"

---

3 North American businessmen also combated the perceived threat of outside agitators by appealing to regional cultural values that resonated among the local populace. For an example to which my analysis is particularly indebted, see John Gaventa, *Power and Powerlessness: Quiescence and Rebellion in an Appalachian Valley* (Urbana, 1980), 104–21.

4 Knight, "The Rise and Fall of Cardenismo," 284–85; Blocker, Nov. 30, 1936, NAW RG 84, Confidential Records, Box 6, who reported "locals [are] closely following events in Spain.... The [employer] group, the three leading daily papers and the conservative thinking citizens undoubtedly favor the 'Franco' Government [*sic*], believing that suppression of radical party in Spain will moderate Cárdenas policies."

and "reaction," each side adopting the mantle of nationalism to rally popular support to its cause.

For Monterrey's industrialists, the radical tone and social policies of Cardenismo cultivated deep-seated anxieties. By early 1936, the conflicts that government reforms generated elsewhere in Mexico had arrived to Nuevo León. The rash of strikes and the union insurgencies at the steel mill and glassworks turned apprehension and dismay into hard reality. Since thousands of locals embraced the boosters' image of a city where class harmony begot economic prosperity, this evidence of class struggle bred genuine fears and heartfelt feelings of betrayal. Citizens once supportive of an earlier, democratic revolution – that of Francisco Madero – bemoaned the excesses of Cardenismo. Jose Saldaña, a local intellectual active in revolutionary politics since the 1910s, abruptly quit his post in Governor Morales's cabinet to protest the latter's sudden endorsement of radicalism. His chronicle of the times eloquently highlights how many middle-class *regiomontanos* perceived this political turn of events.

By Saldaña's account, the Cárdenas government was hijacked by a "team of Marxists [who] slowly added ingredients of the Russian Revolution" to an essentially nationalist-reformist project. The results manifested themselves like a "tempest ... wrapped in smoke and flames. ... In the cities, factory whistles were silenced while streets and plazas echoed with cries of hatred and destruction." Falling industrial production satisfied the radicals, Saldaña believed, because they sought "to finish off everything as a pretext to substitute the constitutional order with a communist [regime]."[5] Suddenly, it seemed to many *regiomontanos*, all they had worked, struggled, sacrificed, and saved for was threatened by outside forces. Astute industrialists recognized the shop-floor roots of industrial conflict.[6] Their workers did as well. Nonetheless, guided as much by custom as the need to rally local support, the industrial elite mobilized the specter of outside agitation to explain the rise of labor protest in the factories and streets of Monterrey.

The industrialists wrapped their resistance in the language of anticommunism. That Communists were proudly active in the labor movement lent credence to their appeals. Party activists soon led Monterrey's three Miners Union locals, the railroaders' Local No. 19, and the Nuevo León Workers Federation. Communist-organized farm workers waged protracted struggles against their employers on the cotton estates north of the city. Communist teachers and physicians also organized during the period. Even the state's Masonic Lodge split into warring factions after the grand master, a prominent surgeon, declared his adhesion to the Communist Party.

5 José P. Saldaña, *Crónicas históricas*, Vol. III (Monterrey, 1982 [1952]), 230.
6 *El Porvenir*, Jan. 1, 1935, noted the "problems with foremen" at the steel and glass plants.

Meanwhile, the strikes and interunion conflicts once confined to small factories spread to the very pillars of industrial Monterrey. And Monterrey's streets echoed with labor protest on a seemingly daily basis. On a single afternoon in January, a *regiomontano* passing through downtown Monterrey encountered steel workers protesting before the state capital, bus drivers marching on city hall, and glass workers converging raucously on their union hall.[7] The violent labor conflicts of 1932, from the hunger marches to the ASARCO sit-down strike, could be explained and dispelled as an aberration, an exceptional response to economic crisis. In the minds of many citizens, however, the events of 1936 confirmed the local media's apocryphal warnings of the dangers posed by communist agitators. How else could one explain the rash of strikes and the sudden ascendancy of militant unionism?

The coming strike at the Vidriera was perceived at the time as a potential watershed in the city's history. The industrialists therefore "initiated an intense publicity campaign, counting on the enthusiastic collaboration of the local press."[8] *El Porvenir* outlined the dangers a strike posed to the economy and society. The plant closure imperiled commerce due to a loss of the glass workers' wages. Bottle shortages posed further problems, from future unemployment for local beverage workers to threats to public health. Most important, they warned, "many more homes will be victimized by the red wave thrashing against Monterrey." Down in Mexico City, newspaper editors emblazoned their front pages with sensational news of the coming strike: "INTENSE AGITATION AND ALARM IN MONTERREY; DISTURBANCES IMMINENT," read *Excélsior*. "[Monterrey] is a city," the influential daily reported, "unaccustomed to seeing its workers press their demands through violence and dissolvent creeds."[9] So did the industrialists present their case to Mexico's reading public.

Nothing proved more troublesome than developments at the state capital. For the local business elite, the governor's late January appointment of Teófilo Martínez Pérez as president of the labor board represented a frontal assault on their local hegemony. Additionally, he was considered a radical lawyer. A few days later, Martínez would oversee the representation election at the glassworks. The businessmen thus hastened to put their organizational unity on display. They convened immediately after Martínez's appointment to plot their antiunion strategy behind the closed doors of the Centro Patronal (Employers Club). Then, on the night preceding the union vote, they took to the streets. In an unprecedented action, 500 of Monterrey's "most significant industrialists and merchants" marched on the state capital, shouting "Down with Martínez Pérez!" They demanded

7 Irma Salinas Rocha, *Mi padre* (Monterrey, 1992), 233–34; *El Porvenir*, Jan. 22, 1936.
8 Saldaña, *Crónicas históricas*, 233.
9 *El Porvenir*, Jan. 29, 1936; *Excélsior*, Feb. 1, 1936.

the governor's swift removal of the labor board's new president. Rebuked, the contingent proceeded to City Hall. Meeting with the mayor, the business leaders protested his recent award of a new bus route to a cooperative organized by former streetcar drivers. The mayor denied their claims that his actions posed a threat to private property. As the discussion grew heated, the mayor warned them to "watch their manners." Infuriated at their "arrogant" treatment by the public servant, the businessmen retreated to their headquarters. There, a local reporter noted, they announced their intention to "place a dike in communist tendencies." "Communism," one speaker promised, "will not find echo in a city like Monterrey, where workers are conscious of their duties and obligations."[10]

The following day, as the strike began at the glassworks, the businessmen reconvened at their Centro Patronal. They plotted their media campaign, reaffirmed Monterrey's spirit of class unity, and subtly contradicted one another. One speaker outlined the need to make the nation aware that the region's industrialists and their capital were "100 percent Mexican." He proposed new categories to define the city's color-coded labor organizations: Mexican unions and Russian unions. The latter, he observed, is a worthy title for those who would "forsake their nationality to become subjects of Stalin."[11] Another declared the "urgent need to tighten their relations with the true workers." He reminded his colleagues that, "We are all the common people, he who works with muscle power, the technician who directs production, and the owner of capital as well." His comrade betrayed a more class-conscious position. He proposed a national campaign to "impress on the workers' consciousness the need that exists to place each individual in the place he belongs." He offered that, "Labor's muscle power would lose its strength without the brains of the business class." Hoping perhaps to alleviate public fears or to instill confidence in his cohorts, a final speaker concluded that "Monterrey's workers, *Señores Comunistas*, are not of malleable substance." Rather, "their level of culture is far superior to that of the agitators who visit us, and that's why, despite their continuous incursions, [the Communists] have never been able to mold them capriciously into rag dolls or lap dogs who would follow them all around."[12] On that note of strident optimism, the business leaders adjourned to await the outcome of union elections at Monterrey Glassworks.

On the first day of February, a Saturday, production halted at Monterrey Glassworks. Company lawyers, unions leaders, and government officials met in the plant's tree-lined courtyard and readied the ballots. Skeleton crews tended the furnaces while their colleagues exited the sprawling

---

10 *El Porvenir*, Feb. 1, 1936.
11 The press adopted the proposal the following day. See for example *Excélsior*, Feb. 2, 1936.
12 *El Porvenir*, Feb. 2, 1936.

workshops. Other workers departed their homes or neighborhood cantinas, converging on the plant gates where a heady air of anticipation awaited. Upon arriving, they encountered federal troops guarding the factory's perimeter. Meanwhile, throngs of railroaders and metal workers gathered on the surrounding streets, exhorting the operatives to support the militant union, ready to adorn the plant gates with the red-and-black flags that mark a stricken plant in Mexico. By then, the press noted, the union elections had become "the obligatory topic of conversation in all quarters of Monterrey."[13] The city thus awaited as the elections transpired into the night. The tabulation of votes endured even longer, until late Sunday.

The initial outcome proved perilously close in the minds of company officials. Loyalists narrowly defeated the militants by a 834 to 777 margin.[14] The plant's "confidential employees" provided the swing votes, prompting a formal protest from United Glass Workers officials. The militants invoked the Federal Labor Law and challenged the legal right of office workers and foremen to place ballots. Their case focused on the nature of the strike. Since the United Glass Workers struck for control of the collective contract, only production workers could vote. The contract, they argued, explicitly excluded the "confidential employees" from its terms. The labor board's president, Martínez Pérez, agreed and he produced a legal precedent to back his resolution. He therefore scratched 144 "white" union votes and ten "red" votes challenged by the company. The results handed the United Glass Workers a 767 to 690 victory. The militants had won.

Who supported the reds? Eighty-three percent of their votes came from workers in the glass-blowing and tempering divisions. The campaign of incentives, intimidation, and ideological persuasion failed to resonate among these workers, who probably based their votes upon their shop-floor experiences. One temperer who supported the reds did so to protest the abusive foremen. But Dionisio Aguilar later affirmed his decision in a more philosophical fashion. "It's a matter of judgment," he explained, "for example, some people have a certain style of thinking, or a way of being, you know, and these people just don't accept any injustices . . . and there are many unjust circumstances in the workers' lives." Aguilar himself joined the reds, he recalled "because some buddies convinced me." But upon further reflection he added that, "look, I don't like injustices either."[15] While 70 percent of the glass blowers and temperers supported the reds, only 8 percent of the glassworks' 200 mechanics followed their lead. Indeed, support for the company union was most conspicuous in the plant's least

13 Ibid.
14 February 1936 Vidriera union election results in AGENL: JCA 58/1788, 60/1815.
15 Aguilar interview.

dangerous departments: packing, carpentry, machine shops, and decorating. Only two of one hundred female decorators supported the reds. Why? For one thing, workers in the female-dominated decorating department recalled the especially warm relations they enjoyed with their Czech supervisor, Mr. Kunte, who shared with them his knowledge of their trade. Moreover, women like Linda Rodríguez earned more as a decorator than did her husband, Angel, who labored as a pattern maker.[16] Furthermore, in contrast to the brewery, the glassworks did not require its female operatives to retire upon marriage. They even elected their own female representatives to the company union, an unusual development in a city where unionism remained mens' work. Even the brewery's company union excluded women from union posts. In the meantime, the red's electoral victory legalized the strike, which would endure for weeks before the company agreed to renegotiate the collective contract.

The militant union's victory at Monterrey Glassworks confounded the people of Monterrey. The union insurgency at the steel mill ten days earlier caused locals to pause and rethink their assumptions about labor relations in the city. Events at the Vidriera, however, represented a formidable setback for the city's preeminent industrialists, the Garza Sada family. The owners of the glassworks redoubled their well-financed, ingenious campaign of resistance to this perceived threat to their local hegemony. Their reaction betrayed the fundamental differences between the city's homegrown industrialists and their counterparts at the Fundidora. A range of variables, from their economic dependence on the state to their historic acceptance of union representation, conditioned the steel mill's acquiescence to the Miners Union. The steel workers, for their part, not only displayed a unified endorsement of revolutionary unionism; they enjoyed the political muscle of a powerful national union. The glass workers, on the other hand, remained divided on the issue of unionism. Meanwhile, Monterrey's industrialists stepped up their the campaign of resistance to Cardenismo.

State Your Position!

The strike at the glassworks provided the *regiomontano* elite the opportunity to broadcast their critical perspective to a nationwide audience. They would do so in dramatic fashion, with an immense "patriotic" demonstration on February 5, Mexico's Constitution Day.[17] On the one hand, the well-orchestrated movement would allow the *regiomontanos* to manifest pride in their national identity and their commitment to constitutional principles. Indeed, one intellectual sympathetic to their interests asserts

16 Aguilar and Rodríguez interviews.
17 Nathan, Feb. 13, 1936, SD 812.00 NL/135.

that the industrialists genuinely perceived their movement as one asserting their patriotism. As Saldaña later recalled, "Everyone forgot about their business affairs. . . . [T]heir *mexicanidad* assumed the one and only place [in their minds]." Long derided for the Americanized way of life, the *regiomontanos* put their patriotism on display in such a way that their actions "reverberated throughout the nation."[18] However, given its timing, most Mexicans certainly perceived the movement for what it was: a protest against Cardenista labor policies.

The rally's organizers mobilized support by articulating a series of cultural values meant to resonate with the *regiomontanos'* patriotic, regional, and masculine identities. Press releases announced the march as a protest against "the preconceived and highly dangerous intrusion of professional communist agitators from Mexico City." These outsiders, locals were reminded by one businessman, "have subverted the local order and overturned the rhythm of cooperation and hard work that has been the base of Monterrey's prosperity." A full-page manifesto in the local daily called upon locals to mobilize for Mexico's defense: "Regiomontanos: the homeland is in danger. The red wave of communism threatens the nation's destruction, the plunder of property, the ruin of our homes, [and] our children's perdition." "The communists neither hide nor disguise their objectives," it went on, "they will change the nation's economic structure . . . replace our glorious flag with their red-and-black rag . . . [and] humiliate the homeland by exchanging our National Anthem for the International Hymn."[19] To punctuate their movement – and display their economic clout – the businessmen resolved to couple the protest with a two-day lockout of local industry and commerce. Only the city's presses would run as usual. Monterrey's local dailies and radio stations were deemed "articles of primary necessity." To that effect, the industrialists devoted a good part of the $20,000 (U.S.) resistance fund to a national public relations campaign. It began in Monterrey, where they attempted to stimulate circulation of the city's probusiness dailies by subsidizing a 50 percent cut in newsstand prices.[20]

Developments in Monterrey received widespread coverage in the national press as well. The *regiomontano* businessmen had cultivated amicable relations with the capital's leading "independent" daily *Excélsior*, whose reporting seemed to set the agenda for the provincial media.[21] The Mexico City press became a battleground where the Monterrey elite and organized

18 Saldaña, *Crónicas históricas*, 232–33.
19 *El Porvenir*, Feb. 3, 1936.
20 Nathan, Feb. 13, 1936, SD 812.00 NL/135.
21 Mexico's paramount nongovernment newspaper had been edited in the late 1920s by Manuel Barragán, the former director of Monterrey's Chamber of Commerce, who briefly administered the Fundidora's welfare benefits program in the 1930s.

labor struggled to define their positions and garner sympathy. On the day of the protest, *Excélsior*'s readers came across an extensive interview with an "impartial" *regiomontano* observer. His succinct history of labor relations in Monterrey told an old story to a new audience. Twenty years earlier, he began, the revolution had "stirred up the social problem [in Monterrey]." Industrial peace returned quickly because workers and employers accommodated their expectations to "the new tendencies of the epoch." The observer then recited the range of benefits offered by the Cuauhtémoc Brewery, as if the benevolent face of paternalism prevailed throughout the city so that "the class struggle has been avoided." Indeed, he concluded, the city experienced no labor conflicts until (national labor leader) Vicente Lombardo Toledano arrived one year before, "sent on instructions from Moscow." True to its proclaimed spirit of impartiality, *Excélsior* offered a forum for the Cardenistas as well. Speaking for organized labor, Lombardo insisted that "the public learn the truth about Monterrey, which for many years has enjoyed a false prestige regarding the conditions of its workers." He then countered with the equally false claim that blue-collar *regiomontanos* "represent last place among Mexican workers" in wages and living conditions. This he attributed to the industrialists' "subversive attitude toward established institutions and legitimate authority."[22] Thus were the literate citizens of Mexico offered conflicting narratives of Monterrey's labor history.

However, an event that allegedly transpired on the eve of Constitution Day certainly shocked the Mexicans' patriotic sensibilities. In an ingenious move, the Monterrey elite used *Excélsior* to alert the nation to the true nature of organized labor in their city. That evening, readers were to believe, a crowd of some 1,500 "red workers" paraded through Monterrey, singing "The International." At some point, they surrounded the office of a local company union. As startled observers watched, the labor mob "ripped the Mexican flag from its standard, threw it to the ground, and defiled it." These "outrages" against the flag continued into the night, forcing "patriotic citizens" to bring their own *tricolores* indoors.[23] The following day, this altogether fabricated incident made headlines throughout Mexico, with the notable exception of Monterrey itself. In the capital of Chihuahua, for example, the editors of *El Heraldo* emblazoned their front page with the news: "Communists Trample Upon Native Ensign."[24] Enraged citizens wired dozens of protests to the president. Telegrams from chambers of commerce, Rotary Clubs, and veterans groups arrived from provincial capitals and even the more remote corners of the republic. For example, school

22 *Excélsior*, Feb. 5–6, 1936.
23 Ibid.
24 *Excélsior*, Feb. 5, 1936; *El Heraldo de Chihuahua*, Feb. 6, 1936.

teachers in the Zacatecan mining town of El Salvador convened a meeting to inform students and parents of the "Communists' cowardly defilement of our beloved national flag." Ninety-five community members – miners, peasants, Masons, and teamsters – signed a telegram demanding that Cárdenas punish "the individuals who committed this act of high treason against the Fatherland." In the meantime, they assured the president that "the gates of this village will remained closed to communism."[25]

The *regiomontano* elite effectively recast the issue of unionism as a patriotic showdown against the forces of communism. The strategy begot some unexpected results. Organized labor responded immediately to the groundswell of patriotism. In Mexico City, Lombardo ordered that the Mexican flag be raised outside CTM headquarters, where the red-and-black banner of labor solidarity previously flew alone. The secretary of public education demanded the immediate removal of the *rojinegro* from masts in front of the Centro Escolar "Revolución," a teacher's training center. Labor activists in Monterrey answered the challenge as well. Days later, a standard bearer carried a massive red-white-and-green *tricolores* at the forefront of a labor parade as followers sang the national anthem.[26] Although nationalism historically served as a rallying point of working-class unification, the unionists now put those patriotic sentiments on public display.

The leaders of Monterrey's Independent Unions cast their nationalist pride with the industrialists. The Independents would mobilize thousands of workers to join in the resistance. His biographer later credited the brewery's Luis G. Sada as the movement's chief organizer. But early reports portrayed the entire movement as a union-led initiative.[27] White union leaders boasted to a Mexico City reporter that the *regiomontano* workers would put down their tools "to defend their place of work . . . [and] support their employers." The industrialists' lockout thus became a "loyalty strike," a walkout to safeguard "the legitimate interests of the working class."[28] The Independent Unions indeed performed a key role in the premarch preparations. While their radio airwaves buzzed with accounts of the red menace, loyal workers helped distribute 100,000 paper flags adorned with the slogan "México Sí, Rusia No!" They passed these out in the factories while volunteers distributed them door-to-door along with lyrics to the national anthem.

The march's promoters also adorned plant gates and city walls with flyers bearing the Independent Unions' signature. "REGIOMONTANO!" one proclaimed, "Now is the time to stand erect – the hour when the virile and

25 Telegrams in AGN: Presidentes, 432.2/184.
26 *El Porvenir*, Feb. 10, 1936; *El Sol*, Feb. 8, 1936.
27 Saldaña, *Constructores de Monterrey*, 153.
28 *Excélsior*, Feb. 3, 1936.

independent worker protects his home, mother, children, and workplace from Stalin's slaves." The Communists, locals were reminded, would spread "class hatred," "dedicate your daughters to free love . . . and turn your sons into slaves." The Knights of Columbus published another handbill that exhorted: "WORKERS OF MONTERREY! Fight the Communists who disbelieve in God . . . Down with the Communist government of Mexico." Other Christian lay organizations, including the Mexican Catholic Youth Association and the Society of Catholic Dames, exhorted their local followers to march in defense of their "Holy Religion."[29] Borrowing a strategy from their central Mexican cohorts, Monterrey's conservatives thus added Christianity to their arsenal of antigovernment barbs. But consistent with local tradition, secular appeals remained the order of the day. The industrialists essentially converted their setback at the glassworks into a patriotic crusade in defense of the homeland. Some who heeded their call remembered the occasion as an "anti-Communist parade." On the day of the march, the American wife of a *regiomontano* merchant recalled the conspiratorial tone with which her mother-in-law insisted that, "We are going to defy Mexico City!" The people of Monterrey, she added, "were in no mood to have organizers from outside arrive in Monterrey by train, harangue the workmen to join the Communist Party and share the wealth, and then take the next train back." Nonetheless, coming as it did on the heels of the red union's victory, the United States consul reported that "there is no doubt that the action of the employers' league, despite protests to the contrary, was intended to have a political effect and impress the authorities so that they will cease upholding the attitude of [organized labor]."[30]

The turnout was indeed impressive. On the morning of February 5, an estimated 50,000 *regiomontanos* turned out for one of the largest antigovernment demonstrations to that point in Mexican history.[31] At the forefront marched the city's most prominent industrialists. Behind them followed "their faithful employees, professional men of all classes, and numerous women and girls who appeared to be school children."[32] People of all ages and walks of life wove through Monterrey's narrow downtown streets. Senior citizens crowded balconies above, armed with their flags and regional pride. A military band added a "martial and patriotic note to the extraordinary event." Other ensembles performed robust *ranchero* tunes and romantic

29 AGN: Presidentes, 432.2/184.
30 Elizabeth Borton de Treviño, *My Heart Lies South* (New York, 1953), 190; Nathan, Feb. 7, 1936, SD 812.00 NL/130.
31 Unless indicated otherwise, details of the march are from *El Porvenir*, Feb. 5, 1936 and *Excélsior*, Feb. 6, 1936. Estimates on the turnout ranged from 60,000 by its local supporters (Saldaña, *Crónicas históricas*, 233) to the United States Consul's calculation of 40,000 (Nathan, Feb. 6, 1936, SD 812.00 NL/129).
32 Nathan, Feb. 6, 1936, SD 812.00 NL/129.

ballads, music that kept the spirits high. When the marchers turned up Juárez Street and lit into the national anthem they evoked "uncontrolled weeps of joy among those watching from the sidewalks."[33] Others expressed their patriotism by shouting *vivas* to President Cárdenas, an indication that many *regiomontanos* perceived the rally as less of an antigovernment demonstration than an opportunity to express their love of the homeland, if not their president.

As the parade progressed, the marchers alternated choruses of the national anthem with defiant cries of "Death to the Communists!" Over their heads sailed the slick banners produced by the event's organizers: "Juárez or Stalin?" "Defend the Embattled Homeland!" "Down with Russian Traitors!" Dressed as bullfighters, members of a bus drivers' union evoked laughter and applause by waging a mock battle with a donkey labeled "Lombardo Toledano." Observers were struck by the diversity of the crowd and astounded by the sight of unexpected arrivals; for the industrialists also mobilized some outsiders deemed acceptable. Organizers trucked in farmers from the surrounding countryside. Leaders of the General Workers Confederation (CGT) arrived from Mexico City. They shared the industrialists' disdain for rival labor leader, Lombardo Toledano. Also present were Nicolás Rodríguez and his fascist shock troops, the Gold Shirts. The Gold Shirts would remain to combat the "invasion of *lombardismo*" in the factories and streets of Monterrey.

The enthusiastic participation of thousands of *regiomontano* workers proved the most conspicuous feature of the day to many observers. Their presence certainly reassured the locals. National labor leaders found a ready explanation for this popular conservatism. A CTM communiqué asserted that since "the regiomontano workers are unaccustomed to struggle, their class consciousness remains weak."[34] Local unionists, whose militance contradicted the CTM's presumptions, cited other motives. They decried the elite's control of the media as a weapon in their antiunion struggle. Big business in fact threatened to boycott commercial broadcasters who lent the airwaves to organized labor. Economic compulsion also helps explain working-class participation. The Cuauhtémoc Brewery, whose operatives were the largest blue-collar contingent of the day, threatened to dock one day's pay for workers who failed to present themselves at the march.[35] At least some workers on hand were in fact red unionists. Dionisio Aguilar had voted in support of the militant United Glass Workers Union several days earlier. He attended what he remembers as "a really powerful

---

33 Saldaña, *Crónicas históricas*, 233–34.
34 Vicente Lombardo Toledano to Lázaro Cárdenas, Feb. 14, 1936, AGN: Presidentes, 432.2/184.
35 Sindicato Industrial de Trabajadores de Monterrey to Francisco Múgica, Mar. 19, 1936 in AGENL: Trabajo – Asociaciones y Sindicatos, 12/100; López and Aguilar interviews.

demonstration" against the Cárdenas government, even though he did not oppose the president's policies. "To the contrary," he later asserted. On the other hand, Constitution Day represented a single, dramatic, and well-publicized moment in a history of such labor mobilizations in Monterrey. Leaders of the Monterrey's forty-two Independent Unions certainly sympathized with the employers' anticommunist diatribes. The rank and filers shared the heartfelt expressions of patriotism heard on that day. The rash of strikes and protracted labor conflicts that threatened to paralyze local industry also frightened and angered many workers. They liked and respected their employers and sought to protect their jobs. Such workers thus sympathized with a banner stating, "We Demand the Right to Work!"

The parade concluded at the state capital, where one American-born local found "it was impossible to get near the Palace of the Governor; streets converging on the square were one heaving, milling, defiant throng."[36] Those in attendance heard a succession of speeches transmitted on local radio. An anonymous worker spoke first. He drew the gathering's attention to the fact that so many of those present were laborers like himself. He praised the heads of the Independent Unions as "labor representatives who have calloused hands, forged through workshop apprenticeships." Turning to the Government Palace and speaking for all *regiomontanos*, he promised to support elected leaders "as long as they behave themselves like true Mexicans." José Saldaña then spoke of the need to "struggle against all foreign hegemonies." The crowd responded with a spontaneous rendition of the national anthem. Angered by a three-hour delay, the protestors coldly welcomed Governor Morales's belated appearance on the capitol's balcony. They shouted down his prepared statement with bold challenges. "State your position!" they cried. "Are you a communist or not?" Unable to finish his speech, Morales retired to his office and met with reporters. Slight and bespectacled, the governor informed them that "here there is no communism or anything like it." He then criticized the city's industrialists for "turning a labor problem into a social commotion." Our workers, he demanded, only want to organize free of employer interference.[37] Organized labor, for its part, disappeared from the streets for a day. Monterrey's red labor central had petitioned authorities for the right to stage a counterparade that afternoon. But permission was denied by General Juan Almazán, the regional military commander.

The following day, the press reported that the industrialists' well-organized lockout silenced factory whistles and cash registers throughout town. But one observer reported nonetheless that "this was anything

36 Borton de Treviño, *My Heart Lies South*, 192.
37 *Excélsior*, Feb. 6, 1936.

but the 'dead city' described in the newspapers." Union strongholds like the smelters and steel mill maintained operations.[38] The next day, people throughout the republic read and heard about the dramatic events that had transpired in Monterrey, interpreting them as an outpouring of patriotism or a trenchant repudiation of the government's labor policies. As one local prone to dramatics concluded, the movement "shook the social and political structures of Mexico" as if the "Grito de Monterrey" had been heard nationwide. Indeed, within a decade, local businessmen would be alluding to their movement's "international repercussions."[39] President Cárdenas certainly heard the "commotion." Indeed, his train arrived in Mexico's industrial capital two days later. He chastised the industrialists for parlaying the question of unionism into a divisive political issue. The dispute at Monterrey Glassworks, the president stated, "was a labor conflict just like any other."[40] But the response it generated – and his own presence in Monterrey – testified to the contrary.

Cárdenas's journey to Monterrey earned renown for his "Fourteen Points" speech, in which he succinctly clarified his government's labor policy. But the president's sojourn also helped cultivate his legendary status among his local working-class supporters. His reputation built less upon the speech than the down-to-earth nature of his visit. Traveling by rail, he arrived unannounced to Monterrey's Union Station and hailed a taxi. One former glass worker asserts that the president then said to the driver, who failed to recognize his famous fare, "Hey there is a strike going on here, isn't there? Well then take me there." A retired steel worker further embellishes the legend by insisting that Cárdenas "came here all alone, he walked around by himself downtown, without anyone, not even his bodyguards, checking everything out, because he heard the employers here in Monterrey didn't care for their workers."[41] The president in fact arrived with a retinue of advisers, including his secretary of labor. But what the workers' testimony highlights in its exaggerated fashion is that Cárdenas did not follow the customary presidential protocol in Monterrey. He neither toured the city's pillars of industry nor did he hobnob with the local elite. Instead, Cárdenas spent the following days touring Monterrey's blue-collar districts, meeting

38 Nathan, Feb. 7, 1936, SD 812.00 NL/130.
39 Saldaña, *Crónicas históricas*, 235–36. At a 1945 business convention a local brick factory manager told his audience that "70,000 souls filled our streets" to protest "the Cárdenas dictatorship," which was "frankly communistic." He went on that, "The news was published in the dailies of Buenos Aires and Paris; that is to say, it had international repercussions." Quoted in Waterman, Oct. 16, 1945, NAW RG 45, Confidential Records, Box 5.
40 *Excélsior*, Feb. 8, 1936.
41 Aguilar and Palacios interviews. Cárdenas' presence was not a direct response to the February 5 demonstration. One week earlier the United States consul reported his scheduled arrival to mediate a labor dispute in the cotton fields north of the city (Nathan, Jan. 31, 1936, SD 812.00 NL/126).

with workers and businessmen, and staging his own rallies at the state capitol.

On his second day in town, the president inspected the Vidriera's company housing and visited workers' homes. Later in the day, he ordered the provisioning of social services to one of the city's more blighted precincts. As an assistant reported, "His arrival generated great enthusiasm and admiration among the barrio's humble inhabitants, who never imagined that General Cárdenas would visit such a place." In another surprise stop, Cárdenas directed his entourage to the Obregón Industrial School, where he promised to address the students' requests, from new machine tools to an electric workers' training program. The president then lectured his captive audience of workers' sons on the merits of unionism: "The union organizes work and yields high returns for the laborer; it provides security for you and future generations."[42] His agenda that day reflected his government's expressed concern to couple its policy of unionization with the improvement of working-class housing, education, and social services. As Sherman acknowledges, those policies and the discourse that accompanied them were intended to counter the conservative opposition's proclaimed defense of family and home.[43] The news of his arrival spread quickly thereafter.

The *regiomontano* workers, "red" and "white" alike, hailed the president's coming with a triumphant spirit. The striking glass workers celebrated his presence with an ad hoc parade through downtown Monterrey, shooting off fireworks and cheering *vivas* to Cárdenas.[44] Union leaders thronged the city's railroad depot, anxious to meet with the president. Cárdenas called an unprecedented reunion of Monterrey's rival labor activists. He reminded them of his plan to unify Mexican workers "so as to end the harm done by inter-union strife." He cited a recent melee on the Tampico docks, where such a struggle left five longshoremen dead, as proof of his urgency. The president then met the industrialists, an encounter that left a lasting impression on the city's business elite. As one witness later admitted: "We all thought we were dealing with some violent, big-shot general, lacking an education, incapable of civility or even understanding issues of paramount importance."[45] They soon thought otherwise. But their assumptions may explain the story that Cárdenas heard next.

42 Report of Francisco Martínez Vásquez, presidential secretary, Feb. 11, 1936 in AGENL: Trabajo – Associaciones y Sindicatos, 12 (quoted); *El Porvenir*, Feb. 8, 1936; Nathan, Feb. 10, 1936, SD 812.00 NL/131.

43 Sherman, *The Mexican Right*, 61, where he quotes a 1935 speech in which Cárdenas stated that "the government is endeavoring to strengthen family ties by making the home an institution protected against poverty, unemployment, and unsanitary living conditions." The author suggests that the discourse was meant to counter that of the *regiomontano* elite.

44 Nathan, Feb. 10, 1936, SD 812.00 NL/131.

45 Cárdenas cited in *El Porvenir*, Feb. 9, 1936; Saldaña, *Crónicas históricas*, 240.

The industrialists reminded the president of their patriotic contributions to Mexican progress and then clarified the threat that Communists posed to Mexico.[46] "Our masses," they feared, "are certain to fall victim to their undeniable propaganda": the red flags, "violent speeches," and singing of the International. "Even the workers of Monterrey," they added, "whose pride and independence are proverbial, are being affected by the propaganda of communistic organizations, which seek to inculcate their pernicious theories." They expressed particular concern for more vulnerable youths. One businessman even charged that communism had "already taken prisoner – the statistics prove it – the youngest workers, whose inexperience and enthusiasm prevents them from guarding themselves against the misleading songs of their unscrupulous leaders." Worse yet, they believed, agents of Moscow had infiltrated "important departments of the government." They quoted the statutes of Mexico's principal labor central and its proposal "to bring about the disappearance of the capitalist regime." "We do not believe it requires a great deal of effort to see a well-defined communist plan in this program."

The industrialists also reiterated the familiar theme of class harmony, albeit with a populist twist. As one explained, "We [and our employees] have always worked together in the workshops," and since "the majority of us have risen from the working class, we understand [labor's] needs quite well." They went on to decry the "artificiality" of local industrial disputes. For years, they argued, "no real disequilibrium" existed between labor and capital in Monterrey, for "we are all Mexicans here." Recently, however, outside agitators had infiltrated their factories, sowing rank-and-file "indiscipline and hatred towards their employers." Acting out of self-interest and political opportunism, these unionists had pitted workers against one another. Their actions posed "grave consequences not only for regiomontano industry, but for the entire nation." The industrialists therefore protested the formation of the national labor central, the CTM, which promised further disruptions of national industrial development.

Cárdenas listened for three hours "with the utmost attention and without interruption . . . his countenance impassive."[47] He agreed with the industrialists on several issues. Cárdenas, for example, affirmed the necessity of combating "bad labor leaders . . . who sell out the workers' just cause to enrich themselves." He nonetheless reiterated the need to unify the workers. Labor unification would arrest the political opportunists and interunion conflicts, benefitting employers and workers alike. Moreover, "stronger unions would strengthen the workers' consciousness of their responsibilities." Then

---

46 *El Porvenir* and *Excélsior*, Feb. 9, 1936; see also their written plea to the president in Centro Patronal
de Monterrey to Lázaro Cárdenas, Feb. 9, 1936, Archivo Plutarco Elías Calles, Mexico City, 142/854.
47 Saldaña, *Crónicas históricas*, 240.

he got to the point about Monterrey: "On the question of communism, you can all be *tranquilos*, because nothing like it exists." Cárdenas contended that "the presence of small groups of communists is neither new or exclusive to our country," and added that these "tiny minorities" exist in Europe and North America as well. He also denied the alleged link between communists and unionism: "Your workers are fighting for a better standard of living and nothing more." Furthermore, he pledged to support "outside" labor organizers because "you have interfered in your workers' right to organize themselves.[48] Thus did he outline his government's labor policy.

The following day, Monterrey's revolutionary unions staged the largest labor rally in the city's history. The demonstration attracted some 25,000 workers, peasants, and their middle-class allies. Cárdenas took the stage after a student activist denounced Monterrey's company unions and the local media. The president's speech informed the nation that no defilement of the Mexican flag ever took place in Monterrey. Indeed, he proclaimed to the gathering, "the workers of Monterrey and the peasants of Nuevo León breath one of the most patriotic spirits in all of Mexico." Cárdenas then identified the Independent Unions as an obstacle to labor solidarity, asserting that "workers should associate with their class to realize their own social betterment and prevent their class enemies from combating [organized labor], as they presently can."[49] Two days later, Cárdenas addressed a second labor rally and delivered his famous "Fourteen Points" speech in his soft-spoken voice. The president echoed his remarks to Monterrey's workers and industrialists, emphasizing that "the government is the regulator and arbitrator" of social relations. He then adjourned his visit to Monterrey with the threat for which the speech derived its renown: "The businessmen who have wearied of the social struggle can hand their industries over to the workers or the government. That would be patriotic; the industrial lockout is not."[50] The address went unreported in the local press.

The "Fourteen Points" speech concluded Cárdenas's final visit to Monterrey as Mexico's president. To punctuate his stay, he ordered a ballot recount at the glassworks. The outcome verified the previous tally and therefore the strike's legality. Five weeks later, a threat to expropriate the plant indeed pressured the Vidriera to negotiate a collective contract with the United Glass Workers Union. The industrialists did, nonetheless, emerge with a victory of sorts. The president decreed Seventh Day Pay as a national labor right. All Mexican workers thereafter enjoyed the obligatory

48 *Excélsior*, Feb. 12, 1936; Saldaña, *Crónicas históricas*, 241–43; for Cárdenas speeches in Monterrey, consult AGN: Presidentes, 432.2/184.
49 *El Porvenir*, Feb. 10, 1936.
50 Saldaña, *Crónicas históricas*, 250.

paid day of rest that the glassworks' owners had conceded to their workers before the strike. Monterrey's industrialists perceived this labor conquest as their own making, further proof that their corporate policies set the standard for Mexican legislators.[51] But the very issue of militant unionism that provoked their showdown with Cárdenas remained unresolved. As an American diplomat concluded, "It is the general impression among industrialists and businessmen that the visit of the President has thus far only heaped coals upon the fire inasmuch as he appears to take the side of the workmen."[52] They therefore continued resisting Cardenista labor policy. But the red unions, galvanized by the president's visit, made further inroads in their factories.

Competing Ideologies and Popular Mobilizations

Monterrey's industrialists never grew weary of the social struggle. The movement they launched on Constitution Day reflected less a culmination than the beginning of their public crusade against unionism. The elite broadened their campaign as the city's revolutionary unions grew more cohesive. At the national level, the *regiomontano* business elite forged closer ties to their cohorts. Within weeks of the February 5 demonstration, similar anti-Communist campaigns transpired in Puebla, Guadalajara, and Tampico. Back at home, the industrialists integrated middle- and working-class locals into their resistance movement with the formation of Nationalist Civic Action (ACN). The ACN appealed to "regiomontanos who cherish order and progress" by pledging to "foster respect for the flag, dignify the home, and preserve the family." Its women's auxiliary, Acción Cívica Femenina, advocated a woman's right to suffrage along with the hope "that she may preserve her place in the home, thereby perfecting her femininity." The ACN also battled unionism on the ideological front by "promoting the recognition of individual effort as the proper means of improving one's economic standing."[53] As one observer reported, the ACN's "ostensible objective" was to promote patriotism; but "the real objective is to combat the alleged communist tendencies" of the Cárdenas regime.[54] Monterrey remained the center of this organizational precursor to the conservative National Action Party, but the ACN soon counted branches throughout the urban North.

51 *El Porvenir*, Feb. 8, 17, 1936.

52 Nathan, Feb. 10, 1936, SD 812.00 NL/131.

53 *Excélsior*, Feb. 7, 1936; César Gutiérrez González, "29 de julio de 1936 en Monterrey: un caso de lucha de clases," *Cuadernos de cultura obrera*, No. 6 (Monterrey, 1983), 37–38; Sherman, *The Mexican Right*, 61.

54 Nathan, July 30, 1936, SD 812.504/1610.

The ACN attracted participants through "popular subscriptions" determined by one's occupation. By late February, the avowedly nonpolitical organization claimed 7,000 members. The local media avidly promoted the cause of the industrialists, broadcasting the ACN's weekly meetings and reaffirming the organization's large working-class membership. In July, an ACN rally in the brewery's Cuauhtémoc Park attracted 20,000 *regiomontanos* "of all social classes." Members sang "modern Mexican songs," heard a child recite the poem "To Work is to Pray," and listened to diatribes against organized labor and its erstwhile national leader, Lombardo Toledano. An unnamed worker who spoke at the rally addressed the issue of popular support, rebuking "those who say the ACN is nothing more than [an elite organization]." "It would be funny," he remarked, "to imagine our bosses standing here in overalls, having just left the workshops stained with oil and cement, sporting their typical *huarache* sandals."[55]

The ACN's "red" rivals denied its popular appeal. Organized labor attributed blue-collar participation to "enormous quantities of money and all the coercive power of mobilization." In fact, the *regiomontano* workers joined the ACN for the same reasons they marched on February 5. Some did so to avoid losing a day's pay.[56] Others acted voluntarily, putting their patriotism on display and safeguarding their city from the threat of communism. After all, the rallies seemed fun and that was where their workmates were going. Nuevo León's governor believed that the ACN's public rituals served more than anything to maintain "the employers' class spirit." Perhaps converting antiunionism into a patriotic duty helped intimidate fellow industrialists, some of whom seemed to acquiesce to militant unionism. ACN activism also challenged those who would question the *regiomontano* elite's national identities. Their local business journal expressed a mounting resentment at the nation's failure to recognize their own and their city's patriotic credentials. "They say that Monterrey is too *pocha* (Americanized)," editors acknowledged, "and to disprove them, take a look at these undeniably Mexican gardens and squares . . . at the maids taking their daily strolls around Zaragoza Plaza. Are these deep-rooted traditions not truly Mexican?" They charged that their critics wanted to "destroy" Monterrey because it offered a "lesson, example and stimulus to other Mexicans." "But the true people have begun to awake," they warned, "and that pueblo will know how to defend Monterrey as the first stage in the rescue of Mexico."[57] The ACN, meanwhile, continued its festive means of reaffirming the locals' spirit of class harmony, regional pride, and civic-minded patriotism.

55 *El Porvenir*, July 1, 1936.
56 Federación de Trabajadores de Nuevo León (FTNL), *La burguesía regiomontana y su verdadero rostro* (Monterrey, 1937), 35 (quoted); López interview.
57 *Actividad*, Dec. 1938.

The upbeat ACN rallies contrasted mightily with the more violent edge of the antiunion campaign. After the 1932 ASARCO strike, violence remained conspicuously absent from Monterrey's labor struggles. Red and white unions waged their jurisdictional struggles peacefully, on the shop floors, in the streets, and in the labor courts. But during their visit with President Cárdenas, the city's red union leaders warned that the industrialists had enlisted the support of the *Camisas Dorados* (Gold Shirts).[58] In February 1936, their national leader, Nicolás Rodriguéz, had arrived to Monterrey with five dozen of his fascist shock troops. Operating under their motto "Mexico for the Mexicans," the *Dorados* emulated Mussolini's Black Shirts. They derived their moniker from their flashy style of dress, one modeled upon that of Pancho Villa's troops. Since the early 1930s, the *Dorados* waged their struggle to save Mexico from "foreign ideologies" by attacking agrarian reformers, union workers, and rural teachers, all considered agents of communism.[59] Public awareness of the indigenous fascist movement emerged dramatically when Mexico City radicals routed the Gold Shirts during a 1935 showdown in the capital's central plaza. The *Dorados* appeared in Monterrey shortly thereafter.

Developments in the northern industrial city proved conducive to their movement. As a city dominated by Mexican-owned industries, the Gold Shirts considered Monterrey a "bulwark" against economic imperialism. They identified the city's ongoing labor conflicts as part of a conspiracy staged by communist labor activists – "the sagacious representatives of the Russian Jews" – to undermine Mexico's industrial development.[60] The Gold Shirts established a conspicuous presence in the city, one that elicited both sympathy and concern. The local press endorsed the Gold Shirts by publishing their daily manifestos. Their leader, Nicolás Rodríguez, manned a local recruiting office, guarded by his heavily armed shock troops. Workers who read the flyers they posted about town learned of the Gold Shirts that "we combat employers who exploit their workers, but we help those who are just, pay well, and treat their workers better." How many workers were recruited by the *Dorados* remains unclear. They certainly coordinated their campaign of intimidation with the Independent Unions. One leader of the Vidriera's company union later admitted his own membership. The city's militant unions, for their part, threatened to expel any member involved with the Gold Shirts. For the reds, the very presence of the Gold Shirts confirmed the fascist demeanor of the city's elite. Indeed, the American consul

---

58 *El Porvenir*, Feb. 9, 1936.
59 Sherman, *The Mexican Right*, 55, 62–64.
60 Mexican Revolutionary Action (Gold Shirts) to Lázaro Cárdenas, Feb. 7, 1936, AGN: Presidentes, 432.2/184.

reported, the industrialists supported them "financially and morally."[61] This alarmed a diplomat whose dispatches then evoked considerably more concern with fascist influences than communist activism in Monterrey. He thus applauded government pronouncements against "an illegal body to combat the labor element." The consul feared that the Gold Shirts would evolve from antiunion thugs into a "fascist movement modeled on the Italian example."[62] Local authorities had more immediate reasons for concern.

The Gold Shirts pledged to settle the union problem swiftly and violently. Upon their arrival, they claimed to possess a list of "twenty-two known Communists" whom they promised to drive out of the city. Nicolás Rodríguez promised that, "We will tell the regiomontano worker what his situation is and how to remedy it, how to defend himself from [labor] leaders, and how to exterminate them."[63] The Gold Shirts put their words into action. In early March, they launched a drive-by shooting against the steel workers' Local 67. That followed on the heels of a shootout with union glass workers and an arson attack on the railroaders' union hall.[64] Fearing more "bloody confrontations," the governor ordered police to close the *Dorados'* headquarters and disarm their members. According to one source close to the elite, the action "incensed many [of those] prominent in local business and industrial circles." Upon searching their archives, authorities claimed to find documents linking the Gold Shirts to the ACN, company union leaders, and local priests. To the governor's dismay, the *Dorados* won a court injunction and reopened their local office.[65] They remained active into mid-1936, publishing diatribes in the local press and promoting interunion conflicts on behalf of the industrialists. But the Gold Shirts met their match in the steel workers. Armed with pistols and iron bars specially crafted in their workshops, Local 67's "revolutionary squadrons" organized a series of "counterattacks" against the unsuspecting Gold Shirts, driving them off the streets of Monterrey.[66] But the labor violence they promoted became an increasingly conspicuous feature of Monterrey's interunion struggles in the months and years to come.

---

61 AGENL: JCA 126/3646; Nathan, Feb. 13, 1936, SD 812.00 NL/135 (file includes Gold Shirt propaganda) (quoted); *El Porvenir*, Aug. 3, 1936.

62 The consul added that, "It would appear the next step the local employers' league might take would be to organize these [Gold Shirts] with a large following into a sort of Fascist group such as formed the original nucleus of a similar element in Italy." Nathan, Feb. 7, Mar. 2, 1936, SD 812.00 NL/130, 142.

63 *El Porvenir*, Feb. 8, 1936.

64 Nathan, Feb. 29, 1936, SD 812.00 NL/141; *El Porvenir*, Mar. 3, 1936.

65 Morales Sánchez to Cárdenas, Mar. 6, 1936 in AGN: Presidentes, 432.2/184; Nathan, Mar. 2, Mar. 16, 1936, SD 812.00 NL/142, 812.5045/273.

66 Elizondo interview.

In the meantime, conservative resistance to Cardenismo paralleled the ascendency of revolutionary unionism in Monterrey. President Cárdenas's own denouncement of company unions and his threats of industrial expropriations emboldened workers and radicalized the union movement. Organized labor broadened its organizational base, inspired by red union victories at the steel mill and glass works. Militant workers attempting to displace company unions now enjoyed the support of the governor and the labor courts. Not only did a prounion judge preside over the tribunal; the revolutionary unions controlled the appointment of worker delegates. Without fear of reprisal, activists launched new campaigns against white unions in major plants. Rank-and-file workers who once waited on the sidelines endorsed militant unionism, drawn by the appeal of a collective contract, their president's exhortations to "associate with their class," or both. In addition to established strongholds – the railroad shops, the steel mill, the smelters, and textile mills – red unions won representation elections in Monterrey's construction, furniture, apparel, and electric power industries.[67] The revolutionary unionists espoused political outlooks as diverse as the industries they represented. But conservative resistance to Cardenismo prompted communist and ruling party unionists to put aside their differences and heed the Cardenista call for labor solidarity.

The Communists' Popular Front strategy bore fruit when Mexico's disparate regional labor centrals and national industrial unions coalesced as the Confederation of Mexican Workers (CTM) in late February 1936. Union leaders did not, as some claim, organize the labor central in response to the antigovernment demonstrations in Monterrey.[68] Nonetheless, the political climate created by the industrialists' showdown with Cárdenas set the stage for the unification of a diverse body of unions whose leaders had been rivals since the 1920s. The CTM unified the Communists' labor central (CSUM), the big industrial unions (railroad, mining-metallurgy, electric, and oil), and leaders of Mexico City's central labor council, headed by Vicente Lombardo Toledano. The Communists had established a strong presence in the industrial unions and their locals. Those unions sacrificed traditions of political independence and union autonomy to ally with an array of regional federations (FROCs) characterized by their centralized control of small unions of tradesmen and service workers. While its statutes pledged otherwise, the CTM collaborated with the Cárdenas regime as its strongest ally. The Communists tenuously and begrudgingly conceded to the policy in the name of proletarian unity.[69]

67 *El Porvenir*, June 6–8, 1936.
68 Shulgolvski, *Mexico en la encrucijada*, 278–79; Sariego, *El sindicalismo minero*, 38.
69 Hernández Chávez, *La mécanica cardenista*, 155; Hamilton, *The Limits of State Autonomy*, 160–62.

In May 1936, Monterrey's revolutionary unions consolidated the Nuevo León Workers Federation (FTNL), the local CTM affiliate. The FTNL replicated the national's unification of diverse unions and antagonistic leaders. To one side were the small, mainly service-sector unions led by officials tied to the ruling party. In the opposing corner stood the industrial union locals, many of whose leaders were then sympathetic toward if not members of the Communist Party. Monterrey's pattern of industrial development lent the industrial unions a powerful voice in the local CTM. Monterrey hosted not only the influential Railroaders Local 19 but three separate Miners Union locals. The muscle assured the election of a radical slate to the FTNL's Executive Committee. Tomás Cueva, a railroad station clerk, and Salvador Rodríguez, an organizer of the 1932 ASARCO strike, assumed the two key posts of secretary general and secretary of organization, respectively.[70] Both were Communists. Their election reflected the unionists' popularity among rank-and-file workers who did not necessarily share their political outlooks.

Workers like Félix Torres recall Cueva, in particular, as a "very honorable and decent man." Torres's fellow electric worker, Zacarías Villarreal, remembered the long-time activist for his convincing May Day speeches. Such oral recollections of past figures build upon the subsequent corruption of many CTM leaders as well as the unscrupulous behavior of certain unionists of the day. Torres, for example, told a tale of one union leader who threatened strikes against small, family-owned tortilla shops to extort money from their owners. Monterrey workers therefore respected activists like Cueva for being "willing and prepared to fight" (*listos y peleadores*), for their *integridad*, and for their oratorical skills. Indeed, one former steel worker remembered that the communist leaders of Local 67 could "talk a lot," and proved particularly effective at articulating their understanding of Mexican labor law. "The majority of workers didn't know anything about the law," he noted, "they didn't know their rights, so [they supported] whoever was well oriented, who said the Federal Labor Law says this or that, who could tell them their rights, even though they were often fibbing because they did not really understand the law [themselves]." But they were considered "honorable," a trait that distinguished them from subsequent union leaders "who really knew the law well but did not have the same principles." We shall see that the qualities that earned Communists their leadership posts in the FTNL also influenced their election to unions like the steel workers' Local 67. As Salvador Castañeda explained, "In all the [red] unions, he who

---

70 Congreso Constitutivo de la Federación de Trabajadores de Nuevo León, May 5, 1936 in AGENL: JCA 126/3646. The FTNL adopted the CTM's statutes with two exceptions that reflected local labor history. The Nuevo León central excluded the national's goal of organizing cooperative societies and added the objective to "fight against white unions."

was not with the Communist Party had practically no legitimacy in the eyes of the workers, it was like a fashion back in those years." That is why the United States consul could emphasize by late 1936 that "the labor unions of Monterrey are fairly well infected with Communists."[71] The industrialists thus had reason for concern, for their presumptions about communist influence in Monterrey rang true.

Activists schooled in union defeats of the 1920s and the insurgency of the Depression years now became major protagonists in Monterrey's labor movement. They found prominent allies among a small but influential sector of the *regiomontano* middle class: college students, professionals, teachers, and feminists. In a city polarized by the issue of unionism, such middle-class activists also chose sides. Some preferred Cardenismo. They were mainly young *regiomontanos* in their twenties and early thirties. Many had seen the lessons taught of the revolution in the 1920s fall prey to the corrupt, right-wing drift of President Calles and his successors. They discovered in Cardenismo the possibility of putting revolutionary promises into practice.[72] As befitted an industrial city, Monterrey's middle-class radicals tied their fortunes to organized labor, just as their conservative counterparts helped administer company paternalism and joined the ACN. Cardenismo became, in their minds, a social movement centered on industrial democracy, political mobilizations, and the cultural transformation of the Mexican proletariat. The Cardenista coalition naturally attracted its share of political opportunists, as all social movements do. Just as their opponents charged, some championed the cause of labor to advance their own political fortunes. However, an equal if not greater number of middle-class Cardenistas became active in the labor movement to empower the working class.

Many were Mexican Communist Party members. PCM membership peaked during the later 1930s. Consistent with its social structure, the Monterrey branch included an unusually high proportion of factory workers as well as the students and teachers who composed much of party's base. As Barry Carr's study concludes, the PCM's small membership figures belied its activists' impact on the social and cultural life of revolutionary Mexico.[73] Among the most noteworthy of Monterrey's PCM activists were Dr. Angel Martínez Villarreal, Humberto Ramos Lozano, and Juan Manuel Elizondo. Martínez was among the most celebrated surgeons of his time in Mexico. In Monterrey, he directed the Medical School and was the rector

71 Interviews with Castañeda, Félix Torres, Nov. 14, 1995, and Zacarías Villarreal, Nov. 18, 1995; Blocker, Dec. 31, 1936, SD 812.00/162 (quoted).

72 Elizondo, *Mi universidad*, 43–61, 123–25.

73 Carr, *Marxism and Communism*. The party's (perhaps exaggerated) figures suggest that the number of dues-paying national members increased from 5,000 to 30,000 between 1936 and 1939. One half of the PCM's Monterrey activists were industrial workers (10).

of the University of Nuevo León during the 1930s. He also entered the "social struggle," speaking at demonstrations, sitting on the local CTM's board, and operating free clinics at the steel mill and smelters.[74] Ramos Lozano organized Monterrey's teachers union during the mid-1930s. He was among those who heeded Cárdenas' call that teachers become not only educators of children but "the guides and directors of the working classes" as well. As Ramos recalls of his fellow teachers, "we always came from the humble classes, from working-class or peasant families in Nuevo León." That background, he believed, "enhanced our capacity to maintain good relations with the underdogs." "You need many skills to be a labor leader," he went on, "but the most important is to have good relations with the *humildes.*" The teacher-activists spoke at union assemblies and taught literacy courses at union halls. They met with unorganized workers as well, especially enthusiastic youngsters, whom "we chatted with about the history of Mexico, the labor movement, and the theories of Marx and Lenin." The teachers proselytized among the nonunion workers through Monterrey's night schools and bolstered attendance by offering courses in drafting and mechanics.[75]

Juan Manuel Elizondo traveled a different road, returning from his university studies in Mexico City to the rambunctious early life of the steel mill's Local 67.[76] While in the capital, he and fellow students became caught up in the radical euphoria of Cardenismo and decided "to enter the social struggle decisively, as professionals." Elizondo later wrote that, "We had the idea of participating as theoretical directors . . . becoming the political representatives of the working class." There was an undeniably elitist tone to their project. Elizondo admits that, "as students, we perceived ourselves as more competent than the [workers'] natural leaders." Communist Party officials sent them out from Mexico City to work with revolutionary unions. Elizondo embraced the practice, for, "rather than writing articles and giving conferences, our idea was to get in touch with the people and thus have a real influence on the working class."

Elizondo returned to Monterrey and joined Local 67. "We already had several comrades of ours" on the union directorship. The union controlled hiring and put Elizondo to work as a chemist in the steel mill's labs. Elizondo also attended to Local 67's legal affairs. But he performed his most important tasks away from the shop floor, organizing the union's cultural programs and speaking before weekly union assemblies. While work at the steel

74 Ramiro Estrada Sánchez, *Buena tarde, Angel* (Monterrey, 1985), 40–50.
75 Cárdenas speech in *El Porvenir*, Feb. 10, 1936; interview with Humberto Ramos Lozano, May 3, 1996.
76 Following paragraph based on Elizondo interviews and Juan Manuel Elizondo, *De historia y política* (Monterrey, 1994), 32–34.

mill entailed a change in lifestyle – "no more running around from cafes to meetings" – Elizondo asserted that "we were better off there than preaching in the desert." To the radicals' further satisfaction, "we were well received by the workers," many of whom already knew Elizondo as the young speaker at the city's labor rallies. For the steel workers, we will see, the arrival of people like Elizondo coincided with the dramatic improvements embedded in their collective contract. They were certainly impressed by the fact that prominent *regiomontanos* took a sincere interest in their condition, however self-interested or politically motivated the Communists' actions may have seemed to the city's elite.

Popular mobilizations continued unabated after Cárdenas's departure from Monterrey, as revolutionary unions extended their inroads in local factories and organized labor became increasingly combative. Worker protest escalated through the mid-1930s. Relatively minor industrial disputes generated impressive displays of solidarity. Union leaders threatened general strikes. They justified their actions by claiming the president's support and reiterated his threat to place factories under workers' control.[77] The revolutionary unions' capacity to mobilize workers had increased tremendously. The presence of smelter, steel, glass, and railroad workers alone guaranteed strong attendance at organized labor's Sunday afternoon rallies, which attracted upward of 20,000 union workers, their families, and local sympathizers. For activists like Elizondo, these *gran manifestaciones* ostensibly countered "the anti-union offensive waged daily by the newspapers and radio." "But *every day*," he emphasized, the media reminded *regiomontanos* that Communists "would devour your children, and that the Russians would do this or that, kill all the priests, and that in Mexico communists received orders from Moscow to liquidate businesses, and they wanted to take away the Mexican flag."

Consistent with the Popular Front strategy, Elizondo perceived their activism in Monterrey as a struggle against "fascism." He also acknowledges the party's influence on their strategies. "The [Communist] International gave everyone the order," he noted, "to get as close to the workers as possible because the fascist propaganda was so powerful and we had no means of gaining access [to the media]." During their weekly rallies, red labor leaders directed their protests against the pillars of the conservative resistance movement. They demanded that the government disband "Nationalist Civic Reaction" and the Gold Shirts, "fascist" organizations that worked to undermine Cardenista reforms. They also highlighted the role of the local media in the elite's campaign. Since the early 1930s, federal communications law prohibited commercial broadcasters from using their medium to promote political agendas. The reds therefore exhorted the state

77 *El Porvenir*, Mar. 17 and 23, Apr. 8, June 11, 18, and 23, 1936.

to seize Monterrey's leading dailies and radio stations and reorganize them as labor-run cooperatives.[78] Cárdenas never complied. But their demands demonstrated the militants' understanding of how important those "modern means of propaganda" had become in the elite's effort to foster antiunion sentiments in Monterrey.

The conservative resistance orchestrated by Nationalist Civic Action and the Independent Unions of Nuevo León thus encountered a rival in Monterrey's Popular Front coalition of red unionists and their middle-class sympathizers. The Popular Front brought strange bedfellows together. The progovernment and communist unionists who vied for power within the FTNL came to an uneasy truce. Their unification reflected a shared commitment to defend Cardenismo against the combative forces of the industrialists and their allies. But in Monterrey the antagonisms within the labor movement were too ingrained to be masked over by popular frontism. Monterrey's railwaymen upheld their distrust of national labor leader Lombardo Toledano, a sentiment they expressed during his late 1935 visit to Monterrey. They had not forgotten the role he played in breaking their strike nearly a decade before.[79] Political factionalism also manifested itself within the FTNL as Communists ascended to leadership positions. The radicals' conspicuous role in the labor movement did not please local ruling party officials either, particularly Governor Anacleto Guerrero, the military veteran elected in mid-1936. Indeed, the state's role in creating the legal and political conditions that made revolutionary unionism possible would soon work against the Communist-led unions.

---

78 Elizondo interviews; SITMMSRM Secciones No. 66 and No. 67 to Lázaro Cárdenas, Jan. 15, 1936 and Sindicato Industrial de Trabajadores de Monterrey to Lázaro Cárdenas, Mar. 9, 1936 in AGN: DGG 2.331.8 (16) 32-A/73; *El Porvenir*, May 2 and 12, 1936; communications law in Hayes, *Radio Nation*, 39, 66–68.
79 *El Porvenir*, Nov. 11, 1935.

9
The Quotas of Power

Organized Labor and the Politics of Consensus

On the evening of July 29, 1936, the Nuevo León Workers Federation staged its weekly labor rally at a new venue. Whereas organizers generally held demonstrations before the state capital, they decided to meet on that night outside the nearby Casino Monterrey, the "exclusive club of the city's 'aristocracy'." As they later claimed, the protesters "wanted to mark the rude contrast of economic reality by presenting overalls and work boots on the front steps of the bourgeoisie's center of vice." Among the other concerns expressed that evening was organized labor's demand that the government disband Nationalist Civic Action for being a "subversive" threat to the "constitutional regime."[1] It just so happened that the ACN was meeting one block away. Some 600 members had convened there to hear the lecture "Mexico Shall be Free in Spite of the Communists." As the two-hour labor rally progressed, speakers were taunted by young ACN activists gathered on a nearby corner. A cordon of steel workers prevented the angered unionists from answering the provocations while orators interrupted their speeches to plead for workers to maintain their composure.

When the labor rally disbanded, an estimated 200 workers marched down the narrow street in front of the ACN's headquarters. The militants shouted revolutionary slogans and, according to later press reports, threw a few stones. Fearing "a bloody confrontation," labor leader Tomás Cueva rushed to the head of the procession and prevented the workers from storming the building. ACN members scurried to lower the metal curtains at their meeting hall's entrance. As the gates came down, volleys of gunfire rang out into the street. Bricks and bullets rained down upon the cornered workers from the rooftop above. And Gold Shirt snipers fired on them from atop the nearby Continental Hotel. Within minutes, two workers lay dead and thirty wounded, one of whom later died. Among the injured was Tomás

---

1 Federación de Trabajadores de Nuevo León, *La burguesía regiomontana*, 38.

Cueva, who survived the gunshot wounds that doctors initially diagnosed as "fatal."[2]

The police arrived promptly from their nearby station. The ACN's subsequent claims of self-defense contradicted the scene discovered by the officers themselves. They therefore sealed the ACN's meeting hall and arrested its 500 inhabitants, among them prominent industrialists, their foremen, and loyal workers. Authorities jailed the alleged perpetrators in the unfriendly confines of the penitentiary, much to the initial satisfaction of the ACN's rivals. But a district judge intervened and ordered their transfer to the military garrison on the edge of town. There, the United States consul reported, the ACN militants "were permitted many liberties." They then mobilized dozens of "lawyers, litigants, and people of high social representation" to win their release.[3] One week later, the district judge acquitted the distinguished defendants after "military experts" testified that the pistols recovered at ACN headquarters had not been fired in years. Labor leaders charged that the police chief had actually "switched the recovered pistols with some old ones [that were] incapable of firing." The case was dropped for "lack of evidence."[4]

The July 29th tragedy marked a watershed in relations between the industrialists, organized labor, and the state in Nuevo León. The violence transpired during another bewildering conjuncture in local politics, one defined by government attempts to check labor militancy. The months following the industrialists' February 1936 showdown with Cárdenas had seen the governor replace the labor board's president, Teofilo Martínez Pérez, with one considered more moderate. In May, General Anacleto Guerrero became governor. The veteran from Nuevo León came from the more conservative wing of the ruling party. But as in other states, such governors were considered loyal to the president and the party.[5] Their nominations were intended to counter the weight of generals who harbored their own political ambitions, men like Juan Almazán, who commanded the northeastern military zone from his Monterrey garrison. Guerrero won a controversial victory over his Liberal Party opponent, Fortunato Zuazua, an outcome tainted by violence and fraud. A federal election inspector reported that Guerrero's strongest support came from the "so-called red workers."

2 Details of the July 29, 1936 events from FTNL, *La burguesía regiomontana*, 39–41; *El Porvenir*, July 30–31, 1936; the legal disposition later filed by FTNL leader Tomás Cueva, in César Gutiérrez G., "29 de Julio de 1936: Un caso de lucha de clases," *Cuadernos de Cultura Obrera* No. 6 (Monterrey, 1983), 83–86; Salinas, *Mi padre*, 229; worker recollections in Sandra Arenal, *En Monterrey no solo hay ricos* (Mexico City, 1988), 42–43.

3 Nathan, July 31, 1936, SD 812.00 NL/153; *El Porvenir*, July 30, 1936.

4 FTNL, *La burguesía regiomontana*, 39; *El Porvenir*, Aug. 7, 1936.

5 Adrian A. Bantjes, *As If Jesus Walked on Earth: Cardenismo, Sonora, and the Mexican Revolution* (Wilmington, 1998), 182–86.

Organized labor had officially sanctioned the ruling-party candidate in tune with its Popular Front strategy.[6] But Guerrero made immediate overtures to the embittered industrialists who had opposed his election. In late July, he gained their approval by publicly chastising Monterrey's communist labor leaders as "ill-fated opportunists" who agitated workers for political ends.[7] His speech earned Guerrero accolades from the Independent Unions and set the tone for the night of July 29th.

Unity at Any Cost

Union workers responded to the July 29th tragedy with outpourings of grief and defiance. Two days later, a general strike paralyzed Monterrey's union factories and commercial establishments. Bus and taxi drivers staged rush hour strikes, blockading traffic in downtown Monterrey. Later that week, 30,000 mourners marched in a funeral procession to honor the fallen unionists – a printer, a machinist, and a waiter by trade. Thousands more filed by their coffins, placed on display in CTM headquarters. Governor Guerrero's conspicuous absence from the events sent a strong, calculated message to communist labor leaders. A mass rally of "some 5,000 reds" marched the next day on the state capital, denouncing Guerrero, insisting on the ACN's closure, and demanding legal justice for their comrades' deaths. Organized labor's indignant response received little attention in the city's press, which hastened to revise its earlier reporting on the July 29th killings. Monterrey's leading daily published a communiqué in which the Independent Unions assailed "red labor leaders" as the "intellectuals authors" of the workers' "assassinations." Readers learned of a "Russian-style assault" on a peaceful ACN meeting, a violent provocation that the businessmen had repelled "to save themselves from being sacrificed on the communist altar."[8]

Since no formal investigation ever took place, the events of July 29th remain shrouded in conspiracy theories. The official account – that of the governor's office and the press – portrays the bloodshed as the unfortunate result of a communist plot to harass the ACN and unseat the Guerrero government by fomenting political instability.[9] Guerrero's charges of a radical conspiracy to provoke a government crisis stand counterposed to evidence strongly suggestive of a well-laid ACN plan to ambush their nemeses. The labor rally's organizers considered it a "suspicious coincidence" that the ACN

6 The 1936 gubernatorial elections and federal inspector's reports in AGN: DGG 2.331 (16)/281; see also Hernández Chávez, *La mecánica cardenista*, 64–67; Saragoza, *The Monterrey Elite*, 174–86.

7 *El Porvenir*, July 25 and 28, 1936; Saragoza, *The Monterrey Elite*, 186–89.

8 Nathan, Aug. 3, 1936, SD 812.504/1611; *El Porvenir*, July 30–31 and Aug. 3, 6–8, 1936; Gutiérrez G., "29 de Julio de 1936," 20.

9 Nathan, July 30, 1936, SD 812.504/1610; *El Porvenir*, July 30, 1936; Saragoza, *The Monterrey Elite*, 186–87.

had convened nearby on that very evening. The daughter of one prominent businessman later wrote that, "perhaps my father knew beforehand what was going to happen," for he advised his employees to stay away from that night's ACN meeting.[10] Organized labor subsequently commemorated the "sacrificed workers" with solemn marches and commemorative publications. A small book published by Local 67, *The True Face of the Regiomontano Bourgeoisie*, explained the circumstances under which "for the first time in Monterrey *patrones* personally murdered workers." At that unique conjuncture in local and national history, Monterrey's industrialists could not turn to the police or army to protect their interests: "Having lost their absolute dominance of the government, frightened by their own tales of communist phantoms, they felt alone, threatened . . . and they fired [upon the workers]." The subsequent impunity enjoyed by the ACN activists illuminated the power of wealth and the shifting winds of local politics.[11]

After July 29th, Monterrey's industrial elite gradually withdrew their antiunion crusade from the public sphere. While the ACN remained active – protected by a court injunction – the industrialists turned their attention back to their factories. Governor Guerrero became a valuable ally. The governor's muted response to the July 29th killings reflected a concerted decision to distance himself from the radicals who dominated the Nuevo León Workers Federation. Indeed, the red labor central's fragile unity unraveled shortly thereafter. By early 1937, the United States consul reported that progovernment leaders were opportunistically seizing "every opportunity to denounce any ties to communism." This partisan fighting fractured the Nuevo León Workers Federation. Unionists loyal to Guerrero accused the labor central's directors of "being under the influence of Moscow" and converting the FTNL into the "executive body" of the Communist Party. The dissidents broke away and established separate headquarters with the governor's moral and financial support.[12]

The schism barely diminished the FTNL's membership because the big industrial unions remained loyal to the communist-led federation. The Communists thus gloated over their base of support within heavy industry, dismissing their adversaries as "nothing more than pork rind and lemonade vendors."[13] Pleased with the turn of events, one Monterrey industrialist ingeniously reclassified the once homogeneous reds as the "beets" and "turnips" – the beets being red to the core.[14] The split prompted organized

---

10 FTNL, *La burguesía regiomontana*, 37; Salinas, *Mi padre*, 231 (quoted).
11 FTNL, *La burguesía regiomontana*, 41.
12 Blocker, Feb. 28, Mar. 31, 1937, SD 812.00 NL/164, 165.
13 *El Porvenir*, Mar. 2, 1937. The dissidents led unions of street vendors, bus drivers, musicians, waiters, and hotel and theater workers. Among the locals with communist leaders were those of railroad, steel, smelter, glass, electric, construction, and furniture workers.
14 Blocker, May 29, 1937, SD 812.00 NL/168.

labor to stage two separate May Day celebrations, with Governor Guerrero presiding over the "official" parade. Denied the right to march, the communist faction met at the railwaymens' union hall, where Tomás Cueva lambasted "fascist" labor bosses in Mexico City for packing the CTM with "corrupt" officials and *"pistoleros"* (gunmen). Cueva also reminded the ranks of Lombardo's "treasonous" past, recalling the role played by the young labor bureaucrat when the Calles regime broke the 1926–27 railway workers' strikes.[15] The feeling endured for the remainder of the Cárdenas years.

The local schism paralleled developments in the capital. In mid-1936, the CTM found itself divided when the communist-led Miner-Metalworker and Railroader Unions broke from the national federation over issues of union autonomy. The industrial unions sought greater political independence from the ruling party and resisted a CTM effort to integrate their locals into regional labor centrals. They organized a dissident federation and elected the *regiomontano* railwayman, Juan Gutiérez, as president. The radical faction took more than half the CTM membership with them, including state labor federations like that of Nuevo León.[16] The CTM split lasted five months. The Communist International finally intervened to save the Cardenistas' labor unification scheme. The Comintern's North American figurehead, Earl Browder, rushed down from the United States to remind his Mexican comrades of the party's "unity at any cost" strategy. They threw in the towel and returned to the CTM corner. But the powerful and historically independent Railroader and Miner-Metalworker Unions remained autonomous. The Communists forsook their posts on the CTM's directorship, conceded to Lombardo's continued tenure as secretary general, and agreed to support PNR candidates for office. Their final endorsement of the unity pledge would be "instrumental in the assembly and maintenance of the Cardenista coalition." Meanwhile, local labor leaders allied with Governor Guerrero gained control of the Nuevo León Workers Federation.[17]

Monterrey's industrialists seized upon this weakening of the labor–state alliance to renew their open-shop drive in their factories. In mid-1937, Local 67's leaders wrote President Cárdenas that "we are not aware of a single labor authority in the republic that registers white unions like they do in this place. . . . They are destroying your work, disorganizing labor, fomenting conflicts between workers, and doing so with the financial and moral support of the [Guerrero] government." The steel workers protested the

15 *El Porvenir*, May 3, 1937.

16 Samuel León and Ignacio Marván, *La clase obrera en la historia de México: En el cardenismo (1934–1940),* 52, 89–90; Hernández Chávez, *La mécanica cardenista,* 154–63; *El Porvenir*, Mar. 20, Apr. 29, and May 13, 1937.

17 Knight, "The Rise and Fall of Cardenismo," 277 (quoted); Hernández Chávez, *La mécanica cardenista,* 162–65; *El Porvenir*, Aug. 20 and Sep. 5, 1937.

labor board's recent decertification of communist-led unions after strikes in the furniture and construction industries. "Furthermore," they lamented to Cárdenas, "we believe that these events are known by yourself." Whether the governor acted independently or with the president's consent remains unclear. But the United States consul confirmed the behind-the-scenes role of Governor Guerrero, who "politically opposed" the leaders of defeated unions. To clarify the shifting tides of local politics, the steel workers observed that, "we workers of Monterrey have seen how *señor* Joel Rocha . . . pompously struts around at the governor's side during the Monterrey Fair."[18] Rocha, a local furniture manufacturer, ACN president, and *"director intelectual"* of the industrialists, had replaced 250 red workers after the labor courts declared their strike illegal. Those displaced workers aimed a more direct attack at Guerrero. The governor, they noted correctly, owed his electoral victory to the support of organized labor. However, "the times are changing, and those who once declared themselves [his] staunchest enemies, now live in peace with [Guerrero], while the workers are subjected to the most hateful reprisals."[19] Safely ensconced in power, Governor Guerrero expressed his contempt for local Communists by conceding to the elite's union-busting activities. He did so by ordering his appointee to the labor courts to decertify communist-led unions.

Monterrey's red worker-activists thus learned that organizing a union and winning certification did not end their struggle. The industrialists preserved their tradition of revising their managerial strategies in ways both cunning and coercive to keep unions out of their plants. United States diplomats reported their efforts to "organize a band of spies . . . to create discord and troubles" in the revolutionary unions. The informers' reports, published in a weekly employers' bulletin, were meant to expose the unions as "Communistic hotbeds" and achieve "the political possibilities resulting therefrom."[20] Nonetheless, far more workers now risked their jobs to maintain their union prerogatives. Workers thus struck to defend their collective contracts or to protest the reprisals to which union officials were subjected by recalcitrant managers. The strikes, as their employers clearly anticipated, permitted the government to resume its role as labor arbitrator. Under Guerrero, the very industrialists who organized resistance to the Federal Labor Law in 1931 would see that labor code serve their ends. By mid-1937, when the reds penned their commemoration to the "July 29th martyrs," organized labor was once again decrying that the labor law "served

18 Sindicato Industrial de Trabajadores Mineros Metalúrgicos, Sección No. 67, to President Cárdenas, June 4 and 12, 1937, AGN: DGG 2.331 (16)/32-A/77 (quoted); Blocker, July 12, 1937, SD 812.00 NL/171.

19 Sindicato Industrial de Trabajadores de las Fábricas de Muebles del Estado de Nuevo León to President Cárdenas, Apr. 30, 1937, AGN: DGG 2.331 (16)/33-A/20.

20 Quoted in Saragoza, *The Monterrey Elite*, 188–89.

only to justify the outrages committed by employers; the right to strike, the workers' only effective weapon, was proscribed." These developments confirmed their historic belief that the law and the state "naturally served bourgeois interests." But as the Communists admitted, the industrialists could also attribute their successful open-shop movement to "a strong and very large faction of *obreros blancos*," the loyal workers who ensured that "in Nuevo León, the bourgeoisie is stronger than the proletariat."[21] Years of organizing experience in Monterrey's factories taught the reds that their initial union conquests would be difficult to maintain. No local company better exemplified this process than Monterrey Glassworks, where the issue of unionism first drew the nation's attention to "Mexico's Chicago."

Meetings, Marches, and Riots

The 1936 glass strike endured six weeks after Cárdenas' historic visit to Monterrey. A bottle shortage at the brewery and government threats to seize their factory pressured the company to agree to the union's key demands. The United Glass Workers won the right to nominate all new hires and to discharge workers through the exclusion clause, prerogatives enjoyed previously by the company union.[22] Shortly thereafter, the rank and file elected a slate of Communist Party militants to lead their union. The glass workers' old collective contract expired six months later. The new one negotiated by the United Glass Workers redressed the grievances that fueled the strike. It secured long-overdue wage hikes, seniority recognition, and new safety regulations. The Vidriera agreed to recognize occupational illnesses and finance a union-operated clinic for workers and their families. The militant union also won the right to name delegates to each department's shop committee. New shop-floor rules provided mechanisms by which the union could petition for disciplinary proceedings against abusive foremen.[23] The collective contract thus promised the glass workers immediate and long-term improvements in their living and working conditions. While contract violations came thick and fast, the months that followed saw rank-and-file support for the United Glass Workers increase.

The red union's victory emboldened workers in subtle but telling ways. As their fear receded, workers like Dionisio Aguilar shed their airs of feigned

---

21 FTNL, *La burguesía regiomontana*, 42.

22 *El Porvenir*, Mar. 14–16, 1936; Nathan, Mar. 16, 1936, SD, 812.5045/273; AGENL: JCA 60/1815.

23 Contrato Colectivo de Trabajo, Vidriera Monterrey and Sindicato Unico de Trabajadores de la Industria Vidriera, Feb. 3, 1937 and Reglamento Interior, Vidriera Monterrey, Feb. 28, 1937 in AGENL: JCA 105/1937. Among other new prerogatives, the minimum wage paid to laborers increased 40 percent (to $2.80); workers won the forty-four hour week (from forty-eight); injured workers received full pay (rather than the legal 75 percent) during periods of convalescence; and, the anniversaries of both the Mexican Revolution and the union's founding became paid holidays.

deference, growing bolder in their demands. As he recalled, "I never asked for anything before the strike." Aguilar remembered being complacent toward perceived indignities – "nothing could be done" – and admittedly "ignorant" of his legal rights. His first bold move came with the strike, when Aguilar joined the red union and supported the walkout. At subsequent union meetings, their leaders explained to the workers the rights they never understood, prerogatives now enshrined in their collective contract. The union also defended those rights in the labor courts, winning workers their legal compensation for occupational illnesses and reinstallations for unjustified dismissals.[24] The United Glass Workers' victory prompted managerial revisions as well. "Things began to change bit by bit," Ricardo Correa remembered. Wages and piece rates gradually improved, keeping in step with inflation. Equally important, the company fired the plant's most notorious foremen. For many workers, militants and loyalists alike, the move provided evidence that the owners were indeed "humane and just" and genuinely ignorant of the abuses transpiring within their factory.[25] But the moment of peaceful conciliation did not last long because management swiftly resolved to break the red union.

Indeed, another interunion conflict began shortly after the United Glass Workers signed their collective contract. Although the state decertified the company union during Cárdenas's visit to Monterrey, old-guard loyalists organized a new one. They could do so because, by Mexican law, the closed shop required only that new hires join the red union. Management then acted to segregate the United Glass Workers' base of support. Recognizing the glass-blowing department for what it was, a stronghold of militant unionism, the Garza Sadas reorganized the plant in late 1936. Overnight, the corporate restructuring transformed the automated bottle, plate glass, and crystalware divisions into three administratively distinct companies: Vidriera, Vidrio Plano, and Cristalería (glass blowing). The company portrayed the reorganization as a means of enhancing administrative efficiency. The militants saw through the argument. As Dionisio Aguilar recalled, "they split the operations in order to get all the whites together." A company loyalist saw things somewhat differently: "The company defended itself by dividing the plant."[26]

The mother company, Vidriera, thereafter employed operatives in the automated bottle plant along with the ostensibly antiunion mechanics, carpenters, and decorators, who had collectively opposed the reds by a 297 to 27 margin. The new division also included 120 office workers, supervisors, and security guards – the "confidential employees" – among the 783 names

24 Aguilar interview; AGENL: JCA 63/1950, 66/2025, 76/2233, 130/3969, 137/3828.
25 Aguilar, Montes Orozco, and Rodríguez interviews.
26 Aguilar and Correa interviews.

on its payroll. Cristalería segregated the glass-blowing crews into a separate entity of 540 unionists. The plate glass division, Vidrio Plano, employed only 242 workers, more than one-third of whom were confidential employees.[27] But two obstacles complicated the management's plan to segregate the workforce along loyalist–militant lines: the 600 temperers and their assistants. All three divisions of the restructured company depended upon these operatives who fed glass products into the tempering ovens. In February 1936, the temperers had backed the red union by a two to one margin. Moreover, the United Glass Workers remained the legal bargaining agent at all three divisions. Only by forcing a strike – and thus another representation election – could management wrest control of the collective contract from the militant union.

Relations between management and militants deteriorated rapidly thereafter. In a move that drew the glass blowers' ire, the company unilaterally drew up new piece rates for the glass-blowing division (Cristalería), thus imposing a de facto speedup on production. The unionists responded with a slowdown movement. Then, in May 1937, security guards turned away the United Glass Workers' chief organizer when he arrived for his shift. The company had the former railroad shop worker fired, he learned, for "promoting indiscipline by distributing propaganda" within the plant.[28] Bowing to the provocation, the union struck. Governor Guerrero intervened eight days into the walkout when Monterrey's revolutionary unions, including the railwaymen, threatened a general strike to protest the employers' offensive. Governor Guerrero convinced the unionists to resume production, promising a just hearing for the fired unionist.[29] But the abrupt eight-day walkout did not strike a sympathetic chord with all union workers. As the local press reminded the community, a strike in support of a single union official cost the workers thousands of pesos collectively. Perhaps for that reason, fifty-six unionists crossed pickets to rejoin company loyalists within the plant. Incensed union leaders expelled the dissidents from the union and then demanded their immediate dismissal in accordance with the collective contract. Management upheld their right to work. Indeed, the company rescinded its contract with the red union, citing the "illegal, unjust, and arbitrary strike" to justify the action. Then, in a move certainly anticipated by management, United Glass Workers officials formally announced their intentions to again strike the plant in protest.[30] Their walkout would force

---

27 AGENL: JCA 58/1788.
28 AGENL: JCA 106/3295; *El Porvenir*, May 15, 1937; for his hearing before the labor tribunal see AGENL: JCA 104/3224. The labor board decided in his favor. He thus received severance pay and returned to his old job as a mechanic in the National Railways shops.
29 Sección 19, Monterrey, to Comité Executivo General del Sindicato de Trabajadores Ferrocarrileros de la República Mexicana, May 15, 1937, AGN: DGG 32-A/77; AGENL: JCA 131/3708.
30 *El Porvenir*, May 14 and June 1, 1937; AGENL: JCA 94/2936, 131/3708.

labor authorities to conduct another round of representation elections, one for each of the company's three divisions.

Now the effects of the corporate restructuring and the government's hostility toward the communist-led union became evident. As in early 1936, the days before the strike saw managers and foremen exhort, cajole, and attempt to bribe workers to oppose the red union. White union leaders canvassed the neighborhoods surrounding the plant, pressuring workers before their families. Then, to further bolster support for the company union, management hired on dozens of new workers. To skirt the union hiring hall, which applied only to production departments, they contracted the laborers for in-plant construction projects. Managers forced the recruits to sign loyalty oaths as terms of employment. Militant glass workers, for their part, faced a quandary. A vote to strike in defense of their union could entail another protracted layoff. By the time of the strike, falling demand for crystal and cut glass was already diminishing production at Cristalería, the new glass-blowing division.[31]

The union elections thus failed to elicit the festive mood of anticipation that enveloped the 1936 strike. For many workers, the walls of deference had fallen fifteen months before. The June 1937 walkout represented a defensive move to maintain the benefits and prerogatives won by their union. The nonunion workers, on the other hand, now embraced the opportunity to reaffirm their belief in the inherent righteousness of their employer, their will to defend their homes and families from communist strikers, or their personal disdain for the militant union's leaders. True to management's designs, the company union recovered its majority status in two of the three glass divisions.[32] The glass blowers defended their union, voting 404 to 227 in support of the strike. Yet to the Garza Sadas' certain surprise, loyalists in the Vidriera automated bottle division defeated the militants by a relatively slim margin (457 to 326). The outcome would have been narrower still had the state not defended the company's interests. Reversing a policy in effect since the 1936 strike, the labor court now authorized the participation of the Vidriera's 120 confidential employees in the union balloting. The labor board also upheld the right of some five dozen contract laborers to participate in the election. That decision alone ensured the red union's narrow defeat in the plate glass division (125 to 117). The United Glass Workers thus lost the collective contract at two of the three plants.

The partial eclipse of militant unionism at Monterrey Glassworks belied one crucial setback for the company. Rank-and-file support of militant unionism had broadened since February 1936. Had the labor board not

---

31 AGENL: JCA 126/3646, 165, 139/3871.
32 Elections results in AGENL: JCA 94/2932 (Cristalería), 94/2936 (Vidrio Plano) and 127/3646 (Vidriera).

upheld the confidential employees' right to vote, the United Glass Workers' margin of victory would have been 837 to 500. Referring to the "red" glass blowers, one company official blamed their militancy on youthful naïveté: "One finds concentrated in that division a great number of young workers easily influenced by communist tendencies." Youngsters in fact filled only the lowest ranks of a glass-blowing hierarchy dominated by workers hired during the mid- to late 1920s. Of course, more than 500 production workers supported the company union. Some did so out of fear, for reprisals against union militants declined but never disappeared in the aftermath of the 1936 strike. Others did so for reasons stated by one glassworker to a local reporter: "We will now earn better salaries through the incentives granted by the company and dedicate to our families the time stolen from us by the reds to attend their meetings, marches, and riots."[33] The tumultuous world of union politics thus led some workers to embrace the tranquility of company unionism.

Monterrey Glassworks thereafter waged a war of attrition against militant workers. Management worked from the top down, systematically firing United Glass Workers officials. Initially, the company sacrificed the large indemnity payments demanded by law to rid the workplace of the experienced union leaders. One eleven-year veteran won a $1,500 severance package for his dismissal, an amount equal to a year's wages for a common laborer.[34] Unionists employed in the bottle and plate glass divisions had limited recourse to their dismissals. They were once again dissidents within workplaces controlled by company loyalists. The glass blowers, on the other hand, resisted management's customary practice of buying off dissent. Union leaders fired from that division challenged their unjustified dismissals by invoking a legal stipulation that permitted a worker to elect reinstallation rather than severance pay. They held out for months until the Supreme Court heard their case and decided in their favor, forcing the company to rehire the glass blowers.[35] The militants thus remain entrenched at Cristalería. However, the red union suffered a rapid depletion of membership in the automated bottle and plate glass divisions. Indeed, the local

---

33 *El Porvenir*, June 11 and 22, 1937 (quoted); AGENL: JCA 94/2932.

34 AGENL: JCA 104/3224, 105/1937. The fired union leaders followed distinct paths out of the plant. One became a cab driver while his colleague collected his severance pay and headed for the United States. Three others organized a glass-decorating cooperative. Two became full-time union organizers. And at least three found employment in Monterrey's railroad shops, where a sympathetic union controlled hiring (Montes Orozco interview; AGENL: JCA 105/3272, 105/3280, 138/3822).

35 AGENL: JCA 119/3518, 125/3644. During the two-year period between 1936–38, the supreme court consistently backed the workers' right to reinstatement. As historians begin mining labor board archives, they may find that the precedent, however brief in duration, helped galvanize the period's mass union drives by alleviating fears of permanent dismissal. Mario de la Cueva, *Derecho del trabajo*, (2 vols., Mexico City, 1967), I, 258–59.

daily soon celebrated the desertion of some three hundred workers from the United Glass Workers' ranks. They did so, one former unionist asserted, to put an end to the "threats of dismissal and frequent reprisals" to which they were subjected by the foremen. They thus became "*libres*," free workers who aroused managerial suspicions by refusing to join the company union.[36]

The jurisdictional struggle escalated once again in 1938, when the two unions both filed petitions to cancel its rivals' certification.[37] As the labor court convened, opposing gangs of workers converged on the Government Palace to await the settlement. As a reporter observed, "The joking around quickly evolved into hard words, whereupon the laborers became a disorderly mob, knives and pistols were brandished, and shots fired." The melee left four workers wounded and one dead when, police claimed, the well-armed company unionists inadvertently fired on their comrades.[38] In the end, the United Glass Workers remained the bargaining agent for the glass blowers while the white union negotiated separate contracts at the other two plants. Those collective contracts underscored the distinctions between revolutionary and company unions.[39] In the glass-blowing division, the union hiring hall remained in effect. So, also, did seniority-based promotions, a union-run clinic, and prohibitions on the use of contract labor. Old customs returned to the other divisions. Management controlled hiring; the company union appointed the shop committees; and seniority went unrecognized as the basis of promotions. Workers employed in the bottle and plate glass divisions thus experienced a resurrection of the very managerial prerogatives that gave birth to the 1934 union drive.

Aside from the United Glass Workers' leaders, the majority of union sympathizers stayed on at the plant. Most did so, Luis Monzón recalled, "due to their pride in being glass workers, for having struggled to master their trade."[40] The negative experience of revolutionary unionism – the "meetings, marches, and riots" – certainly disillusioned others and confirmed their employer's warnings about the violent nature of unionism. Moreover, the "white" workers retained access to the perks of paternalism as well as the concessions offered up by the owners to reinforce the crumbling walls of deference. Those incentives, we shall see, began with the wage hikes that matched those won by the city's revolutionary unions.

36 *El Porvenir*, July 13, 1937; AGENL: JCA 126/3646 and 138/3854.
37 AGENL: JCA 126/3646.
38 *El Porvenir*, Feb. 2, 1938.
39 Contrato Colectivo de Trabajo, Sindicato Unico de Trabajadores de la Industria del Vidrio and Cristalería, S.A., Feb. 17, 1939 in AGENL: JCA 174; Contrato Colectivo de Trabajo, Sindicato de Trabajadores de la Industria del Vidrio y Conexas and Vidriera Monterrey, S.A., Feb. 3, 1939 in AGENL: JCA 190.
40 Monzón inteview.

For the militants, the shifting winds of local politics ensured that the red union's initial victory proved ephemeral. The state's role as final arbitrator of industrial relations permitted management to regain its prerogatives lost in 1936. So, also, did their corporate strategies, be they the shrewd restructuring of the company or their capacity to instill fear among the operatives. Thus did the glass-blowing division, Cristalería, become the lone union outpost in a growing industrial empire that included the glassworks, the brewery, and their respective subsidiaries.

The Quotas of Power

Just as the emergence of Local 67 signaled the dawn of revolutionary unionism in Monterrey, many observers perceived labor's setback at the glass works as a harbinger of its decline. One observer suggested that the labor violence typified by the February 1938 glass workers' shootout was "tending more and more to discredit the CTM in public opinion."[41] In typical fashion, the local press seized on that melee to press home its campaign against red unions. The media portrayed the "spilling of worker blood" as a result of "our local laborers' resistance to the ill-fated influence of outsiders." The Independent Unions adopted their rivals' own language and accused the reds of breaking the "ties that ought to bind brothers of the same race and class." However, while the union's defeat at the glass works signaled the final demise of revolutionary unionism at the Garza Sadas' factories, it did not entail the CTM's "retreat" from Monterrey. As the United States consul later admitted, the reds and whites continued "their never ending battle for supremacy in the manufacturing plants."[42] Meanwhile, the city's revolutionary unionists struggled to overcome their own partisan feuding and resist the open-shop movement.

The 1937 CTM reunification paralleled a rebound in labor militancy, a defensive response to an economic recession and the ongoing struggle to defend earlier union victories.[43] By then, inflation was eroding the wage gains won by industrial workers two years earlier. Collective contracts, Seventh Day Pay, and a new minimum wage boosted earnings for all local laborers between 1934–36. However, six months after the state raised the legal minimum, the United States consul concluded that a 35 percent rise in the cost of living left workers "no better off" than the previous year. In mid-1937, he reported large working-class demonstrations to protest

41 Blocker, June 29, 1936, SD 812.00 NL/169, Feb. 2, 1938, SD 812.504/1702.

42 *El Porvenir*, Feb. 2, 1938; Blocker, Mar. 22, 1938, SD 812.504/1782; Saragoza *The Monterrey Elite*, 189–90, 194, who offers that the CTM "retreated in defeat in early 1937."

43 The years 1937–39 saw workers file an annual average of 850 individual protests and call 230 strikes, mainly in solidarity with other strikers. AGENL: *Informe del Gobernador Bonifacio Salinas Leal, 1939–1940*, 35.

another 25 percent rise in food costs.[44] Furthermore, unemployment became a publicly acknowledged problem for the first time since the Depression. Government records indicate that local joblessness tripled (to 7,000 workers) between 1936 and 1938. Factories reported record job applications as migrants continued arriving to Monterrey from mining zones hit hard by the recession.[45] Meanwhile, real wages continued falling in late 1937 after Governor Guerrero conceded to the industrialists' demands to hold the minimum wage at $2.00 for 1938–39. This, the employers argued, would stimulate industrial development and resolve "the so-called unemployment problem."[46] The economy indeed revived within a year. But Monterrey's factories would not surpass the production bonanza of the mid-1930s until the onset of the Second World War.

In contrast to the early Cárdenas years, worker protest now met the state's disapproval. The United States consul noted in his understated manner that "recent reverses . . . have given labor leaders in this vicinity the impression that unwarranted strikes heretofore permitted . . . are not as popular with [Governor Guerrero] as formerly." President Cárdenas echoed Guerrero's sentiments. Recessionary pressures demanded belt tightening, he now asserted, while "strikes are detrimental to the country and looked upon with disfavor by the government." The president's exhortations reflected the reality of the times: Labor protests, general strikes, and work stoppages had mounted throughout Mexico.[47] In Monterrey, the upsurge in labor combativeness paralleled another factional dispute within the Nuevo León Workers Federation. Ruling party unionists once again defected and established a breakaway central after the "old communistic radical group" won election to the FTNL board of directors. This time, the split lasted into the 1940s. The Cardenista project of working-class unification thus floundered in Monterrey. While an impressive 70 percent of the city's 30,000 workers carried union cards, they split their allegiances between three competing labor centrals. Meanwhile, Governor Guerrero maintained his distance from the reds who elected him to office. By 1938, Guerrero was said to be "riding the fence" between the Independent Unions and the CTM "to keep in the good graces" of Cárdenas.[48]

In fact, ruling-party officials were distancing themselves from radical labor leaders both locally and nationally. A relatively rightward drift in

44 Blocker, July 27, 1937, Aug. 31, 1937, SD 812.00 NL/171, 173.
45 *El Porvenir*, June 22, 1938; Mendirichaga, *Los 4 tiempos*, 374; Blocker, Feb. 27, Oct. 30, 1937, Feb. 28, June 28, 1938, SD 812.00 NL/171, 174, 178, 188.
46 *El Porvenir*, Nov. 29, 1937.
47 Blocker, Nov. 30, 1937, SD 812.00 NL/175 (quoted); Knight, "The Rise and Fall of Cardenismo," 291.
48 Blocker, Mar. 22, 1938, 812.504/1728. The reds still conserved sufficient membership to elect their members to the state labor board.

Cardenista policy after 1937 "owed a good deal" to the efforts of Monterrey's industrialists.[49] The increased militance of organized labor in the factories, mines, oil fields, and farms had generated a conservative backlash, one most visible in Monterrey but spreading across the North, from Tampico to Sonora. Business leaders, conservative generals, and the urban middle classes coalesced into state-level blocs to resist the radical excesses of Cardenismo. The patriotic euphoria motivated by Cárdenas's 1938 oil nationalization briefly masked the deepening polarization of Mexican society. With the ship of state battered by conservative resistance, an economic crisis, and internal feuding, Cárdenas dropped anchor and halted the "forward march of the revolution." Alan Knight thus observes that, "The year 1938, which began in patriotic exaltation, ended with the radicals in retreat." His policies having achieved considerable success, Cárdenas astutely restructured the ruling party to safeguard his reforms and "overcome the factionalism which still gnawed at the vitals of the PNR."[50]

The new Mexican Revolutionary Party (PRM) grouped organized labor, the peasants, and the military into a corporatist political structure meant to contain internal feuding between the party's left and center. Leaders of Mexico's national labor centrals (CTM, CROM, CGT) and the big industrial unions conceded to their locals' integration into the new party apparatus. Miners Union president Augustín Guzmán, for example, overrode union statutes that forbid political alliances by claiming the need to secure a union voice in local, state, and national politics.[51] The election of union workers to political office indeed increased. Meanwhile, Cárdenas's political initiative concluded his program of reforms, the consolidation of the ruling party having been a staple government objective. But the desired effects of party cohesion remained elusive. Monterrey's workers continued to display their own independence in the political arena. By the later 1930s, local resistance to the ruling party came not only from the industrialists but the left wing of the labor movement as well.

Meanwhile, as strike activity escalated, the struggles grew increasingly protracted and violent. Labor authorities delayed hearings on workplace conflicts by classifying them as interunion (as opposed to labor–capital) disputes. Strikes went unresolved while employers organized nonunion workers to drive strikers out of their factories. At the American-owned Carbon Eveready battery plant, company loyalists and strikebreakers armed with Thompson machine guns ousted striking workers as city police stood watch

49 Saragoza, *The Monterrey Elite*, 186–91; Alan Knight, "Social Policy in the 1930s: Lázaro Cárdenas and Mexican Labor (1934–1940)," Paper presented to the American Historical Association, Chicago, Jan. 5, 1995, 9 (quoted).

50 Knight, "The Rise and Fall of Cardenismo," 288–89.

51 Sariego, *El sindicalismo minero*, 38–39.

nearby. One striker died and dozens were wounded. The work stoppage nonetheless continued into its fourth month.[52] At the Garza Sadas' Orión ceramics factory, company loyalists drove pickets away with pistols and clubs. The white unionists then expressed their own political persuasions by replacing the red-and-black flags that adorned the stricken plant's gates with the banner of Spain's fascist Falange Party.[53]

In August 1938, the local CTM petitioned for and received the national's support for a general strike. The action would protest recent events at Carbon Eveready and "halt the perfidious actions of the *patrones*." The citywide strike would also, the unionists hoped, pressure the government to resolve the collective conflicts then pending before an overwhelmed labor board.[54] By August, unions representing 115 plants and workshops had announced their intentions to walk out in solidarity. The government's concern escalated when the electrical workers agreed to strike as well. One observer regarded them as "without question the most radical group in [Monterrey]."[55] Governor Guerrero denounced the general strike as a plot by CTM leader Lombardo Toledano to "provoke discord among Monterrey's laborers." But Monterrey's industrialists privately confided their desire to see the strike proceed. Cutting off power to the city's factories, they explained to one American, would "discredit the CTM once and for all."[56] Guerrero intervened at the final hour. He promised to resolve the cases pending before the labor courts and then denounced the "so-called white unions" as an obstacle to labor's "just aspirations." The governor's discursive turn paid off. Local CTM leaders deferred to orders from Mexico City and canceled the action, allegedly overruling the rank and file's prostrike sentiments. Labor authorities immediately ruled in favor of CTM unions in two of the principal cases that prompted the conflict, including that of the Carbon Eveready strikers. The United States consul nonetheless concluded that "it is difficult to believe that [Guerrero] has suddenly become a convert to the policies of the CTM."[57]

52 Blocker, Apr. 29, 1938, SD 812.5045/744; Carlson, July 30, 1938, SD 812.5045.798; *El Porvenir*, Aug. 3–7, 1938.

53 César Gutiérrez G., "Grupos sindicales y división interna en la FTNL, 1936–1942," in Centro de Estudios del Movimiento Obrero y Socialista (CEMOS), ed., *La CTM en los estados* (Sinaloa, 1988), 34.

54 "Manifiesto de los obreros revolucionarios de Nuevo León y todo el país," Aug. 4, 1938 in *Laborante*, Monterrey, Feb. 1995, 27.

55 Carlson, July 30, Aug. 5, 1938, SD 812.5045/798, 812.5045/802. Six weeks earlier, the electric workers had placed their bargaining power on display with a four-hour blackout to protest the murder of a Ciudad Juárez union leader by ruling party gunmen.

56 Carlson, Aug. 9, 1938, SD 812.4045/804. Only the city's two foreign-owned smelters then enjoyed their own power supplies.

57 *El Porvenir*, Aug. 8–11, 1938; Carlson, July 30, Aug. 5, Aug. 9, 1938, SD 812.5045/798, 812.5045/802, 812.4045/804.

The electrical workers lived up to their radical reputation five weeks later. Early September saw the Nuevo León Workers Federation call another general strike to protest the arrest of a pistol-wielding unionist who assaulted the owner of an apparel factory stricken by CTM workers. National CTM leaders approved the action. They ordered the Monterrey locals to strike until authorities released the organizer, a Mexico City activist. Félix Torres, the electrical workers' union leader recalled that, "It was then that we all realized that Governor Guerrero had gangsters at his service." Torres arrived at the CTM local on the day of the strike to discover the union hall surrounded by ruling-party gunmen. They had entered the hall, pistol whipped the secretary-general, declared the strike over, and ordered all workers out. The electric workers reconvened at their own union local and elected to strike alone. A five-hour power outage convinced authorities to release the jailed activist. The industrialists furiously protested the governor's capitulation as "an abject surrender to the CTM."[58] The local press bemoaned the *fuero* (special privileges) enjoyed by CTM leaders, allowing them to act above the nation's laws and institutions. In a clear indication of how well-organized Mexican business leaders had become, chambers of commerce wired dozens of telegrams to the president's office protesting the action. They echoed Cárdenas's own recent call "to unify the nation's productive forces to achieve Mexico's economic salvation."[59] The state's exhortations to rein in labor militancy failed to quell the tide of rank-and-file combativeness in Monterrey. Multiple and overlapping strikes continued to disrupt the local economy as workers struck in defiance of political authorities and national labor leaders alike. These movements stymied the ruling party's efforts to discipline labor in the year preceding the 1940 presidential elections.

The ruling party's political dominance in Nuevo León seemed well consolidated by the time the Cardenistas reorganized it along corporatist lines in 1938. The Mexican Revolutionary Party's emergence as the state's paramount party held important consequences. Since party candidates ran uncontested, the PRM's internal nominating elections became the decisive event of the electoral season. The city's heavy working-class composition made the labor vote decisive, especially in Monterrey's two congressional districts. Organized peasants largely determined the outcome of gubernatorial races. But even before the ruling party's restructuring, Monterrey's red unions were "taking the lead in selecting candidates [for state office]."[60] Since party statutes limited participation to Mexico's

58 Félix Torres interview in *Laborante*, Feb. 1995, 99–100; Carlson, Sep. 23, 1938, SD 82. 5045/813.

59 *El Porvenir*, Sep. 30, 1938; for a typical example of the protests sent to Cárdenas see Cámara de Industria, Comercio y Trabajo de Nuevo León to President Cárdenas, Sep. 29, 1938, AGN: Presidentes, 432.2/184.

60 Blocker, Mar. 31, 1937, SD 812.00 NL/165.

government-allied labor federations, they necessarily excluded thousands of local workers belonging to the Independent Unions of Nuevo León. Only members of the teachers' union, the industrial union locals, and the red labor federations participated in the electoral process. Individual unions canvassed their members and then delivered the collective votes as a single bloc. The white union's absence did little to diminish the tumultuous world of local labor politics.

The same personal and ideological divisions that divided the revolutionary unions manifested themselves in the political arena as well, where labor activists split their allegiances between leftists militants and "official" candidates whose nominations were approved by Mexico City. Both sides wore their proletarian credentials on their sleeves. The left-independent candidates typically claimed to be "authentic laborers" fighting for a "workers' democracy." In contrast to many "official" nominees, most such candidates were indeed blue-collar workers, who dominated the city council and state congress by the later 1930s. Some entered politics at the behest of workmates. Félix Torres, the communist leader of the electrical worker union, joined the political fray under such circumstances. After completing his primary school education, Torres spent his teenage years working in local construction crews and the cotton fields of South Texas. At eighteen, he was hired by the electric power company and was elected leader of the union eight years later. He entered the state congress at the youthful age of twenty-nine. He continued working his regular eight-hour shift after his 1939 election to Nuevo León's Congress, donning his work clothes after a morning spent in the congressional chambers. Other workers acted out of long-term political ambitions, for a trip to Congress promised a sojourn from the shop floor. Politically aspirant unionists like Local 67's Leandro Martínez regularly shifted loyalties as the political winds altered course. Martinez, who entered the steel mill in 1912, had been a labor activist since the early 1920s. The year 1937 saw the veteran steel worker run for local office on an "independent" slate dominated by leftists. Two years later, Martínez returned to the "official" camp as state congressional candidate.[61]

Labor politics therefore confounded even seasoned observers. The United States consul commented that, "labor squabbles in Monterrey are, to say the least, something of a puzzle.... Thoroughly mixed in intriguing politics, labor groups have lined up against one another... until it is difficult to figure out the various combinations being formed or the final outcome." Electoral results became predictable, in fact. "Official" candidates won, but not without a perennial left-independent challenge to the "party of imposition," as the PRM became known locally. Meanwhile, the passing of the 1937 electoral season "calmed the interunion squabbles" as opponents

---

61 *El Porvenir*, Apr. 5–7, 1937; AGN: DGG 2.331 (16)/281; Torres interview.

waited for the next bell. The following round began in 1939, when the diplomat once again reported "the local labor unions ... [are] engaged in political and factional strife as usual."[62] The 1939 governor's race would manifest just how conflictive labor politics had become. It also exemplified the nationwide jockeying for power between the PRM's left-labor and centrist-military factions, a struggle to define the party's direction and select a successor to Cárdenas in accordance with Mexico's anti-reelection law.

The gubernatorial campaign pitted Juan Gutiérrez, a Nuevo León railroader, against the party's "official" candidate, General Bonifacio Salinas. Salinas, one observer reported, was "said to be hard drinker [who] frequents cafes a good deal." But the Nuevo León native was considered "pliable [and thus] the ideal man for the PRM." Gutiérrez, on other hand, was "very intelligent, shrewd ... [and] a forceful and convincing speaker." According to the United States consul, his experience – a veteran of the revolution, former local and national leader of the Railroaders Union, and then a federal senator – "better prepared him for the executive office."[63] Gutiérrez promised to carry the state's labor vote. His local popularity among workers was second only to that of Francisco Idar, Monterrey's other railroader-cum-senator.[64] By 1938, Gutiérrez sat on the executive committee of the CTM, which officially endorsed his challenge to General Salinas. Indeed, Gutiérrez's one-time nemeses, CTM strongmen Lombardo Toledano and Fidel Velásquez, journeyed to Monterrey to head the 1938 parade that launched the railroader's campaign.

The Gutiérrez candidacy marked a significant challenge by organized labor to the military's erstwhile hegemony within Nuevo León's ruling party. This is certainly how many union activists perceived the Gutiérrez campaign. From their perspective, Salinas was cast from the same mold as Governor Guerrero. Both were one-time Callista generals who shifted their loyalties to Cárdenas after his 1935 showdown with former President Calles. Both, also, were considered "uneducated peasants" by Monterrey's urbanized labor leaders.[65] Moreover, neither general masked his enmity for the labor left nor his sympathies for the industrial elite. Salinas's own promotion of a "just understanding between labor and capital" and his aggressive anti-Communist barbs earned him the radicals' scorn as the

---

62 Blocker, June 29, July 29, 1937, SD 812.00 NL/169, 171; McDonough, Aug. 19, 1939, SD 812.00 NL/209.

63 McDonough, May 31, 1939, SD 812.00 NL/206. General Salinas, a former Callista, earned Cárdenas's trust for the role he played in quelling the 1938 Cedillista military rebellion in nearby San Luis Potosí.

64 *El Porvenir*, Sep. 25, 1938. Idar and Gutiérrez also performed key roles on the senatorial committee that oversaw the 1937 nationalization of Mexico's National Railways, which were briefly placed under union management. Gutiérrez would in fact direct the National Railways.

65 Castañeda, Elizondo, and Ramos interviews.

new "candidate of the rich."[66] Salinas, nonetheless, courted working-class support and found it in Local 67's Leandro Martínez. Salinas named the steel worker to be his campaign manager as well as a congressional candidate on the party's "official" slate. Félix Torres, the communist leader of the electrical worker union, ran as Martínez's opponent, while a United Glass Workers official headed the Gutiérrez campaign. Soon, all the city's major union locals counted pro-Salinas and pro-Gutiérrez committees as the scramble began to secure rank-and-file votes for the crucial election. The left-independents enjoyed a considerable advantage.

Working-class attitudes toward the ruling party (as opposed to President Cárdenas) ran from cynicism to disdain by 1939. Stolen ballot boxes, fraudulent electoral registers, and political violence had been commonplace since the 1920s. Moreover, the recession, inflation, and the attendant fall in real wages further disillusioned local workers. They resented national labor leaders' commitment to political issues rather than their economic grievances, as CTM leader Lombardo Toledano would hear when he ventured to Monterrey in 1939.[67] Working-class resentment evolved into hostility in late 1938, when Francisco Idar was assassinated in Mexico City by ruling-party gunmen. Recall that the Monterrey railroader had won his election to the Senate in 1934 as the Liberal Party candidate. In Monterrey, Idar's support ran strong among workers of all political stripes and union affiliation. His assassination shocked and angered the community. After what one observer described as the largest funeral procession in the city's history, Governor Guerrero had refused to allow Idar's body to lie in state in the Government Palace.[68] These were the circumstances under which the 1939 elections transpired.

The primaries grew heated as the city's revolutionary unions staged their nominating assemblies. Charges of fraud came thick and fast. Salinas supporters accused communist union leaders of wielding "the ignoble and detestable exclusion clause to whip the workers into lackeys" by allegedly threatening to expel them from the unions. The leftists countered that Salinistas employed "official gangsterism" to terrorize pro-Gutiérrez workers. The railwaymen even requested the presence of federal troops lest violence erupt at their union's electoral assembly.[69] Tensions ran especially high when the steel workers convened to cast their ballots. By then, nearly every industrial union local had endorsed Gutiérrez. The collective support of 4,000 steel workers could turn the tide in Salinas's favor. But Local 67's assembly never produced an official endorsement. As soon as the meeting

66 *El Porvenir*, Dec. 11, 1938.
67 *El Norte*, Aug. 7–9, 1939; *El Porvenir*, Aug. 8, 1939.
68 Nathan, Mar. 16, 1938, SD 812.00 NL/179.
69 *El Porvenir*, Mar. 9, 11–13, and 15, 1939; Castañeda and Elizondo interviews.

began, Leandro Martínez breached union statutes by permitting Salinas to speak before the gathering. A heated debate ensued as the candidate entered the stage. The confrontation swiftly escalated into a union hall shootout that left one steel worker dead and five others wounded. Workers in attendance later charged Martínez with instigating the conflict when he fired upon a Gutiérrez supporter who protested the voting procedure. The Salinistas blamed the violence on "Communist instigators." The melee offered a starkly tragic example of Local 67's raucous union assemblies.[70]

Gutiérrez swept Nuevo León's labor vote by a wide margin. The ruling party thus turned to the peasant sector to secure a Salinas victory and, in what became a typical scenario, charges of fraud accompanied the electoral results from the countryside. Party officials in Mexico City determined the final results. As locals expected, Salinas emerged victorious, albeit by margins that defied even his opponents' cynical expectations.[71] The general thus ran uncontested as the PRM's candidate for governor. Salinas's victory brought a sense of closure and relief to Monterrey's industrial elite. In a sign of times to come, they feted his arrival with a postinaugural party at the Cuauhtémoc Brewery's beer garden.[72] However, Gutiérrez and his supporters accepted the results stoically, without protest, because they did not suffer a total defeat. Shortly after the internal party elections, the PRM integrated members of the Gutierrista slate into the party's ticket. As a result, Félix Torres, the union leader who led the electrical workers' strike just six months earlier, won a seat in Nuevo León's Congress. So did the communist leader of the smeltermen's Local 66, who represented Monterrey's Second Congressional District.[73] Perhaps such political concessions to the left were intended to bolster the ruling party's working-class support as national elections loomed on the horizon. If so, they achieved mixed results. In Monterrey, organized labor's response to Cárdenas's more conservative successor proved no more enthusiastic than its reception of his opponent. Both, we shall see, spent considerable effort wooing the industrialists with probusiness, anti-Communist planks that rang quite familiar to *regiomontano* ears. But the concession to Monterrey's more independent-minded, working-class voters also manifested the astute means by which the ruling party negotiated its hegemony to build the enduring political consensus that kept it in power until the early twenty-first century.

---

70 *El Norte*, Apr. 15, 1939.

71 Official electoral results gave Gutiérrez a narrow 8,220 to 7,723 advantage in the labor sector while Salinas carried the state by a 67,258 to 18,202 margin. For voting procedures, reports of fraud, and final electoral results see AGN: DGG, 2.311(16)/281.

72 *El Porvenir*, Oct. 6, 1939.

73 *El Norte*, June 30, 1939; Torres interview. The PRM's concession to the left briefly thwarted the political ambitions of Local 67's Leandro Martínez. He was elected to federal Congress the following year.

Scholars of Mexican labor once perceived the style of "mass politics" engineered by the PRM as a form of "authoritarian populism" by which the state "controlled and manipulated" workers and their unions. They point to the CTM's early and unambiguous alliance with the Cárdenas regime as the moment when labor subordinated itself to the ruling-party machine. The process inhibited the "political maturation" of Mexican workers, whose union leaders subsequently provided blanket endorsements to the postrevolutionary state.[74] The Monterrey case offers evidence of a more complicated process. Locally, the PRM's labor sector included diverse actors with competing agendas. *Regiomontano* workers resisted the imposition of unpopular candidates, doing so by supporting the party's left wing or the independent opposition. As voters, they did not necessarily share the radicals' political convictions. Rather, they supported fellow workers like the Communist, Félix Torres, for the same reason they elected them to union office: for their honesty, integrity, and perceived commitment to blue-collar interests. Their resistance would pressure the PRM hierarchy to proffer political concessions to left-independent candidates. For their part, former Communist Party activists forsook principles for pragmatism, hoping to keep the spirit of Cardenismo alive within an increasingly centrist party structure. This, too, was an astute calculation because the anti-Communist backlash seen early on in Monterrey soon became Mexico's dominant political discourse.

The ruling party institutionalized these "quotas of power," as one *regiomontano* activist labels the political posts apportioned to union workers. After 1939 the steel workers' Local 67 would elect one of its members to Monterrey's city council and another to state congress. So would the railway workers' Local 19. ASARCO's Local 66 earned a permanent seat on the city council as well, thus giving the revolutionary unions what were then nearly half the seats in municipal government.[75] While the consolidation of ruling party hegemony foreclosed the revolutionary hopes of "effective suffrage," internal democracy became a hallmark of such unions as Local 67. Workers embraced union hall democracy because it provided the opportunity to express the political agenda and place their workmates in office. This became a privilege shared only by the revolutionary unions, for thousands of workers belonging to the Independent Unions remained excluded from the ruling-party machine. Indeed, the Cárdenas years witnessed the permanent division of Monterrey's red and white workers along political, organizational, and social lines, a division that was to last for decades to come.

74 Arturo Anguiano, *El estado y la política obrera del cardenismo* (Mexico City, 1975), 62–66; Arnaldo Córdova, *La política de masas del cardenismo* (Mexico City, 1974), 80.

75 Interviews with Elizondo, Castañeda, and Máximo de León Garza, Mar. 17, 1996, from whom I borrow the term *quotas of power.*

10

The Persistence of Paternalism

The two forms of industrial relations consolidated during the 1930s – company paternalism and revolutionary unionism – became the most enduring legacies of Cardenismo in Monterrey. The Cuauhtémoc Brewery and the Fundidora steel mill exemplified that outcome, reflecting the divergent ways in which blue-collar *regiomontanos* and their employers responded to the revolution. The brewery remained an island of class harmony in a sea of industrial conflict. The company reacted to local and national developments by revising its managerial strategies to shield its workers, to the fullest extent possible, from the world of organized labor. It succeeded remarkably well. The brewery operatives upheld their historic mistrust of unions because organized labor offered no preferable alternative to the security of paternalism. Efforts to unionize the plant therefore ran aground on the shoals of company loyalty. The steel workers, on the other hand, became the self-conscious vanguard of organized labor in Monterrey. Local 67's leaders endeavored to defend their *sindicato* by constructing a lasting union identity among rank-and-file workers. The unity they fashioned within this occupational community made Local 67 a tough bargaining agent at the mill. It also became and remained a union with considerable political clout in Monterrey and within the Mexican Miner-Metalworkers Union. Paternalism nonetheless persisted as an integral part of the steel workers' lives, surviving as both a managerial strategy and in the practices of Local 67 itself. We turn first to the Cuauhtémoc Brewery to explore the mechanics of deference, an aspect of working-class culture and industrial relations that has received limited attention by historians of Mexican labor.

The Mechanics of Deference at the Cuauhtémoc Brewery

Nowhere did the industrialists' practices of paternalism achieve greater success than at the Cuauhtémoc Brewery, where relatively consensual labor relations remained the norm during Monterrey's years of defiance. The glass, steel, and smelter workers proved that paternalism in itself produced neither sustained passivity nor unbending loyalty. Their employers' distinct

251

responses to government labor policies did much to shape the outcome of
union struggles in those industries. But a sustained organizing drive never
even developed at Cuauhtémoc in the 1930s. As we saw earlier, the peculiarities of the brewing industry conspired on paternalism's behalf. The
Cuauhtémoc Society's discourse of class harmony percolated down to
the shop floor, where a relatively light work regime underpinned congenial
relations between managers and operatives. Moreover, seasonal downturns
in production enhanced the security delivered by the company's welfare
and savings plans to employees and their families. The perennial layoffs to
which workers had grown accustomed declined during the Cárdenas years,
when the Mexican beer industry enjoyed tremendous growth and prosperity. By 1940, Cuauhtémoc more than doubled the record production level
reached in 1934. Increased sales mirrored the steady expansion of both per
capita beer consumption and the base of urban and rural consumers created
by the Cárdenas government's land and labor reforms.[1]

While the brewery benefited indirectly from government policy, company ideologues nonetheless sustained the idea that state-sponsored unionism posed a new and insidious threat to Cuauhtémoc's prosperity and the
workers' well-being. One of the brewery's few union sympathizers later
recalled hearing that "those who belonged to revolutionary unions here in
Monterrey only wanted to see to it that the company would go broke ... that
the companies lacked the freedom to do what they had to do, that the unions
were really just obstacles placed in the way of the company's progress."[2]
Many operatives apparently agreed. Just as they had marched in protest of
temperance reform in the 1920s, so also did the brewery workers join in the
conservative resistance to government labor policy and unionism during
the mid-1930s. Few recall exactly why.

Decades later, veteran workers like Alejandro Monsiváis will say little
of Monterrey's revolutionary unions except that, "they have a custom of
calling strikes and throwing up their red flags." After five decades of service
to Cuauhtémoc, he upheld his employer's policy of forbidding talk of
unions. "It's prohibited," he quietly explained. His wife, a former operative
who did not share her husband's reticence, remembered of the brewery
that "everything there is very serious, it's work, work, work." María also
recalled marching in the February 1936 protest before Alejandro silenced

1 Cuauhtémoc production climbed steadily from 24,305 to 54,709 liters (1934–40), as falling prices
and rising wages made beer available to a new generation of working-class Mexicans with disposable
incomes. For example, the government's 1936 distribution of expropriated cotton lands to 30,000
farm workers made the nearby Laguna district into a profitable new market for the Monterrey brewery.
Haber, *Industry and Development*, 177–80; Hamilton, *The Limits of State Autonomy*, 331–33; Instituto
Nacional de Estadística, Geografía e Informática, *Estadísticas históricas de México*, Vol. 1 (Mexico City,
1994), 612; Elizondo interview.

2 Carranza interview.

her explanation. "No, no, no," he interjected, "we don't want to go into that.... [W]e know nothing about it." But María did add in a commonsense tone that the owners "formed their own union because they didn't need anyone telling them what to do.... [T]hey knew how to manage their affairs perfectly well."[3] Much like others who remained loyal members of the Cuauhtémoc family, the Monsiváis household benefited mightily from the wages, scholarships, and pensions that came with employment at the brewery.

But in the 1930s, a militant minority did seize upon the state's prolabor overtures to protest latent grievances and practice their right to organize. Cuauhtémoc responded to the challenge posed by Cardenismo and its own workers by refining its system of paternalism to shield the company from the threat of militant unionism. The developments deserve scrutiny because they would soon be replicated throughout the Garza Sada family's diversified industrial dynasty. Indeed, the system of industrial relations perfected by Cuauhtémoc in the 1930s persists to the present day. Over the course of the decade, Cuauhtémoc fashioned new managerial strategies designed to regulate the social world of its workers.[4] The reforms began with company hiring policies. In a development that affected Monterrey's entire working class, Cuauhtémoc began screening out all applicants from union households. Supervisors once hired workers as production so demanded. But a new policy stipulated that all full-time hires have the personnel director's "nod of approval" (*buen visto*).[5] The daughters, sons, or brothers of the city's red unionists were thereafter denied employment at the brewery. The discriminatory practices built upon the family-oriented hiring policy introduced during the 1920s. However, given the subsequent growth of the Garza Sadas' industries, the policy significantly limited later opportunities for thousands of young *regiomontanos*.

A related refinement of company policy forbad the brewery operatives from associating with union workers outside the factory. Cuauhtémoc's female employees, for example, were prohibited by the company from dating union workers. One former steel worker recalled of his youth that, "in those days many women worked at the brewery, and if they had any sympathies, or if their boyfriend was member of a revolutionary union, they were told: either leave that dude (*pelado*) or give up your job."[6] The Cuauhtémoc Society (SCYF) replicated these efforts to shield the workers from union influences. The men, for example, rarely challenged Monterrey's steel workers on the baseball field. According to a retiree from another Garza Sada factory, that

3 Monsiváis and Medrano interviews.
4 The following paragraph is based on Medrano, Monsiváis, Oviedo, and Padilla interviews.
5 AGENL: JCA 153.
6 Castañeda interview.

owed as much to company policy as to the steel workers' own attitude about their nonunion rivals. "They used to call us apathetic in those days," he laughed, "because we were whites, the sons of the bosses, and they were against the bosses."[7] Whatever the cause, Cuauhtémoc's worker–athletes still found plenty of competition in teams from Monterrey's other nonunion factories. In its zeal to shield its members from radical influences, the SCYF also broke its contractual ties with the Orquestra Metrónomo, the popular local swing band that had performed at Cuauhtémoc fiestas since 1930. Why? Because they were union musicians.[8]

Such policies did not necessarily achieve their intended results. The brewery therefore cultivated a network of company spies to more effectively monitor its workers.[9] The so-called *aretes* (earrings) fingered potential troublemakers and reported shop-floor banter to their supervisors. Beyond the factory gates, company police patrolled nearby neighborhoods, chasing away known labor activists, while worker-spies kept an eye on their colleagues in neighborhood cantinas, local dance halls, and other public spaces. One brewery operative, for example, lost his job when an informant spotted him at a CTM labor rally.[10] Brewery workers like María de los Angeles Medrano thus learned to watch their tongues and avoid associating with unionists "because there was vigilance on the outside, too, but one never knew who it was." "If there was someone causing trouble," she believed, the company "knew about it; they knew about everything."[11] Interestingly, former brewery operatives later dismissed these policies of social control less as an infringement upon their freedom than a natural outcome of their independence, a concept that took on new meanings during the 1930s. It no longer implied their mere autonomy from national labor centrals. It also connoted their social insularity from local union workers. As María emphasized, "That is why they called us the white *independent* union, because [the company] did not want us to associate with them, for *any* reason." In a curious but logical way, the operatives ameliorated Cuauhtémoc's top-down regulation of their social lives by turning inward to embrace the intimacy of company paternalism. In the long run, then, these enduring policies of vigilance and selective hiring helped consolidate the familylike nature of brewery work.

Industrial paternalism changed with the times as well, building upon previous practices and matching the benefits won by militant unions. The number of workers living in company-subsidized housing, for example,

---

7 Interview with Francisco Padilla Martínez, Nov. 20, 1995.

8 AGENL: JCA 71/ 2164.

9 Blocker, Feb. 5, 1937, SD 812.00 NL/164.

10 AGENL: JCA 80/2382. Testifying before the labor board, the worker related his "sympathy for [the CTM's] political ideology" to his "unjust treatment" by the brewery.

11 Medrano interview.

increased twofold during the 1930s as the firm developed its own Colonia
Cuauhtémoc on lands near the plant.[12] The workers also saw their wages rise
steadily, received longer vacations, and could now subscribe to improved
healthcare and pension plans. Cuauhtémoc awarded these benefits in rhythm
with those attained by the revolutionary unions in their collective contracts.
The city's union workers grew to resent the tactic, but also gleaned a dose
of pride from the results of their own activism. As one steel worker asserted,
the brewery operatives "were like the butcher's dog, always keeping an eye
out for the scraps of meat that fell to the ground. . . . [T]heir union did
absolutely nothing; they never even knew what sort of profits the company
made. [T]hey just waited for us to carry out the struggle, so that when we
won ten percent [wage hikes], they wouldn't even have to raise their hands
and they gave them eight, nine percent. [T]hey gave them a little less but
then they didn't put up a fight. [T]hey didn't worry about anything, they
just waited until we won so that they would then get theirs."[13] While their
unions never achieved any clout on the shop floor, Monterrey's white union
workers became "free riders," enjoying wages and nonmonetary incentives
similar to those secured by Monterrey's revolutionary unions.

The company magazine, *Work and Savings*, continued to publish dozens
of letters from workers grateful for these benefits and to celebrate the social affairs of the operatives in its column, "Notes From Our Intimate
Lifestyle." As in the 1920s, diatribes against militant unionism and communism continued to remind workers of their "duties" and the need to
"bridle their passions" to avoid "falling prey to demagogic leaders."[14] But
in a notable change from the previous decade, *Work and Savings* now lauded
the brewery's own Cuauhtémoc Workers Union. The company union's leaders, all men, had quickly assumed the local role once performed by steel
workers: directing the Independent Unions of Nuevo León and speaking
on behalf of the city's working class. As long-time leader Jesús Aguirre
stated on the union's fourth anniversary, "we produce practical benefits for
the workers not through violent conflicts and useless exaltations but on a
plane of genuine harmony [with the company]." By doing so, union leaders claimed to defend "the basic principles of the Revolution . . . [and] to
serve as an example, such that the well-being of all Mexicans becomes a
reality." While such pronouncements marked a discursive continuity from
the 1920s, they now rang truer for many Cuauhtémoc workers given the
tumultuous world of revolutionary unionism. Aguirre was a worker well
known for his activism in the SCYF and his starring role as shortstop on
Cuauhtémoc's baseball team. But due to the nature of his union leadership,

12 *Trabajo y Ahorro*, July 30, 1931, Sep. 6, 1937.
13 Carranza and Castañeda (quoted) interviews.
14 *Trabajo y Ahorro*, Sep. 7, 1935.

workers recall Aguirre less as a fellow operative and more as a "company functionary."[15]

Leaders of the Cuauhtémoc Workers Union proved more active outside the brewery than on the shop floor. They directed the Independent Unions of Nuevo León, published manifestos in the local press, and mobilized their ranks to protest the general strikes threatened sporadically by Monterrey's CTM leaders. Company unionists defended Cuauhtémoc's interests on the national level as well. Jesús Aguirre attended three different conventions staged by CTM and Labor Department officials to organize a union of Mexican brewery workers. But during their last reunion, the presiding official concluded that Aguirre's "only reason for attending the meeting is to come and repeal [the industrial union's] creation." Acting in representation of more than one third of the industry's labor force, Aguirre's resistance ensured the project's demise.[16] Back at home, union leaders promoted themselves as ardent defenders of their ranks, heading the resistance against what they called "leaderism," the drive by CTM activists to manipulate workers for their own political ambitions. The company unionists portrayed their actions as a reflection of their manliness and the independent character of the *regiomontano* worker. By resisting the inroads of militant unionism, the male workers not only defended regional norms, values, and a way of life, but protected their homes and families from the destructive designs of the "communist government" and its labor allies.[17] The brewery's unionists made no discursive appeals to the female operatives who comprised one-half of the labor force. Indeed, while women formally belonged to the Cuauhtémoc Workers Union, like all full-time employees, none appeared on its directing board.[18] The females' inconspicuous role in their union reflected a citywide trend, one made all the more notable by their considerable presence at the factory.

In Monterrey, the language of masculinity permeated the discourse of the Independent Unions as well as their red rivals, particularly the steel workers, for whom machismo became an integral part of their union and occupational identities. Monterrey's militants appropriated these gendered ideologies, upholding them to portray revolutionary unionism as a macho endeavor. Cuauhtémoc's male operatives became early and steadfast targets of the their barbs. As veteran brewery workers readily admit, they earned reputations as *tibios*, "pansies" who seemingly acquiesced to their

15 *Trabajo y Ahorro*, Nov. 23, 1935; López and Medrano interviews.
16 AGN: DAT 156/1. The effort to propose a collective contract for Mexico's brewery workers required the approval of two-thirds of the industry's employees. Workers at the country's three principal breweries – Moctezuma (Veracruz), Modelo (Mexico City), and Cuauhtémoc – split their respective loyalties between the CROM, the CTM, and the Independent Unions of Nuevo León.
17 *El Porvenir*, Sep. 17, 1936.
18 *Trabajo y Ahorro*, Oct. 12, 1935, Nov. 21, 1936.

own subordination through their indifference to unionism. The steel workers also capitalized on the conspicuous presence of women at the brewery to further denigrate the male operatives as *medios hombres*, "half-men" who shared their female workmates' presumed docility.[19] The brewery's male workers thus had to swallow their manly pride as the city's militants constructed this emasculated image of their nonunion counterparts. Unlike the steel workers, they offered no collective challenge to their entrenched company union. Nor did they have as much reason to because the shop-floor roots of unionism at the mill did not ferment in the relatively cool and tranquil atmosphere of the brewery.

Those who stayed on longest at Cuauhtémoc were the workers who adhered to the company philosophy of self-improvement, hard work, and thrift. Alejandro Monsiváis and Apolonio López became prototypical Cuauhtémoc veterans.[20] Each gained entry to brewery jobs in customary fashion: via the recommendations of trusted fathers and sisters employed at the plant. Self-taught mechanics, they conformed to the company's vision of the ideal worker: industrious, patient, "self-made" men. Encouraged by his sisters, Monsiváis left his job at a locksmith's shop to enter the brewery as a twenty-year-old laborer. He spent two years sweeping broken glass. But he desired to learn the mechanic's trade. "I began to watch them, seeing how the mechanics were all getting older by then, and I would approach them and try to help, even though the boss was always scolding us, telling us to mind our own business." His constancy won him a mechanic's apprenticeship in the bottling department. Assigned the dirty task of oiling machinery, Monsiváis taught himself basic maintenance through observation and practice. He realized mobility by proving his capacity to tackle more difficult tasks. "You've got to convince the bosses," Monsiváis recalled, "they themselves can tell when you're improving." Then, in tune with company philosophy, he emphasized that "one depends upon oneself." Like Monsiváis, Apolonio López worked his way up the firm's limited occupational hierarchy, eventually landing a job as night-shift mechanic on the labeling machines. More than any factor, López credited his own work ethic for his successful forty-seven-year career at Cuauhtémoc. As he underscored, "The bosses saw that you worked *hard*, and they knew who hung around drinking and dozing off."

Away from the job, López and Monsiváis followed similar paths, avenues that shortened the distance between workplace and home. Both married Cuauhtémoc operatives. Their wives shopped and saved at the commissary. Their children won university scholarships and became professionals. The entire family partook of the social festivities organized by the Cuauhtémoc

19 López and Padilla interviews.
20 The following paragraphs are based upon López and Monsiváis interviews.

Society. Both López and Monsiváis parlayed their savings into home ownership. But thrift did not come naturally. Not only was participation in the company savings plan compulsory for all workers but, in the case of López, pressure came down from his wife. Indeed, while he recalls nothing exceptional about the Cárdenas years, she remembers the period vividly and fondly. For in the 1930s, Cuauhtémoc stopped paying its workers in cash, which Dionisio admittedly squandered at the cantina, but with checks sent to the home. Astonished to learn her husband's true earnings, Elba took charge of the family budget. She parlayed the new savings into a home expansion project, supplementing the family income by taking on boarders. Her own capacity to order foodstuffs on credit at the company store gave her further control of her husband's earnings, a practice promoted by the Cuauhtémoc Society since the 1920s. *Work and Savings* lauded these forms of female empowerment as the surest route to a family's happiness. Thus did the brewery orient their practices of paternalism towards the workers' wives.

In the 1930s, Cuauhtémoc stepped up their pitch. *Work and Savings* encouraged operatives to hand their earnings over to their mothers, wives, or even daughters. Company ideologues chided male workers who refused to divulge their earnings for fear that "your position as head of household be undermined." Management came to understand "the women's capacity to shape the old man's social outlook."[21] They therefore extended the promotion of company loyalty and antiunion sentiments into the home. By doing so, these male managers reaffirmed a traditional gender ideology, one that stressed women's ability to influence and uplift their husbands and sons through moral suasion.[22] Back at home, it was hoped, the women would pressure the men in their families to safeguard their jobs by resisting the economically disruptive forces of unionism. But not all Cuauhtémoc operatives dismissed Cardenismo as a threat to their lifestyles. Some, we shall see, used the political opening to protest the shortcomings of Cuauhtémoc paternalism, prompting their employers to reveal the coercive face of the paternalistic card.

During the 1930s, the brewery's successful maintenance of its well-honed practices of coercion proved exceptional by the standards of the time. Counseled and defended by Monterrey's leading corporate lawyer, the brewery astutely defended its prerogative "to rid themselves of workers unwilling to blindly accept its severe discipline," as one such operative charged.[23] Workers lost their jobs for the most minor of offenses: protesting speedups,

21   *Trabajo y Ahorro*, July 17, 1932, Aug. 11, 1934; Cavazos interview.
22   Andrea Tone, *The Business of Benevolence: Industrial Paternalism in Progressive America* (Ithaca, 1997), 9.
23   AGENL: JCA 80/2382.

demanding wage hikes, talking back to supervisors, or speaking poorly of the company. The prolabor tilt of the arbitration board could complicate the task. But the brewery's lawyers found it possible to avoid severance payments by proving the employee had violated work rules or been hired on a short-term contract. In one case, forty-three workers signed statements supporting the company's case against two *ex-compañeros* who had been "directed and very poorly counseled by their ill-intentioned Communist leaders." In a similar case, five workers admitted to an inquisitive labor lawyer that their foreman pressured them to sign similar oaths to save their jobs.[24] Most typically, the workers provided the legal grounds for their dismissal through their custom of drinking the product of their labor. As many local union activists asserted – and most former brewery workers admit – Cuauhtémoc's employees earned a reputation as *borracheros* (drunkards). Indeed, some former militants attribute the Cuauhtémoc operatives' relative passivity to this peculiarity of brewery work. While the operatives fashioned some clever means of drinking beer on the job, pilfering was in fact a practice well-known and probably accepted by management, for it facilitated the dismissal of troublesome workers.[25]

Their limited confidence in the labor courts and the fear of blacklisting also engendered a degree of quiescence among the operatives. Some workers believed that Cuauhtémoc's owners appealed labor court rulings and bribed district judges to immunize the firm from legal responsibilities. The company did little to dispel the rumors. When one disgruntled worker threatened to file a legal protest, his foremen encouraged him "to do whatever I pleased, because the company has the labor board in its pocket."[26] While recorded cases prove rare, the use of physical violence further perpetuated fear among the operatives, at least one of whom was abducted by city police, beaten, and abandoned in the countryside after he persisted in his legal case against the company.[27] Finally, nearly all workers in Monterrey came to believe that the city's leading industrialists circulated

24 Oviedo interview; AGENL: JCA 48/1383, 80/2382.
25 While local union activists leveled these assertions against the men, on-the-job consumption was by no means a male prerogative. Indeed, given managerial disapproval of female consumption, the women on the bottling line devised truly ingenious means of shirking the supervisors' vigilance. One operative used a miniature pitcher concealed in her work smock to capture beer that flowed through the catch basins. Another, more brazen in her style, sipped her refreshment through a straw extending from a hollowed orange shell (Oviedo, López, Carranza, and Castañeda interviews).
26 Carranza interview; AGENL: JCA 194, 212 (quoted).
27 AGENL: 4/234; AGN: DGG 2.331 (16)/63A/13. Another perhaps apocryphal tale alleges that Cuauhtémoc jailed troublesome workers in subterranean cells beneath the brewery. This assertion is made by veteran labor activists like Juan Manuel Elizondo and Salvador Castañeda, both of whom attribute the failure to unionize the brewery less to the operatives' resistance than to the company's sway over its workers. Castañeda thus argued that, "Those *cabrones*' domination of their workers was so powerful that they couldn't liberate themselves even with the government's support."

a blacklist. When they fired a worker, one operative claimed, "they would also give them the black ball, as they used to say, so that they couldn't get work anywhere else."[28] While bribery, bullying, and the blacklist left few archival trails, the workers' widespread belief in these allegations suggests their potential effectiveness.

Cuauhtémoc revised its labor policies in the manner described thus far for two reasons. On the one hand, the company responded to developments extraneous to the brewery. The Garza Sadas genuinely (and correctly) feared that organized labor had targeted the factory in its drive to unionize Monterrey workers. The managerial reforms also responded to pressures from the operatives themselves. Neither paternalism nor the company union immunized the brewery from worker grievances and workplace conflicts. The protests were either individual acts of resistance or collective drives by workers struggling to gain their own inclusion into the company's practices of paternalism. Benevolence generated expectations. And those who protested loudest were the workers with the least to lose, the contract laborers whose part-time status excluded them from company welfare benefits.

During the 1920s, the brewery had replaced dozens of skilled workers with laborers contracted by several plant supervisors. While they entered to perform specialized stints as mechanics, electricians, or welders, the majority stayed on for years. Working without the formality of written contracts, these *eventuales* shuttled between tasks throughout the plant. "Let's go do this job," the foremen would say, "and we'll move on to another."[29] Not only did the practice reduce labor costs. Their part-time status facilitated the dismissal of skilled workers with union sympathies. In no other department was the contract workers' presence more conspicuous than in the general workshops, where the foreman, Roberto Salas, "always brought in his own people."[30] Salas's father was among the "Group of 22" workers who helped Luis G. Sada found the Cuauhtémoc Society. He hired on the skilled workers who built and repaired machinery throughout the brewery and its subsidiary packaging and malt plants. The story of Manuel Carranza, one of his hires, typifies the background and experience of these contract workers. His is also an exceptional tale of a Cuauhtémoc worker who, like some young *regiomontanos* of his generation, became a lifelong revolutionary union activist.[31]

As with so many labor contractors in his day, Salas recruited Carranza directly from his welding class at Monterrey's Obregón Industrial School. Salas hired the student in 1935 for a specific task: to construct the aluminum

28 Oviedo interview.
29 AGENL: JCA 153, 199.
30 Medrano interview.
31 Unless indicated otherwise, the following account is based upon Carranza interviews.

bar – shaped as a giant keg – that became a centerpiece of Cuauhtémoc's public beer garden. Impressed by the sixteen-year-old's talent as a welder, Salas kept Carranza in his employ for three more years, assigning the young welder new and more complex tasks as his confidence in him grew. In those days, Carranza remembered, some fifty other workers of all trades labored for different contractors in the workshops. They came to share similar grievances. They worked alongside and performed the same tasks as the brewery's full-time employees, workers who earned twice their wages and enjoyed Cuauhtémoc's celebrated welfare benefits. Not only were the contract laborers excluded from the perks of paternalism, they received neither paid vacations nor Seventh Day Pay, despite contributing up to four years of steady service to the company. Some contractors did not even pay the legal minimum wage to their less-skilled hires. Worse yet, management often forced them to join and pay dues to the Cuauhtémoc Workers Union, even though its contract did not cover the *eventuales*.[32]

While the contract workers valued the steady employment, they increasingly talked amongst themselves of their unequal treatment. In the mid-1930s, they began filing protests with the labor courts to win full-time status. Their resistance would achieve lasting consequences by the close of the decade. At first, company lawyers defended the practices, successfully denying any contractual ties or legal responsibility for the part-time workers.[33] However, four years after the protests began, a Supreme Court decision found Cuauhtémoc liable for the laborers' interests and awarded the plaintiffs a hefty financial settlement. By then, management had ordered the intermediaries to conform rigidly to the labor code. The contractors subsequently paid their hires Seventh Day Pay, legal vacation packages, and overtime. Waivers in their contracts thereafter enshrined the part timers' limited job security. As the union delegate to the labor board understood, "It is already well known by this tribunal that the company customarily forces its workers to sign the waiver to shun its legal responsibilities." The personnel manager also began screening subsequent hires to the contractual positions.[34] Manuel Carranza had joined in the protest that led to this outcome.

In 1938, Salas assigned Carranza to work with a team of seasoned mechanics to assemble an imported bottle-capping machine. Salas explicitly informed his laborers that they "worked for him and not the brewery." As

32 AGENL: JCA 173, 178, 194.
33 AGENL: JCA 48/1383.
34 In the 1939 case, a higher court concluded four years of appeals and counterappeals by establishing a contractual tie between Cuauhtémoc and the contract workers. The judges ordered Cuauhtémoc to pay more than $10,000 in severance pay and back wages to the three claimants – a sum equal to roughly four years' earnings for each dismissed worker. AGENL: JCA 65/1989 (quoted), 199.

Carranza acknowledged, "We recognized Salas as our immediate boss. . . . The brewery had nothing to do with us . . . yet." After three years of steady labor in the workshops, Carranza felt deserving of the higher wages and fringe benefits earned by full timers. "That is how the discord began with Salas," he recalled. But the will to act upon his grievances emerged only when "I threw in my lot with the revolutionaries." Carranza recalls that by the time the brewery rehired him, "I already had quite a bit of union consciousness. . . . [T]hen I started reading, I read a lot of revolutionary pamphlets. I began to understand better what fighting unions (*sindicatos de lucha*) were all about. I saw all the benefits, how they defended workers and everything, and it was around that time that I started going to the labor rallies . . . and I became more and more involved [in the union movement]." Carranza had first learned of the benefits of revolutionary unionism from fellow students at the Obregón Industrial School who belonged to the steel mill's Local 67. Thereafter, the nineteen-year-old immersed himself in left-wing labor politics and learned his rights as a worker. The times and the education radicalized Carranza.

Back at the brewery, Carranza soon learned that his workmates – part timers like himself – were union sympathizers as well. They resolved to challenge their contractual status. They halted work on the bottle-capping machine, approached Salas, and demanded higher wages and full benefits. Salas fired them. Carranza and his workmates hired a lawyer and filed claims against the brewery. Cuauhtémoc settled immediately with Carranza's companions, giving each the three-month severance pay required by law.[35] However, the company decided to retain Carranza's services, believing perhaps that the youngster had naively followed the older militants. Consistent with the firm's managerial philosophy, brewery representatives visited the Carranza home. As he recollected, "They were company police. They came to see my mother and tell her that I should stop once and for all, that I shouldn't be involved with such people, that I forget about it already." His mother convinced Carranza to drop the case when Cuauhtémoc offered him a full-time position as a welder.

With full-time status came an obligatory membership in the Cuauhtémoc Society. Carranza thus immersed himself in the brewery's company culture. He excelled as a tennis player, having learned the game from his American employers when he worked as a twelve-year-old errand boy at ASARCO's Matehuala smelter. The young welder challenged the brewery's office clerks at tennis, coached the women's squad, and represented Cuauhtémoc against teams from throughout northern Mexico. Carranza also enlisted in the Cuauhtémoc Workers Union, like all full timers at the closed-shop plant. Unlike most operatives, he attended union

35 AGENL: JCA 178.

assemblies. His memory filtered through a subsequent life of leftist labor activism, Carranza recalled the union's leaders as being "more devoted to the company than to the workers themselves." When queried, he admitted that they put forth "some very simple demands, such as requesting more funding for sports, this or that, anything except wage increases." Down on the shop floor, the very abuses that Monterrey's militants struggled to overcome – from arbitrary treatment to a lack of seniority rights – went unchallenged by the union. Instead, union officials encouraged workers to settle their grievances directly with management. Union shop committees, as even Cuauhtémoc loyalists like María de Jesús Oviedo admit, functioned only to discipline or dismiss troublesome workers through the exclusion clause.[36] His impressions confirmed, Carranza set out to organize a "truly independent union."

The moment seemed opportune for organizing. Carranza reminisced that, "Those were years of union effervescence. A lot of organizations were surging forth... protected, of course, by the government of General Lázaro Cárdenas." Lacking experience as an organizer, Carranza visited the local Casa del Obrero Mundial (House of the World Worker). "That was the center where we went to learn about organizing unions," Carranza explained, "from other *compañeros* who already had the experience.... We went there in the evenings after work, and they explained what the benefits would be once we were in a revolutionary organization, independent of the brewery, a union of brewery workers who would appoint their own leaders and then put forward a petition demanding the brewery's compliance with the rights workers had in those days." Two veteran activists – union organizers and Communist Party members – outlined the obstacles ahead. They told him, "Look, Carranza, to organize the brewery has been our principal objective for years. It's difficult but not impossible. You guys aren't the first ones to develop [labor] activity there. You aren't the first and you won't be the last." They counseled Carranza to organize a base of support in the workshop before approaching workers in other departments. Through practice, Carranza quickly grasped the amount of patience that successful organizing entailed. He would learn that, "to carry out union work within the factory one needs a great deal of time, to earn the workers' confidence, to become friends, *compañeros*, so that they trust in you, and there just wasn't enough time to do this at the brewery." Furthermore, he realized, company work rules prohibited shop workers from visiting other departments during his shift. Carranza's quixotic union drive met passive resignation – neither sympathetic nor hostile – from his immediate workmates. Veteran workers simply warned the youngster to "watch out for yourself," that his activities would lead to trouble. They soon did.

36 Oviedo interview.

His previous transgression alerted brewery officials to remain vigilant. By the end of the year, Carranza recalled, "they no longer considered me a trust-worthy worker." Carranza returned as a full-time welder and found himself surrounded by company loyalists. Ostensibly his assistants, "they were really there to tell the company everything I spoke about." Meanwhile, other "informants" discovered Carranza's after-hours visits to the Casa del Obrero Mundial. Carranza not only recognized the vigilance; he saw his union drive floundering. He proceeded nonetheless, for Carranza had little to risk but his dignity. As a skilled worker and the youngest son of a large family, Carranza's future shone brightly. He ultimately fell victim to his own youthful naïveté.

One morning, his supervisor assigned Carranza the task of welding a fermentation tank. Entering the chilly department, he encountered the foreman, Orozco. "[Orozco] was the one in charge of getting me drunk," he recalled with a chuckle. "We're not going to work today, Carranza," his foreman greeted him, "we're going to drink beer." Following a department custom – albeit in exaggerated fashion – Carranza and Orozco drank fresh lager throughout the day. By the close of the shift, Orozco had finished his task and Carranza stumbled to the showers. Minutes later, Cuauhtémoc's personnel manager and a company lawyer appeared at the door. "How are you feeling, Mr. Carranza?" they sarcastically inquired. "Well you see how I am!" he laughed, sobering to the reality of his imminent discharge. Carranza filed a petition to protest his subsequent dismissal. "My defense was that everyone used to drink beer there and the brewery knew it, that my getting drunk inside wasn't a rare thing." "Moreover," he went on, "they incited me." "But," he admitted, "I was also to blame, knowing how the company had me." Carranza in fact understood that the law overrode custom. That is why the young welder never even attended his labor court hearing. He quickly found work at another local factory and Cuauhtémoc ridded itself of an unreconstructed unionist.

Carranza was not the only Cuauhtémoc worker to embrace the union cause during the mid-1930s. Former workers also recall that two young workers in the bottling department, the Cárdenas sisters, organized a drive around demands for equal wages for women. María de Jésus Oviedo emphasizes that their challenge to gendered wage differentials struck a sympathetic chord among the female operatives. But the sisters' attempt to rally their workmates failed to elicit active support and they lost their jobs. The company apparently responded to the challenge because María recalls that by the 1940s women in her department earned wages equal to their male counterparts.[37] A lone militant in Cuauhtémoc's packaging division met a more antagonistic response than the Cárdenas sisters. His colleagues "grew disgusted at my idea of forming a red union to defend our interests."

37 Elizondo and Oviedo interviews.

One workmate succinctly reminded him that "[the company] gave us the bread to live by and that he was quite comfortable with the white union." Furthermore, the dissident learned, "he had already reported me [to management]."[38] The Cuauhtémoc operatives who embraced unionism during the Cárdenas years were not all youngsters like Carranza. Several were veterans with up to twenty years experience at the brewery.[39] But all were exceptions to the rule of deference because the majority of Cuauhtémoc workers resisted unionism as a cause antagonistic to their interests.

Cardenismo thus had a paradoxical impact at the Cuauhtémoc Brewery. While the operatives upheld their own independence from organized labor, they experienced new and enduring restrictions on their freedom. But they were awarded material benefits that matched those of the revolutionary unions. Moreover, the company's discriminatory hiring policies ensured that their sons and daughters enjoyed privileged access to the perks of paternalism. The corporate labor policies fashioned by Cuauhtémoc would be extended throughout the Garza Sadas' industrial empire and replicated by such large-scale, nonunion employers as CEMEX cement and La Moderna Cigarettes, both national leaders in their respective industries. This system of industrial relations came about in a subtle and piecemeal fashion. Therefore, in contrast to Monterrey's revolutionary unionists, the 1930s did not mark a watershed in the lives of the city's "white" workers. That may be why President Cárdenas left no lasting impact on their collective memory. Linda Rodríguez, the former glass decorator, acknowledges that "many people appreciate him a lot because frankly it was he who did more for the people [than any other president]." "In Michoacán," she went on, "they love him dearly, the call him Tata Cárdenas, but not so much here [in Monterrey]." Few brewery workers even remembered that, at that time, they formally belonged to a company union and were thus covered by its collective contract. When queried about Cardenismo, one retired operative quietly claimed that, "I never knew anything about that." Instead, they speak with great pride of their Cuauhtémoc Society and in reverential terms about the late Luis G. Sada (1884–1941), the plant manager and SCYF founder whom they still associate with the extensive welfare benefits provided by the company.[40]

Building New Identities at Local 67

Those *regiomontanos* who did organize revolutionary unions developed clear and passionate memories of the Cárdenas government. That is because

38 AGENL: JCA 212.
39 AGENL: JCA 80/2382, 212.
40 Monsiváis (quoted), Oviedo, and Padilla interviews.

Monterrey's steel, smelter, electric power, and railroad workers all experienced Cardenismo as a radical and enduring break with the past. They thus direct their reverence toward a "heroic" president who, for Félix Torres, "was like a teacher who energized the labor movement in Monterrey." Or, as the iron worker Salvador Castañeda believes, "the emancipation of Mexico's workers surged forth in the mid-1930s under the shadow of General Lázaro Cárdenas." For Castañeda, "workers began to have rights due to a president who was genuinely revolutionary, as we called someone with just and righteous intentions, because before Don Lázaro Cárdenas workers had no rights in Mexico." Workers of this generation universally attribute their successful union struggles to the support of a government with a "progressive outlook." Dionisio Palacios asserted that, "We owe all our union conquests to Don Lázaro because the employers' association was very powerful here in Monterrey." He thus agrees with his friend, Castañeda, that "of every president we have had since Santa Anna, no *cabrón* except Don Lázaro Cárdenas has been truly patriotic."[41] Consistent with Myrna Santiago's assessment of Mexican oil workers, these blue-collar *regiomontanos* fashioned a collective memory of Cárdenas that highlighted how he "more than any president before or after him, had made a real, tangible difference in their lives."[42] This selective memory of Cárdenas owed as much to the workers' experience with subsequent governments as to the dramatic changes ushered in by revolutionary unionism.

Few experienced the process more dramatically than the steel workers, who perceive the years "before 1936," when they established Local 67, as an extension of the old Porfirian regime. Cardenismo thus assumes legendary status in their memories. That legend built upon both myth and reality. The changes were real indeed. Much like the city's smelter or electric workers, the steel workers' Local 67 secured immediate improvements in their living and working conditions. Moreover, their affiliation with the militant Miner-Metalworkers Union introduced them to a new world of labor politics and rowdy union assemblies, and a workplace where they ostensibly enjoyed "the freedom to voice our grievances without fear of reprisal."[43] However, the Cárdenas years did not entail a complete rupture with the past. Paternalism remained pervasive in their lives. As retired workers recognize, unions like Local 67 emerged "under the patronage" of President Cárdenas, whose *estado papá* endeavored to protect workers as the weaker party in their relations with employers. Moreover, the means

---

41 Castañeda, Palacios, and Torres interviews.
42 Mynra Santiago, "Strike Breaker or Working-Class Hero? Lázaro Cárdenas and the Mexican Oil Workers, 1924–1940," Paper presented to the Latin American Studies Association, Chicago, Sep. 24, 1998.
43 Quiroga interview.

by which Local 67 endeavored to transform rank-and-file identities and build enduring union loyalties was reminiscent of the cultural practices of company paternalism. Indeed, welfare capitalism persisted at the steel mill, as Local 67 cooperated with management in the administration of the welfare benefits inherited from the 1920s.

Rank-and-file allegiance to Local 67 built first and foremost upon the conquests enshrined in the union's first collective contract. The 1936 contract, as union organizers promised, boosted and leveled wage rates dramatically.[44] It also improved pension plans, extended paid vacation days to fourteen, and brought accident compensation rates in line with the Federal Labor Law (rather than the state's 1906 Accident Law). The Fundidora expanded its welfare programs as well. The company built an additional school and, in the early 1940s, opened a maternity hospital named by the workers in honor of company director Adolfo Prieto's wife, María Josefa. The Cooperativa Acero and its savings and loan program persisted, albeit under union control. Then, in 1939, the company conceded to union demands that it develop further worker housing in what became Colonia Buenos Aires, the vast neighborhood of steel workers across the river from the mill. Finally, the union constructed its own funeral home for the exclusive use of its members' families. Such welfare programs thus ensured the survival of what the company had long promoted as the Great Steel Family.

All of Monterrey's revolutionary unions secured new prerogatives that would not be matched by the city's nonunion factories. One was that "we now practiced union democracy," an important departure from the days of company unionism. One electrical worker thus recalled that "we ensured that the immense majority [of workers] turned out for union assemblies, and that the people spoke and expounded on their ideas and problems." This happened because "the company could no longer fire us [for protesting]" and the workers thus "had no fear" of speaking their minds.[45] Another key aspect of industrial democracy was the companies' recognition of seniority as the basis of promotions. This was a right that trade unionists had demanded since the 1910s. For that reason retired steel and electrical workers commonly cite it as the foremost conquest enshrined in their collective contracts. In the case of the steel mill, managers naturally abhorred Local 67's "blind adherence to seniority rights," which they believed would threaten "the plant's development" by promoting "incompetent workers." In fact, workers eligible for a promotion were subjected to a "competency trial" administered by joint committees of supervisors and union delegates. Unlike the "old system," Antonio Quiroga noted, "determining who was competent

44 The following paragraphs are based upon collective contract in AGN: DAT 209/4; Castañeda, Elizondo, Palacios, Quiroga, Reyna, and Solís interviews.
45 Félix Torres in Arenal, *En Monterrey no solo hay ricos*, 44.

was no longer in the company's hands." For most workers, seniority meant an end to favoritism and, for union leaders, it therefore promoted greater rank-and-file unity.[46] More important, the union stewards who sat on such committees – once appointed by the company union – were now elected by workers in their departments. The Fundidora also agreed to employ two such unionists as part-time business agents to handle the daily grievances filed by the reconstituted shop committees. Shop-floor relations thus changed dramatically. Work remained highly dangerous, Rafael Reyna noted, because a system that linked bonuses to tonnage output "accelerated production excessively." But the new benefits of revolutionary unionism better compensated the steel workers for the sacrifices made in the workshops, rolling mills, and furnaces.

Retired workers like Reyna therefore speak of 1936 as a year of "emancipation," a watershed when the union became strong enough and willing to challenge customary managerial prerogatives. In Antonio Quiroga's recollection, the moment signaled the end of "tyrannical" foremen and "self-appointed" union leaders "who did nothing in defense of the workers." As Salvador Castañeda depicts the period, "'Don Lázaro' Cárdenas [had] liberated the workers from years of ignorance and misery." Notably, both Quiroga and Castañeda later directed the union, one that fashioned a quasi-mythical narrative of past labor relations to construct and maintain rank-and-file loyalty to Local 67. Manuel Carranza later recognized that the benefits had come from "years of struggle by the workers." But such working-class agency is absent from most oral testimonies. Young workers who experienced the union's controversial emergence speak of it as a "political affair," a factional struggle won by the "reds" due to the paramount support of the Cárdenas government.[47]

That Local 67's leaders included former company union activists did not, for rank-and-file steel workers, lessen the significance or breadth of the change. For one thing, union officials were now elected by the workers. Furthermore, people like the union's first secretary general, Leandro Martínez, possessed the "experience, education, and preparation" to lead Local 67.[48] While Martínez later adopted the "Porfirian" leadership style characteristic of the company union, workers nonetheless recall him as "a spearhead who taught the workers how to resist." Equally important,

---

46 Some workers opposed seniority rights for reasons different than the company. Rafael Reyna had entered the mill in 1934 after graduating from the Obregón Industrial School. He already had greater skills than many old timers, but the new system meant that "one would have to keep waiting" to move up the occupational ladder. Interviews with Quiroga, Reyna, Solís, Villarreal; company protests in Evaristo Araiza, Gerente General, Fundidora Monterrey, to Gregorio Esparza, Secretario General del SITMMSRM, Sep. 28, 1938, in AGN: DAT 209/4.

47 Carranza, Castañeda, Quiroga, and Reyna interviews.

48 Castañeda interview.

Reyna points out, was that "the government's support of the workers permitted the union to strengthen itself." Internal democracy, thereafter a hallmark of the union, ensured a degree of rank-and-file control of the leadership. As in all Miners Union locals, the steel workers elected a Vigilance Committee whose power paralleled that of the union board. Committee delegates oversaw the leaders' compliance with union statutes. The steel workers also nominated workmates for union posts. They elected those who earned respect for their "rectitude" and "honor," or displayed a certain swagger at union assemblies, where many a union leader was taken to task by the workers.[49] The freedom to dissent and hold union officials accountable thus made the institution of Local 67 more important than the leaders themselves. That was of paramount importance because personal, political, and generational antagonisms often divided the union leadership.

The Cárdenas years witnessed relentless struggles for supremacy between communist and government-allied leaders in all of Monterrey's revolutionary unions. Local 67 typified the process. Two years after the union's founding, the steel workers elected to replace Leandro Martínez and his allies with a left-wing slate of directors. Heading the executive committee was Guadalupe Rivas, a former miner and union organizer from Zacatecas. Rivas became the "best union leader of his time," in the judgment of Dionisio Palacios.[50] Whereas his predecessors came from the ranks of skilled labor, Rivas was a third-grade molder's assistant. "They were people who were not well educated," one worker said of many union leaders at the mill, "but they had good intentions; they were fighters." "Back then," Castañeda added, "we didn't go around asking 'how well prepared are you?' A worker stood out when he stood up to the company." Rivas developed his renown for militancy while a union delegate on the foundry's shop committee. He also earned a reputation as a "hard worker," an exceptional union leader who continued laboring in the foundry during his tenure as secretary general. "[Union officials] generally did not want to work after that," one worker recalled. Finally, Rivas's popularity built upon his machismo, a cultural trait shared and acted out by most steel workers. His hard character derived from past experience. Rivas was said to have killed a man during his organizing days in the mining camps, an episode that prompted his flight to Monterrey. He subsequently proved his tough demeanor by aggressively challenging Leandro Martínez during Local 67's earliest assemblies. Thus did the former miner earn the reputation that resulted in his election as the union's secretary general.

49 Carranza, Castañeda, and Reyna interviews.
50 *El Porvenir*, Apr. 4, 1938. Analsysis of union leadership based on Castañeda, Elizondo, Palacios, and Solís interviews.

Machismo became an enduring quality of the steel workers' union identity. Their exaggerated masculinity spilled over into Local 67's union assemblies. As former steel workers remember, the weekly reunions were *"muy pesadas,"* heavy, raucous and, potentially violent affairs held at the close of the day shift. Mandatory attendance ensured the presence of some 4,000 exhausted, sometimes inebriated, and often armed steel workers. The meetings could potentially evolve into melees like that which erupted at the time of the 1939 gubernatorial elections. Rank-and-file workers therefore elected fellow unionists who, in Salvador Castaneda's words, "had balls big enough to confront the issues and handle the workers. . . . [I]t wasn't easy to manage those people; you had to do it more with bravado than reason." Tough leaders ensured the union's strength and cohesiveness. Retired workers thus attribute the emergence of leaders like Rivas and his rival, Leandro Martínez, to their skills at maintaining unity through sharp oratorical skills and a macho demeanor. Despite their partisan rivalries, all union leaders shared a commitment to revolutionary unionism. They had seen how divided loyalties undermined union victories in other local industries. They thus worked together to build enduring union identities among a rapidly expanding number of rank-and-file workers.

Just as industrial paternalism built upon working-class traditions of mutual aid, so did Local 67's cultural programs evolve from a foundation established by the Recreativa Acero during the 1920s. The Recreativa endured as a social and recreational center for white-collar employees and their families. But the collective contract placed most aspects of company culture under the administration of the union's secretary of education and cultural affairs. Baseball, for example, remained immensely popular among the steel workers. Fundidora athletes now donned jerseys emblazoned with their union affiliation rather than their employer's name. Other cultural practices reminiscent of the Great Steel Family survived under union auspices as well. Local 67 organized a Feminine Group and a Miners Youth association to integrate the workers' wives and children into union culture. Observers commented upon their noteworthy presence at the labor rallies and parades sponsored by the union. By the late 1930s, they also remarked on the "Miners militias," the contingents of uniformed steel workers and their martial bands that marched in the labor parades of the time.[51] Local 67 thus painted a radical political culture on the customary practices of paternalism.

51 *El Porvenir*, May 2, 1938, Nov. 21, 1939; *El Norte*, Feb. 13 and Sep. 17, 1939; Elizondo and Palacios interview. The CTM organized the militias, which survived into the mid-1940s, in response to a perceived threat of "indigenous fascism" and the fear of a military rebellion against the ruling party. "We always had to march in those days," recalled Palacios. During the war, participating steel workers went through their formations after every shift, led by "worker-sergeants" trained at the nearby military garrison.

Consistent with Cardenista policy, the union also became a school for the making of the new Mexican worker as well as several labor leaders who went on to direct the national Miner-Metalworkers Union. Local 67 endeavored to forge the "men of steel" into a different kind of "aristocracy" than that envisioned by company director Adolfo Prieto. The mandatory union assemblies became the workers' classroom. Local 67's leaders abandoned the discourse of class harmony and taught the rank and file a revised history of the mill, one that highlighted cruel foremen, complacent labor leaders, and "imposed" collective contracts. According to one of the project's organizers, Juan Manual Elizondo, the history of Local 67 and the benefits that resulted from the union's founding would instruct workers "to care for and protect the union." For decades thereafter, union leaders endeavored to remind the ranks that theirs was "a union that was created not without great difficulty, it was created with sacrifice . . . to give us what we had." Manuel Carranza entered the mill in 1942 and learned the union's history from Gabriel Espinoza, one of the workers who was briefly fired during the 1936 organizing drive. Carranza became Local 67's leader in the 1970s and emphasized that "those legends served as the pith, the backbone, to convince the workers *how* the union was created and *why* we have these benefits and by means of *who* we are enjoying these prerogatives and *why* we have a collective contract . . . so they understood why we must take care of our own union, you know." Activists also endeavored to demonstrate the union's "social value." That meant its role not only as the workers' bargaining agent but as a vanguard union dedicated to issues external to the steel mill, from supporting local strikers to raising funds for political causes.[52] The curriculum assumed a distinctly left-wing hue when Communists directed the union and turned to middle-class sympathizers to help fashion their strategies.

College students like Juan Manuel Elizondo and his *regiomontano* classmate, Antonio García Moreno, joined Local 67 during this period. They were inspired by a desire "to put our ideas of the working class, its development, and its destiny [into practice]."[53] Leaving behind their studies in Mexico City, Elizondo and García returned to Monterrey as Communist Party (PCM) activists. They entered into the life of the steel mill "when the party gave everyone orders to integrate themselves into unions." Fellow student activist and future governor, Raul Rangel Frías, convinced Elizondo to take a job at the mill. "He told me, look, the Fundidora has 4,000 employees and you are running around in the cantinas looking for a couple of workers to talk with." The steel workers were familiar with student activists like Elizondo and García, who would be employed respectively in the chemistry

---

52 Carranza, Castañeda, and Elizondo interviews.
53 Elizondo, *De historia y política*, 33.

lab and machine shops. Both were regular speakers at Monterrey's red labor rallies and had coauthored *The True Face of the Regiomontano Bourgeoisie*, the publication written in honor of the "July 29th martyrs" and distributed to all the mill's workers by Local 67. Despite Elizondo's local renown, he remembered, "I was very careful not to come across as the know-it-all man." Here, from the elite's perspective, were the outside agitators, a status that belied their *regiomontano* origins but neatly characterized the intents of their activism. The former students played a key role in the life of the union. Elizondo served as a legal counselor and business agent while García became Local 67's secretary of education and cultural affairs. They also addressed union assemblies, speaking to the steel workers on issues both practical (local politics, collective contracts) and theoretical (the theory of surplus labor value, explained through a parable in which the black pig grows fat at the expense of a red one).[54]

Nothing exemplified Local 67's politics more clearly than its first publication, *La Pasionaria*. The magazine's editors named it in honor of Dolores Ibarruri, the Spanish Communist Party leader whose female representatives visited the Fundidora in 1936 to solicit support for the Republican cause. Lessons of the Spanish Civil War became an integral part of the steel workers' schooling in the 1930s. It also became a destination for their union funds. In 1938, Local 67 and other revolutionary unions donated $2,000 of clothing and toys to the orphaned children of Republican soldiers. On another occasion, the steel workers provided arms, cash, and truck repairs to a group of North American and Spanish radicals passing through Monterrey with a cache of weapons destined for the front in Spain.[55] The pages of *La Pasionaria* certainly reflect the topics discussed in the union hall, from local strikes to national politics to critiques of Mexican labor leaders. One article thus reprimanded ruling party union bosses, calling upon them "to invigorate the labor movement by returning to the working masses, consulting and obeying them . . . rather than selling them out for simple political compromises." The history of industrial relations at the mill was also integral to the discourse. As *La Pasionaria's* editors wrote in one issue: "Our bosses, who say they are the most benevolent [employers] in the country, would never admit that the 1917 Constitution obligated them to pay overtime, provide workers' compensation for accidents, and respect the seven-hour shift for night work. . . . These

54 Elizondo interviews. The Communists apparently used their shop-floor popularity to enlist workers into the party. By 1938, the PCM claimed 150 active members working at the mill (*El Machete*, Aug. 22, 1939).
55 *La Pasionaria*, Mar. 1938; Elizondo interview; Nathan, Feb. 28, 1937, SD 812.00 NL/164. Aside from its politics, *La Pasionaria* retained much in common with the company press of the 1920s: slick packaging, sophisticated graphics, and (to the Chamber of Commerce's dismay) advertisements from local merchants "of great respectability and liberalism" (*La Pasionaria*, Dec. 1936).

conquests they portray as gifts, when they were in fact won through struggle."[56] Thus did Local 67's leaders offer their own "populist" interpretation of Mexican history, much like those contemporary observers who perceived working-class mobilizations rather than top-down reforms as the catalyst of the revolutionary process.

The union hall and the company press thus offered forums where worker–activists endeavored to build union identities by teaching workers the value of and need to defend Local 67. The Fundidora's directors had acquiesced to revolutionary unionism. But, in the later 1930s, the future seemed uncertain. While the Cárdenas government gradually retrenched on its earlier radicalism, the city's powerful industrialists discovered seeming allies in Nuevo León's more conservative governors. Moreover, union leaders certainly knew that the city's industrialists employed paid labor observers to report on their activities and foment discord within the unions.[57] Recall that no sooner had Local 67 won legal recognition when old-guard union leaders launched the resistance movement that ultimately cost them their jobs. Their successors therefore guarded the union from future dissent. They did so through the very strategies fashioned by the industrialists and their white unions. The collective contract served as their principal tool.

The contract's admission and exclusion clauses were the most radical and controversial conquests of Mexico's revolutionary unions. They placed the right to hire and fire workers – the most fundamental of managerial prerogatives – under union control. The admission clause established the union hiring hall. Local 67 reserved 50 and 25 percent of job vacancies for members' sons and brothers, respectively. Ten year's seniority earned each steel worker the right to bring a relative into the mill. Local 67 allocated the remaining openings to fellow unionists, notably workers laid off from other union plants or activists blacklisted by the city's nonunion factories.[58] Manuel Carranza, the young welder discharged by the Cuauhtémoc Brewery, entered the steel mill under these auspices. Scholars often perceive the admission clause as the basis of subsequent union boss corruption in Mexico.[59] It indeed had this consequence in many industries, most famously within the "black gold mafia" that the Mexican Oil Workers Union became. In Monterrey, union hiring sustained occupational communities of industrial workers, ensuring that high-paying jobs at the steel mill or smelters were passed down from father to son. More important, it protected

56 *La Pasionaria.*, Dec. 1937, Mar. 1938.
57 Blocker, Mar. 13, 1937, SD 812.504/1642.
58 Carranza, Castañeda, and Solís interviews.
59 Knight, "Social Policy in the 1930s," 6, who also quotes the manager of a Coahuila coal company where unionists employed the clause "to send for all the men who had been fired by other companies to put them on our books."

the families of union workers from the discriminatory hiring practices developed by the city's industrial elite during the Cárdenas years. As one electric power worker thus recalled, "We used the admission clause to protect ourselves and to fight against the [industrial elite's] black list."[60] Just as the industries of the Garza Sada clan restricted hiring to workers of impeccably nonunion blood, so too did generations of steel workers bring their sons into the mill, ensuring that all new hires hailed from union households.

Revolutionary unions employed the so-called *cláusula de exclusión* in more notorious fashion. The militants used their right to discharge members – and thus dismiss them from their jobs – for the same reason as Monterrey's Independent Unions: to discipline workers and eliminate dissent. Local 67 used it to expel the former leaders of the Federated Steel Unions. The United Glass Workers applied it against members who crossed picket lines during the 1937 Vidriera strike. The Railroaders Union threatened to discharge workers who joined the ACN or the Gold Shirts. Unions like Local 67 also wielded the exclusion clause when the threat of monetary sanctions failed to elicit regular attendance at union assemblies or labor rallies. In exceptional cases, it became a weapon in the hands of unscrupulous union officials. One steel worker, Salvador Castañeda, lost an earlier job at Monterrey's railroad shops for assaulting a corrupt union official who stole his free railroad tickets allocated by the company.[61] Revolutionary unionists could thus use the exclusion clause to punish personal enemies or enforce political conformity. From the unionists' perspective, the right to fire dissident workers maintained unity within the ranks. The rank and file did not adapt to the culture of revolutionary unionism without a bit of prodding. Many certainly preferred to retire to the cantina after a shift at the mill rather than file into a stifling union hall for the weekly assemblies. Over time, the steel workers grew accustomed to mandatory attendance at union assemblies. It was, after all, their union. Local 67 officials nonetheless ensured steady turnouts at the union hall and political rallies by threatening to sanction workers who were persistently absent.[62]

Such policies supplied ammunition for the media's persistent blasts against Monterrey's revolutionary unions. The conservative daily *El Porvenir* emerged as a champion of rank-and-file interests. Its coverage of union meetings and interviews with disgruntled workers provide insight into the causes of discontent. Anonymous dissidents criticized the use of fines to bolster union hall attendance or coerce workers into supporting a union

---

60 Villarreal interview.

61 *El Porvenir*, Aug. 3, 1936, July 7, 1937; Castañeda interview.

62 Union statutes stipulated monetary sanctions for workers absent from three consecutive assemblies (AGENL: JCA 126/3646).

leader's political campaign.[63] One steel worker with seventeen years at the mill lost his job for refusing to join Local 67. He remained recalcitrant "in virtue of considering myself a free man." As the proud veteran wrote to *El Porvenir*, "I went off to fight the Revolution when these people who pretend to direct [the union] were not even born." While his dismissal aroused rank-and-file protests, Local 67's leaders garnered the necessary two-thirds vote required by union statutes to apply the exclusion clause.[64] But the new union prerogative rarely served this coercive function and, in the case of Local 67, only after consulting the ranks.

It was the use of union funds that became the greatest cause of rank-and-file discontent. Thus when inflation began eroding real wages in 1937, union workers protested their leaders' subordination of bread-and-butter issues to their own political agenda. According to press accounts, the workers' dues served not for their own benefit but to finance political campaigns or to underwrite union delegations to Moscow.[65] However, for the most part, workers dissented less to the political uses of union funds than to the causes to which they were directed. The occasional resolution to contribute one day's wages toward the Republican cause in Spain or the settlement of Spanish refugees generated notable complaints. Mexico's workers, after all, harbored a historic disdain for Spaniards.[66] Rank-and-file workers thus proposed more "patriotic" alternatives. One suggested financial support for the families of workers killed in a Coahuila mine blast. Dissenting railroaders, fearing that union officials in Mexico City would skim the money, demanded that their dues instead purchase Christmas gifts for the local poor.[67] As elsewhere in Mexico, Monterrey's workers rallied around the hallmark of Cardenista patriotism: the expropriation of the foreign-owned oil companies. The steel workers alone donated eight-day's hard-earned wages – a total of $104,000 – to help finance the Cárdenas government's purchase of the oil companies.[68] For the most part, though, the union dues financed more mundane endeavors. At the steel mill, Local 67 employed union funds to make legal counsel available to

63 *El Porvenir*, Aug. 4, Sep. 6, Nov. 23, 1936, July 7, 1937.

64 *El Porvenir*, Nov. 3, 1938.

65 Monterrey's Railroaders and Miners Unions collected $3,500 through a special levy to send union delegates to Moscow. Upon his return, José Arizpe, a railroad worker, penned a highly critical account in *El Porvenir* of the miserable conditions suffered by Russia's workers. Blocker, Nov. 30, 1937, SD 812.00 NL/174; *El Porvenir*, Dec. 17, 1937.

66 *El Porvenir*, Dec. 6, 12, 1936. Union leaders thus expounded upon the difference between the "evil Spaniards (*gachupines*) who only come here to enrich themselves," and the freedom fighters, political refugees, and orphans of Republican Spain, hundreds of whom were settled in Monterrey. *El Norte*, Aug. 8, 1939.

67 *El Porvenir*, Jan. 6, 1937, Nov. 29, 1936.

68 *El Porvenir*, Apr. 1, 1938.

workers and their families, to build a funeral parlor, to purchase a printing press, and to construct a union assembly hall. The latter became necessities after Governor Guerrero curtailed the union's access to a state-owned assembly hall and closed government printing offices to *La Pasionaria*'s editors.[69]

Local 67's proclaimed position at the vanguard of Monterrey's revolutionary union movement earned it the enmity of the state's conservative government. That owed as much to the presence of Communists on the union's board as to Local 67's unambiguous support of local strikes. Indeed, one of the principal uses of the members' dues was to augment the union's "resistance fund." "We were the treasury of many other unions," Salvador Castañeda noted. Local 67 used the fund to offer both financial sustenance and legal support to striking workers. More than any other cause, such labor solidarity underscored the union's "social value." Among the greatest beneficiaries were the ASARCO smelter workers. Their common affiliation with the Miner-Metalworkers Union had resurrected the ties of solidarity first forged by Monterrey's metal workers in the late 1910s. Twenty years later, a rash of industrial disputes at the smelter again threatened a general strike of Monterrey's metallurgical industries. Company intransigence, union combativeness, and the government's reluctance to mediate the conflicts caused persistent strikes at ASARCO. The years 1937–39 saw Local 66 stage labor actions to force the company to meet its economic demands when contract revisions came due. Each time, national Miners Union leaders intervened to prevent a sympathy strike at the steel mill. In 1938, ASARCO responded to a series of one-hour sit-down strikes by firing 280 workers at its Monterrey plant. That specific strike developed in the context of Mexico's expropriation of the foreign-owned oil companies, a precedent that Miners union activists desired for their own industry. The Cárdenas regime, financially crippled by the oil nationalization and dependent on mineral tax revenues, declared the strikes illegal. The Monterrey smeltermen were out three months before labor authorities pressured the company to reinstate them.[70] Local 67 sustained the striking workers with their own "resistance fund."

The steel workers' support of their fellow *metalúrgicos* became another duty of revolutionary unions, a policy that steel workers expected Local 66 to reciprocate. But it met management's objection. Indeed, when another strike paralyzed ASARCO in 1939, the Fundidora threatened to dismiss steel workers who "morally and materially supported" the smeltermen. They

69 *El Porvenir*, Mar. 18, 1937; Solís interview.
70 Castañeda interview; for details of the ASARCO conflicts see Blocker, Mar. 18, Mar. 21, Mar. 26, 1938, SD 812.5045/706, 713, 715; Daniels, Mexico City, Apr. 17, 1938, SD 812.5045/723; *El Porvenir*, Sep. 27, Dec. 2, 1937, Mar. 16–23, 1938, Jan. 26, 1939, Mar. 17–23, 1939.

did so when Local 67's leaders started voicing their own grievances during rallies in support of the ASARCO strikers. Not only did the steel workers now seize the opportunity to protest violations of their collective contract. Local 67 threatened a strike of its own. The militancy of Monterrey's metal workers drew the unfavorable attention of government officials as well. The secretary of labor exhorted the steel and smelter workers to "recognize the economic straits through which the nation is passing."[71] President Cárdenas also appealed to working-class patriotism in his own pleas for labor peace. In a letter sent to the Miners locals, the president chastised union leaders for acting like "a labor aristocracy" by pressing "excessive demands" and maintaining the ranks in "a constant state of agitation." The metalworkers' "unpatriotic acts," he warned, would undermine "the prestige and respectability of the government's revolutionary policies."[72]

Union leaders' commitment to revolutionary nationalism could temper the militance of Local 67. When they renegotiated the collective contract in 1937, the steel workers limited wage demands in compliance with Cardenista calls for patriotic sacrifice. They did not, however, limit their concerns to bread-and-butter issues. Nor did Local 67 secure all labor conquests at the negotiating table. The steel workers improved their working conditions through collective action as well, a confrontational attitude that exasperated their supervisors. Local 67 often won workplace reforms through *paros locos*, well-coordinated but illegal wildcat strikes. In 1938, for example, the union's safety commission demanded a revision of work rules in the rolling mill. They presented their demand – longer breaks for the rollers and their assistants – during a mid-shift visit to company offices. The timing and nature of the demand surprised plant managers, who refused to restructure work rules during the middle of a shift. The blast furnace workers therefore sounded the plant whistle one hour later and the operatives, on cue, halted production in every department. A two-hour standoff ensued before management acquiesced to Local 67's demand that longer and healthier rest periods be conceded to the rolling crews.[73]

Such workplace actions violated legal restrictions on the right to strike and supplemented the Fundidora's mounting charges against its workers. As the company protested to Miners Union officials in Mexico City, "the cooperation expected on the part of the [national] union has been effectively demonstrated . . . however, the same cannot be said for many of your [local] workers, who fail to reciprocate the confidence we place in them." The Fundidora complained of unspecified "loopholes" in the contract that permitted workers to shirk, leave early, and miss work "with impunity." The

---

71 *El Norte*, Jan. 11, Feb. 8–13, 1939; *El Porvenir*, Jan. 1 and 26, Feb. 13, Mar. 10, 17, and 22, 1939.
72 Cárdenas circular quoted in Stewart, Mexico City, Apr. 5, 1939, SD 812.5045/872.
73 Palacios and Castañeda interviews.

company's agent continued that, "They may be a minority, but [the militants'] attitude has spread to their workmates and affects the efficiency of the plant, with repercussions for the entire economy of a nation that expects hard work and perseverance from its sons."[74] Local 67 officials voiced complaints of their own. Writing to President Cárdenas, they charged that national Miners Union leaders had formed a collaborative alliance with Fundidora officials in Mexico City. The nature of the company's relation with the national remains unclear. But Augustin Guzmán, who organized and directed the union during its militant early years, had been succeeded in 1938 by Gregorio Pérez Esparza, whom one U.S. official called "a conservative compared to his predecessor." Prodded by the government, Esparza actively mediated industrial relations in order to forestall strikes in the conflictive mining and metallurgical industries.[75]

Strikes loomed at the mill with each two-year revision of Local 67's collective contract. These were moments when union leaders would selectively prove their commitment to either "responsible unionism" or their militant understanding of Cardenismo, depending upon economic conditions. In 1937, inflation was eroding the steel workers' earlier wage gains and the state cut public works by 38 percent. The Fundidora's post-Depression bonanza suffered a momentary setback.[76] Cárdenas, meanwhile, pleaded for workers to tighten their belts, warning that "illegal and unwarranted strikes are detrimental to the country and looked upon with disfavor by the government." Local 67 complied. Union leaders responded to rumors of an "imminent strike" at the Fundidora by staging a rally before the state capital to profess their respect for their president's appeal.[77] Both the economy and demand for Monterrey steel rebounded shortly thereafter. The Fundidora workers responded by setting new production records. Two years later, they would cash in on their patriotic sacrifices.

In late 1939, the steel workers voted unanimously to strike the mill. The threat had loomed since February. Whereas unionists then complained of contract violations, notably the supervisors' failure to comply with safety regulations, they added a new list of demands as the December 1 strike deadline approached. Local 67 called for the dismissal of the blast furnace's general foreman, long despised for his "cruel, inconsiderate, and hateful attitude towards his subordinates." The union also insisted upon the replacement of a company doctor whose "habitual drunkenness" jeopardized

74 Compañía Fundidora de Monterrey to SITMMRM, Mexico City, Sep. 23, 1939, AGN: DAT 290/4.
75 Sección No. 67, SITMMRM, to President Cárdenas, Sep. 14, 1938, AGN: Presidentes 431.7; Stewart, Mexico City, Apr. 5, 1939, SD 812.5045/872.
76 AHFM: *Informe de la Compañía Fundidora de Fierro y Acero de Monterrey*, May 29, 1942; Knight, "The Rise and Fall of Cardenismo," 291; Haber, *Industry and Underdevelopment*, 177, cites a drop in the mill's utilization of installed capacity from 80 percent (1936) to 54 percent (1937).
77 Blocker, Nov. 30, 1937, SD 812.00 NL/175; *El Porvenir*, Nov. 11, 1937.

the workers' health. The workers also pressed for a 25 percent wage hike.[78] The economic issue eventually stalled negotiations in Mexico City and prompted the strike call.

The onset of war in Europe had by then halted North American imports to Mexico and transformed Monterrey steel into an article of primary necessity. Company officials pleaded that a stoppage would reverberate throughout Mexico's economy, hampering public works projects and forcing layoffs at companies dependent upon Fundidora production. The steel workers rejected these appeals to their patriotic sentiments. Not only had productivity risen considerably, they argued, so had the value of Fundidora stock and dividends paid to shareholders. Local 67 rolled off a lengthy and detailed series of figures to back their wage demands and convince labor authorities to sanction the strike. Union officials also called management's attention to the "fabulous salaries" paid out to supervisors and technicians, "who produce practically nothing and in fact constitute a burden on the workers... who could readily perform [their] duties with greater effort, knowledge and efficiency."[79] This became a common lament as the steel mill modernized the plant and recruited dozens of young engineers to supervise production.[80]

The steel workers then cultivated their president's support by appropriating his language of revolutionary nationalism to sanction their movement. Union officials drew the president's attention to the "bonanza" then enjoyed by "Mexico's monopolistic iron and steel company." They celebrated their own role as producers of the steel upon which Mexico's industrial progress depended. The steel workers reminded Cárdenas that their employer was maximizing profits as a result of wartime production in the United States. Consistent with their subsequent philosophy, they expressed their pride in manufacturing steel for creative, nation-building ends rather than the destruction of "defenseless pueblos." Now, Local 67 wrote Cárdenas, "our members only aspire to reap a minimum part of the copious profits obtained at the expense of our noble, sincere, and patriotic efforts." The company's "fabulous earnings enrich a minority" of shareholders, they went on, including Monterrey's "magnates of national industry, the principal owners of Fundidora stock."[81] The steel workers reminded Cárdenas of the union struggles that engulfed Monterrey in February 1936, harking back to "the memorable occasion when you harshly reprimanded [the *regiomontano* industrialists] for their failure to cooperate in Mexico's progress." Finally,

78 Sección No. 67, SITMMRM to Evaristo Araiza, General Manager, Fundidora Monterrey, Nov. 24, 1939, AGN: DAT 290/4.
79 Ibid.
80 Castañeda and Contreras interviews.
81 Monterrey's industrial elites were in fact relatively minor shareholders in the firm.

they concluded, "our Local 67 emerged from that formidable battle . . . and placed itself at the vanguard of the working masses, setting a palpable example of unity, brotherhood, and the collective strength of labor." The steel workers concluded with an appeal to the president's "unbreakable will to heed the workers' call."[82]

Monterrey braced for a strike at the city's largest employer. The threat prompted "a wake-up call in all sectors of society." As the press noted, a strike at the mill would reverberate in the companies that supplied the Fundidora and merchants dependent upon steel worker wages. Moreover, the shift to wartime production in the United States had already impacted local industry. Shortages of industrial material forced several major employers to reduce operations to three-day weeks. Two days before the strike, as negotiations dragged on in Mexico City, Local 67 called for the smeltermen to organize "union guards" to protect plant gates from strikebreakers. The ASARCO workers elected to continue working to provide "resistance funds" to their Miners Union comrades. The reciprocated solidarity proved unnecessary. At 4:00 A.M. on December 1, eight hours before the strike's deadline, labor authorities in Mexico City intervened and the walkout was averted.[83] The Mexican economy's dependence on Monterrey steel certainly prompted the intervention. Most important, the company offered a 20 percent wage hike and agreed to Local 67's contract proposals. The Fundidora also pledged to construct new company housing, augment the pension fund, and concede to the union's long-time demand that workers receive full-wage payments as accident compensation.[84] Labor peace thus reined as the Fundidora entered into a new phase of development prompted by wartime exigencies.

The president who Monterrey's steel workers credited for their "emancipation" left office shortly thereafter. While "Don" Lázaro departed, the spirit of Cardenismo lived on in the furnaces, workshops, union hall, and neighborhoods inhabited by the "men of steel." Adolfo Prieto, who pledged in 1926 to forge them into "the genuine aristocracy of the national proletariat," saw his promise realized by the time of his death. The steel workers certainly fit Prieto's vision of an aristocracy of relatively affluent proletarians who mastered their specialized trades. Moreover, the Cárdenas years saw the steel workers' Local 67 supplant Monterrey's railroaders as the vanguard of Monterrey's revolutionary union movement. Thus the conservative and respectable labor aristocrats who forged their workmates into the Great Steel Family of the 1920s gave way to a new generation, one that shaped the

82 Sección No. 67, SITMMRM to President Cárdenas, Dec. 14, 1939, AGN: DAT 290/4.

83 *El Norte*, Nov. 22–Dec. 2, 1939; *El Porvenir*, Nov. 29–Dec. 2, 1939, Jan. 2, 1940; Carlson to State Department, October 10, 1939, SD 812.00 NL/213.

84 *El Norte*, Jan. 2, 1940.

subsequent history of labor relations at the Fundidora guided by the ideals of Cardenismo. That was a development that Prieto never foresaw but accepted nonetheless, consistent with his liberal ideals of industrial relations. In fact his company's acquiescence to the dramatic shift from conservative to revolutionary unionism did much to uphold the steel workers' loyalty to the Fundidora and their respect for "Don Adolfo."

Upon his passing in 1945, Prieto would thereafter be credited as a man who took charge of the Fundidora in 1907 and guided the mill through nearly four decades of immense challenges and change. Thus when eulogizing Prieto, the company could rightly claim that, "The workers of the Monterrey plant always displayed respect and fond sympathy for him, and he always remembered the help and solidarity with which they all collaborated with him during the Fundidora's most difficult times." His nephew, Carlos Prieto, would inherit control of a company that remained one of Mexico's most renowned and successful industrial enterprises for decades to come. Much like the brewery workers, the "men of steel" continued to take immense pride in their and their employer's role in helping Mexico achieve a degree of economic independence. And just as the Cuauhtémoc operatives credited Luis G. Sada with their impressive welfare benefits, so also did rank-and-file steel workers later acknowledge Prieto for the housing, athletic programs, maternity hospital, and schools that were hallmarks of Fundidora paternalism. One thus remembered him as a "cultured and visionary man . . . [who] demonstrated great affection for the workers and their families."[85] The steel workers did so because those benefits ensured that their children enjoyed the life opportunities and standards of living to which they had long aspired. But their union made sure that future generations knew that this outcome was as much a product of paternalism as of revolutionary unionism.

85 AHFM: *1944 Informe*, March 27, 1945, 15; Gabino Martínez Lozano, *La Maestranza: Crónica de Fundidora* (Monterrey, 2000), 19; Castañeda, Contreras, and García interviews; Domínguez interview in Arenal, *Diéz años después*, 31.

The Institutionalized Revolution

Histories of Mexico's revolution often conclude the story with President Cárdenas's retirement from public life. The year 1940, then, marks a watershed, the moment when so many revolutionary hopes had been fulfilled and the revolutionary project therefore concluded. In the six years following his inauguration, the state sanctioned the unionization of hundreds of thousands of workers. The government distributed millions of acres of land to farm workers and peasant villages. Key industries like the railways and oil had been nationalized by the state. The Cárdenas regime established the foundations for stability by taming the last of the rebellious generals and by fashioning a corporatist political machine that ran on the votes of loyal workers, peasants, and a growing middle class. A party that ruled for the rest of the century safeguarded the reforms that did away with Porfirian Mexico and ushered in a new, postrevolutionary order, the one of political stability and economic growth known as the "Mexican miracle." So read the "official" history of the revolution, the one fashioned by ruling party ideologues and taught to generations of Mexican schoolchildren. The story endured because much of it rang true.

By the late twentieth century, few events in modern Latin American history had produced greater scholarly output than the Mexican Revolution. Scholars who witnessed the upheaval portrayed it as a "social revolution." In this "orthodox" view, the common people struggled "to carve a new and better world for themselves and in doing so destroyed the visible forms of an older society."[1] The revolution thus abolished the old order and transformed social relations. The scholarly consensus changed by the 1970s. Revisionist scholars downplayed the popular nature of revolution, disputed its "official" history, and even denied its revolutionary character. They portrayed the upheaval as an intraelite struggle whose victors formed a more centralized state and resumed the prerevolutionary process of capitalist development.[2]

---

1 Frank Tannenbaum, *Mexico: The Struggle for Peace and Bread* (New York, 1950), 51, 55.
2 Adolfo Gilly, *La revolución interrumpida* (Mexico, 1972); Arnaldo Córdova, *La política de masas de cardenismo* (Mexico, 1974); Ramón Eduardo Ruiz, *The Great Rebellion, Mexico 1905–1924*

Whereas orthodox scholars saw trade unions or land reform as products of popular agency, the revisionists perceived social reform as a top-down means by which an authoritarian state coopted the masses and defeated their popular and democratic aspirations. These rival schools both echoed contemporary views. The revisionist paradigm of corporatist subordination proved remarkably consistent with the government's own critics in the 1930s, be they conservatives or communists. Likewise, union activists of the era typically portrayed their conquests as the result of working-class mobilizations rather than top-down reforms or benevolent rewards. Therein lies the value of a "postrevisionist" historiography that synthesizes the orthodox emphasis on popular movements and the revisionist accounts of state formation. As the Monterrey case demonstrates, government policy implementation entailed an interactive process of negotiation amongst political authorities, local elites, and rival groups of workers. Thus both company paternalism and revolutionary unionism were historical outcomes forged in the struggles between industrialists, the working class, and the revolutionary government.

Consider paternalism. Monterrey's unique system of welfare capitalism marked the intersection of working-class culture and corporate resistance to state labor policy. Their employers may have financed it, but veteran workers collaborated in the establishment and administration of company welfare programs. Building on traditions of mutual aid, it satisfied rank-and-file aspirations to self-improvement, recreational diversions, education for their children, and social security for their families. The state thus sanctioned a system that abetted its project of working-class cultural transformation. Yet laborers also aspired to working conditions that were as safe as their industries permitted. They chafed at arbitrary treatment by tough and overbearing foremen. They resented unilateral speedups and rationalization schemes. Workplace grievances cut against the benevolent grains of paternalism and transformed the shop floor into a crucible of working-class militance. Like the rural poor struggling for land, the urban proletariat depended upon grass-roots organizing, experienced leadership, and state mediation to overcome elite resistance.[3] Their actions pressured the revolutionary state to make good on what workers perceived as its constitutional obligation to defend labor's rights. The shifting political winds could limit or sustain the effectiveness of popular mobilizations. Union aspirations that predated Cardenismo were thus achieved in the 1930s. But the achievement of revolutionary unionism owed as much to popular

(New York, 1980); Alan Knight offers a critical synthesis of the historiographical debate in "The Mexican Revolution: Bourgeois, Nationalist, or Just a 'Great Rebellion'?" *Bulletin of Latin American Research* 4 (1985), 1–37.

3 See Paul Friedrich, *Agrarian Revolt in a Mexican Village* (Chicago, 1970).

aspirations and rank-and-file solidarity as to the government's drive to unify Mexican workers. After all, it was not only elite resistance, but opposition from brewery and glass workers, that led the same government to abandon its project of working-class unification in Monterrey.

The urban polarization generated by state labor policy proves consistent with research on the Mexican countryside. The government's agenda of agrarian reform and anticlericalism turned villages against one another and provoked factional divides within communities. So too did the issue of unionism divide Monterrey and engender fervent rivalries among workers. Many perceived militant unionism as a self-defeating cause. Fear became an important factor in their calculations. The industrialists fired labor activists, enlisted the violent tactics of the Gold Shirts, and organized their "white" unions to resist the inroads of Cardenismo. Their actions led Mexican revolutionaries to relegate the Monterrey elite to the same counterrevolutionary pantheon as the wealthy landowners who resisted state policy through organized violence.[4] But some peasants protested agrarian reform as well. And those who waged economic struggles against the rural elite could prove as obstinately conservative in defense of their own cultural values and traditions. Their defiance stymied many a revolutionary project in the Mexican countryside.[5] The Monterrey case extends our understanding of popular conservatism to urban, industrial Mexico. The *regiomontano* workers' resistance to unionism, their participation in antigovernment rallies, and their enlistment in Nationalist Civic Action reflected something more than the industrialists' powers of coercion. Workers manifested their own independent disposition to preserve social stability, preferring the gradual evolution of paternalism to the risks of militance. Revolutionary unions threatened their economic security, the interests of families, and ultimately the cultural values and regional identities that underpinned a history of class collaboration. As in many rural communities, these urban proletarians mobilized to defend a way of life threatened by an alien and intrusive state. As John Sherman suggests, the "fundamentally conservative nature" of the post-Cardenista state becomes more understandable given the apparent breadth of these sentiments in 1930s Mexico.[6]

When that decade ended, there remained much to be resolved. The advent of union bossism and working-class "cooption" that scholars attribute to Cardenismo remained an uncertainty in the 1930s. Monterrey's

---

4 John Sherman, *The Mexican Right: The End of Revolutionary Reform, 1929–1940* (Westport, CT, 1997), 41, 56.

5 See Mary Kay Vaughan, *Cultural Politics in Revolution: Teachers, Peasants, and Schools in Mexico, 1939–1940* (Tucson, 1997); Jennie Purcell, *Popular Movements and State Formation in Revolutionary Mexico* (Durham, 1999).

6 Sherman, *The Mexican Right*, xiii.

revolutionary unionists had long voiced their fears of sacrificing their political independence to Mexico City. For that reason, the emergence of corporatism did not lead to a smooth working-class integration into the ruling party. It was a process of negotiation through which workers won their "quotas of power" from the Cárdenas regime. Historians may relate the corporatist labor–state alliance to his government. But the workers who lived through the experience credit "Don Lázaro" more for their "emancipation" from Porfirian labor practices than the subordination of their interests to those of the ruling party. They look back to the 1930s and recall the radical promises of Cardenismo, a moment when they pressured a tutelary state to sanction their drive for industrial democracy. Monterrey's unionists reminisce upon the years when they elected blue-collar workers like Félix Torres to Nuevo León's Congress. They laud the electrical worker for having returned from the corridors of power to his working-class roots. Many came to deplore the "professionals who came out of universities" and parlayed their CTM posts into lucrative careers in politics. Recalling the 1930s and 1940s, Manuel Carranza remembers that, "Back then the unions acted honestly, effectively, and cleanly. . . . [T]hey were genuinely revolutionary unions that assumed the role for which they were created, because they were organizations created by the workers themselves."[7] His testimony neatly bridges the orthodox and revisionist historiographies of Mexico's revolution. Like Carranza, many *regiomontanos* experienced the social revolution that orthodox historians described. They subsequently struggled to keep the spirit of Cardenismo alive. But by the end of the 1940s most had seen their popular and democratic aspirations defeated. It is that crucial and transitional decade in Mexican history that we now examine.

From Contention to Conciliation

Looking back from the early twenty-first century, the Cárdenas years loom as an exceptional epoch that cast a long shadow over modern Mexican history. In a remarkably brief period the Mexican people witnessed the dramatic socioeconomic reforms and the consolidation of a ruling party that became Cárdenas's legacy. It proved to be a unique moment, one that therefore ensured the president's legendary status among his government's benefactors and supporters. But Cardenista policy also exacerbated a condition that the revolution had created: the polarization of Mexico's politics and society. Monterrey was but a highly visible reminder of the state of the nation. Cárdenas had responded to the conservative winds blowing out of the North and across urban Mexico by shaving the radical edge from government policy. The moderation that began in 1938 set the backdrop

---

7 Villarreal and Carranza interviews.

for presidential succession in 1940. Restrained from reelection by constitutional principle and personal choice, Cárdenas acquiesced to his more conservative successor, Defense Secretary Manuel Avila Camacho. So did the Mexican left. CTM and Communist Party leaders both asserted the need to consolidate Cardenista reforms given the fascist threat at home and abroad. As Alan Knight suggests, "conciliation had a definite logic" given contemporary fears of a military coup and the global context of a world at war. Just as the leftward tilt of President Cárdenas's policies responded to popular mobilizations and personal priorities, so was Avila Camacho "moved by circumstances and inclination to the right."[8]

The policy of moderation would prompt a significant working-class defection from the ruling party coalition. It also did little to placate the Mexican right or an urban middle class pressed by economic recession and embittered by political corruption. Thus did a multifaceted coalition of disaffected unionists, business conservatives, lay Catholics, and fascist sympathizers rally behind General Juan Almazán, the millionaire opposition candidate whose lucrative business ventures blossomed during his ten-year command of the Monterrey military garrison. However, while Almazán berated the government for corrupting the "promises of the revolution," his vague promises of reform differed more in tone than substance from those of the "official" candidate. Having been crafted by its labor wing, the ruling party's new Six-Year Plan seemed to conservatives to promise a continuity of Cardenismo. But the candidate's campaign-trail stumping suggested otherwise.

Avila Camacho abandoned the Cardenistas' pugnacious language of class for one of national unity. His rhetoric of conciliation, anti-communism, and respect for family and religion rang familiar to *regiomontanos*. Indeed, Avila Camacho visited Monterrey at least five times during the course of his campaign in a "conscious, conspicuous attempt to court the businessmen of Monterrey."[9] The industrialists financed the new Partido Acción Nacional (PAN), the conservative opposition party founded in 1939. But they courted Avila Camacho as well, feting the candidate at a lunch after he toured the brewery and glassworks. The candidate, in turn, praised the *regiomontanos* as business leaders "who dream and plan for the prosperity and greatness of Mexico."[10] Like his opponent, Avila Camacho promised to defend working-class gains, hedging his populism with warnings against militancy. After all, he claimed, "the laboring class has been able to progress in this city

8 Knight, "The Rise and Fall of Cardenismo," 295, 307; see also Ariel José Contreras, *México 1940: Industrialización y crisis política* (Mexico, 1977); Luis Medina, *Historia de la Revolución Mexicana, 1940–1952: Del cardenismo al avilacamachismo* (Mexico, 1978), 48–136.
9 Saragoza, *The Monterrey Elite*, 193.
10 Quoted in Knight, "The Rise and Fall of Cardenismo," 297.

without such struggles as had taken place in other parts of the country."[11] The city's CTM leaders dutifully endorsed Cárdenas's successor. But reports from the industrial union assemblies indicated widespread rank-and-file apathy if not opposition toward the ruling-party candidate. Meanwhile, the international press predicted that an Avila Camacho government would retreat from social reformism and attempt to discipline labor to promote private capital investment.[12] The pundits proved to be right.

The ruling party won the most visibly fraudulent election in modern Mexican history. While Almazán garnered massive support in the cities, ballot stuffing, coerced voting, and the mobilization of the rural electorate allowed the PRM to claim its disputed victory. Despite the political violence that ensued (and claimed dozens of lives), Almazán's was the last viable challenge to ruling party dominance for decades to come. The eclectic nature of the opposition ensured its short-term survival, the rightist PAN being a largely ineffective exception until the 1980s. Meanwhile, the federal government indeed moderated its policies on nearly every front, from education and church–state relations to agrarian reform and labor. Thus did conciliation begin. It begot results by mollifying the regime's middle-class and conservative critics. Cardenista reforms had integrated union workers and farmers into Mexico's "revolutionary family." But it fell upon the rulers of the 1940s to negotiate an enduring political consensus and thereby institutionalize what became an effectively *post*revolutionary order. The government's capacity to maintain that consensus owed a good deal to the steady economic growth that began during the Second World War and was abetted by a fivefold increase in federal spending in the 1940s alone.[13] Thus began the so-called "Mexican miracle" of sustained growth and political stability that distinguished Mexico from its Latin American neighbors for the next forty years.

The state now hinged Mexico's future not on economic redistribution but on development and production. As in earlier times, a new generation of policymakers saw industrialization as the key to the country's recuperation. Labor and the left endorsed a project that promised to liberate Mexico from the clutches of backwardness and dependency. So did the private sector, whose boosters rekindled the prerevolutionary ideal that "the salvation of Mexico lies in industry." Industrial development would not only generate national wealth and create jobs; it promised to combat illiteracy and uplift those downtrodden Mexicans "who only wear sandals and unbleached cotton, sleep on the floor, and live in straw and wooden huts." Poverty remained

---

11 McDonough, May 31, Sep. 6, 1939, SD 812.00/NL 206, 211.

12 *El Norte*, Aug. 25–28, Sep. 4, 13, and 25, 1939; *The New York Times*, Feb. 4, 1940.

13 Stephen R. Niblo, *Mexico in the 1940s: Modernity, Politics, and Corruption* (Wilmington, 1999), 89–141.

endemic and industry was the cure. The government put rhetoric to effect with protective tariffs, tax concessions, and a labor policy meant to enhance the investment climate. Industrialization thus proceeded apace, bolstered as much by government policy as wartime restrictions on American exports. During Avila Camacho's term alone, industrial investments quintupled, manufacturing and construction output grew nearly 60 percent, and earnings on capital soared. By 1950, this policy of import-substitution industrialization made the nation largely self-sufficient in consumer goods.[14] Mexico thus began its transformation from a predominantly agrarian to a relatively urban, industrial society. But the process demanded sacrifice on the part of workers, whose considerable hardships galvanized unprecedented levels of protest during and after the war.

Hardship, Profits, and Protest in Wartime Monterrey

Industrial Monterrey was already booming in the early 1940s. "Business in 1941 is expected to be the best for years," the United States consul reported. He then added, in a tone reminiscent of the 1920s, that "interest in political affairs is not so active here as it appears to be in some other parts of Mexico. . . . The people of Monterrey want to be free to work and hope that they will not be hampered by adverse laws or policies."[15] By the time Mexico entered the war in early 1942, Monterrey's workers were again producing record levels of steel, glass, and beer. Their "battle for production" would be Mexico's contribution to the Allied cause. Nearly every local industry boomed during the war, as the conflict curtailed imports and opened new markets in Europe and the Americas. The Fundidora, for example, constructed a second blast furnace, doubling the mill's capacity, and increased its payroll to more than 4,000 workers. The Garza Sadas extended their industrial empire as well. They opened subsidiary brewing and glass plants in Guadalajara and Mexico City. And they further diversified their local holdings, launching Mexico's first major chemicals company (CYDSA) and a steel division (HYLSA) that would one day rival the Fundidora.[16] In the meantime, the rapidity by which Monterrey entered its second phase of industrialization brought unexpected consequences.

In contrast to the prerevolutionary phase of development, securing labor proved a limited obstacle to wartime industrialization. Most local employers

---

14 Confederation of Industrial Chambers quoted in Bohan, Mexico City, SD 812.50/June 8, 1948; Knight, "The Rise and Fall of Cardenismo," 309–10; Enrique Cárdenas, *La hacienda pública y la política económica, 1929–1958* (Mexico, 1994).

15 McDonough, Dec. 31, 1940, SD 812.00 NL/228.

16 Javier Rojas Sandoval, "La industria siderúrgica en Monterrey: HYLSA (1943–1985)," in Mario Cerutti, ed., *Monterrey: Siete estudios contemporáneos* (Monterrey, 1988), 55–90; AHFM: *Informe*, Mar. 27, 1945; Waterman, Jan. 4, 1943, NAW/RG 84 General Records, 1936–1948, Box 62.

simply drew on a rapidly expanding pool of *regiomontano* youth and incoming migrants. Monterrey's population more than doubled during the 1940s, to 350,000, a pattern that was repeated throughout the twentieth century. Some migrants came to seek work in the labor-starved United States, as Monterrey hosted one of three recruitment centers for the Bracero (guest worker) Program. But most of the newcomers were reportedly "farmers [who] continue to desert their properties in favor of industrial work in the city." Despite a boom in residential construction, rural migration strained the city's housing stock. By the end of the war, Monterrey had "outgrown its capacity for providing adequate public utilities in the necessary margin of safety for a city of this size." Its twenty-year-old bus system was "rundown and dangerous." Electrical power outages were common. Moreover, it was reported that "for the first time in its history Monterrey is faced with a serious water shortage." By 1948, authorities had ordered *regiomontanos* to refrain from watering their gardens and filling their swimming pools. That was a short-term solution to what became a persistent crisis, one that eventually transformed the once flood-prone Río Santa Catarina into a dusty riverbed.[17] These urban-industrial ills were compounded by the daily hardships caused by the war.

Mexicans had been warned of a coming spell of disciplined productive effort and belt-tightening sacrifice. And by the mid-1940s, shortages, long lines, and inflation became the common lot of workers and the middle classes alike. By war's end, the retail price index had risen by more than 260 percent, pushing real wages to historic lows. Writing from Mexico City, an American diplomat observed that, "the average Mexican can stand a lot of suffering, but there must be a limit to what even he can stand." Bad harvests worsened their plight. His colleague in Monterrey reported as early as 1942 that, "wives of working people were spending almost their entire day in front of small stores in the hope that some corn would be delivered."[18] Despite the generalized wartime inflation, he found prices to be "without reason" and attributed it to corruption. Poorly enforced price controls offered little reprieve as "hoarding and black market operations dominate the everyday living picture here." Thus four years later, prices of basic commodities remained high and "the cost of living shows no signs of diminishing." Locals were by then charging that the very government agencies "designed to protect the 'man in the street' have themselves been guilty of profiteering." Such hardships contrasted with the conspicuous consumption of those

17 Waterman, May 7, 1946, SD 812.50/5-746; De Zengotita, Mexico City, Sep. 6, 1946, SD 812.50/ 9-646; Moffet, June 18, 1948, NAW/RG 84 General Records, Box 87; for the city's failure to address the long-term water crisis, see Vivienne Bennett, *The Politics of Water: Urban Protest, Gender, and Power in Monterrey, Mexico* (Pittsburgh, 1995).
18 Ailshie, Mexico City, Jan. 9, 1945, SD 812.504/1-945; Waterman, July 1, 1942, NAW/RG 84 General Records, Box 53; Knight, "The Rise and Fall of Cardenismo," 310–11.

Mexicans who prospered during the war. In Monterrey, the "popular temper" thus came to a "breaking point because of the inability to live decently in the face of such apparent wealth as exists in this district." Hunger marches and antigovernment protests became common. In mid-1943, for example, rioting broke out and buses were burned when the municipal government issued fare hikes for public transit. One year later, protest erupted again in response to compulsory wage deductions through which union workers subscribed to a new national health system that offered few immediate rewards.[19] Despite the United States consul's pessimistic forecast, the war's conclusion would bring a measure of relief to *regiomontanos*. It would also unleash an unprecedented level of strikes throughout Mexico.

At the outset, wartime exigencies achieved the formal, albeit tenuous, industrial peace for which many locals had longed. In 1942 Monterrey's red labor leaders signed on to a National Unity Pact under which strikes would be curtailed and the government pledged to defend union rights and safeguard working-class living standards.[20] It failed to achieve the latter objective. But workers indeed adhered to the no-strike pledge during the early years of the war. Throughout 1942, for example, an American observed "a manifest lessening of labor agitation." This owed perhaps to popular support for the Allied cause, one that union leaders endorsed and that President Roosevelt's visit to Monterrey helped bolster. But the United States consul also attributed industrial peace to the changing mood of the labor boards. In contrast to the "lush days of the Cárdenas regime, when only the voice of labor was heard in the courts," they "now render decisions adverse to labor when the circumstances justify."[21]

This was a nationwide trend. Supported by a Supreme Court stacked with conservatives, government arbitrators increasingly rendered decisions favorable to business. This did not, for the United States consul, mean that working-class attitudes had changed. Indeed, "[t]he constant dinning into the minds of labor for a period of years that the patron is his enemy . . . cannot be eradicated immediately." But "the fact that strikes have not been successful, and frequently cost labor more than they have produced, is having a sobering influence."[22] The spell lasted briefly. By 1944, Monterrey was "menaced with complete paralyzation" as "strikes and threats of strikes" were said to be "the order of the day." After two years of hardship, local

---

19 Waterman, July 7, 1946, SD 812.50/5-746; Waterman, June 2, 1943, NAW/RG 84 General Records, Box 62; Knight, "The Rise and Fall of Cardenismo," 311.

20 Waterman, Jan. 31, 1942, SD 812.00 NL/242.

21 Waterman, July 1, Aug. 3, 1942, NAW/RG 84 General Records, Box 53.

22 Waterman, Sep. 1, 1943, NAW/RG 84, General Records, Box 62; for cases filed and resolved in Nuevo León's labor courts during the war, see Luz María Echevarría Reyes, *La paz laboral como activo social: Catálogo de la Junta de Conciliación y Arbitraje, 1941–1948* (Monterrey, 1998).

workers forsook their no-strike pledge to protest falling wages and contract violations. Labor unrest intensified as the war drew to a close, accelerated thereafter, and affected every sector of Monterrey's economy. Of paramount concern were the railroads, an industry plagued by mismanagement, outmoded equipment, and persistent cost-of-living strikes. The state's efforts to resolve the conflicts were complicated by intense interunion quarrels among Local 19's communist leaders and their progovernment rivals.[23] But a series of walkouts at the Fundidora garnered the most attention due to steel's strategic contribution to wartime production and national industrial development.

Like all workers employed by Monterrey's largest industries, the steel workers certainly fared better than most Mexicans during the war. For one thing, their consumer cooperative helped alleviate the effects of hyperinflation. The *cooperativas* not only offered credit but claimed to hold their prices 30 percent below prevailing wholesale costs. Moreover, collective contract revisions boosted the steel workers' average wage 110 percent between 1939 and 1945, setting the standard for other industries to follow.[24] But those wage gains did not simply reflect the company's considerable wartime profits. They also resulted from the steel workers' own militancy. Having established itself as the vanguard of organized labor in Monterrey, Local 67 put its organizational unity and political influence to work. The steel workers struck the mill three times during the mid-1940s, including a two-month walkout to resist management's attempt to curtail the union hiring hall and abrogate seniority rights. Workers who experienced it recall 1948's "strike of 69 days" as a defining moment in their union's history, a walkout that brought immense hardships to the workers' families but reinforced rank-and-file loyalties to Local 67. Looking back, Manuel Carranza recalled that "we would have a great collective work contract precisely because of the hard and tenacious struggles that the union put up" in the 1940s. Its leaders also upheld the union's "social value" by organizing protests against the cost of living, supporting local strikers with legal counsel and "resistance" funds, and walking out in solidarity when Mexican mineworkers struck. Dionisio Palacios remembered of these final years of his own career that, "Local 67's power was so great that [the government] had to put on a good face, whether they liked it or not."[25] Indeed, with nearly 7,000 members employed in the strategic steel and smelting industries, Monterrey's three Miners Unions locals enjoyed

23 Waterman, Mar. 31, May 2, 1944, NAW/RG 84, General Records, Box 70.
24 AGENL: JCA 357/2; AHFM: *Informe*, Mar. 14, 1946.
25 Carranza, Castañeda, Palacios and Solís interviews; Ailshie, Mexico City, Jan. 9, 1945, SD 812.504/1-945; Moffit, June 25, July 2, 20, 23, Aug. 6, 20, Sep. 10, 1948, NAW/RG 84 General Records, Box 87; AHFM, *Informes*, Mar. 27, 1945, Apr. 7, 1949.

considerable clout with the local ruling party and within the national union.

Never again in its subsequent history would Local 67's leaders be more unified nor enjoy greater backing from the national leadership in Mexico City. Leftist militants still dominated Mexico's big industrial unions and their locals through the 1940s. Thus a decade after they joined Local 67, former student activists like Juan Manuel Elizondo and Antonio García Moreno had become seasoned and respected union officials. García Moreno then labored as a machinist, led the Fundidora union, and served in Nuevo León's Congress. He was also considered among the "principle Communists in Monterrey," one who was "intelligent and possibly convinced of his ideas."[26] Meanwhile, the Miners Union was led in those crucial years by none other than Elizondo. After departing Monterrey in 1939, the *regiomontano* had organized mine workers throughout western and northern Mexico. The experience earned Elizondo sufficient support to win his controversial election as the union's secretary general. Despite protests from his own minister of labor and anti-Communists within the union, President Avila Camacho intervened to sanction Elizondo's victory. His college education, strong legal background, and sincere efforts to "work for peace in the mining industry [and] secure maximum benefits for union members" reportedly earned Elizondo the president's confidence. Indeed, Avila Camacho informed one American diplomat that "if all labor leaders in Mexico were like that young man, the country would be saved."[27] Elizondo was therefore an anomaly among labor leaders during a transitional period when the ruling party began to distance itself decisively from the Mexican left.

Elizondo tapped into the president's own nationalism when justifying his union's militant stance toward Mexico's foreign-owned mining companies, which reaped immense profits as labor's earnings declined. As a union independent of the CTM, the Miners refused to subscribe to a no-strike pledge which, in Elizondo's eyes, violated the workers' constitutional rights. Under his leadership, for example, the Miners Union staged a twenty-five-day national strike that paralyzed 105 mines and foundries, including Monterrey's steel mill and smelters. The 1944 strike achieved 30 percent wage hikes and standardized collective contracts for all mine and metal workers. One year

---

26 Lee, Mexico City, Oct. 3, 1944, NAW/RG 84 Confidential Records: 1936–49, Box 5. As late as 1949, well after the PCM's national demise, the detailed reports filed by a concerned U.S. Embassy indicated a strong communist presence in Monterrey's Miners, railroader, electrical workers, and teachers unions.

27 Ironically, the president reportedly did so at the behest of Nuevo León Governor Bonifacio Salinas, whose election Elizondo had opposed in 1939. Avila Camacho subsequently named Elizondo as Mexico's representative to the 1945 Chapultepec Conference and then supported his 1946 election to the Federal Senate. Holland (quoted), Mexico City, June 1, 1945, SD 812.504/6-145; Niblo, *Mexico in the 1940s*, 122–23; Elizondo interview.

later, the government pressured the companies to acquiesce to the union's demand that employers cover workers' contributions to the national health system (IMSS). The Monterrey locals also convinced the IMSS to construct a local clinic for the exclusive use of the city's steel and smelter workers. Those achievements, as well as Elizondo's commitment to internal union democracy, led workers like Salvador Castañeda to reminisce that "the national Miners Union was never in better hands than in the epoch of Juan Manuel Elizondo."[28] That democratic legacy, we shall see, came to an end after Elizondo's tenure. But the unity achieved within Local 67 and with the national leadership allowed the steel workers to defend and strengthen their collective contract. That legacy survived as Mexico's industrialization promised a strong and enduring demand for Monterrey steel.

There Were Many Betrayals

The labor militancy that had seemingly defined the Cárdenas years thus persisted through the 1940s. But the political climate was changing along with the causes of worker protest. Unions were on the defensive, struggling to restore lost wages and safeguard earlier conquests. Organizing drives were rare and proved unsuccessful. As they had during the 1920s, Monterrey's leading industrialists swiftly dismissed union activists with severance pay, a legal strategy that labor courts condoned once again. But such resistance could cost them dearly.[29] They therefore preempted union activism with high wages, good benefits, effective vigilance, and selective recruitment. Indeed, the industrialists had become "so careful regarding the labor ideology of the men they hire that they [did so] only through a cooperative central body that maintains a black list of undesirable workers." When the Garza Sadas opened their HYLSA steel plant, for example, they recruited their initial 700 employees from the family's other subsidiaries. They then contracted North Americans to train the new recruits. Monterrey industrialists would subsequently transfer the recruitment policies wherever they invested capital. Thus when they opened petrochemical plants in Tampico, they reportedly "investigate[d] the family backgrounds of every person who presents a job application to be sure they don't come from 'a radical PEMEX [oil worker] family'." As their industrial empire expanded, they introduced thousands of new workers to the practices of paternalism and enlisted them in a rechristened National Federation of Independent Unions. Indeed, the employers' labor recruitment agency, itself a "subsidiary of the Chamber

28 The 1944 strike in Ailshie, Mexico City, Jan. 9, 1945, SD 812.504/1-945; AHFM: *Informe*, Mar. 27, 1945; Castañeda, Elizondo, and Palacios interviews; Elizondo, *De historia y política*, 33–34; IMSS benefits in AHFM: *Informe*, Mar. 14, 1945.
29 AGENL: JCA 242/6, 410/4, 411/6, 415/5.

of Commerce . . . also assist[ed] in the formation of company unions." By the late 1940s, Monterrey's business leaders could rightly boast that the majority of their industrial workers were "controlled" by white unions.[30]

The revolutionary project of working-class unification remained unfulfilled. But state labor policy did produce one unforseen consequence: the corporate solidarity and activism of Monterrey's industrial elite. By the 1940s, ruling party policies to promote industrialization and tame union militancy promised profitable returns. But the businessmen upheld their mistrust of central government authority. The future remained uncertain. President Cárdenas, after all, had been expected to follow his predecessors' policies. Moreover, the consolidation of a local ruling-party machine over which they enjoyed minimal influence meant that the gap separating their political and economic clout was and remained vast. The industrialists therefore organized themselves and took measures to ensure the long-term success of their corporate labor strategies. Monterrey's pioneer of paternalism, the brewery's Luis G. Sada, had passed away. His extended family's growing industrial empire demanded a new generation of managers, engineers, and personnel specialists. Thus did his cousin, Eugenio Garza Sada, found a private university, the Monterrey Technological Institute (ITESM). Opened in 1943 and modeled on his American alma mater, M.I.T., the "Tec" became Mexico's leading business and engineering school. Its monthly journal, *Relaciones Industriales*, quoted American management experts, analyzed Mexican labor disputes, and preached the gospel of company paternalism.[31]

By the mid-1940s, Monterrey's industrialists were said by their American golf partner to be "gradually and successfully spreading their influence throughout the republic."[32] Excluded from the ruling party apparatus, they nearly all belonged to the political vehicle of Mexican conservatism, Partido Acción Nacional. They also remained the primary ideological and financial force behind the Mexican Employers Confederation, the only business association to remain independent of the new corporatist political framework. Founded as a defensive response to state labor policy, the COPARMEX staffed a legal office to counsel employers on the labor law. By 1945, they were demanding that the labor code be reformed to restrict the right to strike and proscribe union participation in electoral politics. But there were limits to their influence. Unlike the Monterrey Group, much of Mexico's growing industrial bourgeoisie needed government protection

30 De Zengotita, Mexico City, Feb. 26, 1947, SD 812.5043/2-2647 (quoted); Rojas Sandoval, "La industria siderúrgica," 61; for Tampico hiring practices, see *Forbes*, Oct. 1979, cited in Nuncio, *El Grupo Monterrey*, 231.

31 *Relaciones Industriales*, Feb., Aug. 1948 in AGN: DGG 2/331 (16)/63-A/33.

32 Waterman, Oct. 16, 30, 1945, NAW/RG 84 Confidential Records, 1936–1949, box 5.

and supported a degree of state intervention to maintain labor peace. Their progovernment manufacturers' association (CNIT) thus agreed to renew their wartime unity pact with the CTM, which the COPARMEX "almost considered class treason." The Monterrey elite would have no truck with organized labor. Indeed, against this backdrop, they had renewed their low-intensity assault on the lone outpost of red unionism in the Garza Sada's empire: the Cristalería glass-blowing division. By early 1946, CTM leaders saw the looming conflict as the opportune moment to "strike [the COPARMEX] at the very heart of its power."[33] Once again, a dispute at the glass works drew nationwide attention to Monterrey.

Conflicts between the United Glass Workers and management had simmered throughout the war. As in other local industries, the wage issue topped labor's list of grievances. Union officials claimed that as the company reaped its wartime profits, its members were forced to work overtime to meet their families' basic needs. But they also protested a history of contract violations that predated the war: the use of "confidential employees" to perform union jobs; the hiring of contract laborers in violation of the union hiring hall; and, the foremen's refusal to recognize their shop committees. They also demanded the owners close the company store, which competed directly with a union-run cooperative, and pay workers' contribution to the IMSS health system. The union put these issues forth in their new collective contract proposal. When negotiations stalled, fifty-five unionists walked off the job in protest. They were fired for "sabotage." The union thus called a strike, which rank-and-file workers supported by a unanimous vote.[34]

One month later, in late May 1946, the national CTM entered the fray. Its leaders called a nationwide general strike for June 7 in solidarity with the striking glass workers. In Mexico City, the conservative press reported the looming strike as a "communist plot" by CTM leaders "to 'conquer' the industrial center of Monterrey." But American officials understood the broader political context. With national elections on the horizon, the CTM sought to impress its strength on the future president. Given "the intransigent attitude of the Monterrey industrialists toward organized labor," it chose the industrial center "for its show of strength."[35] The president intervened and convinced CTM leaders to cancel their strike call. His labor officials rushed to Monterrey to mediate the dispute, doing so at the company's apparent request. But the owners refused to accept the wage accord. By then, an American official reported, "it is generally conceded in businesses circles

33 On COPARMEX see Ben Ross Schneider, "Why Is Mexican Business So Organized?" *Latin American Research Review* 37:1 (2002), 85–89; Medina, *Del cardenismo al avilacamachismo*, 329–39 (quoted).

34 AGENL: JCA 356/4, 357/2.

35 Ailshie, Mexico City, June 18, 1946, SD 812.5045/6-1846.

[in Mexico City] that Monterrey industrialists are unreasonably tightfisted and that workers were entitled to wage increases." In fact, the Garza Sadas proved willing to make a considerable sacrifice rather than permit organized labor to enhance its prestige. They thus held out and, in response, the local CTM announced their own intentions to paralyze Monterrey. By then, the railway union was already "refusing to move freight sent by or destined to Monterrey industry." Thus it was expected that the government would "adopt a firm attitude" since a general strike in Monterrey "would seriously damage the national economy."[36] On the evening of June 10, the citywide strike began. When the electrical workers elected to join the walkout, the governor intervened. In an act of dubious legality, he seized the glass factory, placed it under state management, and signed a contract with the union that conceded to all its demands. Ten years after the elite's 1936 showdown with President Cárdenas, the government's threat of industrial expropriation had materialized. But the political climate that generated that historic confrontation had long since passed. The Garza Sadas filed suit against the government and, months later, the Supreme Court declared the Cristalería seizure unconstitutional.[37]

By then, however, the state had returned the factory to its owners and rank-and-file sympathies for revolutionary unionism had waned considerably. One observer summarized that, "to the joy of the Monterrey business community, things went from bad to worse for the Governor and the intervened plant."[38] Production fell to half its normal levels during the five-month "appropriation." According to the governor's report, the owners cut fuel supplies from their adjoining bottle plant. They also launched an "economic blockade." Their suppliers refused to ship raw materials and their customary purchasers rescinded their orders. The state-appointed manager blamed the fiasco on the white-collar employees. Indeed, he fired thirty-four technicians and supervisors for manifesting their "puritanical loyalty" toward the owners through an alleged campaign of "organized sabotage within and outside the plant." Taken together, these forms of resistance caused production to fall and thus a significant decline in the bonus earnings upon which the glass workers depended. Nuevo León's government spent some two million pesos just to meet payroll and import raw materials. As a result, "the Governor had no alternative but to return the plant to its owners." As soon as he did, the strike began anew. It lasted another two

---

36 Ailshie, Mexico City, May 31, June 14, 1946, SD 812.5045/5-3146, 812.5045/6-1446; Waterman, July 1, 1946, SD 812.5045/7-146.

37 Events leading up to strike in AGENL: *Informe del Gobernador Arturo B. de la Garza, 1946–1947*; AGENL: *Periódico Oficial del Gobierno*, Monterrey, June 10, 1946; Medina, *Del cardenismo al avilaca-machismo*, 338–39.

38 De Zengotita, Mexico City, Jan. 14, 1947, SD 812.5045/1-1447.

months before the labor courts resolved it. The outcome was considered a "clear moral victory for the company."[39] The settlement forced Cristalería to meet the union's wage demands. But the company was not required to pay the back wages that workers demanded. Nor would it reinstate the fired union officers and nearly 200 other laborers, all of whom received their indemnity due by law. Nine months after the initial walkout began, the glass workers returned with a 15 percent pay raise.[40]

Several years later, the "red" union lost its collective contract at Cristalería. Perhaps the company's hard bargaining during the contract negotiations was a calculated attempt to provoke a strike and break the union. If so, the strategy succeeded. The drawn-out conflict proved costly for the owners, but more so for their workers. Those who remained therefore acquiesced to company unionism. The red union's earlier victory failed to deliver the rewards they expected. Supervisors violated the collective contract with impunity and neither the labor courts nor union militancy offered a resolution. Moreover, some workers came to resent the red union's practices as well. As a shop steward, Dionisio Aguilar was pressured to lie on behalf of colleagues who violated work rules by drinking or sleeping on the job. "Even though they were my friends," he lamented, "I felt ashamed for the injustices I had to commit." He recounts the experience and his feelings of betrayal to explain his equally anguished decision to quit the union. Remarking on the strike's aftermath, Aguilar then recalled that, "Within two or three years, everything went back to how it was. . . . [T]he abuses continued, although they were a little more measured." Indeed, the company learned from its earlier setbacks. While they cast a critical eye back on the harsh conditions they endured, retired glass workers universally acknowledge that the Sadas were "just" and "honest men."[41] They remember that the company had fired its most notorious foremen because management understood the role their abuses played in fomenting support for the reds. By the end of the 1940s, former union militants like Aguilar and Juan Montes Orozco had been made foremen themselves. The tactic apparently achieved the intended results. Come the 1970s, a new generation of militants would acknowledge Orozco as a particularly "humanitarian" supervisor within a work environment that once again proved conducive to unionism. He and Aguilar went on to long careers as glass blowers.[42] As such, they both remained beneficiaries of the welfare benefits that their youthful militancy had helped procure.

---

39 AGENL: *Periódico Oficial del Gobierno*, Nov. 13, 1946.
40 Intervener's report and strike settlement in AGENL: JCA 357/2, 365/8.
41 Aguilar, Montes Orozco, Monzón, and Rodríguez interviews.
42 In Garza H., *Cristal quebrado*, 123, a worker recalled of his foreman that he was "very strict but a good person."

The demise of the United Glass Workers was the epilogue of revolutionary unionism in the Garza Sadas' industries. Ruling party officials continued to decry white unions as a violation of labor's constitutional rights. Nuevo León's governor, for example, acknowledged the "better salaries and benefits" offered by local employers. "But with these," he claimed to an audience of metal workers, "they not only pay for labor, but also for the conscience of the worker, knotting his throat, and silencing his protest."[43] In 1947, the Mexican congress even proposed legislation to proscribe company unions. But the minister of labor informed an American that they no longer posed a concern to his government. The diplomat understood why. He reported that their members enjoyed "wages and conditions of work comparable, if not superior" to workers belonging to "national unions." "Indeed," he went on, "single-plant unions are frequently found in enterprises that are outstanding for furnishing their workers with club houses, clinics, and athletic parks and facilities." "This is especially true in Monterrey," he claimed, "where the recreational and medical facilities afforded their employees by some companies cannot be matched elsewhere in the world." For that reason, he concluded, "their workers are vehement in opposing tenders of affiliation from what they consider the corrupt or communistic national bodies."[44]

The outcome of the Cristalería conflict led the American labor attaché to foresee the long-term survival of company unionism in Monterrey. "Regardless of what can be said as to the harm done to labor in the long run," he remarked, "it will be very difficult to convince members of company or independent unions that they would be better off in national or industrial groups." The glass strike demonstrated the limits and risks of state intervention, for which the strikers "paid by being out of work . . . and receiving for that time only a fraction of their wages." The diplomat therefore anticipated "that as long as the situation in Monterrey remains what it is today, the Monterrey workers may be expected to spurn [organized labor] and will be better off for it."[45] His prediction proved correct. Revolutionary unions persisted in those industries for which Monterrey had long held renown: steel, smelting, and railroads. But the times had changed. While the grievances that led the glass workers to once endorse a militant union persisted, the political and social climate had not. Those *regiomontanos* who had taken to the streets in February 1936 could rest contented. A decade after they protested the "communist government of Mexico," a president who shared their conservative political outlook finally arrived at the National Palace.

43 Governor Arturo B. de la Garza quoted in De Zengotita, Mexico City, May 26, 1947, SD 812.5043/5-2647.

44 De Zengotita, Mexico City, Apr. 10, 1947, SD 812.5043/4-1047.

45 De Zengotita, Mexico City, Feb. 26, 1947, SD 812.5043/2-2647.

The Miguel Alemán government would institutionalize Mexico's political system. With his 1946 inauguration, the language of class harmony, anticommunism, and business patriotism so familiar to *regiomontanos* became the ruling party's own mantra. While his predecessor hedged such talk with conciliatory policies toward labor, Alemán's government backed it with uncompromising action.[46] Industrial progress demanded disciplined workers, and labor–state relations thus reached a critical juncture. Throughout Mexico, wildcat strikes, contract disputes, and interunion conflicts threatened to paralyze key industries like the railroads and oil. That militancy defied government policies meant to check wages and promote industrial development. The government claimed communist agitation as the cause of union indiscipline. Its allies in organized labor offered a solution to its dilemma. In the early 1940s, CTM founder Lombardo Toledano had relinquished leadership to Fidel Velásquez and his clique of Mexico City unionists. The so-called five little wolves were staunch anti-Communists with reputations for corruption, opportunism, and a practiced disregard for union democracy. Indeed, after one brief interlude, Velásquez maintained a self-perpetuating hold on the CTM reins until his death in 1997. At the time, however, the labor central's future seemed uncertain. With the ascension of the conservative union bosses, the internal rivalries that had long divided CTM leaders proved beyond reproach. By mid-1948, the railroad, oil, and miner-metalworker unions had all declared their independence from the CTM. As a result, half the confederation's remaining membership hailed from Mexico City alone.[47] Moreover, the militants who led the national industrial unions pledged their formidable support to an independent labor central and to a new party of the Mexican left, the Partido Popular. While their industrial militancy challenged the state's economic project, the dissident unions could have threatened the corporatist foundation of the ruling party itself.

The militants' challenge thus begot the decisive union takeovers known as *charrazos*. The process had immediate ramifications in Monterrey. It began with the state's de facto intervention of the railroad union. Backed (if not instigated) by the government, a rival faction seized the union's Mexico City headquarters in late 1948. The takeover was led by an opportunistic rodeo fan named Jesús Díaz de León, alias *"El Charro"* (The Cowboy). He and his anti-Communist allies charged their opponents with corruption and won official recognition from the ministry of labor. They then seized union

46 The following draws on Ian Roxborough, "Mexico," in Leslie Bethell and Ian Roxborough, eds., *Latin America Between the Second World War and the Cold War, 1944–1948* (Cambridge, 1992), 190–216; Barry Carr, *Marxism and Communism in Twentieth-Century Mexico* (Lincoln, 1992), 164–78; Jorge Basurto, *La clase obrera en la historia de México: Del avilacamachismo al alemanismo (1940–1952)* (Mexico City, 1984).

47 De Zengotita, Mexico City, Nov. 13, 1947, SD 812.5043/11-1347.

locals, purged them of leftists, and negotiated a new collective contract that offered workers docile leadership in exchange for job protection.[48] One year later, a similar fate befell the oil workers' union, resulting in the ouster of communist leaders and the appointment of their progovernment rivals. As in earlier times, Mexican unionists were shaping their strategies in rhythm with Mexico's shifting political winds. Some were opportunists inspired by promises of wealth and power. Others were sincere anti-Communists who discovered relief in the nascent Cold War climate. Whatever their motives, the unions' new *"charro"* leaders herded the railway and oil workers back to the CTM's corral.

In early 1950, delegates from Monterrey's steel mill and smelters arrived in the capital for their union's national assembly. They were sent on a mission: to support a leftist slate headed by their fellow *regiomontano*, Antonio García Moreno. While personal and political animosities had long divided Miners Union leaders, it was also observed that, "in the election of officers and the determination of policy, the democratic process is given full play" in what had become the "lone wolf" of the organized labor movement.[49] But when they arrived at the union hall, delegates representing four-fifths of the union's 50,000 members were denied entry. The militants convened elsewhere and elected the Monterrey steel worker as their secretary general. The defiant gesture marked a symbolic end to the Miners' history of union democracy. The state endorsed their anti-Communist rivals. This *charrazo* met resistance. Months later, 6,000 miners struck the Coahuila coal fields. The government sent in the army, strike funds were seized, and the *charro* leaders started a custom of supplying union strikebreakers. But the miners held out, counseled by García Moreno, and sustained by aid from the Monterrey locals. In early 1951, they staged a fifty-day "hunger caravan" that took some 4,000 miners and metal workers through nearby Monterrey and on to Mexico City. But the government held firm and "the last gasp of militant unionism" collapsed.[50] In its aftermath, the Miners Union applied the exclusion clause against its high-profile militants. Among them were García Moreno and Juan Manuel Elizondo. As Local 67's new president, it fell upon Salvador Castañeda to formally expel his workmates. "He wanted to wash his hands of the deed," Castañeda explained of the national leader. "'You're screwed (*jodido*),' I told him, but he threatened me as well." His voice filled with sorrow, Castañeda simply recalled of the time that, "There

48 For the takeover of Monterrey's Local 19 see *El Norte*, Oct. 22–28, 1948; Moffet, SD 812.504/Oct. 29, 1948; Moffet, Nov. 12, 1948, NAW/RG 84 General Records, Box 87, who reported "much pleasure in local press over reorganization of railroad union and elimination of communists."

49 Ailshie, Mexico City, Jan. 9, 1945, SD 812.504/1-945; De Zengotita, Mexico City, Apr. 10, 1947, SD 812.5043/4-1947.

50 Roxborough, "Mexico," 213 (quoted); Basurto, *Del avilacamachismo*, 226–27.

were many betrayals." He then added that, "We don't always know how to do justice to those who deserve it . . . but [Elizondo and García Moreno] will always have a special place in the memory of Local 67."[51]

The union takeovers of 1947–50 marked a watershed in the history of Mexican labor. The system of industrial relations subsequently known as *charrismo* accomplished three long-term objectives of the ruling party and its labor allies. Since the 1920s, they had perceived unionization as a means of disciplining workers so as to promote Mexico's industrialization. The *charros* also brought their tamed industrial unions into the CTM fold. And, by doing so, they integrated the workers of Mexico's largest and most strategic industries into the newly christened Institutional Revolutionary Party (PRI). Efforts to forge an independent labor central collapsed, thus denying the leftist Partido Popular its potential base of support. Union leaders thereafter delivered blue-collar votes to the PRI and pledged their patriotic support to the government's nationalist industrial policy with a new CTM motto: "For the Emancipation of Mexico."

That workers imbued with the spirit of Cardenismo acquiesced to *charrismo* owed far less to coercion than the success of that economic model. For the next quarter-century, a Mexican "miracle" of sustained growth brought higher wages, expanded social services, and the government concessions necessary to limit rank-and-file dissent. Their living standards rose while many a union worker's children entered Mexico's growing middle class. It has thus been acknowledged that even a tamed union "could be seen to deliver some of the goods; and to many it seemed preferable to a perilous, quixotic militancy."[52] Much like the paternalistic coin proffered by Monterrey's industrialists, *charrismo* had its tarnished flip side as well. The militants who fashioned an enduring Mexican labor movement lost their positions of leadership. Militant unionism would no longer be tolerated in this, a truly *post*revolutionary Mexico. But the activism of the Cardenista generation resulted in the constitutional rights and enduring benefits enshrined in their collective contracts. While workers may have lamented the seeming defeat of democratic unionism, they continued to defend the hard-fought achievements of the 1930s and 1940s, a history of struggle they bequeathed to future generations.

Postscript, Monterrey

The Mexican "miracle" ushered in twenty years of unparalleled peace and prosperity. Come the 1950s, as Monterrey joined in the world's postwar economic boom, civic boosters could look back and take pride in the locals'

51 Castañeda interview.
52 Knight, "The Rise and Fall of Cardenismo," 319.

history of taking on and overcoming obstacles to progress. The challenges had been considerable; and there were more to come. Their ancestors had weathered the region's legendary climate to make the desert bloom into "Mexico's Chicago." Then, in the early twentieth century, revolution and its consequences posed another challenge to the march of industry. But two generations of *regiomontanos* struggled through civil war, meddlesome government policies, political polarization, and wartime hardships to uphold their city's renown as the "Sultan of the North." Monterrey was thus poised to build on its past and capitalize on its unique historical development. In 1951, the city's boosters celebrated the golden anniversary of their famous steel mill. The press embraced the moment to contrast Monterrey with other Mexican cities renowned for their rich colonial heritage but "where time seems to stop with great frequency." Editors admitted that Monterrey "has almost no historical monuments to pride itself on; it lacks archeological ruins ... cathedrals ... and the baroque Mexico of the sixteenth century." "However," they offered, "Monterrey can rightfully boast of some of the most beautiful – even artistic – monuments of our age: the great factories that scrape the sky with their smoking chimneys, the steel towers of the blast furnaces ... and the wonder of its machinery, so perfect, so beautiful, such a friend of man that it almost, almost, has its own soul." Monterrey was thus "a modern city whose watch is perfectly synchronized with our times."[53]

By the century's close, those monuments to industrial progress surrounded many Mexican cities. But the *regiomontanos'* per capita contribution to the nation's gross national product still outpaced that of their Mexico City rivals. Indeed, Monterrey's industrialists extended their economic influence well beyond their hometown. They launched subsidiary steel, brewing, glass, cement, and chemicals plants throughout Mexico and in other Latin American markets. The local elite diversified their holdings as well, branching out into banking, tourism, retail, and media holdings. "Much of this extensive industrial empire," it was noted, "can be traced back to a red brick building in the heart of Monterrey: the Cuauhtémoc Brewery." Industry remained the foundation of their dynasty. And the results of the *regiomontanos'* hard work and entrepreneurial spirit were most evident in Monterrey, where economic opportunity lured "thousands of people who know how to plough but have no idea how to handle a lathe."[54] By the 1990s, rural migrants had transformed the one-time commercial outpost

53 *El Porvenir*, 1951, quoted in AHFM: *Di-Fundidora*, company magazine, May 1, 1982.
54 With less than 4 percent of the population, Monterrey-based companies produced a reported 20 to 25 percent of Mexico's gross national product by the later twentieth century. See *Los Angeles Times*, July 15, 1979 (quoted); *Forbes* (1979); and *Wall Street Journal* (1981) reports in Nuncio, *El Grupo Monterrey*, 216–40; John Davidson, "City Apart," *Mexican Business*, Apr. 1995, 52.

into a sprawling metropolis of more than three million residents. It had also become one of the most polluted cities in the Americas. Through it all, however, foreign observers still encountered a place that they described much like their prerevolutionary predecessors. Monterrey thus retained its image as a producer of steel and beer, and as "Mexico's most American city." Yet it was the unique culture – the *regiomontanos'* "strong sense of regional pride" – that struck journalists most when they reported on Monterrey.[55]

Like so many a manufacturing center, the city's past came to be defined by its captains of industry. "The story of Monterrey," Alan Riding wrote in the 1980s, "has been inseparable from that of the Garza and Sada families." A century of intermarriage between these and a handful of other prominent families ensured the survival of Mexico's most tightly knit clan of elites. They left their stamp through their patronage of museums, private schools, and the sports-crazed city's professional baseball teams, the *Sultanes* and the *Industriales*. Unified by the leadership of Eugenio Garza Sada, this Monterrey Group also "came to symbolize the industrious no-nonsense approach" of the *regiomontanos*.[56] Throughout the second half of the twentieth century, visitors commented frequently on the locals' "habit and pride of work." "Monterrey citizens are proud of their old families," Erna Ferguson found, "but they are proud too that their city lacks the tradition of the leisure hacendado class."[57] "This city," another observed, "is marked by punctuality and efficiency. . . . [T]he mentality of 'leaving things for *mañana*' doesn't exist here." A Mexico City resident informed one reporter that, indeed, the *regiomontanos* were hard working and industrious. But like other *chilangos*, he considered the northerners to be "often stingy, always in a hurry . . . and sometimes we think that they are hardly even Latinos." To those charges, one *regiomontano* businessmen countered that "we're Mexican from head to toe." Indeed, another boasted, "it's as if we were chosen to guide Mexico toward progress." Visitors found that this work ethic and regional chauvinism were displayed by all *regiomontanos*. Be they "corporate executives" or "assembly line workers," they all "share the same values," distrusting central government authority and believing in "hard work, family, education, [and] efficiency."[58] Thus did Monterrey's identity reflect the self-image of its

55 Davidson, "City Apart," 52; Riding, *Distant Neighbors*, 285.

56 Riding, *Distant Neighbors*, 285.

57 Erna Ferguson, *Mexico Revisited* (New York, 1955), 91.

58 David Bertugli, "Monterrey: Mexico's Industrial Dorado," *Town and Country*, Nov. 1980; Davidson, "City Apart," 52; for commentary on the unique qualities of *regiomontano* workers, see Sanford Mosk, *Industrial Revolution in Mexico* (Berkeley, 1950), 272; Jorge Balan, et al., *Men in a Developing Society: Geographic and Social Mobility in Monterrey, Mexico* (Austin, 1973), 36–38; Philip Anderson, "The City That Works," *Maclean's* 110 (1997), 42–47; and Davidson, "City Apart," who considered Monterrey's to be the "most stable, educated, and skilled work force in Mexico" (55).

industrial magnates, whose mastery of public relations ensured the visitors' frequent commentary on company paternalism.

Travelers who toured the brewery sixty years after its founding still considered it "the model factory that all visitors must see." Like those who arrived in the decades to come, they would enjoy a cool Carta Blanca in Cuauhtémoc's shady beer garden and hear a promotional discourse that highlighted the owners' benevolence. They therefore repeated Monterrey's renown as a city that pioneered national standards for welfare benefits and compliance with Mexican labor law. Visiting the Cuauhtémoc Society in the 1950s, Ferguson marveled at the library, theater, billiards hall, and an athletic complex that "offers all sorts of sports fields for women and children as well as men." Nearly three decades later, another reporter found that the industrialists still awarded their "loyal workers with benefits unimaginable in most countries." The companies not only delivered discounted foodstuffs to workers' homes. By then, their subsidized stores offered furniture, electronics, and sporting goods on credit. The expanded colonias of company housing were "luxurious in comparison to working-class standards." Indeed, it was claimed, the industrialists' efforts "to ensure loyalty . . . [and] to keep unions out had created perhaps the most spoiled labor force in the world." But *regiomontano* businessmen belittled the antiunion motives. A glass company executive thus informed a journalist that the Garza Sadas have "always seen these benefits as a way of recognizing our gratitude toward our vast family of robust workers." In fact, he boasted, "North American companies can't compete with us in terms of what we give [our employees]."[59] Other large employers, including General Motors, did indeed offer their postwar Mexican workforce the kind of welfare benefits, educational programs, and cultural activities familiar to *regiomontano* workers.[60] But their early and enduring endeavors lent credence to the *regiomontanos'* claims to be Mexico's pioneers of paternalism.

A system of paternalism once inspired by the North American model later attracted students of labor management from the United States itself. They discovered that the practices instituted after the revolution remained firmly entrenched at century's close. As one study of the brewery observed, "Through recreational activities, the elite transmits its ideology and values to the working class in an informal manner. . . . [T]he [Cuauhtémoc Society] not only pressures the worker and his family to spend free time at the club,

---

59 Ferguson, *Mexico Revisited*, 95; *Los Angeles Times*, July 15, 1979 (quoted); Bertugli, "Monterrey."

60 GM executives also underscored their corporate strategies with the discourse of national industrial progress and working-class betterment heard in Monterrey since the 1920s. See Steven J. Bachelor, "Toiling for the 'New Invaders': Autoworkers, Transnational Corporations, and Working-Class Culture in Mexico City, 1955–1968," in G. Joseph, A. Rubenstein, E. Zolov, eds., *Fragments of a Golden Age: The Politics of Culture in Mexico Since 1940* (Durham, 2001), 273–326.

but it decides how much money the worker can spend on groceries, where he can live, and how he can conduct his private business." The social control of the brewery operatives' lives remained a customary practice. It also, as the analysis suggests, applied principally to men. The mechanization of Cuauhtémoc's bottling and packaging divisions had eliminated "female" work on the production lines by the 1970s. Women remained in clerical positions. But as in earlier times, marriage marked the end of the secretaries' careers. They were forced to retire "because it is believed that a married woman might not to be as pleasant to her boss and be a bad influence on young single women."[61] Perhaps this belief that marriage erodes docility explains the brewery's historical policy of compulsory retirement.

The subsequent masculinization of Cuauhtémoc's workforce proceeded smoothly from management's perspective. Like their counterparts at the glass works, the male workers remained as fearful and distrustful of red unions as their forefathers learned to be. As in earlier times, some workers perceived benefits like housing, loans, company publications, and social festivities as "methods of manipulation and control." One glass worker attributed his workmates' "conformity" to their largely rural backgrounds, because "their earnings and treatment were almost always better than what they received in the countryside."[62] Erna Ferguson also met a brewery worker who countered the claims of company publicists. He informed her, for example, that some workers earned but a third of what the company declared. He also remarked that the "company unions have a good spy system." He therefore chose to remain anonymous, warning her "that he would lose his job if his employer knew he had talked freely." Paternalism thus elicited criticism from workers and at least one satirical polemic from a dissident member of the Garza Sada family itself. However, as another journalist reported, "while some workers complain about this paternalism, none are ready to fight it." Given the relative docility and corruption that came to define the mainstream labor movement, unionism offered limited rewards and considerable risks. The anonymous worker interviewed by Ferguson may have turned a critical eye on the brewery, but he harbored no illusions about organized labor. Their leaders, he believed, "have gone into politics, and proved [to be] traitors to their people."[63] By then, his was a sentiment shared by many red union workers as well.

61 Maria de Lourdes Melgar Palacios, "Economic Development in Monterrey: Competing Ideas and Strategies in Mexico," (Ph.D. diss., Massachusetts Institute of Technology, 1993), cited in Davidson, "City Apart," 54.

62 Garza H., *Cristal quebrado*, 140–50.

63 Ferguson, *Mexico Revisited*, 95–96; Bertugli, "Monterrey." For a biting yet humorous satire of the elite and their labor policies ("If you give your workers everything, they will ask for nothing. Begin by giving them a union."), see Irma Salinas Rocha, *Los meros meros de Monterrey: Manual de conducta para multimillonarios* (Mexico City, 1988), esp. 158–65.

Given the national prominence of the Monterrey elite, it was their story of success and the benefits bestowed on workers that garnered international acclaim. But had journalists ventured to the east-side neighborhoods surrounding the Fundidora, they would have discovered a past and present that often countered Monterrey's master narrative. Paternalism certainly persisted at the steel mill, albeit under joint union-company administration. With Don Adolfo's death in 1944, control of the firm and Prieto's "liberal" managerial style passed to his nephew. Carlos Prieto would relocate the corporate offices to Monterrey. But Fundidora executives remained conspicuously aloof from the organizational life of the local business elite.[64] Moreover, aside from their high standard of living, the working-class culture that locals identified with the "men of steel" departed notably from that of Monterrey's white union workers.

As a long-time union physician later remarked, "being born strong, healthy, hardworking, and rebellious at the Fundidora also meant studying in the company schools, playing sports on its fields . . . occupying your father's place at work, [and] entering fully into union activities." Many a steel worker encouraged his children to pursue careers in the professions. But throughout the postwar years, the appeal of high-paying jobs and the macho image of steel work lured third- and fourth-generation workers into the mill. Aurelio Arenas, for example, could count seventy family members who had labored at the plant by the 1970s. Such life choices remained a prerogative of the workers' sons.[65] But María de Robles Cantú asserted that "being the daughter of a Fundidora worker was like knowing you had a secure future." "We were all part of a big family," she reminisced, "and even more so because we lived in a neighborhood of employees . . . and we all eventually dated and then married steel workers." With that life came material well-being, and bouts of anxiety. "All of us wives of Fundidora workers lived in constant fear of accidents," one recalled, "and when the accidents happened they were no small deal." Those anxieties heightened when sons followed fathers into the mill. Like María, her children and grandchildren were born in the company's maternity clinic and attended Prieto School. The males became steel workers. But unlike María, her daughters came of age in an era when they could continue their careers in commerce or nursing despite having families of their own.[66]

The "Great Steel Family" had fashioned working-class traditions not unlike that of many brewery or glass workers and their kin. What distinguished the former was the "strong tradition of union struggle" that became

---

64 Waterman, Oct. 30, 1945, NAW/RG 84, Confidential Records, Box 5.

65 Castañeda interview; physician and Arenas interviews in Sandra Arenal, *Fundidora: Diéz años después* (Monterrey, 1996), 97, 160.

66 Robles interview in Arenal, *Fundidora,* 223–29; Arenal, *En Monterrey no solo hay ricos,* 62.

a "common value" among steel workers. This aspect of their identity "frightened, was repudiated by, and caused constant uneasiness for the country's most conservative business group." After all, a local physician noted, "such a bad example dared to exist in the same city where the regiomontano employers walk hand in hand with their workers' representatives."[67] Yet the Monterrey elite could do little to proscribe this unwelcome remnant of Cardenismo. They simply refused employment to the steel workers' kin and reminded their own employees of their paternalistic benevolence. Local 67's leaders, on the other hand, made sure that young workers knew that their standard of living was as much a product of paternalism as of revolutionary unionism. "Although the work was really rough," Manual Carranza recollected, "the Fundidora always allowed me to have a good salary, good benefits, and the best schools for our children." "But all that," he went on, "owed to the fact that we had the best collective contract, which was itself the product of many years of struggle by the Miners Union workers."[68] Those benefits and conquests endured as the steel mill entered into the prosperous postwar decades.

Partisan struggles for union leadership survived as well. Indeed, the advent of *charrismo* may have concluded the struggles for power between leftists and progovernment leaders in Mexico City. But if the Fundidora offers a representative case, it did little to diminish the battles for supremacy within Mexico's industrial union locals. Out in the provinces, the internal democracy for which the Miners Union was renowned survived the 1950 *charrazo*, albeit in a fashion that mirrored Mexico's own system of one-party rule. The union held elections regularly and enforced the no-reelection clause in its statutes. But union posts alternated between two rival factions who both earned reputations as *charros* for their unambiguous support for the ruling party. Salvador Castañeda acknowledges that "those of us chosen to lead the union in those years were called *charros* by the people that opposed us, and *charro* in our language means servile, being the company's errand boy." The leaders were so labeled for practicing what Castañeda considered to be "honorable" and "disciplined unionism." Rather than put forth "excessive demands," he argued, "the union was like the administrator of the Fundidora's interests." Latin America's oldest mill was no longer Mexico's monopoly steel producer. Come each contract revision, Local 67's leaders therefore studied the company's production, costs, and earnings, and "the union never asked for a wage increase that was not justified by the profits."[69] Nor did they defy the ruling party. Instead, union officials used their allotted

67 Arenal, *Fundidora*, 97.
68 Carranza interview.
69 Castañeda interview, who also claims that his post-1950s successors within the union leadership forsook the principles of honor that had guided his generation.

posts on the city council, in the state Congress, and on the regional branch of the federal labor court to defend working-class interests. From a rank-and-file perspective, they apparently delivered the goods; for even their leftist rivals admitted that their voice remained a minority one within Local 67.

Dissidents called this system by which rival PRI factions alternated in power "*charrismo* disguised as democracy." They blamed it on national union leaders, who sanctioned a process that kept their allies in power and helped defuse internal disputes. Their resistance mainly expressed itself in union assemblies. There, they took leaders to task for abuses of power that ranged from shop-floor favoritism to taking kickbacks from wholesalers who supplied the union-run cooperative. The dissidents also castigated their leaders for "tampering with politics and forgetting about the workers' problems." From their perspective, it was their rivals' ongoing competition for the "quotas of power" and the "booty" they skimmed from the cooperative that divided Local 67. The leftists dissidents put forth their own slates during union elections. "Of course we lost," Manuel Carranza admitted, "but we really put up a tough fight in the assemblies." Their opponents labeled them "divisionists" and "anti-unionists." But they rarely silenced the incipient opposition "because that way they could claim that we had democracy in the union." So the dissidents persisted. They struggled as much against *charrismo* as rank-and-file passivity. Among them was Jesús Medellín, whose great uncle was among Local 67's founding organizers. Medellín later noted that while "discontent" was evident on the shop floor, attendance at union assemblies declined in the 1960s as workers came to sense that "the local's assemblies were nothing but a show."[70] But their union democratization movement progressed as the political climate in Mexico grew increasingly tense.

By the 1970s, a new generation of social activists were challenging the postwar political consensus in the union halls, campuses, and streets of urban Mexico. What underpinned these movements was a growing sense of indignity at a corrupt system of authoritarian rule. What galvanized them was the government's schizophrenic response. Outright repression proved rare by Latin American standards. But instances like the 1968 massacre of hundreds of student protestors in downtown Mexico City radicalized the left. Two years later, the government tried to cure the PRI's tattered credentials with a dose of populism. Contemporaries likened the process to the political opening of the Cárdenas years. Policy rarely matched the rhetoric, which included tacit support for union democratization. But the opening prompted an upsurge of militant activism, especially in the provinces and, most notably, in Monterrey. Leftist students struck the University of

---

70 Carranza interview; Manuel Domingúez, Rafael Duéñez, and Jesús Medellín interviews in Arenal, *Fundidora*, 35–37, 113–17, 136–38.

Nuevo León and a communist guerrilla movement, the September 23rd League, tried to destabilize the government through urban terrorism. In 1973, they killed the city's eighty-year-old industrial patriarch, Eugenio Garza Sada, during an aborted kidnaping in front of the brewery. Some 150,000 *regiomontanos* turned out for his funeral in a massive outpouring of public grief. The swift repression that ensued disbanded the communist guerrillas. But it was against this political backdrop that young workers challenged their entrenched union leaders. They failed at Cristalería, where the punitive dismissal of 400 dissident glass blowers concluded a rare attempt to overthrow a company union. The same issues that prompted the 1936 strike, from abusive foremen to workplace safety issues, prompted their movement. Moreover, as in earlier times, the glass workers had drawn inspiration from events at the steel mill.[71]

In fact, the Fundidora insurgency resembled the one that gave birth to Local 67 itself. In 1965, the dissidents established the "5th of February" Centro de Orientación Sindical (COS), a "union school" modeled after the clandestine labor circles organized by Spanish Communists during Franco's dictatorship. According to Carranza, they named the COS "in honor of our Constitution, since that's where our rights are written and we, the working class, had the duty to enforce them." Their movement began with some seventy workers, who circulated a newspaper and staged informal meetings in the back of local cantinas. Among the unenforced "rights" they protested were their leaders' failure to address grievances related to workplace dangers in the increasingly antiquated mill. They also defended the "*eventuales*," hundreds of young workers who labored at the mill but enjoyed neither full-time status nor union rights. They were angered by recent layoffs and, as concerned workers knew, some *eventuales* were tied to student militants and the September 23rd League.[72] As the insurgency spread, so did the divisions among the brazenly "corrupt and anti-democratic" leaders themselves. As Medellín recalled, "the corruption became so barefaced that some of the traditional leaders rebelled against the others." Several had their union rights suspended and joined the dissident COS movement. Then disaster struck the mill. In November 1971, a faulty crane malfunctioned and dumped a kettle of molten steel on dozens of furnacemen. Seventeen workers died in the gravest industrial accident in Monterrey's history. Generalized discontent gave way to widespread indignation. That was the moment, Medellín remembers, "when everybody unified to demand changes."[73]

71 Javier Rojas, "Luchas obreras y sindicalismo en Monterrey," *Cuadernos de cultura obrera* 1 (1980), 19–42; Garza H., *Cristal quebrado*.
72 Carranza, Arenas, and Ignacio Briseño interviews in Arenal, *Fundidora*, 66–69, 78–82, 161–65. [February 5th is celebrated as Constitution Day in Mexico].
73 Medellín in Arenal, *Fundidora*, 138–40.

Three months later the steel workers turned *charrismo* on its head. After a protest before the mill, a group of *eventuales* marched on Local 67, chased off its leaders, and seized the union hall. They then turned to the COS activists, who called workers out of the plant for a special assembly. They stripped the leaders who fled of their union rights and elected Manuel Carranza as secretary general.[74] Pressured by Nuevo León's governor, the national Miners Union sanctioned the new leadership. Thus did Carranza, the once youthful rebel fired by the brewery in 1938, become the leader of Local 67. Militancy returned to the Fundidora during Carranza and his successors' tenures. The steel workers struck the mill twice during the mid-1970s to protest contact violations. The union extended legal advice and financial support to other rebellious Miners locals, much to the annoyance of national leaders. Local 67 also renewed its tradition of international solidarity, donating considerable union funds to leftist rebels in El Salvador and Nicaragua.[75] But the renewal of revolutionary unionism coincided with the decline of the Mexican "miracle." The company had responded to mounting financial troubles in the early 1970s by instituting a modernization program that increased plant capacity by 50 percent but failed to stem the Fundidora's descent into bankruptcy. That, in turn, prompted the two costly strikes. In 1977, the federal government assumed the company's mounting debt and integrated the mill into Mexico's state-owned steel complex. Labor relations between Local 67 and the workers' new employer, the government, deteriorated rapidly thereafter. The global economic crisis of the early 1980s soon pushed the state itself to the edge of financial insolvency. The consequences fell hardest on the Mexican working class.

As interest rates soared, Monterrey's debt-burdened industrialists closed factories and laid off tens of thousands of workers. Those who stayed on saw inflation pummel their earnings. In response to the prolonged crisis, the state adopted a privatization program to alleviate its foreign debt. Steel was among the first industries placed on the auction block. On the evening of May 10, 1986, steel workers tuned in to the evening news and heard a stunning development. The Fundidora was bankrupt and the eighty-six-year-old mill would be closed rather than sold to private investors. With the announcement, Local 67's leaders forsook their old antagonisms to save the workers' jobs. Their daily protests rallied family and community to their cause. But the workers' newfound solidarity achieved little where it mattered most, in Mexico City. Miners Union leaders refused to discuss the mill's closure nor give the steel workers a voice at their national convention. Federal officials remained firm in their decision. By the end of the month,

74 Medellín in Arenal, *Fundidora*, 140–42; Jorge Basurto, *La clase obrera en la historia de México: En el regímen de Echeverría: Rebelión e independencia* (Mexico City, 1983), 181–82.
75 *El Diario de Monterrey*, May 10, 1996; Carranza interview.

workers' hopes for a reopened mill gave way to panic, nostalgia, a few tears, and much uncertainty about the troubling future ahead. In a symbolic act of defiance, the steel workers concluded their final protest march by dancing around a bonfire as they burned their PRI credentials.[76]

Scholars attribute the mill's controversial closure to an array of causes, from mismanagement to global overproduction to the pollution created by an inner-city steel mill. For those reasons, rumors of the plant's imminent demise had circulated for a year. At the time, the government, the press, and the city's industrialists blamed the "death" of the Fundidora on union militancy and corruption.[77] Local 67's leaders considered it a politically motivated decision meant to "finish off a fighting union so that nothing but the sold-out CTM remained." After all, they note, a company that by then employed 11,000 workers had produced record levels of steel just one year earlier. Whatever the cause, unemployed steel workers thereafter suffered the elite's "vengeance" for the culture of militancy in which they took such pride. The restrictive hiring policies adopted by the industrialists in the 1930s returned to haunt the "men of steel." By the late 1980s, open-shop employers had detected and fired the few steel workers who managed to "deceive" their blacklist. Many turned to self-employment. Others joined the mass Mexican immigration to the United States. A few committed suicide. Meanwhile, their families struggled to overcome their loss of the high wages, welfare benefits, and company schools that had promised security to generations of steel workers.[78] Today, the notion that Local 67 caused the Fundidora's demise is firmly entrenched in public opinion. Indeed, Monterrey's captains of industry and their loyal workers make the claim with a sense of pride, as if the mill's closure sanctioned decades of paternalistic bonding and company unionism. That system of labor relations now stands as the revolution's most enduring local legacy.

By the 1990s the postrevolutionary order had reached its final hour. Embattled by a second economic crisis, widespread corruption, and an indignant citizenry, the government succumbed to grass-roots pressures to democratize Mexico's system of one-party rule. By "liberalizing" the economy, the government may have paved a new road to recovery. But cutbacks

---

76 Arenas and Cantu interviews in Arenal, *Fundidora*, 167–79, 228–29.

77 Scholars also note that the government soon bailed out the Garza Sadas by absorbing much of their steel company's debt. HYLSA benefited mightily from the Fundidora's closure. Rosa Albina Garavito, "Fundidora: La reconversión como castigo," *El Cotidiano* 12 (1986), 22–26; Francisco Zapata, *El sindicalismo mexicano frente a la restructuración* (Mexico, 1995), 112–13; Zapata Novoa, *La muerte de la Fundidora*, 111–30; Raúl Rubio Cano, "La muerte de la Fundidora: la verdadera historia," *El Porvenir*, May 5, 1988.

78 Interview with Aurelio Arenas, February 8, 1996; Robles interview in Arenal, *Fundidora*, 222–29; interviews with anonymous steel workers in *El Porvenir*, January 1, 1988; *El Diario de Monterrey*, May 9–10, 1996.

in government spending undermined the politics of patronage and divorced the ruling party from its pillars of support. When given a meaningful political voice, workers, farmers, and middle-class Mexicans opted for change and abandoned the PRI. The majority chose the alternative with roots in Monterrey and its resistance to Cardenismo, the National Action Party. Like many *regiomontanos*, the PAN advocated hard work and individual effort over intrusive state policies. And by the late 1990s, Mexicans could look to Monterrey and perhaps see the nation's future. Capitalizing on Mexico's economic opening, the city's family-owned industries became national export leaders. But unlike earlier times, recovery now depended as much on local initiative as on foreign capital investment. Those multinational executives chose Monterrey because "this is a working culture" and "[w]e hardly have any labor problems here."[79] Indeed, by century's close, the steel mill, smelters, and railway shops that once nurtured a culture of labor activism had all been shuttered. Their disappearance marked the final chapter of militant unionism in twentieth-century Monterrey.

Those workers who had resisted unions could thus take comfort in the security of company paternalism. As retirees, they continued to reside in the homes that they purchased with decades of hard work and loyalty to their employers. Their pensions and health benefits sustained them in old age. And they still returned to the company recreational centers they had enjoyed since their youth. But Mexico's crisis and recovery came at a cost. Forced to trim expenses, Monterrey's new generation of industrialists downsized their paternalistic perks. Paternalism persisted; but housing developments stalled, benefits were cut, and the fiestas became fewer. The incentives that gave birth to paternalism, from militant unions to a meddlesome government, had ceased to exist. Moreover, as the city grew, the *regiomontano* elite moved their homes and offices to new suburban enclaves and seemingly "forgot about how and where their workers lived." Contrasting her own experience to that of her glass-worker son, Linda Rodríguez recalled of her employers that "they treated workers much differently, like family. In those days they recognized all the employees and they always watched out for the people." "Now it's different," she lamented, "today the bosses don't even know their own workers."[80] Much as the ruins of the Fundidora cast their shadows upon Monterrey's past, so did personalism become a bygone ingredient of company paternalism.

Today the rusted blast furnace that marked Mexico's entry into the era of industrial modernity stands as a reminder of a nation's dreams of economic independence. The massive workshops where laborers once toiled now house a museum and cinema, while the lands once occupied by rail lines, rolling

79 "The City That Works," *Maclean's*, July 7, 1997, 43.
80 Zapata Novoa, *Tercos y triunfadores*, 91; Rodríguez interview.

mills, and mountains of coal host an amusement park, a Coca-Cola Theater, and a Holiday Inn. Retired steel workers still gather to reminisce in the neighborhood clubs and cantinas that surround their old workplace. Several blocks away, teachers at the Obregón Industrial School prepare the next generation of workers for jobs in the export-oriented industries that accent the city's outskirts. Other youngsters may find work in the factories that thrive in the very heart of Monterrey. The ASARCO smelter chained its gates shut in the early 1990s. The once bustling railroad yards were relocated long ago. But trucks still ramble across the tracks laden with cases of beer and shipments of glass. And the *regiomontanos* continue to pride themselves on the local origins of their industries, their entrepreneurial spirit, and the culture of work and savings that makes Monterrey prosper. In their minds, their hometown remains Mexico's preeminent industrial city, a blue-collar metropolis that celebrates calloused hands and a skyline punctuated by smokestacks.

Select Bibliography of Primary Sources

Archives

Archivo General de la Nación (AGN), Mexico City
   Departamento de Trabajo (DT)
   Dirección General del Gobierno (DGG)
   Ramo de Presidentes
Archivo General del Estado de Nuevo León (AGENL), Monterrey
Archivo Histórico Fundidora Monterrey (AHFM)
Archivo Municipal de Monterrey (AMM)
Bibliteca, Sociedad Cuauhtémoc y Famosa (SCYF), Monterrey
Biblioteca Universitaria (BU), Universidad Autónoma de Nuevo León
Centro de Estudios del Movimiento Obrero y Socialista (CEMOS), Mexico City
Hemeroteca Nacional (HN), Mexico City
State Department Records, National Archives, College Park, MD
   Central Files (Record Group 59)
   Foreign Service Post Files (Record Group 84)

Periodicals (archival location)

Actividad, Monterrey (AMM)
Colectividad, Monterrey (AHFM)
CYPSA, Monterrey (AHFM)
Defensa Proletaria, Mexico City (CEMOS)
Di-Fundidora, Monterrey (AHFM)
El Diario de Monterrey
El Economista Mexicana, Mexico City (HN)
Excélsior, Mexico City (HN)
El Machete, Mexico City (CEMOS)
Monterrey News (BU)
El Norte, Monterrey (HN)
La Pasionaria, Monterrey (BU)
El Porvenir, Monterrey (HN)
El Sol, Monterrey (HN)
Trabajo y Ahorro, Monterrey (SCYF)
Triunfaremos, Monterrey (AHFM)
La Unión, Monterrey (BU)
La Voz de Nuevo León, Monterrey (BU)

Oral History Interviews

All interviews were recorded in Monterrey and translated to English by the author, with the exception of Elizondo, which was conducted in collaboration with Raul Rubio Cano. Citations include interviewees' names, place of employment and/or union affiliation, and dates of interviews.

Dionisio Aguilar, Vidriera Monterrey, Mar. 20, 1996
Linda Alba de Rodríguez, Vidriera Monterrey, Apr. 25, 1996
Aurelio Arenas, Fundidora, Feb. 8, 1996
Ing. Gabriel Cárdenas Coronado, Fundidora, June 18, 2001
Manuel Carranza, Cuauhtémoc Brewery/Fundidora, Jan. 4 and 11, 1996
Salvador Castañeda Medina, Fundidora, Nov. 14, Dec. 5, 1995, Mar. 13, 1996, June 13, 2001
Lic. Luis Alfonso Cavazos, Sociedad Cuauhtémoc, Mar. 17, 1996
Gerónimo Contreras, Fundidora, Dec. 5, 1995
Ricardo Correa Vidaurri, Vidriera Monterrey, May 8, 1996
Juan Manuel Elizondo, Fundidora, Apr. 9, 1996, June 16, 2001
Jesús García Martínez, Fundidora, Nov. 13, 1995
Manuel González Caballero, Fundidora, June 30, July 4, 1995, May 8, 1996
Apolonio López Galván, Cuauhtémoc Brewery, Dec. 11, 1995
Antonio Martínez Chapa, Vidriera Monterrey, Apr. 29, 1996
Francisco Martínez Padilla, Cementos Mexicanos/Fábricas de Monterrey, Nov. 20, 1996
María de los Angeles Medrano, Cuauhtémoc Brewery, Dec. 11, 1995
Alejandro Monsiváis Rodríguez, Cuauhtémoc Brewery, Dec. 11, 1995
Juan Montes Orozco, Vidriera Monterrey, Apr. 4, 1996
Luis Monzón, Vidriera Monterrey, Mar. 20, 1996
María de Jesus Oviedo, Cuauhtémoc Brewery, May 23, 1996
Estela Padilla, Cuauhtémoc Brewery, Nov. 20, 1995
Dionisio Palacios Moya, Fundidora, Mar. 13, 15, and 18, 1996
Antonio Quiroga, Fundidora, Mar. 26, 1996
Humberto Ramos Lozano, teachers union, Jan. 15, 1996
Rafael Reyna Ramírez, Fundidora, May 22, 1996
Angel Rodríguez González, Vidriera Monterrey, Apr. 25, 1996
Salvador Solís Daniel, Fundidora, Nov. 14, 1995
Felix Torres, electrical workers union, Nov. 14, 1995
Zacarías Villarreal Dávila, electrical workers union, Nov. 18, 1995

Index

Acción Cívica Nacionalista (ACN), *see* Nationalist Civic Action

alcohol, *see* temperance reform

Alemán, Miguel, 299

Almazán, Juan Andreu, 130, 287; 1940 elections, 230, 286

American Smelting and Refining Company (ASARCO), 6, 134; and Mexican state, 148–9, 150, 159; *see also* ASARCO; foreign capital

anarchism and anarchists, 28, 44, 121, 135; *see also* Casa del Obrero Mundial

anticlericalism, 86, 284

anticommunism, 96–7, 204, 209–10, 217, 222, 231, 247–8; and government policy, 185–6

ASARCO, Monterrey smelter, 14–15, 110; and Local 66 (SITMMRM), 184, 250, 280; and paternalism, 57, 147–8; strikes at, 41, 47–8, 145, 159, 276; working conditions at, 151–2

ASARCO Production Workers Union, 150, 157, 181

Avila Camacho, Manuel, 286–7

Calles, Plutarco Elías, 175; labor policy of, 60, 113, 123; in Monterrey, 86, 130; opposition to, 124, 176–8

Camisas Dorados, *see* Gold Shirts

Campa, Valentín, 112, 118–19, 146, 160, 164

Cárdenas, Lázaro, 176, 177, 277; collective memory of, 189, 265–6, 268, 285; labor policy of, 167–8, 217–19, 242–3, 245, 250, 266–7, 285–6; in Monterrey, 166–7, 215–19; opposition to, 203–4, 208–15, 284–5; support for, 178, 213, 216, 218

Casa del Obrero Mundial, 36, 263

Cementos Mexicanos (CEMEX), 140–1, 189fn

Cervecería Cuauhtémoc, *see* Cuauhtémoc Brewery

charrismo, 299–300, 301, 307–8

Church: Catholic, *see* religion

class, 39, 121–2, 142–4, 185–6

Communists, 137, 166, 204, 218, 226–7; and union leadership, 224–6, 232, 276, 292, 300; *see also* anticommunism; Campa, Valentín; Elizondo, Juan Manuel; Partido Comunista Mexicana

company housing, 70, 89, 151, 267

company paternalism, *see* paternalism

railroad workers, 86–7, 117–18,
120, 193; influence on labor
movement, 36, 45, 123–6;
unions of, 24, 28–9, 49, 51, 61,
122, 172, 224, 274, 299–300;
see also Campa, Valentín; Cueva,
Tomás; Gutiérez, Juan
regionalism, 8–12, 112, 114–16,
131, 155, 176, 209, 302–5, 313;
and Monterrey working class,
26–7, 43, 52; and organized
labor, 116–19, 139, 185–6; *see
also* identity formation
religion, 131, 212; and
paternalism, 56, 57; *see also*
anticlericalism
Reyes, Bernardo, 13, 17, 24, 25,
26, 27
Rocha, Joel, 157

Sada, Luis G., 42, 57, 58, 60, 62,
64, 138, 158, 211, 265, 294
Sada, Roberto, 195
Sáenz, Aarón, 111–12, 129, 130–1,
177
Sindicato Industrial de
Trabajadores Ferrocarrileros de la
República Mexicana, *see* railroad
workers
Sindicato Industrial de
Trabajadores
Mineros-Metalúrgicos de la
República Mexicana, *see*
Miner-Metalworkers Union
Sindicato Unico de Trabajadores de
la Industria de Vidrio, *see* United
Glass Workers Union

Sociedad Cuauhtémoc y Famosa
(SCYF), *see* Cuauhtémoc Society
sports, 72, 94–5, 170
Steel Unions (Federación de
Sindicatos de Acero), 135, 139,
179–84, 187
students: university, 175, 225;
see also Elizondo, Juan Manuel;
Universidad de Nuevo León

teachers union, 226
temperance reform, 68, 95

unemployment, 155–6, 242
unions, *see specific unions*; company
unions; labor activists; organized
labor
United Glass Workers Union, 197,
207, 218, 235–40, 295
Universidad de Nuevo León, 175,
308–9

Velásquez, Fidel, 247, 299
Vidriera Monterrey, 6, 16, 23;
interunion conflicts at, 190,
195–7, 240; labor relations at,
192–3, 235–40; and
paternalism, 193–5; strikes at,
206–8, 296–7, 309, working
conditions at, 191–3, 197–9;
see also United Glass Workers
Union

welfare capitalism, *see* paternalism
women: in labor force, 63–4, 72,
75–8, 208, 264, 305; *see also*
gender